Social Movements of the Sixties and Seventies

Edited by Jo Freeman

Longman
New York & London

Social Movements of the Sixties and Seventies

Longman Inc., 95 Church Street, White Plains, N.Y. 10601
Associated companies, branches, and representatives
throughout the world.

Developmental Editor: Nicole Benevento
Editorial and Design Supervisor: Diane Perlmuth
Interior Design: Eileen Beirne
Manufacturing Supervisor: Marion Hess
Production Supervisor: Ferne Y. Kawahara

Concepts of buttons in chapters 13, 14, 15, 16, and 18 by
Cindy Fried, with graphics by Eileen Beirne.

Library of Congress Cataloging in Publication Data
Main entry under title:

Social movements of the sixties and seventies.

  Bibliography: p.
  Includes index.
  1. Social movements—United States—History.
I. Freeman, Jo.
HN59.S625   303.4'84   81-18586
ISBN 0-582-28091-5   AACR2

Manufactured in the United States of America

Copyright Acknowledgments

To Toni,
          Vicky,
                    and Cathy,
with whom I learned my
first lessons in social movements.
And to
          J. T.
who first encouraged me to write about them.

Contents

Foreword

This important collection of essays on the social movements of the Sixties and Seventies is clearly a significant contribution to the understanding of a turbulent period in American history. It may be something else as well: part of a new process in which theories, like the ones developed here, not only describe a reality but also set forces in motion which then help to transform that reality.

In one standard academic paradigm—the *plus ça change, plus c'est la même chose* view of reality—bursts of social energy come and go in a stately, cyclic progression. Thus Samuel Huntington wrote in *American Politics: The Promise of Disharmony* that there have been four periods of "creedal passion" in our history: the Revolutionary, Jacksonian, Progressive, and S&S (Sixties and Seventies) eras. Given this periodicity, Hungtinton noted, the next age of social movements will not occur until the second or third decade of the twenty-first century. That is a classical interpretation with roots in Aristotle's *Politics* and Plato's *Republic* with their theories of the inevitable rise and decline of various political forms.

I think Henry Adams is closer to the truth in his perception that time has speeded up in the twentieth century and become much more volatile (like H_2O in the transition from ice to water to steam). That is why I think this book might be relevant to the future as well as to the recent past it describes. It is significant, for instance, that many of the authors in this book come from the movements they analyze and are not merely detatched observers. That is to say, social movements in the late twentieth century have become more self-conscious, and this is one of the reasons why America might not have to wait fifty or more years for another period similar to the Sixties and early Seventies.

It is, for instance, possible to reconstruct the Reformation as a social movement. Scholars with diverse points of view—Max Weber, Franz Borkenau, and Antonio Gramsci—have done so brilliantly. Yet the movement itself was not aware of what it was doing. The Calvinists in giving glory to God through an inner-wordly asceticism, Weber argued, unwittingly completed the "disenchantment of the world"; their abstemious puritainism provided the motivation for an economic system that was to create the most hedonistic society the world has ever known. The unintended consequences of their actions turned out to be more momentous than they intended. Saints promoted secularism.

It was, of course, the nineteenth century, and Karl Marx in particular, that began to understand this kind of unconscious dialectic. So it was that socialism defined itself as the first self-conscious social movement in history. Even so, that consciousness was, more often than not, most precise and developed in the minds of middle-class intellectuals who dedicated themselves to the proletariat, like Marx himself, than in the actual consciousness of the proletarians. So it was that when George Lukacs wrote that the working class was the first social class ever to have an objective and total view of its place in society, he had to distinguish between this ideal consciousness and the actual empirical consciousness of the workers. The ideal consciousness, he argued, in terms of a fateful distinction, is to be found in the party, not in the working class as it is.

Actual working-class consciousness, Barrington Moore has recently documented in a study of German socialism, often had little to do with Lukacs' (or Marx's) ideal. In a sense that was inevitable because, as Marx had pointed out, the workers in capitalism (and the exploited classes in every social order) normally internalize the norms and values of their rulers. If, then, socialism was a much more self-conscious movement than, say, the Reformation, there were still limits upon that self-consciousness. What is remarkable about the movements described in this book is that they thought of themselves as part of history almost from the beginning. Indeed, at times the claims were grandiose to the point of absurdity, as when a student strike leader at Columbia University spoke in the name of the majority of the people of the world.

All social movements have, of course, been led by articulate, usually literate, people. What is new—what is described here—is the emergence of movements in which the rank and file are also literate and articulate. That can give rise to rhetorical delusions of grandeur, as that Columbia student proves. It also marks the impact of a new, and educated, stratum upon political life. In the demonology of American conservatism, such movement people are pictured as the hypocrites of a "new class" who speak in lofty universals in order to secure their own privelege and power. One problem with this thesis is that it is usually developed by individuals who have the same sociological profile as those whom they denounce, a fact that subverts their sociological explanation of their enemies.

My point in emphasizing the self-consciousness of the new social movements is not to exalt them above the less educated, to assign them a moral and intellectual superiority as against "mere" workers or blacks or Hispanics. It is only, but emphatically, to suggest that these social movements will be different, that the old rules—including the old cycles à la Huntington—no longer apply. And that is why I regard this book as an event in the present and the future as well as a depiction and analysis of the past. It is the theoretical consciousness of participant-observers, and it therefore has an ongoing relevance to the lives, not just the minds, of both the authors and the readers.

The French revolutionaries of 1789 thought of themselves as born-again Roman republicans. The Russian revolutionaries of 1917 pictured themselves as Marxist Jacobins. In the 1980s there are already young movement activists who look back to the ancient days of the 1960s as to a Camelot. They—and everyone else, even those who want only to understand the world but not to change it—will find an excellent exemplar of our new living history, of our self-conscious social movements, in this indispensable collection of essays.

Michael Harrington

Preface

The 1960s was one of those decades that occurs two or three times a century and has a profound transformative effect on society. It was a decade that spilled over into the seventies and whose effects are still rippling through some of our more remote social bayous even as the reaction to those effects dominates the societal center. The sixties was marked, above all, by public discontent organized into protest movements.

The civil rights movement that began in the late fifties was the first of these movements, and it set the tone and style for what was to come. Organized by and for southern blacks, the civil rights movement nonetheless sought a reaffirmation of such basic American values as equal rights and individual dignity. This reaffirmation by a movement that targeted as its enemy a practice—segregation—typical of a region that itself was stigmatized by the rest of the nation made it easy for a population still appalled by the atrocities of Hitler's Germany to view the movement's achievements as a goal and not a threat. It was not until black protest "went north" that serious national opposition appeared.

In the meantime, the civil rights movement captured the imagination of a public jaded by a decade of conformity, particularly the post-World War II generation attending college. The young people who found an answer to President Kennedy's call to "ask what you can do for your country" through participation in the civil rights movement began to apply the concepts and values they had learned from that movement to other segments of society. These values were initially expressed in the Port Huron Statement, adopted in 1962 by the Students for a Democratic Society. It urged "the establishment of a democracy of individual participation governed by two central aims: that the individual share in those social decisions determining the quality and direction of his life; that society be organized to encourage independence in men [sic] and provide the media for their common participation...."

SDS went through many changes before finally self-destructing in 1969. But the values expressed in the Port Huron Statement did not die with it. These values emphasized the politicization of society, individual fulfillment, and the legitimation of dissent in a sharp break with the previous era's stress on privatization and conformity. Such a change has proved enduring even while conservatives organize their own movements in reaction to the successes of the sixties and seventies.

Politicization and individual fulfillment as values probably had their greatest effect in the women's movement, which expressed them in the phase "the personal is political" and acted them out in ways that began to violate other basic American values such as patriarchy. Although this movement began in the sixties, it did not become public until 1970, and in the decade of the seventies it reached its peak and greatest influence. More than any other movement of the last two decades, it deprivatized what had heretofore been perceived as personal problems.

Although the sixties is viewed as the decade of protest, it was really the seventies that saw the greatest flowering of movements on a wide variety of issues, attracting segments of the population that had condemned the sixties' protestors as "commies." Some of those movements are discussed in this book. Often small or local movements, they did not achieve the national publicity of the sixties' movements. But that was not the only reason they were not publicized. Often the press simply chose to ignore movements or protest actions that in the sixties would have been on the front pages. For example, the arrest of civil rights demonstrators in the early sixties for local actions was often quickly known across the country. The arrest of over a thousand demonstrators at a nuclear plant in Seabrook, New Hampshire, in 1977 got a ten-second play on the nightly news and at best back-page coverage in the major newspapers. I spoke at three different campuses in the West shortly after that demonstration and barely a handful of people in my audience knew about it.

Geographic distance is not the sole explanation of this lack of awareness. In 1978, fifteen thousand people marched on the Supreme Court to urge it to overturn the *Bakke* decision by a lower court that had eliminated the University of California at Davis Medical School's affirmative action program. The television news that night and the headlines the following day blared forth the theme "sixties reenacted on the Washington Mall." What they were referring to was not the first truly integrated march on Washington since 1963 but the gathering of young people for a free rock concert given by the producers of the forthcoming movie *Hair*, a concert given in exchange for allowing the producers to film them for the movie's crowd scenes. The editors of several media had simultaneously decided to ignore the march on the Supreme Court—a serious political reenactment of the sixties—in favor of a spoof.

Although the seventies' movements were much more diverse and were marked by more conflicting goals than the sixties' movements, they weren't necessarily smaller. Four marches on Washington between 1960 and 1980 drew over one hundred thousand participants: a civil rights march in 1963, an antiwar demonstration in 1969, an ERA march in 1978, and an antinuclear march in 1979. While accurate figures aren't available, there were probably more marches and demonstrations in the District of Columbia in the seventies than the sixties. Gays, antiabortionists, farmers Indians, Iranians (on several sides), and religious fundamentalists all saw Washington as the place to make their presence felt. Thus, while the press may have persuaded the general population that times had cooled, the people and politicians in the nation's capital knew better. They complained that single-issue protestors were replacing the traditional power brokers and overloading the political system in the process.

The eruption of movements in the seventies testified to the success of the sixties' movements in several ways. First, the sixties' movements legitimated dissent itself. Protestors are no longer stigmatized as subversive; at worst they are dismissed as troublemakers. Second, the use of mass demonstrations and even civil disobedience was perceived as effective. Participants may have seen few immediate benefits from their actions, but they attracted the attention of many others who had neither the skills nor the knowledge to use the traditional methods of political insiders. Last, but hardly least, the gains achieved in the sixties stimulated a backlash.

The sixties' movements were largely from the left. Those of the seventies were from the right as well as the left, and other movements were unclassifiable on a left-right spectrum. That the right should respond to movements it perceived as disrupting the status quo was only to be expected. The last century of American history has seen three great eras of "progressive" movements, all of them followed by reactionary ones. The immediate targets of reaction are not easily predictable. The targets for the seventies backlash were movements or issues that were still publicly prominent. Initially the right focused on busing, abortion, and the ERA. Eventually, it expanded to include gays and foreign policy issues (e.g., the Panama Canal treaty). Most recently it has attacked contemporary economic policy and social policies that regulate the freedom of business enterprises to control their own operations (e.g., affirmative action, health and safety programs).

This pantheon of issues is broader than those raised in the sixties, but it does reflect the basic difference in perspectives between the left and the right on the role of government or the state. Essentially the left believes the government should regulate economic activities and stay out of people's private lives. The right believes the government should regulate personal decisions insofar as they deviate from traditional norms (e.g., abortion and homosexuality) but should stay out of economic activities. Only the libertarians consistently believe the government should stay out of both, and they've never attracted a large following. As we move into the eighties, it remains to be seen whether this basic difference will be crystallized into two distinct ideologies, each a unifying umbrella for various constituency movements, or whether American movements, like American society, will continue to be highly pluralistic, each group pursuing their own ends, sometimes in alliance with others, but not in concert.

* * *

This book was originally conceived to meet my need for a teachable textbook for a course I was giving on social movements. All the books available in the mid-seventies were either too narrow, too broad, too expensive, or too old; so in 1975 I boldly announced I would produce my own. I decided to edit an anthology rather than write a textbook myself because I wanted to focus on the contemporary American social movements that had caught the imagination of my students, and I knew I could not do the necessary field research alone. Instead, I sought to draw upon the work of young scholars who were writing dissertations on these movements but hadn't yet published everything they had to say.

Getting the word out was easier said than done because at that time there was no viable network of social movements scholars. The well-known authors were largely from the collective behavior school and had stopped writing on social movements years ago. The less well known were not political scientists, as I was, and thus I could not reach them through my professional grapevine. I began with a search of the published literature of the period, for which I received invaluable assistance from Paula Hane, librarian at the college where I was teaching, and Naomi Katz, my student assistant. I also collected papers, some of which are published here, at the annual meetings of relevant professional associations.

The fact that I was looking for a rather unusual product complicated the search. Most articles on social movements tend to be primarily theoretical generalizations or broad analyses of specific movements. I was looking for pieces that combined theory and data, using each to analyze the other. I also wanted articles on specific topics. While I tried to include as many major movements as possible, when I could not find pieces on both the movements and the topics I was trying to cover, the topics took precedence. Consequently, some movements are discussed in this book more than once, and some that I wish were in it, aren't. (Other movements, such as the environmental and gay rights movements, aren't represented because the people commissioned to write about them didn't come through.) Nonetheless, this book should not be seen as a survey of all the relevant topics. Even if one could accurately define the universe, editorial discretion had to be exercised, and not all topics are equally popular all the time.

This book received a major boost in 1977 when I was invited by Mayer Zald and John McCarthy to present a paper at a national symposium on social movements at Vanderbilt University. The work of some of the people I met there is in this book. Other papers came from irregular seminars of social movement scholars in New York and Washington, D.C., that the symposium generated.

More important, this symposium created the rudiments of a network of social movements scholars, which has now been institutionalized into a Social Movements Section of the American Sociology Association. Even before this crystallized, word of the book was traveling over this emerging grapevine, and several people wrote and asked if they could contribute.

Manuscripts began to arrive and the book to take shape in 1979—the year I started law school. For my entire legal education, my idea of "rest and recreation" was to edit articles on social movements. My student status gave me access to the New York University library, for which I was grateful. But I discovered that there is a great difference between producing a book as a student and as a professor. The handicap is not lack of time; frankly, I had more discretionary time than when I was teaching. The handicap is lack of institutional resources. Faculty library and mailing privileges, an office, copying equipment, a telephone, a secretary, and colleagues all took on an importance they did not have when I had them in abundance. I'm most grateful to my publisher, Longman, for filling part of this need by permitting me to use their facilities on occasion, yet the sheer logistics of doing so made me cognizant of how much easier it is to produce a book when institutional support is readily available. I'm also grateful to those contributors who understood the constraints under which I was editing the book and readily responded to rewrite requests within my time schedule.

This book reflects the state of contemporary social movements analysis as much the state of contemporary social movements. Social movements were traditionally studied within the framework of collective behavior. While those grounded in this tradition did not all agree on what a social movement was, or what the key elements of analysis ought to be, they did share a common distaste, often subtle, for movements and their participants. By and large these writers came of age politically and academically in the thirties and forties when the prevalent movements were extremist in nature. Fascism, communism, and other totalitarian movements shaped their perception of social movements and the questions they considered central to their analyses. The literature of this period will not be reviewed here, as partial reviews are found throughout the book, but it contains a set of core concerns. These include sources of discontent (structural dysfunctions that caused movements), motives for participation (personality dysfunctions), ideology, and leadership.

The current generation of movement scholars has had its perceptions shaped by the movements of the sixties and seventies. Unlike the previous generation, most of the newer writers are very sympathetic to the movements they studied. Many were participants, or had friends who were. Consequently, there is now a new "movement" among social movement scholars that asks very different questions than were traditionally asked, questions of more immediate interest to movement participants. Their core concerns of mobilization, organization, strategy, and social control are reflected in the table of contents of this book. Thus, unintentionally, this book is not only about movements, but is part of a movement; it is to that intellectual movement, as well as the social movements of the sixties and seventies, that my final expression of gratitude must go.

Introduction

One of the most difficult problems in analyzing social movements is defining exactly what a social movement is. Participants generally know that theirs is a movement, but movements are so diverse that it is difficult to isolate their common elements and incorporate them into a succinct definition. Virtually all movement theorists have differing definitions, and one entire book has been devoted to this problem.[1] Nonetheless, there are some common themes and elements that recur in case studies and theoretical analyses, although not always with a common emphasis.

Spontaneity and structure are the most important elements. Spontaneity has been emphasized by sociologists, especially those in the collective behavior tradition. This tradition has lumped together as similar phenomena fads, crowds, panics, riots, and social movements. The latter have been seen as more organized versions of collective behavior, but not distinctly different from it. One classic description views social movements as the end result of a transition from more elementary forms of collective behavior. During its development, a social movement "acquires organization and form, a body of customs and traditions, established leadership, an enduring division of labor, social rules and social values—in short, a culture, social organization, and new scheme of life."[2] Yet because the analytic emphasis is on the commonality of spontaneity, little attention has been given to how this structure is acquired, and more important, what the consequences of the kind of structure acquired are for the movement's goals and participants.

What sociologists see as the end product of a developmental process, political scientists see as the beginning. Social movements are "nascent groups"[3] that are not truly interesting until they have "crossed the threshold into organizational life."[4] Eventually some movements mature into interest groups with a well-defined membership, stable funding, a permanent staff, and, above all, a knowledge of how to operate within the political process. Such organized groups have long been perceived as fundamental components of the American political process,[5] but political scientists have paid little attention to what prompted their organization or sustained them during the nascent phase.

It is much more useful to think of all the above forms of social action as existing along a continuum. At one end are those forms marked by their contagious spontaneity and lack of structure, such as fads, trends, and crowds. At the other end are interest groups whose primary characteristic is a well-developed and stable organization often impervious to spontaneous demands from their members. In the middle are social movements that, however diverse they may be, exhibit noticeable spontaneity and a describable structure, even if a formal organization is lacking.[6] It is often hard to identify the exact amount of structure necessary to distinguish a social movement from a crowd or trend, and often harder to distinguish a social movement organization from an interest group, but those distinctions are crucial. It is the tension between spontaneity and structure that gives a social movement its peculiar flavor. When one significantly dominates the other, what may one day be, or may once have been, a social movement, is something else.

Conceptualizing a social movement as the middle of a continuum does not mean there is a natural progression from the spontaneous end to the organized one, as "natural history" theorists postulate. As some of the case studies in this book illustrate, the organization can exist before the movement. While it is unusual for a highly formalized organization to become a social movement organization, it is even more unusual for a totally unorganized mass to become one. Chapter 1 examines the relationship between preexisting organizations and movement development.

A social movement has one or more core organizations in a penumbra of people who engage in spontaneous supportive behavior which the core organizations can often mobilize but less often control. When there is spontaneous behavior with only embryonic organization, there may be a premovement phenomena awaiting the right conditions to become a movement, but there is no movement per se. When the penumbra of spontaneous behavior has contracted to no more than the core organizations, or has not yet developed, there is also no movement. An organization that can mobilize only its own members, and whose members mobilize only when urged to action by their organization, is lacking a key characteristic of movements. Regardless of whether structure or spontaneity comes first, or if they appear simultaneously, the important point is that both must exist.

Although structure and spontaneity are the key components, they are not the only ones. Several other important elements shape the form and content of a social movement. Whether all are necessary to label a collective action a movement is open to debate. But these elements are so prevalent that they cannot be overlooked.

Of utmost importance is the consciousness that one is part of a group with whom one shares awareness of a particular concern. Individuals acting in response to common social forces with no particular identification with one another may be setting a trend, but they are not part of a movement. It was said by sixties' activists that "the movement is a state of mind." As Roberta Johnson demonstrates in her analysis of the disabled, it is a common state of mind and a sense of identification with others who hold similar views that make possible the common acts of movement participants, even when they are out of communication with each other. Government agents in the 1960s often attributed concurrent eruptions of protest on the campus as the result of some underlying control by agents of a well-organized subversive group. The real culprit was the press, which by publicizing the actions of students on one campus gave new ideas for actions to students with a common state of mind on other campuses. The spontaneous activities that subsequently occurred may not yet have been a movement, but they drew upon the common consciousness that was later forged into a movement.

Alternatively, a movement can create consciousness. The desire to do this by spreading the movement's message is another key component. This missionary impulse is not restricted to social movements but when it is lacking, it usually indicates that the movement has been successfully repressed or is stagnating. It may also mean that what ought to be a movement has never become one. Gross et al.'s data on the men's movement describe a phenomenon with apparently all the necessary components of a social movement, but one that neither grows nor dies. Few of its participants have the evangelistic urge to expose potential recruits to the ideas of the movement or see much benefit in constant expansion. There is a reason social movements are called "movements." Without the missionary impulse they seldom move.

The message carried is another important element—some would say the most important. Smelser, for example, defined collective behavior "as mobilization on the basis of a belief which redefines social action."[7] Highly developed movements usually embody their message in an elaborate ideology that often antedates the movement, though is also responsive to it. Such an ideology has several parts. It specifies discontents, prescribes solutions, justifies a change from the status quo, and may also identify the agents of social change and the strategy and tactics they are to use. Not all movements have a complete ideology, nor is one necessary. What is necessary is identification of a problem, and, if the movement is to grow beyond its initiators, some vision of a better future. These alone can create a belief system of extraordinary power.

Both the importance and the power of a belief system were documented by the collective behavior theorists, though only Smelser organized his entire theoretical structure around the nature of generalized beliefs. More contemporary social movements analysts have tended to downplay the importance of ideology, and, like interest-group theorists, to view it as an optional tool in the organizer's arsenal.[8] This is why there is so little on ideology in this book. It does not mean, to paraphrase Daniel Bell, that the era of ideology has ended. It more accurately reflects the fact that ideology is taken for granted. With a few notable exceptions, the belief systems of most movements in the sixties and seventies were extensions of basic liberal concepts that dominate our public philosophy. Contemporary analysts have simply not seen their motivating force as requiring an explanation. As movements develop whose ideology is inconsistent with liberal values, we can expect to see greater attention paid to belief systems. Perhaps the next generation of theorists will agree with Smelser that "the beliefs on which collective behavior is based ... are ... akin to magical beliefs."[9]

Whether magical or practical, agreement within a movement on the content of the belief system is sometimes lacking. As Gerlach and Hine point out, ideologies exist on two levels.[10] The upper level contains the concepts on which there is basic agreement. These generally include identification of the problem and a vision of the future. Such a vision, even for movements whose explicit goals are immediate benefits for their members (e.g., worker's compensation for black and brown lung disease), is almost always expressed in terms of general social improvement. The second level may be highly varied and the source of much factionalism. Disagreements over strategy and tactics, the proper agents of social change, and immediate goals exist on this level. Sometimes cleavages in the second level are shifted to the first. When this occurs, it is problematic whether there is one movement or two.

Precisely because movements are so volatile, defining the point at which a transformation or a true split has occurred is both necessary and difficult. Organizational cleavages are usually quite public, but don't always reflect true movement cleavages. For example, during the late fifties and early sixties blacks in the South organized into a movement for integration and equality called the Civil Rights Movement. In the late sixties and early seventies, blacks in the North organized into a movement stressing separation and self-enhancement, which never acquired a commonly accepted name. It was occasionally called the Black Power Movement, but most participants and observers recognized that it was not appropriate to call it a civil rights movement. Had the movement of the early sixties changed into the movement of the late sixties, or were there two different movements? Some of the major organizations in the civil rights movement survived intact, even though they were forced to rethink a few of their goals. But some did not. The Congress of Racial Equality (CORE) was totally transformed, perhaps reflecting the fact that it was based in the North to begin with. The Student Non-Violent Coordinating Committee (SNCC) tried to transform itself by eliminating white participants and removing the word "Non-Violent" from its name, but did not survive the process.

I would argue that there were two different movements and that the former stimulated the formation of the latter but was not transformed into it. Despite their volatility, a certain amount of movement stability is another key component. The people in movements may change, and the objectives may change, but if both these factors change, it is not the same movement. In other words, no matter how much a movement may evolve in response to internal dynamics and external pressures, there must be a continuity of persons or objectives. New segments of the population may adopt the movement's objectives, or its original social base may change theirs, but when both change, it is because there is a new movement that only superficially resembles the old. Thus any analysis of the history of contemporary black protest must look at two separate phenomena.

This simple characterization is not always simple to apply. Everyone agrees that the women's movement had two branches with two separate origins. Does this mean there were two separate movements? The social base of both was primarily among college-educated employed women. But there was a decided difference of age and orientation, reflecting the generation gap of the sixties. This gap is no longer socially important, nor is it reflected in current movement participation. Does that mean the branches have merged or that one has ceased to exist and the other is attracting all the newly available participants? If one looks at objectives to provide guidance, there is even greater confusion. Participants of the younger branch claimed that their goals were much more radical than the reformists of the National Organization for Women (NOW) and related groups. Yet surveys do not show clear differences between the beliefs and goals of movement participants by organizational affiliation. Whether or not the disagreements were on the upper level of problem identification and vision—indicating two separate belief systems—or that of strategy, tactics, and short-range goals—indicating only normal movement flux—is a crucial question that will probably never be definitely answered. Nevertheless, the attempt to answer questions like these makes social movements analysis one of the more dynamic, if not systematic, fields of knowledge.

NOTES

1. Paul Wilkinson, *Social Movement* (New York: Praeger, 1971).
2. Herbert Blumer, "Social Movements," in *Principles of Sociology*, ed. Alfred McClung Lee (New York: Barnes and Noble, 1951), p. 199.
3. Theodore J. Lowi, *The Politics of Disorder* (New York: Basic Books, 1971), p. 54.
4. Ibid., p. 42.
5. James Madison, *Federalist Papers* # 10; Alexis de Tocqueville, *Democracy in America* (New York: Vintage, 1945); David Truman, *The Governmental Process* (New York: Knopf, 1958).
6. Political parties exist on the edge between social movements and interest groups. Normally they are quite staid, with a well-defined organization, recognized leaders, and a distaste for unpredictable or uncontrolled actions by their members. But when they gear up for campaigns, most parties become mobilizing institutions often attempting to organize a temporary social movement for their candidates.
7. Neil J. Smelser, *Theory of Collective Behavior* (New York: Free Press, 1962), p. 8.
8. In an unpublished paper Myra Marx Ferree and Fred Miller particularly chide the resource mobilization perspective for ignoring the importance of ideology. See their "Winning Hearts and Minds: Some Social Psychological Contributions to the Resource Mobilization Perspective on Social Movements."
9. Smelser, *Theory of Collective Behaviour*, p. 8.
10. Luther P. Gerlach and Virginia H. Hine, *People, Power, Change: Movements of Social Transformation* (Indianapolis: Bobbs-Merrill, 1970), p. 165.

Voter Registration Drive, Alabama, 1966.

National Women's Conference, Houston, 1977.

Part 1
Origins

1

On the Origins of Social Movements

Jo Freeman

Most movements have inconspicuous beginnings. The significant elements of their origins are usually forgotten or distorted by the time a trained observer seeks to trace them out. Perhaps this is why the theoretical literature on social movements usually concentrates on causes (Gurr 1970, Davies 1962, Oberschall 1973) and motivations (Toch 1965, Cantril 1941, Hoffer 1951, Adorno et al. 1950), while the "spark of life" by which the "mass is to cross the threshold of organizational life" (Lowi 1971, p. 41) has received scant attention.

From the implicit assumptions in the literature one would postulate either a "spontaneous generation" theory or an "outside agitator" theory of movement formation. The first asserts that if grievances exist and the social structure is conducive to movement activity, a movement will automatically occur. Conversely, if movement activity does not occur, it is because the political system provides adequate channels to pursue solutions or because grievances are insufficient. The second theory assumes that there are always grievances; outsiders translate them into action. Remove the outsiders, or their outside funding sources, and movements will cease (Kornhauser 1959, McCarthy and Zald 1973).

All these assumptions contain grains of truth, but they must be separated out, subject to microsociological analysis, and reformulated into testable propositions. This in turn requires that we identify the phenomena to be analyzed.

Recognizing with Heberle (1951, p. 8) that "movements as such are not organized groups," it is still the structured aspects that are more amenable to study, if not always the most salient. Turner and Killian (1957, p. 307) have argued that it is when "members of a public who share a common position concerning the issue at hand supplement their informal person-to-person discussion with some organization to promote their convictions more effectively and insure more sustained activity, a social movement is incipient" (see also Killian 1964, p. 426). Such organization(s) and other core groups of a movement not only determine much of its conscious policy but serve as foci for its values and activities. Just as it has been argued that society as a whole has a cultural and structural "center" about which most members of the society are more or less "peripheral" (Shils 1970), so, too, can a social movement be conceived of as having a center and a periphery. An investigation into a movement's origins must be concerned with the microstructural preconditions for the emergence of such a movement center. From where do the people come who make up the initial, organizing cadre of a movement? How do they come together, and how do they come to share a similar view of the world in circumstances that compel them to political action? In what ways does the nature of the original center affect the future development of the movement?

Before answering these questions, let us first look at data on the origins of four social movements prominent in the sixties and seventies: civil rights, student protest, welfare rights, and women's liberation. These data identify recurrent elements involved in movement formation. The ways in which these elements interact, given a sufficient level of strain, would support the following propositions:

Proposition 1: The need for a *preexisting communications network* or infrastructure within the social base of a movement is a primary prerequisite for "spontaneous" activity. Masses alone do not form movements, however discontented they may be. Groups of previously unorganized individuals may spontaneously form into small local associations—usually along the lines of informal social networks—in response to a specific strain or crisis. If they are not linked in some manner, however, the protest does not become generalized but remains a local irritant or dissolves completely. If a movement is to spread rapidly, the communications network must already exist. If only the rudiments of a network exist, movement formation requires a high input of "organizing" activity.

Proposition 2: Not just any communications network will do. It must be a network that is *cooptable* to the new ideas of the incipient movement.* To be cooptable, it must be composed of like-minded people whose backgrounds, experiences, or location in the social structure make them receptive to the ideas of a specific new movement.

Proposition 3: Given the existence of a cooptable communications network, or at least the rudimentary development of a potential one, and a situation of

---

* The only use of this significant word appears rather incidentally in Turner (1964, p. 123).

strain, one or more precipitants are required. Here, two distinct patterns emerge that often overlap. In one, a *crisis* galvanizes the network into spontaneous action in a new direction. In the other, one or more persons begin *organizing* a new organization or disseminating a new idea. For spontaneous action to occur, the communications network must be well formed or the initial protest will not survive the incipient stage. If it is not well formed, organizing efforts must occur; that is, one or more persons must specifically attempt to construct a movement. To be successful, organizers must be skilled and must have a fertile field in which to work. If no communications network already exists, there must at least be emerging spontaneous groups that are acutely attuned to the issue, albeit uncoordinated. To sum up, if a cooptable communications network is already established, a crisis is all that is necessary to galvanize it. If it is rudimentary, an organizing cadre of one or more persons is necessary. Such a cadre is superfluous if the former conditions fully exist, but it is essential if they do not.

THE CIVIL RIGHTS MOVEMENT

The civil rights movement has two origins, although one contributed significantly to the other. The first can be dated from December 7, 1955, when the arrest of Rosa Parks for occupying a "white" seat on a bus stimulated both the Montgomery Bus Boycott and the formation of the Montgomery Improvement Association. The second can be dated either from February 1, 1960, when four freshmen at A & T College in Greensboro, North Carolina, sat-in at a white lunch counter, or from April 15–17, when a conference at Shaw University in Raleigh, North Carolina, resulted in the formation of the Student Non-Violent Co-ordinating Committee. To understand why there were two origins one has to understand the social structure of the southern black community, as an incipient generation gap alone is inadequate to explain it.

Within this community the two most important institutions, often the only institutions, were the church and the black college. They provided the primary networks through which most southern blacks interacted and communicated with one another on a regular basis. In turn, the colleges and churches were linked in a regional communications network. These institutions were also the source of black leadership, for being a "preacher or a teacher" were the main status positions in black society. Of the two, the church was by far the more important; it touched on more people's lives and was the largest and oldest institution in the black community. Even during slavery there had been an "invisible church". After emancipation, "organized religious life became the chief means by which a structured or organized social life came into existence among the Negro masses" (Frazier 1963, p. 17). Furthermore, preachers were more economically independent of white society than were teachers.

Neither of these institutions represented all the segments of black society, but the segments they did represent eventually formed the main social base for supplying civil rights activists. The church was composed of a male leadership and a largely middle-aged, lower-class female followership. The black colleges were the homes of black intellectuals and middle-class youth, male and female.

Both origins of the civil rights movement resulted in the formation of new organizations, despite the fact that at least three seemingly potential social movement organizations already existed. The wealthiest of these was the Urban League, founded in 1910. It, however, was not only largely restricted to a small portion of the black and white bourgeoisie but, until 1961, felt itself to be "essentially a social service agency" (Clark 1966, p. 245).

Founded in 1909, the National Association for the Advancement of Colored People (NAACP) pursued channels of legal change until it finally persuaded the Supreme Court to abolish educational segregation in *Brown* v. *Board of Education*. More than any other single event, this decision created the atmosphere of rising expectations that helped precipitate the movement. The NAACP suffered from its own success, however. Having organized itself primarily to support court cases and utilize other "respectable" means, it "either was not able or did not desire to modify its program in response to new demands. It believed it should continue its important work by using those techniques it had already perfected" (Blumer 1951, p. 199).

The Congress of Racial Equality, like the other two organizations, was founded in the North. It began "in 1942 as the Chicago Committee of Racial Equality, which was composed primarily of students at the University of Chicago. An off-shoot of the pacifist Fellowship of Reconciliation, its leaders were middle-class intellectual reformers, less prominent and more alienated from the mainstream of American society than the founders of the NAACP. They regarded the NAACP's legalism as too gradualist and ineffective, and aimed to apply Gandhian techniques of non-violent direct action to the problem of race relations in the United States. A year later, the Chicago Committee joined with a half dozen other groups that had emerged across the country, mostly under the encouragement of the F.O.R. to form a federation known as the Congress of Racial Equality" (Rudwick and Meier 1970, p. 10).

CORE's activities anticipated many of the main forms of protest of the civil rights movement, and its attitudes certainly seemed to fit CORE for the role of a major civil rights organization. But though it became quite influential, at the time the movement actually began, CORE had declined almost to the point of extinction. Its failure reflects the historical reality that organizations are less likely to create social movements than be created by them. More important, CORE was poorly situated to lead a movement of southern blacks. Northern-based and composed primarily of pacifist intellectuals, it had no roots in any of the existing structures of the black community, and in the North these structures were themselves weak. CORE could be a source of ideas, but not of coordination.

The coordination of a new movement required the creation of a new organization. But that was not apparent until after the Montgomery bus boycott began. That boycott was organized through institutions already existing in the black community of Montgomery.

Rosa Parks's refusal to give up her seat on the bus to a white man was not the first time such defiance of segregation laws had occurred. There had been talk of a boycott the previous time, but after local black leaders had a congenial meeting with the city commissioners, nothing happened—on either side

(King 1958, pp. 37–41). When Parks, a former secretary of the local NAACP, was arrested, she immediately called E. D. Nixon, at that time the president of the local chapter. He not only bailed her out but informed a few influential women in the city, most of whom were members of the Women's Political Council. After numerous phone calls between their members, it was the WPC that actually suggested the boycott, and E. D. Nixon who initially organized it (ibid., pp. 44–45).

The Montgomery Improvement Association (MIA) was formed at a meeting of eighteen ministers and civic leaders the Monday after Parks's conviction and a day of successful boycotting, to provide ongoing coordination. No one then suspected that coordination would be necessary for over a year, with car pools organized to provide alternative transportation for seventeen thousand riders a day. During this time the MIA grew slowly to a staff of ten in order to handle the voluminous correspondence, as well as to provide rides and keep the movement's momentum going. The organization, and the car pools, were financed by $250,000 in donations that poured in from all over the world in response to heavy press publicity about the boycott. But the organizational framework for the boycott and the MIA was the church. Most, although not all, of the officers were ministers, and Sunday meetings with congregations continued to be the main means of communicating with members of the black community and encouraging them to continue the protest.

The boycott did not end until the federal courts ruled Alabama's bus segregation laws unconstitutional late in 1956—at the same time that state courts ruled the boycott illegal. In the meantime, black leaders throughout the South had visited Montgomery, and out of the discussions came agreement to continue antisegregation protests regularly and systematically under the aegis of a new organization, the Southern Christian Leadership Conference. The NAACP could not lead the protests because, according to an SCLC pamphlet, "during the late 50s, the NAACP had been driven out of some Southern states. Its branches were outlawed as foreign corporations and its lawyers were charged with barratry, that is, persistently inciting litigation."

On January 10, 1957, over one hundred people gathered in Atlanta at a meeting called by four ministers, including Martin Luther King. Bayard Rustin drew up the "working papers." Initially called the Southern Leadership Conference on Transportation and Nonviolent Integration, the SCLC never developed a mass base even when it changed its name. It established numerous "affiliates" but did most of its work through the churches in the communities to which it sent its fieldworkers.

The church was not just the only institution available for a movement to work through; in many ways it was ideal. It performed "the central organizing function in the Negro community" (Halloway 1969, p. 22), providing both access to large masses of people on a regular basis and a natural leadership. As Wyatt Tee Walker, former executive director of SCLC, commented, "The Church today is central to the movement. If a Negro's going to have a meeting, where's he going to have it? Mostly he doesn't have a Masonic lodge, and he's not going to get the public schools. And the church is the primary means of communication" (Brink and Harris 1964, p. 103). Thus the church eventually came to be the center of the voter registration drives as well as many of the other activities of the civil rights movement.

Even the young men and women of SNCC had to use the church, though they had trouble doing so because, unlike most of the officers of SCLC, they were not themselves ministers and thus did not have a "fraternal" connection. Instead they tended to draw many of their resources and people from outside the particular town in which they were working by utilizing their natural organizational base, the college.

SNCC did not begin the sit-ins, but came out of them. Once begun, the idea of the sit-in spread initially by means of the mass media. But such sit-ins almost always took place in towns where there were Negro colleges, and groups on these campuses essentially organized the sit-in activities of their communities. Nonetheless, "CORE, with its long emphasis of nonviolent direct action, played an important part, once the sit-ins began, as an educational and organizing agent" (Zinn 1964, p. 23). CORE had very few staff in the South, but there were enough to at least hold classes and practice sessions in nonviolence.

It was SCLC, however, that was actually responsible for the formation of SNCC; though it might well have organized itself eventually. Ella Baker, then executive secretary of SCLC, thought something should be done to coordinate the rapidly speading sit-ins in 1960, and many members of SCLC thought it might be appropriate to organize a youth group. With SCLC money, Baker persuaded her alma mater, Shaw University, to provide facilities to contact the groups at centers of sit-in activity. Some two hundred people showed up for the meeting, decided to have no official connection with SCLC beyond a "friendly relationship," and formed the Student Non-Violent Co-ordinating Committee (Zinn 1964, pp. 32–34). It had no members, and its fieldworkers numbered two hundred at their highest point, but it was from the campuses, especially the southern black colleges, that it drew its sustenance and upon which its organizational base rested.

THE MOVEMENT

The term "the Movement" was originally applied to the civil rights movement by those participating in it, but as this activity expanded into a general radical critique of American society and concomitant action, the term broadened with it. To white youth throughout most of the sixties, "the Movement" referred to that plethora of youth and/or radical activities that started from the campus and eventually enveloped a large segment of middle-class youth.

The imprecise use of the term is illustrative of the imprecise definitions of the Movement. In some ways, it was several movements operating under the same rubric with a certain affinity, if not always agreement. In other ways, it was an ill-matched pairing of a social base in search of an ideology and an ideology in search of a social base. The Movement is also referred to as "the student movement" and "the New Left," reflecting the respective social base and ideology.

It has been argued that students have good reason to feel estranged from American society *in their role as students*; that they have specific complaints of inequities to them upon which they could build a powerful movement. But the demand for "student power" that should have represented this drive was a short-lived one and in fact was aborted by the very organization that was seeking to use students as its social base. Conversely, the New Left is essentially an intellectual movement whose analyses were not always welcomed or adopted by the students who marched under its banners. Consequently, the New Left became a home for all who called themselves radicals, without ever having to direct itself to the mobilization of a specific body of people to make gains for themselves. Instead, its more general framework of political analysis led students, and ex-students, to provide the troops for many other movements while often denying they had the right to make demands for themselves.

Because of its diverse nature, the "core groups" of the Movement are more plentiful and less significant than core groups of other movements discussed here. Although it did work through organizations, the Movement was much more spontaneous and undirected than any of the others. Many an investigating committee tried to pin a "conspiracy" theory on the rapidly spreading campus sit-ins, failing to realize that the mass media were really the culprits. Students so readily recognized the community of interests they shared with other students on other campuses that mere awareness that something was happening could be enough to prompt imitation.

Nonetheless, there were "core groups," and the most important of them, the Students for a Democratic Society, played a significant enough role to allow its origin to speak for much of the movement. And its formation illustrates another interesting twist on the pattern we have been observing so far.

In some ways a student movement didn't need to develop the intricate communications network that preceded movement formation among other groups. Like southern blacks, students had a natural network. The campus was the place they shared their concerns. It was the natural focal point of organizing. But it was a large place, for the most part, so at least at the beginning the basic units had to be smaller and the ties between them more definitive than was necessary once the movement was more developed.

In the late 1950s several things happened that presaged a new intellectual and/or campus movement. With the abatement of the McCarthy scare, liberal and socialist groups of students on different campuses formed new organizations. SLATE appeared at Berkeley, POLIT at Chicago, and VOICE at Michigan. Student journals, such as *New University Thought* and *Studies on the Left*, modeled after the *New Left Review* in London, also emerged. After the Bay of Pigs fiasco, Fair Play for Cuba chapters were started on several campuses. The groundwork was laid for a campus peace movement after the Berlin crisis in the summer of 1961, the resumption of nuclear testing, and the push for a massive civil defense program. As a result, the Student Peace Union and the student branch of SANE sprouted many campus chapters (O'Brien 1969, pp. 4–5).

Yet these groups were not themselves a student movement, merely the student branches of "adult" organizations. As one early leader commented,

"We must not be led into the popular characterizations of our activity as a 'spontaneous new mass movement.'... In many of the protests—civil defense, capital punishment, the Uphaus conviction—what students did was to translate the undramatic campaigns of various adult organizations into dramatic student demonstrations. The direct action of the great peace movement has been similarly under adult auspices: The Committee for Non-Violent Action, the War Resisters' League, and the American Friends Service Committee. These movements were thus neither spontaneous nor strictly a student movement; the new thing is that students are involved at all" (Haber 1966, pp. 35–36).

What focused these isolated groups on different campuses was the southern sit-ins of 1960. "These actions had a powerfully inspiring effect on many socially concerned, intellectually sensitive white students, who were galvanized almost immediately into a variety of activities in support of the Southern civil rights struggle. Aside from their inspirational effect, the sit-ins served as a mechanism for bringing such students together for the first time for practical interaction over political issues. It did not take long for a mood of activism to take root among significant pockets of students on many campuses, once the prevailing pattern of political apathy had been disrupted" (Flacks 1970, p. 1).

In 1960 SDS was just one of several "national" student political groups. It had recently changed its name from the Student League for Industrial Democracy (SLID), but still remained the relatively insignificant youth affiliate of an aging social democratic clearinghouse for liberal, prolabor, anticommunist ideas. What put life into this moribund group were two University of Michigan students, Al Haber and Tom Hayden. In the late spring of 1960 Al Haber organized a conference at U.M. on "Human Rights in the North." "This conference began SDS's long association with SNCC and recruited some of the young people who subsequently became the 'old guard' SDS leadership" (Kissinger and Ross 1968, p. 16).

Shortly after the conference, the United Auto Workers donated $10,000 to SDS, which used the money to hire Haber as an organizer. He corresponded widely, mimeographed and mailed pamphlets, gave speeches, and generally made contacts with and between others (Sale 1973, p. 35). Both Hayden and Haber argued that the different issues on which activists were working were interconnected, that a movement had to be created to work for broad social change, that the university was a potential base and agency in a movement for social change, and that SDS could play an important role in this movement (O'Brien 1969, p. 6).

Despite this potential, SDS "remained practically non-existent as an organization in the late 1960-to-1961 school year. Then, in the summer of 1961, the 14th Congress of the National Student Association was held in Madison, Wisconsin.... It was regional and national meetings of NSA which first brought together Northern white radicals" (Kissinger and Ross 1968, p. 16).

What followed were years of hard organizing effort, stimulated by civil rights activity and campus protests (Sale 1973). In the early years SDS had many competitors for the affections of students, but none in the form of organizations claiming to represent students as students. The others were largely youth groups of national liberal and socialist organizations. SDS's activities were never confined solely to the campus, and usually sought to channel student activity to the support of other movement efforts. But its formation does illustrate once again the pattern found elsewhere.

The campus provided one form of communications network, but it was an unrefined one. The development of local radical activities and the southern sit-ins selected out of the mass of students those most likely to be receptive to organizing efforts. Hayden and Haber had access to resources from LID and organized labor to finance an office and embryonic staff until SDS eventually broke away in 1962 to stand by itself. More than SDS, the multitudinous events of the sixties served to goad students into political activity, but SDS provided them with a structure in which to engage in it. And an assist in all this, in the beginning, was the "established" student organization, the NSA, its "University Press Service . . . the press work of CORE, the NAACP and other adult groups . . . [which] combined to tell the world about student actions, and so to spread the movement" (Haber 1966, p. 35).

THE NATIONAL WELFARE RIGHTS ORGANIZATION

The welfare rights movement is an excellent example of movement entrepreneurship and government involvement in movement formation. If ever a movement was *constructed*, this one was. The building blocks of its construction were the Great Society antipoverty programs and the plethora of black and especially white civil rights workers who were left "unemployed" with that movement's alternation and decline (Piven and Cloward 1971, p. 321). Many local welfare protest groups originated in antipoverty agencies in order to get more money for the poor. Many others came out of community organizations formed by liberal church groups and urban civil rights activists a few years before. These groups were widely scattered throughout the country and not linked by any communications mechanism.

The entrepreneur who linked them in order to create a movement was George Wiley, a former chemistry professor and civil rights activist who left CORE after losing his bid to become national director. Attracted to the idea of organizing welfare recipients by a pamphlet written by Columbia social work professor Richard Cloward, later published in the *Nation*, Wiley organized the Poverty/Rights Action Center in Washington in May 1966. Shortly before the P/RAC office opened on a $15,000 budget, a conference on the guaranteed annual income had been held at the University of Chicago. Organized by three social work students, it brought together organizers and representatives of welfare groups, community organizations, and poverty workers. Although not specifically invited, Wiley came and was given a place on the conference program. When the participants seemed receptive to his ideas, Wiley announced to the press that there would be national demonstrations on June 30 in support of an Ohio march for adequate welfare already being organized by the Cleveland Council of Churches (Piven and Cloward 1977, pp. 288–91).

Wiley volunteered his new organization to coordinate the national support actions. Drawing upon his contacts from the civil rights movement and those he met at the conference, his "support activities" were highly successful. "On the morning of June 30, when they finally reached Columbus, the forty marchers were joined by two thousand recipients and sympathizers from other towns in Ohio. On the same day in New York two thousand recipients massed in front of City Hall to picket in the hot sun.... Groups of recipients in fifteen other cities...also joined demonstrations against 'the welfare'" (Piven and Cloward 1971, p. 323).

This action was followed by a national conference of a hundred people in August that elected a Co-ordinating Committee to plan a founding conference for the National Welfare Rights Organization. "The organizers were members of Students for a Democratic Society, church people, and most prominently, VISTA and other antipoverty program workers" (Piven and Cloward 1977, pp. 291–92).

VISTA volunteers continued to be the NWRO's "chief organizing resource" (Piven and Cloward 1971, p. 329). But they were not the only resource supplied by the government. "If the NWRO developed as a by-product of federal intervention in the cities, it later came to have quite direct relations with the national government. In 1968, the outgoing Johnson Administration granted NWRO more than $400,000 through the Department of Labor, a sum roughly equivalent to the total amount raised from private sources after the organization was formed.... Federal officials were aware that the money would go toward strengthening local relief groups" (Piven and Cloward 1971, pp. 329–30). In effect, the federal government was supporting a social movement organization whose purpose was to extract more money from state and local governments.

This intimate connection between the federal government, the NWRO, and recipient groups lasted only a few years. The NWRO eventually faced organizational problems it was unable to surmount, and antipoverty programs were dismantled by the Nixon administration (Piven and Cloward 1977). But while they lasted, local recipient groups were forged into a movement by experienced civil rights activists and government-funded volunteers under the direction of a single well-trained organizer with an entrepreneurial instinct.

THE WOMEN'S LIBERATION MOVEMENT[*]

Women are not well organized. Historically tied to the family and isolated from their own kind, only in the nineteenth century did women in this country have the opportunity to develop independent associations of their own. These

[*] Data for this section are based on my observations while a founder and participant in the younger branch of the Chicago women's liberation movement from 1967 through 1969 and editor of the first (at that time, only) national newsletter. I was able, through extensive correspondence and interviews, to keep a record of how each group around the country started, where the organizers got the idea from, who they had talked to, what conferences were held and who attended, the political affiliations (or lack of them) of the first members, and so forth. Although I was a member of Chicago NOW, information on the origins of it and the other older branch organizations comes entirely through *ex post facto* interviews of the principals and examination of early papers in preparation for my dissertation on the women's liberation movement. Most of my informants requested that their contribution remain confidential.

associations took years and years of careful organizational work to build. Eventually they formed the basis for the suffrage movement of the early twentieth century. The associations took less time to die. Today the Women's Trade Union League, the General Federation of Women's Clubs, the Women's Christian Temperance Union, not to mention the powerful National Women's Suffrage Association, are all either dead or a pale shadow of their former selves.

As of 1960, not one organization of women had the potential to become a social movement organization, nor was there any form of "neutral" structure of interaction to provide the base for such an organization. The closest exception to the former was the National Women's Party, which has remained dedicated to feminist concerns since its inception in 1916. However, the NWP has been essentially a lobbying group for the Equal Rights Amendment since 1923. From the beginning, the NWP believed that a small group of women concentrating their efforts in the right places was more effective than a mass appeal, and so was not appalled by the fact that as late as 1969 even the majority of avowed feminists in this country had never heard of the ERA or the NWP.

The one large women's organization that might have provided a base for a social movement was the 180,000-member Federation of Business and Professional Women's Clubs. Yet, while it has steadily lobbied for legislation of importance to women, as late as "1966 BPW rejected a number of suggestions that it redefine . . . goals and tactics and become a kind of 'NAACP for women' . . . out of fear of being labeled 'feminist'" (Hole and Levine 1971, p. 89).

Before any social movement could develop among women, there had to be created a structure to bring potential feminist sympathizers together. To be sure, groups such as the BPW, and institutions such as the women's colleges, might be a good source of adherents for such a movement. But they were determined not to be the source of leadership.

What happened in the 1960s was the development of two new communications networks in which women played prominent roles that allowed, even forced, an awakened interest in the old feminist ideas. As a result, the movement actually has two origins, from two different strata of society, with two different styles, orientations, values, and forms of organization. The first of these will be referred to as the "older branch" of the movement, partially because it began first and partially because it was on the older side of the "generation gap" that pervaded the sixties. Its most prominent organization is the National Organization for Women (NOW), which was also the first to be formed. The style of its movement organizations tends to be traditional with elected officers, boards of directors, bylaws, and the other trappings of democratic procedure. Conversely, the "younger branch" consisted of innumerable small groups engaged in a variety of activities whose contact with one another was always tenuous (Freeman 1975, p. 50).

The forces that led to NOW's formation were set in motion in 1961 when President Kennedy established the President's Commission on the Status of Women at the behest of Esther Petersen, then director of the Women's Bureau. Its 1963 report, *American Women*, and subsequent committee publications documented just how thoroughly women were denied many rights and opportunities. The most significant response to the activity of the President's commission was the establishment of some fifty state commissions to do similar research on a state level. The Presidential and State Commission activity laid the groundwork for the future movement in two significant ways: (1) It unearthed ample evidence of women's unequal status and in the process convinced many previously uninterested women that something should be done; (2) it created a climate of expectations that something would be done. The women of the Presidential and State Commissions who were exposed to these influences exchanged visits, correspondence, and staff, and met with one another at an annual commission convention. They were in a position to share and mutually reinforce their growing awareness and concern over women's issues. These commissions thus provided an embryonic communications network.

During this time, two other events of significance occurred. The first was the publication of Betty Friedan's *The Feminine Mystique* in 1963. A quick best seller, the book stimulated many women to question the *status quo* and some women to suggest to Friedan that an organization be formed to do something about it. The second event was the addition of "sex" to the 1964 Civil Rights Act.

Many thought the "sex" provision was a joke, and the Equal Employment Opportunity Commission treated it as one, refusing to enforce it seriously. But a rapidly growing feminist coterie within the EEOC argued that "sex" would be taken more seriously if there were "some sort of NAACP for women" to put pressure on the government.

On June 30, 1966, these three strands of incipient feminism came together, and NOW was tied from the knot. At that time, government officials running the Third National Conference of Commissions on the Status of Women, ironically titled "Targets for Action," forbade the presentation of a suggested resolution calling for the EEOC to treat sex discrimination with the same consideration as race discrimination. The officials said one government agency could not be allowed to pressure another, despite the fact that the state commissions were not federal agencies. The small group of women who desired such a resolution had met the night before in Friedan's hotel room to discuss the possibility of a civil rights organization for women. Not convinced of its need, they chose instead to propose the resolution. When conference officials vetoed it, they held a whispered conversation over lunch and agreed to form an action organization "to bring women into full participation in the mainstream of American society now, assuming all the privileges and responsibilities thereof in truly equal partnership with men." The name NOW was coined by Friedan who was at the conference doing research on a book. When word leaked out, twenty-eight women paid five dollars each to join before the day was over (Friedan 1967, p. 4).

By the time the organizing conference was held the following October 29 through 30, over three hundred men and women had become charter members. It is impossible to do a breakdown on the composition of the charter membership, but one of the officers and board is possible. Such a breakdown accurately reflected NOW's origins. Friedan was president, two former EEOC commissioners were vice presidents, a representative of the United Auto Workers Women's Committee was secretary-treasurer, and there were seven past and present members of the State Commissions on the Status of Women on the twenty member board. One hundred twenty-six of the charter members were Wisconsin residents—and Wisconsin had the most active state Commission. Occupationally, the board and officers were primarily from the professions, labor, government, and communications fields. Of these, only those from labor had any experience in organizing, and they resigned a year later in a dispute over support of the Equal Rights Amendment. Instead of organizational experience, what the early NOW members had was experience in working with and in the media, and it was here that their early efforts were aimed.

As a result, NOW often gave the impression of being larger than it was. It was highly successful in getting in the press; much less successful in either bringing about concrete changes or forming an organization. Thus it was not until 1970, when the national press simultaneously did major stories on the women's liberation movement, that NOW's membership increased significantly.

In the meantime, unaware of and unknown to NOW, the EEOC, or the State Commissions, younger women began forming their own movement. Here, too, the groundwork had been laid some years before. The different social action projects of the sixties had attracted many women, who were quickly shunted into traditional roles and faced with the self-evident contradiction of working in a "freedom movement" but not being very free. No single "youth movement" activity or organization is responsible for forming the younger branch of the women's liberation movement, but together they created a "radical community" in which like-minded people continually interacted or were made aware of one another. This community provided the necessary network of communication and its radical ideas the framework of analysis that "explained" the dismal situation in which radical women found themselves.

Papers had been circulated on women and individual temporary women's caucuses had been held as early as 1964 (see Hayden and King 1966). But it was not until 1967 and 1968 that the groups developed a determined, if cautious, continuity and began to consciously expand themselves. At least five groups in five different cities (Chicago, Toronto, Detroit, Seattle, and Gainesville, Florida) formed spontaneously, independently of one another. They came at an auspicious moment, for 1967 was the year in which the blacks kicked the whites out of the civil rights movement, student power was discredited by SDS, and the New Left was on the wane. Only draft resistance activities were on the increase, and this movement more than any other exemplified the social inequities of the sexes. Men could resist the draft. Women could only counsel resistance.

At this point, there were few opportunities available for political work. Some women fit well into the secondary role of draft counseling. Many didn't. For years their complaints of unfair treatment had been forestalled by movement men with the dictum that those things could wait until after the Revolution. Now these political women found time on their hands, but still the men would not listen.

A typical example was the event that precipitated the formation of the Chicago group, the first independent group in this country. At the August 1967 National Conference for New Politics convention a women's caucus met for days, but was told its resolution wasn't significant enough to merit a floor discussion. By threatening to tie up the convention with procedural motions the women succeeded in having their statement tacked to the end of the agenda. It was never discussed. The chair refused to recognize any of the many women standing by the microphone, their hands straining upwards. When he instead called on someone to speak on "the forgotten American, the American Indian," five women rushed the podium to demand an explanation. But the chairman just patted one of them on the head (literally) and told her, "Cool down, little girl. We have more important things to talk about than women's problems."

The "little girl" was Shulamith Firestone, future author of *The Dialectic of Sex*, and she didn't cool down. Instead she joined with another Chicago woman she met there who had unsuccessfully tried to organize a women's group that summer, to call a meeting of the women who had halfheartedly attended those summer meetings. Telling their stories to those women, they stimulated sufficient rage to carry the group for three months, and by that time it was a permanent institution.

Another somewhat similar event occurred in Seattle the following winter. At the University of Washington an SDS organizer was explaining to a large meeting how white college youth established rapport with the poor whites with whom they were working. "He noted that sometimes after analyzing societal ills, the men shared leisure time by 'balling a chick together.' He pointed out that such activities did much to enhance the political consciousness of the poor white youth. A woman in the audience asked, 'And what did it do for the consciousness of the chick?'" (Hole and Levine 1971, p. 120). After the meeting, a handful of enraged women formed Seattle's first group.

Subsequent groups to the initial five were largely organized rather than formed spontaneously out of recent events. In particular, the Chicago group was responsible for the formation of many new groups in Chicago and in other cities. Unlike NOW, the women in the first groups had had years of experience as trained organizers. They knew how to utilize the infrastructure of the radical community, the underground press, and the free universities to disseminate women's liberation ideas. Chicago, as a center of New Left activity, had the largest number of politically conscious organizers. Many traveled widely to left conferences and demonstrations, and most used the opportunity to talk with other women about the new movement. In spite of public derision by radical men, or perhaps because of it, young women steadily formed new groups around the country.

ANALYSIS

From these data there appear to be four essential elements involved in movement formation: (1) the growth of a preexisting communications network that is (2) cooptable to the ideas of the new movement; (3) a series of crises that galvanize into action people involved in a cooptable network, and/or (4) subsequent organizing effort to weld the spontaneous groups together into a movement. Each of these elements needs to be examined in detail.

COMMUNICATIONS NETWORK

The four movements we have looked at developed out of already existing networks within their populations. The church and the black college were the primary institutions through which southern blacks communicated their concerns. In the North the church was much weaker and the black college non-existent, perhaps explaining why the movement had greater difficulty developing and surviving there. The Movement, composed primarily of white youth, had its centers on the campus because this was where that constituency could readily be found. Nonetheless, campuses were too large and disconnected for incipient movement leaders to find each other. Instead they fruitfully used the national and regional conferences of the CIA-financed National Student Association to identify and reach those students who were socially conscious. Of course, once the Movement took hold, it developed its own conferences and networks, so the subsequent exposé of the NSA came too late to stifle its growth. The welfare rights movement, much more than the others, was created by the conscious efforts of one person. But that person had to find constituents somewhere, and he found them most readily in groups already organized by antipoverty agencies. Organizers for the national movement, in turn, were found among former civil rights activists looking for new directions for their political energies.

The women's liberation movement, even more than the previous ones, illustrates the importance of a network precisely because the conditions for a movement existed *before* a network came into being, but the movement didn't exist until afterward. Analysts of socioeconomic causes have concluded that the movement could have started anytime within a 20 year period. Strain for women was as great in 1955 as in 1965 (Ferriss 1971). What changed was the organizational situation. It was not until new networks emerged among women aware of inequities beyond local boundaries that a movement could grow past the point of occasional, spontaneous uprisings. The fact that two distinct movements, with two separate origins, developed from two networks unaware of each other is further evidence of the key role of preexisting communications networks as the fertile soil in which new movements can sprout.

References to the importance of a preexisting communications network appear frequently in case studies of social movements, though the theoretical writers were much slower to recognize their salience. According to Buck (1920, pp. 43–44), the Grange established a degree of organization among American farmers in the 19th century that greatly facilitated the spread of future farmers' protests. Lipset has reported that in Saskatchewan, "the rapid acceptance of new ideas and movements . . . can be attributed mainly to the high degree of organization. . . . The role of the social structure of the western wheat belt in facilitating the rise of new movements has never been sufficiently appreciated by historians and sociologists. Repeated challenges and crises forced the western farmers to create many more community institutions (especially co-operatives and economic pressure groups) than are necessary in a more stable area. These groups in turn provided a structural basis for immediate action in critical situations. [Therefore] though it was a new radical party, the C.C.F. did not have to build up an organization from scratch" (1959, p. 206).

Similarly, Heberle (1951, p. 232) reports several findings that Nazism was most successful in small, well-integrated communities. As Lipset put it, these findings "sharply challenge the various interpretations of Nazism as the product of the growth of anomie and the general rootlessness of modern urban industrial society" (1959, p. 146).

Indirect evidence attesting to the essential role of formal and informal communications networks is found in diffusion theory, which emphasizes the importance of personal interaction rather than impersonal media communication in the spread of ideas (Rogers 1962, Lionberger 1960). This personal influence occurs through the organizational patterns of a community (Lionberger 1960, p. 73). It does not occur through the mass media. The mass media may be a source of information, but they are not a key source of influence.

Their lesser importance in relation to preexisting communications networks was examined in one study on "The Failure of an Incipient Social Movement" (Jackson, Peterson, Bull, Monsen, and Richmond 1960). In 1957 a potential tax protest movement in Los Angeles generated considerable interest and publicity for a little over a month but was dead within a year. According to the authors, this did not reflect a lack of public notice. They concluded that "mass communication alone is probably insufficient without a network of communication specifically linking those interested in the matter.... If a movement is to grow rapidly, it cannot rely upon its own network of communication, but must capitalize on networks already in existence" (p. 37).

A major reason it took social scientists so long to acknowledge the importance of communications networks was because the prevailing theories of the post-World War II era emphasized increasing social dislocation and anomie. Mass society theorists, as they were called, hypothesized that significant community institutions that linked individuals to governing elites were breaking down, that society was becoming a mass of isolated individuals. These individuals were seen as increasingly irresponsible and ungovernable, prone to irrational protests because they had no mediating institutions through which to pursue grievances (Kornhauser 1959).

In emphasizing disintegrating vertical connections, mass society theorists passed lightly over the role of horizontal ones, only occasionally acknowledging that "the combination of internal contact and external isolation facilitates the work of the mass agitator" (Kornhauser 1959, p. 218). This focus changed in the early seventies. Pinard's study of the Social Credit Party of Quebec (1971) severely criticized mass society theory, arguing instead that "when strains are severe and widespread a new movement is more likely to meet its early success among the more strongly integrated citizens" (Pinard 1971, p. 192).

This insight was expanded by Oberschall (1973), who created a six-cell table to predict both the occurrence and type of protest. As did the mass society theorists, Oberschall said that even when there are grievances, protest will not occur outside institutional channels by those who are connected, through their own leadership or patron/client relationships, with governing elites. Among those who are segmented from such elites, the type of protest will be determined by whether there is communal, associational, or little organization. In the latter case, discontent is expressed through riots or other short-lived violent uprisings. "It is under conditions of strong... ties and segmentation that the possibility of the rapid spread of opposition movements on a continuous basis exists" (p. 123).

The movements we have studied would confirm Oberschall's conclusions, but not as strongly as he makes them. In all these cases a preexisting communications network was a necessary but insufficient condition for movement formation. Yet the newly formed networks among student radicals, welfare recipients, and women can hardly compare with the long-standing ties provided by the southern black churches and colleges. Their ties were tenuous and may not have survived the demise of their movements.

The importance of segmentation, or lack of connection with relevant elites, is less obvious in the sixties' movements. The higher socioeconomic status of incipient feminists and Movement leaders would imply greater access to elites than is true for blacks or welfare recipients. If Oberschall were correct, these closer connections should either have permitted easier and more rapid grievance solutions or more effective social control. They did neither. Indeed, it was the group most closely connected to decision-making elites—women of the Presidential and State Commission—who were among the earliest to see the need of a protest organization. Women of the younger branch of the movement did have their grievances against the men of the New Left effectively suppressed for several years, but even they eventually rejected this kind of elite control, even when it meant rejecting the men.

Conversely, Piven and Cloward show that the establishment of closer ties between leaders of local welfare rights groups and welfare workers through advisory councils and community coordinators led to a curtailment of militance and the institutionalization of grievances (1977, pp. 326–31). They also argue that the development of government-funded community programs effectively coopted many local black movement leaders in the North and that federal channeling of black protest in the South into voter registration projects focused the movement there into traditional electoral politics (ibid., p. 253). In short, the evidence about the role of segmentation in movement formation is ambiguous. The effect may be varied considerably by the nature of the political system.

CO-OPTIBILITY

A recurrent theme in our studies is that not just any communications network will do. It must be one that is co-optable to the ideas of the new movement. The Business and Professional Women's (BPW) clubs were a network among women, but having rejected feminism, they could not overcome the ideological barrier to new political action until after feminism became established. Similarly, there were other communications networks among students than that of the NSA, for example fraternities and atheletic associations. But these were not networks that politically conscious young people were likely to be involved in.

On the other hand, the women on the Presidential and State Commissions and the feminist coterie of the EEOC were co-optable largely because their immersion in the facts of female status and the details of sex discrimination cases made them very conscious of the need for change. Likewise, the young women of the "radical community" lived in an atmosphere of questioning, confrontation, and change. They absorbed an ideology of "freedom" and "liberation" far more potent than any latent "antifeminism" might have been.

NSA does not appear to have been as readily co-optable to the Movement as the new women's networks were to feminism. As an association of student governments, its participants had other concerns besides political ones. But while it didn't transform itself, it was a source of recruitment and a forum for discussion that gave the early SDS organizers contacts on many campuses.

While no data are available that would identify specific networks within the black churches and colleges that were co-optable to the emerging civil rights movement, we can reasonably assume there were some. Not all blacks initially supported the Montgomery boycott or agreed that the protests should be extended. The MIA and SCLC had to find like-minded people and then coordinate their actions.

Exactly what makes a network co-optable is harder to elucidate. Pinard (1971, p. 186) noted the necessity for groups to "*possess* or *develop* an ideology or simply subjective interests congruent with that of a new movement" for them to "act as mobilizing rather than restraining agents toward that movement," but did not further explore what affected the "primary group climate." More illumination is provided by the diffusion of innovation studies that point out the necessity for new ideas to fit in with already established norms for changes to happen easily. Furthermore, a social system that has as a value "innovativeness" (as the radical community did) will more rapidly adopt ideas than one that looks upon the habitual performance of traditional practices as the ideal (as most organized women's groups did in the fifties). Usually, as Lionberger (1960, p. 91) points out, "people act in terms of past experience and knowledge." People who have had similar experiences are likely to share similar perceptions of a situation and to mutually reinforce those perceptions as well as their subsequent interpretation. A co-optable network, then, is one whose members have had common experiences that predispose them to be receptive to the particular new ideas of the incipient movement and who are not faced with structural or ideological barriers to action. If the new movement as an "innovation" can interpret these experiences and perceptions in ways that point out channels for social action, then participation in a social movement becomes the logical thing to do.

THE ROLE OF CRISES

As our examples have illustrated, similar perceptions must be translated into action. This is often done by a crisis. For blacks in Montgomery, this was generated by Rosa Parks's refusal to give up her seat on a bus to a white man. For women who formed the older branch of the women's movement, the impetus to organize was the refusal of the EEOC to enforce the sex provision of Title VII, precipitated by the concomitant refusal of federal officials at the conference to allow a supportive resolution. For younger women there were a series of minor crises.

While not all movements are formed by such precipitating events, they are quite common as they serve to crystallize and focus discontent. From their own experiences, directly and concretely, people feel the need for change in a situation that allows for an exchange of feelings with others, mutual validation, and a subsequent reinforcement of innovative interpretation. Perception of an immediate need for change is a major factor in predisposing people to accept new ideas (Rogers 1962, p. 280). Nothing makes desire for change more acute than a crisis. Such a crisis need not be a major one; it need only embody collective discontent.

ORGANIZING EFFORTS

A crisis will only catalyze a well-formed communications network. If such networks are embryonically developed or only partially co-optable, the potentially active individuals in them must be linked together by someone. This is essentially what George Wiley did for local recipient groups and what other SDS organizers did with the contacts they made in NSA and on campuses. As Jackson et al. (1960, p. 37) stated, "Some protest may persist where the source of trouble is constantly present. But interest ordinarily cannot be maintained unless there is a welding of spontaneous groups into some stable organization." In other words, people must be organized. Social movements do not simply occur.

The role of the organizer in movement formation is another neglected aspect of the theoretical literature. There has been great concern with leadership, but the two roles are distinct and not always performed by the same individual. In the early stages of a movement, it is the organizer much more than any leader who is important, and such an individual or cadre must often operate behind the scenes. The nature and function of these two roles was most clearly evident in the Townsend old-age movement of the thirties. Townsend was the "charismatic" leader, but the movement was organized by his partner, real estate promoter Robert Clements. Townsend himself acknowledges that without Clements' help, the movement would never have gone beyond the idea stage (Holzman 1963).

The importance of organizers is pervasive in the sixties' movements. Dr. King may have been the public spokesperson of the Montgomery Bus Boycott who caught the eye of the media, but it was E.D. Nixon who organized it. Certainly the "organizing cadre" that young women in the radical community came to be was key to the growth of that branch of the women's liberation movement, despite the fact that no "leaders" were produced (and were actively discouraged). The existence of many leaders but no organizers in the older branch of the women's liberation movement readily explains its subsequent slow development. The crucial role of organizers in SDS and the National Welfare Rights Organization was described earlier.

The function of the organizer has been explored indirectly by other analysts. Rogers (1962) devotes many pages to the "change agent" who, while he does not necessarily weld a group together or "construct" a movement, does many of the same things for agricultural innovation that an organizer does for political change. Mass society theory makes frequent reference to the "agitator," though not in a truly informative way. Interest groups are often organized by single individuals and some of them evolve into social movements. Salisbury's study of farmers' organizations finds this a recurrent theme. He also discovered that "a considerable number of farm groups were subsidized by other, older, groups. . . . The Farm Bureau was organized and long sustained by subsidies, some from federal and state governments, and some by local businessmen" (Salisbury 1959, p. 13).

These patterns are similar to ones we have found in the formation of social movements. Other organizations, even the government, often serve as training centers for organizers and sources of material support to aid the formation of groups and/or movements. The civil rights movement was the training ground for many an organizer of other movements. The League for Industrial Democracy financed SDS in its early days, and the NSA provided indirect support by hiring many SDS organizers as NSA staff. The role of the government in the formation of the National Welfare Rights Organization was so significant that it would lead one to wonder if this association should be considered more of an interest group in the traditional sense than a movement "core" organization.

From all this it would appear that training as an organizer or at least as a proselytizer or entrepreneur of some kind is a necessary background for those individuals who act as movement innovators. Even in something as seemingly spontaneous as a social movement, the professional is more valuable than the amateur.

REFERENCES

Adorno, L. W., et al.
  1950   *The Authoritarian Personality.* New York: Harper & Row.
Bird, Caroline
  1968   *Born Female: The High Cost of Keeping Women Down.* New York: McKay.
Blumer, Herbert
  1951   "Social Movements." In A. M. Lee, ed., *New Outline of the Principles of Sociology.* New York: Barnes and Noble.
  1957   "Collective Behavior." In Joseph B. Gittler, ed., *Review of Sociology: Analysis of a Decade.* New York: Wiley.
Brink, William, and Louis Harris
  1964   *The Negro Revolution in America.* New York: Simon and Schuster.
Buck, Solon J.
  1920   *The Agrarian Crusade.* New Haven: Yale University Press.
Cantril, Hadley
  1941   *The Psychology of Social Movements.* New York: Wiley.
Clark, Kenneth B.

1966 "The Civil Rights Movement: Momentum and Organization." *Daedalus*, Winter.

Cloward, Richard
1966 "A Strategy to End Poverty." *Nation*, 2 May.

Coleman, James
1957 *Community Conflict*. Glencoe, Ill.: Free Press.

Currie, Elliott, and Jerome H. Skolnick
1970 "Critical Note on Conceptions of Collective Behavior." *Annals of the American Academy of Political and Social Science* 391 (September): 34–45.

Dahrendorf, Ralf
1959 *Class and Class Conflict in Industrial Society*. Palo Alto, Calif.: Stanford University Press.

Davis, James C.
1962 "Toward a Theory of Revolution." *American Sociological Review* 27, no. 1: 5–19.

Dawson, C. A., and W. E. Gettys
1929 *An Introduction to Sociology*. New York: Ronald Press.

Edelsberg, Herman
1965 "NYU 18th Conference on Labor." *Labor Relations Reporter* 61 (August): 253–55.

Ferriss, Abbott L.
1971 *Indicators of Trends in the Status of American Women*. New York: Russell Sage Foundation.

Firestone, Shulamith
1971 *Dialectics of Sex*. New York: Morrow.

Flacks, Richard
1970 "The New Left and American Politics: After Ten Years." Paper presented at the American Political Science Association convention, September.

Frazier, E. Franklin
1963 *The Negro Church in America*. New York: Schocken.

Freeman, Jo
1975 *The Politics of Women's Liberation*. New York: Longman.

Friedan, Betty
1963 *The Feminine Mystique*. New York: Dell.
1967 "NOW: How It Began." *Women Speaking*, April.

Griffiths, Martha
1966 Speech of 20 June, *Congressional Record*.

Gurr, Ted
1970 *Why Men Rebel*. Princeton: Princeton University Press.

Haber, Robert A.
1966 "From Protest to Radicalism: An Appraisal of the Student Movement: 1960." In Michael Cohen and Dennis Hale, eds., *The New Student Left*. Boston: Beacon Press.

Hayden, Casey, and Mary King
1966 "A Kind of Memo." *Liberation*, April.

Heberle, Rudolph
1951 *Social Movements*. New York: Appleton-Century-Crofts.

Hoffer, Eric
1951 *The True Believer*. New York: Harper & Row.

Hole, Judith, and Ellen Levine
1971 *Rebirth of Feminism*. New York: Quadrangle.

Holloway, Harry
1969   *The Politics of the Southern Negro.* New York: Random House.
Holzman, Abraham
1963   *The Townsend Movement: A Political Study.* New York: Bookman.
Jackson, Maurice, et al.
1960   "The Failure of an Incipient Social Movement." *Pacific Sociological Review* 3, no. 1: 40.
Killian, Lewis M.
1964   "Social Movements." In R. E. L. Faris, ed., *Handbook of Modern Sociology.* Chicago: Rand McNally.
King, C. Wendell
1956   *Social Movements in the United States.* New York: Random House.
King, Martin Luther, Jr.
1958   *Stride Toward Freedom.* New York: Harper & Row.
Kissinger, C. Clark, and Bob Ross
1968   "Starting in '60: Or From SLID to Resistance." *New Left Notes,* 10 June.
Kornhauser, William
1959   *The Politics of Mass Society.* Glencoe, Ill.: Free Press.
Lang, Kurt, and Gladys Engle Lang
1961   *Collective Dynamics.* New York: Cromwell.
Lionberger, Herbert F.
1960   *Adoption of New Ideas and Practices.* Ames: Iowa State University Press.
Lipset, Seymour M.
1959   *Agrarian Socialism.* Berkeley: University of California Press.
Lowi, Theodore J.
1971   *The Politics of Discord.* New York: Basic Books.
McCarthy, John, and Mayer N. Zald
1973   *The Trend of Social Movements in America: Professionalization and Resource Mobilization.* Morristown, N. J.: General Learning Press.
Oberschall, Anthony
1973   *Social Conflict and Social Movements.* Englewood Cliffs, N. J.: Prentice-Hall.
O'Brien, James
1969   *A History of the New Left, 1960–68.* Cambridge, Mass.: New England Free Press.
Pinard, Maurice
1968   "Mass Society and Political Movements: A New Formulation." *American Journal of Sociology* 73, no. 6 (May): 680–92.
1971   *The Rise of a Third Party: A Study in Crisis Politics.* Englewood Cliffs, N.J.: Prentice-Hall.
Piven, Frances Fox, and Richard Cloward
1971   *Regulating the Poor: The Functions of Public Welfare.* New York: Pantheon.
1977   *Poor People's Movements: Why They Succeed, How They Fail.* New York: Pantheon.
Rogers, Everett M.
1962   *Diffusion of Innovations.* New York: Free Press.
Rudwick, Elliott, and August Meier
1970   "Organizational Structure and Goal Succession: A Comparative Analysis of the NAACP and CORE, 1964–1968." *Social Science Quarterly* 51 (June).
Sale, Kirkpatrick
1973   *SDS.* New York: Random House.
Salisbury, Robert H.

1969 "An Exchange Theory of Interest Groups." *Midwest Journal of Political Science* 13, no. 1 (February).

Shils, Edward
1970 "Center and Periphery." In Center for Social Organization Studies, *Selected Essays*. Chicago: University of Chicago Press.

Smelser, Neil J.
1963 *Theory of Collective Behavior*. Glencoe, Ill.: Free Press.

Toch, Hans
1965 *The Social Psychology of Social Movements*. Indianapolis: Bobbs-Merrill.

Turner, Ralph H.
1964 "Collective Behavior and Conflict: New Theoretical Frameworks." *Sociological Quarterly*.

Turner, Ralph H., and Lewis M. Killian
1957 *Collective Behavior*. Englewood Cliffs, N. J.: Prentice-Hall.

Zinn, Howard
1964 *SNCC: The New Abolitionists*. Boston: Beacon Press.

Levitate the Pentagon Vigil, 1967.

Part 2
Mobilization

Among the most important problems facing movements is how to recruit participants, how to maintain their active allegiance to the movements, and how to channel their energy into common tasks. Many movements have taken it for granted that their supporters are committed to the goals of the movements and that commitment alone is sufficient to sustain activism. This is often the case, at least when a movement is well organized, under attack, and when support is needed for only a short time. But movements operating on the premise that commitment is all that is necessary are movements that eventually fail. Commitment by itself rarely proves sufficient to sustain powerless groups trying to change the status quo. As the studies in this section amply illustrate, much more is necessary.

Judkins and Jenkins compare several attempts at organizing by underprivileged groups with clear and discrete grievances. Judkins looks at the Black and Brown Lung movements of Appalachia, and Jenkins compares three separate attempts to organize farmworkers in California. Their data show that these groups did not have the knowledge or material resources to organize themselves into a successful movement. Only when there was an ongoing infusion of outside resources did a movement become feasible. These resources included knowledge of the problem (e.g., that coal and cotton dust cause disease), financial support for permanent staff, access to professional expertise, and expressions of legitimacy from outside authorities.

But the data also make it clear that an even more important resource was an understanding of why people join organizations and an ability to provide members with rewards for their participation. Successful organizations offer not only opportunities for members to demonstrate their commitment to the cause but opportunities for members to share experiences and socialize with others of similar backgrounds. These solidary incentives are the "glue" that hold movement organizations together even when victories are few and far between.

Gross, Smith, and Wallston show that too much of a good thing can be counterproductive, however. The phenomenon they call the men's movement is all glue and no substance. Except for a small core of committed activists, participants enjoy the benefits of sharing without expending the effort and taking the risks of reaching out to others. This failure is probably not due to a lack of resources because, unlike mill and farmworkers, participants are largely well-educated professionally employed white men. But their grievances are vague and diffuse, their potential sympathizers hard to locate, and their purposive incentives largely lacking.

Johnson attacks this question from a different perspective by examining how the disabled were able to organize in one part of the country but failed to do so in others. She attributes success in the Bay Area to a change of consciousness that did not occur to the same degree elsewhere. Like Jenkins and Judkins, she also points to the importance of elite legitimation and the existence of preexisting networks to facilitate mobilization.

Thorne is more concerned with mobilization as strategy than with the strategy of mobilization. She compares two draft-resistance groups in Boston, one offering draft counseling and the other public noncooperation, to highlight the conflict between gaining legitimacy and gaining public attention.

Each of the articles in this section makes it clear that the spontaneity that is characteristic of movements must be organized to maximize effectiveness.

2

Mobilization of Membership: The Black and Brown Lung Movements

Bennett M. Judkins

THE THEORETICAL ISSUE

A traditional focus in the study of social movements has been on how people are recruited and are retained long enough for the movement to accomplish its goals. This focus has been a major one in part because the dominant theoretical approaches have emphasized why an individual engages in collective action. The emphasis on the psychological characteristics of movement participants as the causal factor for a movement's existence has generated a great deal of literature but little consensus on why people join movements.

Early psychoanalytic approaches stressed that individuals prevented from attaining their goals developed attitudes of aggression. As a result, they were apt to "find release by participation in a social movement which may direct aggressive tendencies at conditions or groups which are not responsible for the initial causes of frustration" (Herberle 1951, p. 107). A recurrent social psychological explanation is the concept of relative deprivation. According to Denton Morrison,

> The basic notion is that feelings of deprivation, of discontent over one's situation, depend on what one wants to have; that is, deprivation occurs in relation to desired points of references, often, "reference groups," rather than in relation to how little one has. In turn, social movements are thought to emerge and flourish when groups of persons experience relative deprivation. (Morrison 1971, p. 675)

Another major influence was Gustave LeBon (1960), who asserted that individuals act differently and more rationally alone than in collectives. His interpretation dominated the study of social movements for almost a century. The collective behavior approach came under withering attack in the 1960s and seventies as evidence mounted that participants in social movements were neither irrational nor psychologically less stable than nonparticipants. Indeed, participants were usually better educated, more likely to be active in their communities, and had a high sense of political efficacy (see Obershall 1973, pp. 135–37; Geschwender 1971, pp. 156–57).

Consequently, a new theoretical perspective called *resource mobilization** emerged that moved away from the social psychology of collective behavior to look closely at the process by which people with grievances are mobilized into social movements. This added a sociological framework to the already existing attempts of many movement leaders and activists to develop guidelines and principles on the problems of membership recruitment and movement development. The traditional emphases on structural strain, generalized belief, and deprivation, which had ignored many of the ongoing problems and strategic dilemmas of social movements (Zald and McCarthy 1979, p. 1), was rejected. The new approach viewed movement formation not as a "simple knee-jerk response to social conditions" (Wilson 1973, p. 90) but as a complex process of the mobilization of resources—of which movement participants were only one —† necessary for the survival and success of a social movement.

This chapter looks at the mobilization of people into two occupational health movements that have emerged in the last two decades to address problems resulting from workers' exposure to detrimental environmental conditions: the Black Lung movement in the coal mining industry and the Brown Lung movement in the textile industry.

The discussion is organized around three hypotheses prominent in the resource mobilization perspective. First, there is an explicit recognition of the importance of involvement by individuals and organizations from outside the collectivity a social movement represents. Second, individual involvement in social movement activity is explained by the costs and rewards of participation. Third, recruitment differs with the form of organization of the move-

---

* The research mobilization perspective is represented in the works of John Wilson, Charles Tilly, Williams Gamson, Anthony Oberschall, Michael Lipsky, and John McCarthy and Mayer Zald. It reflects an interest in the dynamics and tactics of social movement growth, decay, and change and emphasizes both societal support and constraint of social movement phenomenoa (Zald and McCarthy 1979).

† Advocates of the resource mobilization perspective, particularly McCarthy and Zald, emphasize the declining significance of the membership base to the development of modern social movements. They see the rise of professional movement organizations made up primarily of personnel committed to social movement careers as more important than individual citizen participation to the vitality of a social movement. It is the assumption of this author, however, that although the resources other than beneficiary membership are important to the success of a movement, and even to the mobilization of membership, as is described in this chapter, the essence of a "social movement" implies participation by large numbers of people. If the professional social movement organization, or "interest group," as political scientists might call it, fails to mobilize a large number of beneficiary constituents, then it remains "interest group" even if the manipulation of the press results in the appearance of a mass movement.

ments. An analysis of the two movements demonstrates how these factors—outside involvement, costs and rewards, and form of organization—influence recruitment of potential supporters into social movements. A final section of the chapter analyzes the impact of participation in the movement on the retention of active participants.

Before any discussion of the two movements, let us take a look at a brief history of the environment in which the movements developed.

OCCUPATIONAL HEALTH IN AMERICA

The problem of occupational illness in America received very little attention until the 1970s. This was true in part because the field of occupational health had historically been concerned with work safety rather than occupational disease. Treatment was generally restricted to those emergency measures necessary for the worker to complete the workday. Also, occupational health programs were usually handled by company doctors with both an economic relationship with their employer and a potential economic conflict with the worker's personal physician. Moreover, occupational health research was until recently poorly funded. In 1972, only 36 cents per worker was spent annually on the detection, control, and prevention of occupational disease (Kerr 1972, pp. 12–13).

An awareness of the problems of occupational illness was strengthened by the 1969 Federal Coal Mine Health and Safety Act and the 1970 Occupational Safety and Health Act. These laws not only raised the consciousness of American workers, medical professionals, government agencies, and industries but led to guidelines and standards for industries to follow. A regulatory agency, the Occupational Safety and Health Administration (OSHA), was established to oversee the industries and protect the health of America's workers.

Nonetheless, acknowledgment of occupational health problems was limited. This was especially true of coal workers' pneumoconiosis, or "black lung," a respiratory disease caused by the inhalation of coal dust from underground mines. Great Britain recognized and provided compensation for pneumoconiosis in the early 1940s, but little information on it appeared in American medical journals until the 1960s. Partly this reflected a long-held conviction that only silica and dust containing silica were injurious to health. Also, the appellation "coal workers' pneumoconiosis" was British in origin, and much confusion existed about its applicability to the U.S. coal industry. But Dr. Lorin Kerr, former director of occupational health and safety for the United Mine Workers, suggests that the attitude and influence of employer-oriented physicians "resulted in an avoidance of known facts about the ravages of coal dust in human lungs because to do otherwise would cost money" (Kerr 1969, p. 3).

The situation with byssinosis, or "brown lung," was much the same. Byssinosis is a respiratory disease that textile mill workers contract as a result of breathing in dust from processed cotton. Again, Great Britain recognized and provided compensation for byssinosis in the early 1940s, but it was not until 1971 that North Carolina, the nation's largest textile-producing state, allowed cotton textile workers with pulmonary insufficiency due to byssinosis to file claims for workmen's compensation. Compensation for industry-related injuries has been a part of American society since the early 1900s when many states set up programs to provide adequate income maintenance for workers disabled by occurrences arising out of their employment. But work induced illnesses have been difficult to prove and have become a noticeable part of compensation cases only recently.

Coal workers' pneumoconiosis was officially recognized as a compensable disease in West Virginia, the nation's largest coal mining state, in 1969 and later that year by the Federal Coal Mine Health and Safety Act, which established a federal benefits program for miners disabled by the disease. Byssinosis became compensable in North Carolina in 1971 and in South Carolina in 1977; legislation is currently pending in several other states to enact similar compensation laws.

From their inception, the various compensation programs never ran smoothly. Matters were complicated by the tremendous confusion among physicians on these diseases, their character, and the disease components that contributed to disability. Moreover, each party interpreted the diseases consistent with their self-interest. Industry tended to minimize the severity of the diseases and maximize the costs of compensation and meeting proposed regulations. Workers, wanting both compensation and a clean workplace, emphasized the prevalence and severity of the illnesses. Industry opposition to cleaning up the workplace and the failure of programs to adequately and efficiently compensate workers who contracted these diseases encouraged the formation of social movements in both the coal and textile industries. Although the movements began approximately five years apart, they developed in similar ways. Three factors determined how successful the movements would be.

OUTSIDE INVOLVEMENT

The mere existence of a social problem does not create a social movement. At the minimum, those most directly affected must be aware that the problem exists. In the beginning stages of both the Black and Brown Lung movements, few workers were aware that the respiratory problems they were experiencing were occupationally induced, or if they were aware of it, they did not know what to do about it. Initial involvement from the outside was required for the workers to learn more about their plight.

In the coal mining communities, this knowledge was provided by three physicians: I. E. Buff, Donald Rasmussen, and Hawey Wells. The three doctors worked independently of one another for several years, trying to increase public awareness of the disease. Dr Buff's involvement began in the 1950s after coal companies introduced new cutting machinery that created more dust in the mines (Trupp 1969, p. 102). A heart specialist, Buff treated many miners who had collapsed on the job. The company assumed that they had had heart attacks, a noncompensable disease, but Buff found that they were suffering from diseased lungs. When he tried to so inform the industry, miners, and the mining communities, he met with much resistance. Rasmussen and Wells, pulmonary specialists who had done research on pneumoconiosis for the Public Health Service in 1964 and 1965, testified at a 1968 Senate hearing on a proposed occupational health and safety bill. Their pleas that provisions protecting miners be included in the proposed legislation went unheeded.

During this same period, issues of miners' health and safety had been brought before the leadership of the United Mine Workers, but union contracts seemed to be negotiated with more of a concern for traditional "bread and butter" issues. Two disasters encouraged several miners to take further action and eventually link up with the work of the three physicians.

In May 1968, twenty-five men were trapped in a mine at Hominy Falls, West Virginia. Rescue attempts were partially successful, but four men died. A meeting was called in Clifftop, West Virginia, a nearby town, to discuss issues of health and safety. Dr. Buff, who was beginning to be known through reports of his work printed in the newspapers, was invited to speak. The miners had become aware of problems in the compensation system as a result of attempts to obtain compensation for silicosis, a lung disease caused by the inhalation of silica from underground rocks. Although silicosis had been compensable since 1933, the miners were recently experiencing difficulty in getting compensation. Buff told them about pneumoconiosis and how the law did not recognize it as a distinct entity from silicosis.

A much bigger mine disaster occurred in November 1968 when seventy-eight men were killed in a coal mine explosion in Farmington, West Virginia. The disaster had a tremendous impact on the American public because the ordeal of attempted rescues was shown for several days on television during the Thanksgiving holidays. Like major disasters of the past, this one prompted a government response, with a conference on mine safety called the following month by the U.S. Department of the Interior. Buff, Rasmussen, and Wells were in attendance, and as a result formed a committee called The Physicians for Miners' Health and Safety. The purpose of the committee was to press for improved conditions in the mines, but the doctors were specifically interested in addressing the problems of coal workers' pneumoconiosis. They embarked on a heavy speaking schedule in the mining communities, emphasizing two major points: Coal dust causes respiratory diseases, and black lung should be made compensable (Trupp 1969, p. 104).

Whenever possible, the three physicians appeared together at protest meetings held all over West Virginia. Buff would attack the coal industry, the inaction and corruption of the UMW's leadership, and the horrors of black lung disease. Rasmussen gave less oratorical presentations on the exact nature of the disease. His expertise legitimized the group and their activities. Wells usually concluded the meetings with a call for political action. To stir the miners' emotions he would crumble dried sections from diseased black lungs in front of them, indicating that the material was like a slice of their own lungs (Denman 1974, pp. 67–71).

The major thrust of the doctors' efforts was dissemination of information about the disease and the need for political action to change the compensation law. The formation of the movement organization was done by the coal miners themselves. Joe Malay, a miner and original member of the Black Lung Association, said in an interview:

> The reason that we formed the Black Lung Association is that we knew that we was going to have to write a bill of our own. We went down to talk to Paul Kaufman (a local lawyer) because Dr. Buff recommended him to us . . . then the union come along with a bill, and of course, they asked us not to support the one that we was getting up, to forget about it, and not to give Paul Kaufman no money. So in order to get money, you had to have some kind of organization, see, to pay the money into, so that's why we formed the Black Lung Association.

The significant role played by the coal miners was reaffirmed in an interview with Rasmussen, who indicated that "the people who really did the work were the rank-and-file coal miners. Woody Mullins, Ronny Sturgill, and the Halls . . . the rank-and-file miners got the whole thing going, it was their own idea; nobody talked them into starting the Black Lung Association."

The Black Lung Association was officially introduced at a rally in Beckley, West Virginia, on January 19, 1969. The first statewide rally occurred ten days later in Charleston, the state capital, with over five thousand miners in attendance. The major speakers were not miners but Paul Kaufman, a lawyer, Ken Heckler, a U.S. congressman (who also read a letter from Ralph Nader), and members of the physicians' committee. These well-known speakers attracted a lot of media attention, which in turn helped unite all miners in West Virginia to this common cause. The statement of Ralph Nader seemed to symbolize the direction of the movement:

> Your gathering here makes it clear to the coal mine operators and those groups and individuals that do their bidding that no longer are you going to tolerate a situation that makes coal miners cheaper than coal. . . . You are not going to tolerate puppet-like physicians, employed by the coal operators, disgracing their profession by saying black lung is not all that bad and miners can learn to live with it. From now on, the coal miners whose bodies are being abused and whose lungs are being destroyed are going to be the ones who say how bad black lung is.

Nader was also a key figure in bringing the problem of brown lung to the attention of the American public. His 1971 article in The Nation outlined the history of the disease and attacked the textile industry for its reluctance to acknowledge the problem and seek a solution. Students working through PIRG (Public Interest Research Group, a Nader-funded campus organization) also contributed much of the early research on the problems of cotton dust and compensation for byssinosis in the Carolinas. Not until late in 1974, however, did a concerted effort begin to organize textile workers to address these problems. Although the actual door knocking was conducted by two veteran organizers who had recently worked with coal miners in their strike against the Brookside mines in Harlan County, Kentucky, support for this effort came from many activists in the southern region, and monetary support came from the United Church of Christ and the Campaign for Human Development (a Catholic organization).

To recruit workers into the movement, the organizers held screening clinics to examine people for possible cases of byssinosis. This strategy, which was quite successful, is explained in one of the organizing documents:

A Brown Lung screening clinic is an important event in the development of a Brown Lung Association chapter, but it is only part of a whole process. Every event that people participate in, every meeting, is an educational experience. People don't learn just from being told or taught things, they have to *experience* things. And the experiences have to be repeated and they have to build on each other for people to really learn and understand.... A clinic shows brown lung victims that a lot of people are on their side, that brown lung disease *is* important, and most of all, that a doctor or medical professional *does* believe that they have the disease.

The screening clinics were important because they brought necessary information to the textile workers about their breathing difficulties, what caused them, and what could be done. The workers had not been informed by the industry about their condition or about the dangers of cotton dust. Interviews with workers repeatedly revealed that they did not know anything about brown lung or compensation until they were contacted by a representative of the Brown Lung Association.

This information in itself was not sufficient to promote a movement among southern textile workers. Active workers did not have the protection of a labor union in most parts of the industry, and the historical failure of labor organizing had left its impact on the ability of workers to come together in any form of collective action. Some have characterized this as a sense of "fatalism," but one of the original brown lung organizers saw it somewhat differently:

They're not fatalistic, they are realistic. If you have very few options, to pretend that you have them is to be a fool. It is being practical to know what your options really are.... Here is the possibility of rainbow and here is the possibility of hell. And the textile industry made the possibility of hell greater than the possibility of rainbow. They brought in troops and they killed people, and when you are not really sure about that rainbow, but you are fairly sure that you might get hurt or lose your job, and maybe killed, it's just being practical not to jump for the rainbow.

Partly for this reason, few active workers came to screening clinics or joined the Brown Lung Association. Organizers had to build the movement with retired and disabled textile workers, who had little to fear from the industry and much to gain by getting compensation for their illness. Within less than a year after the initial organizing efforts were begun, a Bi-State Board of the Brown Lung Association was created. It was composed of retired and disabled textile workers from four communities in North and South Carolina. From that point on, the major decisions of the movement were decided by this group.

Still "outside organizers" continued to play an important role. As the movement grew larger (fifteen chapters in four states in 1981) and acquired more funds (over $300,000 in 1981), the professional paid staff increased (to close to forty in 1981). Staff members became more specialized with some personnel doing medical research, some doing legal research, others raising funds, and still others engaged primarily in administration. The struggle to change the compensation laws and fight for a cotton dust standard to reduce the dust levels in the mills required highly sophisticated medical and legal knowledge. This necessitated hiring personnel that could put this information into terms that the millworker leadership of the movement could understand and utilize in its decision-making processes. Although staff members were paid salaries below those of most active textile workers, the Brown Lung Association became a desirable training ground for many young activists interested in the increasingly important issues of occupational health.

The Brown Lung Association was able to expand to such a large social movement organization in part because of the availability of federal funding. In 1977 the organization received a large training grant from CETA (Comprehensive Employment and Training Act), which allowed for an expansion into three new communities in North Carolina. The association also received grants from OSHA under its New Directions Program, which supported several staff members working primarily with active workers. Finally, the Brown Lung Association was able to acquire several VISTA workers; although these jobs paid less than those on the regular staff, the VISTA workers served in many of the same positions.

The Black Lung movement was also supported by the federal government, although to a somewhat lesser degree. In addition to VISTA workers, the movement was supported by a program called Designs for Rural Action (DRA), a federally funded community action agency responsible for assisting community-related projects in Appalachia. The agency was formed in 1968 to facilitate the work of Dr. Rasmussen of the physicians' committee and Arnold Miller, who later became a president of the Black Lung Association and eventually president of the UMW. The offices of the DRA in Charleston, West Virginia, became the central office of the Black Lung Association, where the movement's newsletter was published and which eventually served as a central coordinating office for the chapters of the growing movement.

Federal funding, then, was important to the growth of both movements. The acquisition of federal funds, however, required a knowledge of funding sources not usually possessed by either mine or mill workers. This knowledge—and the proposals themselves—had to be supplied by a support staff of outside organizers educated in universities and other movements, rather than in the mills or the coal mines. The problem was not simply a lack of special skills but also what one organizer referred to as a "terrible insensitivity to the way the rest of the world works" on the part of funding agencies, both public and private. Although most agencies want proposals to be "from the people," they also want them "perfectly typed in gorgeous paragraphs." Rather than take on the funding world and teach them to be receptive to working-class people, organizers generally wrote the proposals themselves.

Yet why would the federal government fund political organizations such as the Black Lung and Brown Lung Associations? In the case of the DRA, it is probable that because of the many bureaucratic levels in government, high-level federal officials were not aware of what was happening in the organization. Perhaps equally important is that funding criteria for government agencies change with each administration. During the late sixties, when "war on poverty" programs were still in full swing, VISTA and other community action agencies encouraged the poor to participate in programs to change the status quo. When the Nixon administration dismantled these programs, the trend changed. Under the Carter administration, the philosophy was again reversed. Carter's appointee to head ACTION (of which VISTA is a part) was Sam Brown, a former antiwar activist, who encouraged a policy of support to social change organizations. Carter's OSHA also believed that workers should help themselves. Because the Brown Lung Association was already in the field, it was funded by OSHA to educate workers about byssinosis. Much of the monetary and manpower support the Brown Lung Association had been receiving during the Carter administration was removed in the Reagan administration, which opposed organizing poor people "in a confrontational mode." This fluctuation in external funding can have a dramatic impact on the strength of the modern social movement.

Industry tried to discredit the Black Lung and Brown Lung movements by attacking their monetary and staff support as "outside agitation." Movement supporters, both organizers and workers, tried to minimize the importance of outside influence by crediting results to the workers. Even though the use of outside resources can generate controversy, the importance of monetary and personnel support for the movements to begin, much less to grow and be successful, cannot be ignored. When a movement's constituency is poor and powerless, these resources must come from outside. For these movements to be composed of the true beneficiaries of the movement, the money and personnel must be used to organize those members of the affected constituency who may not automatically see the benefits of joining. Whether someone will join is a function of the costs and rewards of involvement.

THE COST/BENEFIT OF PARTICIPATION

Major participants in both movement organizations were the retired rather than the active workers. Active workers were not immediately interested because the major goal of the organizations—to provide workmen's compensation—was of little concern to them. The diseases generally took several years to develop, and symptoms evolved gradually. Even if an active worker developed the disease, she or he would be unlikely to file for compensation or join an organization like the BLAs because of the risks involved. Cleaning up the work environment, too, was a long-range goal with few immediate benefits.

One woman I interviewed was diagnosed by company doctors as having byssinosis in August 1979. She was put on sick leave and given $50 a week for thirteen weeks. Almost a year later, when a representative from the Brown Lung Association contacted her, she learned that she could receive compensation for the disease. The company had terminated her employment and failed to tell her anything about her condition. An active worker who filed for compensation faced even greater risks. Textile workers were especially vulnerable; they had no union and could be fired or transferred to a less desirable shift or job, and without a guarantee of compensation. In over 80 percent of the cases filed, the industry appealed the workers' claims in court.

An active worker who chose to join the Brown Lung Association appeared to be advocating a change in the worker-management relationship that was very similar to union involvement. That the Brown Lung Association was viewed in a similar way to a union by industry is supported by a former president of the North Carolina Textile Manufacturers Association and mill owner who stated, "We're opposed to sitting down with any third party, as far as discussing the working conditions of our people.... We're smart enough to do right by our people, to the extent that we can afford it. We don't entertain that we need some outside help from someone who is going to mediate.... We are not going to put up with them [the Brown Lung Association] at all. They are adversaries ... and our people don't need a damned outside source to come talk to us and they know it." Members of the Brown Lung Association were labeled "anarchists, hippies, Communists, damn Catholics, and labor union agitators" by various industry representatives. An active worker who joined such a group incurred great social and economic costs.

In contrast, coal mining has a long history of unionism that supports the idea of workers organizing collectively. But the existence of a union posed special risks of its own. The UMWA (United Mine Workers of America) constitution provided that a member could be expelled from the union for joining any organization deemed "dual" to the union (Hume 1971, p. 111). The Black Lung Association was seen by the union leadership as composed of "hippies, scabs, and slick suave lawyers" (McFeatters 1972, p. 1), and they actively opposed its growth. This opposition emerged after leaders in the Black Lung movement charged the union leadership with a failure to address the problems of occupational health and safety and with corruption in union management. Eventually, the union leadership promised to introduce a bill in the West Virginia legislature to provide workmen's compensation for miners afflicted with pneumoconiosis. Consequently, many miners felt that it would be unwise to take any action that might be interpreted as undercutting the official policy of the organization. To join the Black Lung Association could mean a loss not only of union membership but also of job and pension and hospital benefits. As Brit Hume (1971), author of *Death in the Mines*, stated, "It was a punishment few members were willing to risk."

Unlike most active workers, retirees could receive immediate material benefits in the form of workmen's compensation. Many joined the movement organizations because of the assistance provided in the sometimes complicated and litigious claims process. Second, retired workers could join without fear of the economic sanctions that threatened the active worker. Third, retired workers had more time to spend in movement activities, although poor health limited this involvement significantly. Finally, movement organization meetings were an opportunity for retired workers to enjoy association with others while doing something constructive. A common sentiment was expressed by the president of one of the local chapters of the Brown Lung Association who, in answering a question on why she stayed in the organization, responded, "I love it. I love working with people.... If I never get a dime, I love it and I love to stay in it, and I love to visit people." This cultural norm of visiting and talking with people was important to the movement's organization because a large part of the work of building the movement required these skills. But retired workers became involved in many new experiences that were also rewarding to them personally and helped build the strength of the movement. The same retired worker who loved to visit and help people also enjoyed more militant expressions of the movement's activities: "We toted posters and signs around.... I never had done that until I got into brown lung, but let me tell you now, I am not ashamed of it.... And I think we should do it more often and get out here and worry the textile people to death until they have to come across and pay us. I wish there was some way that we could just worry them to death, and let them know we ain't scared of them."

Others found satisfaction in more traditional political activities that had not generally been open to the average textile worker. An account of a Carolina Brown Lung Association (CBLA) visit to Washington, D.C., in Mimi Conway's *Rise Gonna Rise* demonstrates this point:

> ...the North Carolina chapters of the CBLA went to the Capitol to visit their congressmen. A reception room had been arranged with rows of straight backed chairs facing a long table for the legislators. The brown lung group turned the chairs to form a semicircle, creating an informal atmosphere. Lucy Taylor walked over to the table and took the center seat. One by one, the North Carolina congressmen came in and sat to the left or right of her. It was clear that she, and not they, was chairing this meeting.
>
> Lucy introduced her fellow CBLA members.... Then she laid it on the line. She asked each legislator if he would work for the brown lung legislation that Senator Ernest Hollings had just promised the South Carolina chapters of the CBLA he would introduce. The CBLA wanted to know who was for it and who against. To underscore the point, Lucy added in the rasping voice, "If we didn't have confidence in you, you wouldn't be here." Just as she said this, North Carolina's senior senator, Jesse Helms, appeared at the door and, as unobtrusively as possible, took a chair in the back of the room. Lucy Taylor, as alert a politician as Helms, spotted him. He was the one she wanted.... "There's a seat for you up here, right by me, Senator Helms," Lucy Taylor said. (Conway, pp. 70–71)

Retired and disabled workers had much to gain and little to lose from participation in the Black and Brown Lung Associations. It provided for the possibility of material gain, for interaction with fellow human beings struggling under similar circumstances, for social status and political power, and was a once-in-a-lifetime chance to express feelings about the work and the industry that had taken away their health.

THE MOVEMENT ORGANIZATION

The structure of a social movement can take many forms.* The form it takes greatly influences the process of mobilizing people and other resources.

---

* Traditional movement theory had accepted the Weber-Michaels model of increasing oligarchization as a social movement grows and develops. Zald and Ash (1966) have questioned this assumption, and Roberts and Kloss (1979) suggest that many contemporary movements may actually be antibureaucratic movements seeking more equitable forms of social organization.

The Black Lung and Brown Lung Associations exemplify a social movement structure identified as decentralized, segmented, and reticulate (Gerlach and Hine 1970). Let us briefly look at this structure because it was important to the recruitment process in both the Black Lung and Brown Lung movements.

Both movement organizations were very decentralized. Formal structure was present but served primarily to facilitate communication, not decision making. A form of participatory democracy was generally preferred by both organizers and workers because of negative experiences with bureaucracies. For example, one bureaucracy with which coal miners had much experience was the Social Security Administration (SSA). In an early issue of the *Black Lung Bulletin*, the association's newsletter, an editorial reflected their resentment of this kind of structure: "For efficiency's sake, workers in the SSA operate almost like machines. A decision is made, a button is pushed, and the workers do what they are told—losing the ability to understand the people with whom they are dealing."

Members were organized into chapters, but the chapters were not subject to central direction. Because each chapter developed independently, ways of operating and ideologies were sometimes quite different between chapters. Although each chapter was initially established by an organizer sent to a local area from the state organization, the development of that chapter was left to the members. The result was a highly segmented movement whose chapters were often in conflict. In the Black Lung movement this internal conflict manifested itself in struggles over political power within the movement organization. In the Brown Lung movement, which had more monetary resources and professional staff, the struggles were over the distribution of available funds and personnel.

The movements were held together, not by central control, but through a network of personal relationships and intergroup linkages. Appalachia, the geographical area where most coal is mined, is a culturally cohesive area. The occupation of coal mining with its mining camps, labor struggles, and dangerous work has served to unify coal miners and their families. When retired and disabled coal miners came together in the Black Lung movement there was a sense of identification and belonging, which was reinforced by these cultural and occupational similarities. They served to facilitate communication, interaction, informal group structure, and trust—all of which were important commodities in the successful completion of the movement's goals.

Textile workers did not have the same unifying experiences, but they did have a unique history of oppression and violence, which was buttressed by the culture of the mill village. Isolation and paternalistic control produced common life situations and life experiences. Also, high labor turnover rates in the mills resulted in an extensive network of occupational affiliations in different mill villages. Even though mill workers frequently quit their jobs, they usually signed on at another mill soon after.

A decentralized, segmented, reticulate movement structure recruits participants through their natural community relationships. They are not recruited into the movement per se (Gerlach and Hine 1970, p. 97) but into specific cells in the organizational network, generally the local chapter. For coal miners, union locals were the source of new recruits. Although the national union leadership ignored the miners' request for action, many rallies were organized around union locals. Textile workers lacked a formal organization like the union, which may explain why their movement took longer to emerge and grow. But an informal structure of communication and interaction linked textile workers together. As Lacy Wright, one of the first converts to the movement, said at an initial meeting of retired textile workers: "Back in the old days, we used to sit around and talk 'cotton mill talk.' People would tell each other their problems and complaints because there wasn't much that could be done to change things. We want to talk some 'cotton mill talk' today but now we think there is something that we can do to change some of our problems and make life a little easier."

This informal communication and interaction structure was important to legitimizing much of what coal miners and mill workers read and heard about. Even if information was made available to them through the mass media, they rarely acted on it without checking it out with their neighbors. This also made it difficult for "outside organizers" to effectively recruit new members into the movement without utilizing this network. As one textile worker told me, "If a member of the staff knocked on my door and wanted to interview me about compensation... I'd say that I am not interested. A person would be suspicious of someone who was telling them how to get some money for their breathing problem. If there hadn't been someone else with a breathing problem the same as mine, I wouldn't have talked with them." This suggests that workers who are old and sick may have a certain respect and trust in one another that, if recognized, can facilitate movement formation.

IMPACT OF MOVEMENT INVOLVEMENT

The process of mobilizing movement membership does not stop with the initial recruitment period. The successful movement organization requires that members be retained for a sufficient time to accomplish the movement's goals. Involvement in a social movement, however, may alter the reasons for participation, especially if the movement has multiple goals. The Black Lung and Brown Lung movements had very similar aims. First, both associations fought to increase the probability that worker's afflicted by either black lung or brown lung would receive compensation for their illness. Second, because these diseases were occupationally induced, the organizations wanted the work environment cleaned up and dust levels reduced to prevent future workers from contracting the disease. Because of the inclusive nature of both movements (i.e., there were no mandatory requirements for membership), people would most likely join these movements with a variety of commitments to the major goals.

The decentralized nature of the movements encouraged a high level of freedom for members to design the nature of their involvement. Members could work at the local, state, or regional level of the associations and could participate in any number of different tasks: organizing other workers, raising funds, maintaining the chapter office, lobbying in state and federal legislatures, and so forth. They were able to do what they enjoyed doing, what they had the skills to do, and what they were able to do physically.

Although most people who joined these associations filed claims for either benefits or compensation, many members did not have an occupational disease and thus did not file claims. And many claimants diagnosed as not having byssinosis or pneumoconiosis remained active. Some of this may be attributed to simple altruism. As one staff member indicated, "Everybody likes the idea of doing something that lasts beyond their lifetime. They make change, and I think people like that." This sentiment was supported by the thoughts of one mill worker, who stated, "They will write something on my tombstone besides that I was born and that I died." Although retired workers would not benefit from the success of the second major goal of both movements—to clean up the workplace—their children and grandchildren, and the children of other miners and mill workers, might. Their continued involvement adds support to the suggestion by Fireman and Gamson (1979) that an assessment must be made of what a movement participant's *group* may gain or lose, as well as what participants may gain or lose as individuals.

The desire to produce social change comes not just from simple altruism but from an understanding of the process of oppression as well as the mechanics of social change. Participation in a social movement can increase one's awareness of issues that the nonparticipant may not be exposed to. Even the initial involvement of concerned "outsiders" can be a significant factor in influencing the involvement of the potential member. As one retired textile worker confessed:

> I never thought anything would come along that could help. It has always been put down, put down. . . . Well, when I went into the Brown Lung [Association] there, and began to attend these meetings, I said, "Wait a minute here." You know, I just got enthused myself, it really made me feel great, because there was people who were educated who was doing something for these poor working people who had never had anybody to take an interest in them or to help them in any way. I never dreamed that it would really happen, I really didn't.

Further participation in the Brown Lung Association revealed many things to the retired and disabled textile workers that helped them to understand what caused their problem and why it continued. As Essie Briggs, a retired mill worker from South Carolina, once testified:

> When we did find out that it was the dust that made us sick we found ourselves faced with an industry that did not want to take responsibility for our sickness and laws that made it difficult, at best, to get compensation. Occupational disease in the Carolinas is treated like the bastard child of the compensation system. And like the illegitimate child, no one wants to take the responsibility. Lawyers shrug, legislators throw up their arms, industrial commissions duck, and the industry tries to pretend that there is no problem. Well, we are living proof.

Participation in the Black Lung movement revealed similar injustices to the coal miner, which ultimately resulted in an additional goal for the Black Lung Association: the reform of the miners' union. As one retired miner exclaimed:

All big corporations and political bureaucrats are organized against the miner, whether active, retired, or disabled. It is time we look and see whether or not we are getting the benefits due us and what should we do about it. . . . Many of us miners fought with our own hands and spent our own meager money to get our union. Our union has sold out to the political tinhorns and yellowdogs. Let us once again unite.

The nature of participation within a social movement, then, can have a significant impact upon whether the membership will remain actively involved in the movement's activities. The inclusive nature of the Black Lung and Brown Lung movements and the relatively decentralized structures allowed for a wide variety of participation. For those whose involvement resulted in an increased awareness of the nature of injustice and the forms of oppression that control workers' lives, the reasons for participation may be altered, and new goals for the movement may emerge.

CONCLUSION

This chapter has attempted to look at some of the factors that influenced membership mobilization in two occupational health movements. The factors on which the discussion has been based are not exhaustive but exemplify some of the external variables that influence the recruitment process. The basic argument is that movements emerge, grow, and survive out of more than just feelings of frustration or deprivation on the part of an aggrieved population.

In the first place, many movements require some outside assistance in the form of funds or personnel to serve as a catalyst for the movement process. Forms of social control, insufficient information, and lack of experience in movement activities may necessitate certain resources that are unavailable to the aggrieved group. As in the case of the Black and Brown Lung movements, the complexity of the issues addressed may make the continued involvement of professional staff mandatory.

Second, whether a person joins a movement is somewhat dependent on an evaluation of the costs/benefits of participation. Active workers had little immediate gain from involvement in either the Black or Brown Lung movements—and much to lose. Retired workers had much to gain in the form of compensation and less to risk from company retaliation. In addition, both movement organizations provided opportunities for association and interaction that encouraged continued involvement.

Third, the structure of the movement organization also affects the recruitment process. The decentralized and segmented nature of the Black and Brown Lung movements encouraged recruitment into one of the many cells, usually local chapters, of the movements. This was accomplished through preexisting networks of personal and occupational relationships. The inclusivity of the movement, coupled with the opportunity for autonomy and decision-making power at the local level, allowed for much initiative on the part of most movement members.

Finally, the nature of movement participation can greatly influence the retention of a movement's membership. Initial reasons for involvement can be expanded as the member becomes more aware of the issues that encouraged the movement in the first place and the forces that hinder the movement's goals. The essence of this process is summed up in the words of one of the organizers in the Brown Lung movement, who said, "If you're a movement, then you have to be about people learning something and that changing them, and then they try to change the society that had denied them something, and then change themselves as they do it, and include more and more people, who are also about changing themselves and changing society."

REFERENCES

Conway, Mimi
    1979   *Rise Gonna Rise: A Portrait of Southern Textile Workers*. Anchor Press/Doubleday, Garden City, New York.

Denman, William N.
    1974   *"The Black Lung Movement: A Study of Contemporary Agitation."* Dissertation, Ohio University.

Fireman, Bruce, and William A. Gamson
    1979   "Utilitarian Logic in the Resource Mobilization Perspective." Pp. 8–44 in *The Dynamics of Social Movements*, edited by Mayer N. Zald and John McCarthy. Cambridge, Mass.: Winthrop.

Gerlach, Luther P., and Virginia H. Hine
    1970   *People, Power and Change: Movements of Social Transformation*. Indianapolis: Bobbs-Merrill.

Geschwender, James A.
    1971   *The Black Revolt: The Civil Rights Movement, Ghetto Uprisings and Separatism*. Englewood Cliffs, N.J.: Prentice-Hall.

Herberle, Rudolf
    1951   *Social Movements: An Introduction to Political Sociology*. New York: Appleton-Century-Crofts.

Hume, Brit
    1971   *Death in the Mines*. New York: Grossman.

Kerr, Lorin E.
    1969   "The Occupational Pneumoconiosis of Coal Miners as a Public Health Problem." *Virginia Medical Monthly* 96 (March): 121–26.
    1972   "The Neglect of Occupational Health: A National Scandal." Paper presented at the National Tuberculosis and Respiratory Disease Association Annual Meeting in Kansas City, Missouri, 23 May.

LeBon, Gustave
    1960   *The Crowd: A Study of the Popular Mind*. New York: The Viking Press.

McCarthy, John D., and Mayer N. Zald
    1973   *The Trend of Social Movements in America: Professionalization and Resource Mobilization*. Morristown, N.J.: General Learning Corporation.

McFeatters, Dale
    1972   "Boyle's Campaign Aimed at 'Outsiders!" *Knoxville News Sentinel* (November 20): 1, 2.

Malay, Joe
    1969   Tape recording of interview provided by Thomas Rhoddenbaugh.

Morrison, D. E.

1971 "Some Notes Toward Theory on Relative Deprivation, Social Movements and Social Change." *American Behavioral Scientist* 14 (May/June): 675–90.

Nader, Ralph
1971 "The Cotton-Mill Killer." *The Nation*, 15 March, pp. 335–37.

Oberschall, Anthony
1973 *Social Conflict and Social Movements.* Englewood Cliffs, N.J.: Prentice-Hall.

Rasmussen, Donald
1972 Tape recording of interview provided by William Denman.

Roberts, Ron E., and Robert Marsh Floss
1979 *Social Movements: Between the Balcony and the Barricade.* 2nd ed. St. Louis: The C. V. Mosby Company.

Trupp, Philip
1969 "Dr. Buff Versus the Black Lung." *Reader's Digest*, June, p. 102.

Wilson, John
1973 *Introduction to Social Movements.* New York: Basic Books.

Zald, Mayer N., and Roberta Ash
1966 "Social Movement Organizations: Growth, Decay, and Change." *Social Forces* 44 (March 3): 327–41.

Zald, Mayer N., and John D. McCarthy
1979 *The Dynamics of Social Movements.* Cambridge, Mass: Winthrop.

3

The Transformation of a Constituency into a Movement: Farmworker Organizing in California

J. Craig Jenkins

On the afternoon of July 29, 1970 Cesar Chavez and twenty-nine growers assembled at the headquarters of the United Farm Workers Union on the outskirts of Delano, California, to sign union contracts covering the majority of the farmworkers in the table grape industry. The optimistic rhetoric of the growers about the "common interests" of employers and workers hardly concealed the fact that a major transformation in the structure of economic and political power was in the making. For the first time in the long history of farmworker insurgency, a farmworker movement had finally brought sufficient power to bear against growers to force significant concessions. Though it took five more years of struggle to consolidate these gains, the United Farm Workers had clearly entered the first solid wedge in the seemingly impenetrable armor of California agribusiness.

Why did the United Farm Workers succeed where so many previous challenges had failed? To answer this question, this chapter compares the three farmworker challenges launched in California since World War II: the National Farm Labor Union (NFLU), active from the spring of 1947 through the winter of 1952; the Agricultural Workers Organizing Committee (AWOC), launched with the strong sponsorship of the AFL-CIO in the winter of 1959, but effectively collapsing by the winter of 1961; and the United Farm Workers Union (UFW), which began in the early 1960s as the National Farm Workers

Association (NFWA), a community organization of Mexican farmworkers organized by Cesar Chavez. My comparison will show that farmworker movements have traditionally failed because of structural obstacles to the mobilization of farmworkers, systematic political repression, and at least for the AWOC, major strategic errors. The crucial ingredients for the UFW's success were the strategy of mobilization adopted by the organizers and major changes in national politics that enabled the UFW to mobilize sufficient external resources to compensate for the powerlessness of farmworkers.

THE STRUCTURAL POWERLESSNESS OF FARMWORKERS

The structure of the farm labor market has made farmworkers economically deprived, socially fragmented, and subject to powerful social controls. The agricultural production cycle creates a division of labor—and interest—among a small nucleus of "permanent" workers, seasonal "locals" who supplement farm labor income with other part-time work, and migrant workers who move from harvest to harvest. Because of the depressed wage scales and the erratic and seasonal nature of the work, all are economically insecure and few possess the material resources to support a strike. Of the three groups, seasonal local workers possess the greatest potential for mobilization.

Migrant workers lack community ties, are the most vulnerable to grower coercion, and are frequently the victims of discrimination. There have been two major systems of migrant labor recruitment: the *bracero* program and the labor contracting system. Between 1942 and 1964 the *bracero* program administered the importation of over a million seasonal contract workers from Mexico. The growers used the program to collectively "fix" wages and to systematically repress dissidence. Until it was terminated in 1964, the program was used to break farmworker strikes and depress the entire wage structure (Galarza 1964, Craig 1971). The growers then turned to the labor contracting system, an arrangement developed in the late 1800s to recruit short-term immigrant workers from China and Japan. Because of language barriers, only the contractors could communicate with both growers and immigrant workers. Contractors assumed primary responsibility for recruitment, supervision, and payment, and for the provision of housing and transportation to the workers. Because contractors' income derives from a fee levied against farmworkers' wages and charges for support services, contractors are opposed to union controls over hiring. They also have an economic interest in recruiting workers who are so deprived that they cannot furnish their own transportation and housing. Recently, illegal aliens have been the favored recruits. The extreme dependence of these immigrant workers, coupled with their marginal occupational commitment as short-term workers, guarantees their willingness to break strikes.

Permanent workers, or "hands," are employed year-round on a single "ranch" building canals, leveling land, and doing chores. During the harvest they often assume supervisory positions as foremen and contractors. Despite their greater economic security and stronger ties to work and community, permanent workers are subject to the paternalistic control of growers. Growers offer them steady employment, better jobs and wages, cheap housing, emergency loans, small gifts, and a show of personal concern in exchange for personal loyalty. Simultaneously, because of their authority and relative privilege among farmworkers, permanent workers tend to be the informal or "natural" leaders of the community. They have therefore been used by the growers to coopt dissidence by sounding workers for grievances, pressuring quiescence, mediating individual complaints, and if these moves fail, recruiting a new crew. Because permanent workers constitute one-fourth or more of the work force, their support is invaluable for strikes.

The greatest potential for mobilization has been among local seasonal workers. They live in local residential communities, and because they have their own transportation and housing, are rarely dependent on labor contractors. They generally derive their income from nonfarm or multifarm jobs, and so supporting a strike does not necessarily endanger their livelihood. These local workers, however, constitute less than half of the harvest labor force. An effective strike requires the solid support of other workers, especially migrants.

The mobilization of farmworkers is further hampered by ethnic rivalries among workers, which overlap with occupational distinctions. This ethnic division of labor is a product of the intense competition among successive immigrant groups that have entered the agricultural labor market and discrimination by growers. The sharpest conflicts have been between domestic or more settled workers and the more recent immigrants. Because of low aspirations and short-term commitments, immigrants are readily available to break strikes. Growers have also promoted conflict by recruiting new groups whenever any one group has become numerous enough to pose a strike threat, by playing on group loyalties, and by discouraging acculturation or the forging of ties between different groups. For example, in the 1920s Mexicans and Filipinos were the new, strikebreaking groups, but by the 1930s their strikes were broken by Anglo "dust bowlers," who promptly assumed the more desirable jobs (Stein 1973). Over the last three decades, new farm labor has come primarily from Mexico, first *braceros*, then "green card" immigrants who held temporary visas, and recently, illegal aliens. Domestic workers—Anglo, Filipino, and Mexican American—have found their strikes undercut by Mexican immigrants.

These structural features of the labor market illuminate three factors that affect mobilization: group cohesiveness, social controls possessed by opponents, and resources controlled by the group. Group cohesion provides a basis for communication, facilitates the formation of common definitions of grievances, and fosters commitments to collective interests over individual gain. Members of a group fragmented along ethnic and occupational lines are not inclined to view problems as collective ones. Individuals are inadequately aware of others' grievances and are inclined to compete for the benefits that already exist rather than cooperate for new benefits.

Opponents employ both authoritative and coercive controls to counter mobilization. Growers have developed personal ties with their contractors and permanent hands to ensure their loyalty and have relied on coercion, threatening illegals and *braceros* with deportation. When these controls have failed, violent attacks have been mounted, ranging from police harassment of pickets to vigilante raids and assassinations.

Resources, such as disposable "free time," an economic margin, expertise, and communication facilities are crucial to any social movement. The fewer resources a group has, the more powerless it is and the more it needs an infusion of outside resources to mount an effective challenge. Two resources are central: power resources, such as organized strikes that enable the movement to apply leverage against opponents; and organizing resources, such as experienced cadres that facilitate the pooling of power resources. While farmworkers possess considerable potential power in the harvest because of the perishability of most crops, organizing resources are extremely scarce. Farmwork is the lowest-paid occupation in the United States, consistently below the federal poverty line (Dunbar and Kravitz 1976, p. 23). Workers with experience in political action are rare. After fourteen-hour days, few workers have the time to invest in organizing efforts.

Between the NFLU and the UFW challenges the structure of the farm labor market changed, slightly improving the chances of organizing. Between the late 1940s and the 1960s the proportion of farmworkers who were migrants declined from approximately one-third to around 20 percent, and that of permanent workers declined from around 40 percent to less than one-third. The *bracero* program came to an end in 1964, forcing growers to depend on the less controllable "green card" immigrants and illegals for strikebreakers. By the time that the UFW began organizing, local seasonal workers increased to over half of the labor force.* Because these workers were enmeshed in local neighborhoods and were less dependent than other workers on the growers, the UFW was able to mobilize a significant base of support.

These changes were also accompanied by a slight reduction in ethnic diversity. During the NFLU's challenge, approximately one-half of the workers were "Anglos," most of whom were permanent hands and locals. The majority of the migrants were ethnic minorities—black Americans, Filipinos, Mexican immigrants, Portuguese and West Indians. These workers readily broke the Anglo-supported NFLU strikes. By the late 1960s, the Anglo workers had largely moved out of agriculture. They composed less than one-quarter of the labor force and held permanent positions. Black Americans, once concentrated in cotton production, had largely abandoned the fields. Filipinos remained prominent among the migrants but had declined to less than a quarter of the migrant labor force. Filling these positions, the Mexican workers took over the majority of both migrant and local seasonal jobs. By the early 1970s, Mexican workers comprised almost two-thirds of the total labor force.† While a potential rivalry existed among the Mexican workers—between older immigrants who had become locals or permanent hands and the recent "green card" or

---

* Derived from *Annual Report of the California Farm Placement Service, Department of Human Resources* (1946–1975).
† Derived from Metzler and Sayin (1948: 23), Metzler (1964: 23), and the report of the California Assembly (1969: 23–25).

illegal immigrants—this was partially muted by common nationality. Still, the increased cohesion of the labor force brought about by these changes was not so great that the UFW strikes would receive solid support.

THE POLITICS OF CONTAINMENT:
THE NATIONAL FARM LABOR UNION

The NFLU challenge was launched in the spring of 1947 under the sponsorship of the American Federation of Labor and with financial support from a foundation and several international unions. The president of the NFLU, H. L. Mitchell, had been the principal organizer of the Southern Tenant Farmers Union, a depression era union of Arkansas and Missouri tenant farmers. Mitchell was the main contact with organized labor and the liberal political community. Key organizers were veterans of union drives of the 1930s: Henry ("Hank") Hasiwar, a former organizer of auto and hotel workers; Bill Becker, former labor director of the Socialist Party; and Ernesto Galarza, previously the key liaison between the AFL and Latin American union movements.

The NFLU's initial strategy was an orthodox industrial union approach: Organize a majority of the workers in the largest enterprise, offer the economic gains of a union contract as the major incentive, build a strike fund from member dues, and strike as soon as the employer was vulnerable. The first strike target was the 1,100-acre DiGiorgio ranch located near Arvin. Because of its size and mix of crops, over half of the 2,200 workers employed at the harvest peak were permanent hands or local workers. Two-thirds of these were "Anglos" who had secured their positions by breaking Mexican strikes during the 1930s. On October 1, 1947, the NFLU struck the DiGiorgio ranch with the Anglos providing the major base of support. The first day, over two-thirds of the workers marched out, but the picket line held firm for only a week. The DiGiorgio manager promptly called on the Mexican consul, who instructed the 130 *braceros* to return to work or face deportation. Though *braceros* were legally barred from employment in labor disputes, the *bracero* program officials ignored the union petitions. DiGiorgio also dispatched a squad of labor contractors who shortly returned with over four hundred workers, mostly illegals from Mexico and Mexican workers from the Los Angeles *barrios*. Hampered by court injunctions barring mass picket lines and the use of sound equipment, the strikers turned back few of the strikebreakers. Within a month the plum harvest had been completed, and though DiGiorgio had suffered major losses, the ranch was operating with nearly a full staff.

The NFLU also lacked strike relief to support the strikers. The strike pool of $3,000 was immediately depleted. The California Federation and local unions initially provided generous strike relief, but by the winter their interest waned as it become clear that the picket lines were not holding. Contributions plummeted, leaving the union able to support only a handful of loyal members. With strike morale at an ebb, the strikers began to melt away. By the spring of 1948 the picket line had dropped to less than a hundred workers, a symbolic effort to keep the union visible.

The NFLU then attempted to mount a boycott against DiGiorgio and to raise funds from the liberal community. But the DiGiorgio Corporation mounted an effective political counterattack, obtaining an injunction barring the boycott as illegal under the National Labor Relations Act, despite the exemption of agriculture from the Act. By the time the injunction was overruled a year later, the union challenge was in disarray. DiGiorgio also convinced a prominent California senator to investigate the union's political affiliations. Though allegations of Communist ties were unfounded, the "red smear" campaign weakened remaining liberal and labor support. Vigilantes then attacked, critically wounding the president of the DiGiorgio local in a midnight raid. Shortly afterward, DiGiorgio filed a multimillion-dollar libel suit against the NFLU and its labor supporters, charging that a film produced by the Hollywood Film Council and shown at public rallies throughout the state had "misrepresented" the corporation's labor policies. The California Federation refused to fight the suit, agreeing behind the scenes to scuttle its support for the NFLU if DiGiorgio would drop the suit (Galarza 1970). By the fall of 1949 the NFLU was politically isolated, cut off from liberal and labor allies.

Over the next three years the NFLU mounted several strikes but failed to build a membership. The leaders shifted to a new strategy of "area strikes" that focused on wage demands and the withdrawal of *braceros*. Mobilization focused on the domestic migrants, offering the incentive of short-term economic gains. While the strikes secured wage increases, these were soon rescinded, and the strikes produced only a handful of loyal members. By the winter of 1951 Hasiwar and Galarza decided to embark on another course. Focusing on the expanding *bracero* program that was displacing the domestic migrants who wintered in the Imperial Valley, the organizers experimented with a broader mobilizing strategy, offering citizenship training and counseling to the Mexican workers. The new incentives were highly successful. The Mexican workers responded en masse, and on May 12, 1952, the NFLU challenged the growers, demanding that they grant hiring priority to domestic workers or face a strike. Though the domestic workers were solidly organized, the growers controlled over five thousand *braceros*. Protected by the local police, the growers transferred the *braceros* from field to field. Labor contractors imported additional crews of illegals. The U.S. Department of Labor turned a deaf ear to the NFLU's petitions, rejecting the findings of the California Conciliation Service that a strike existed and authorizing the "drying out" or conversion of illegal aliens into *braceros*. By the end of the four-week harvest, the majority of the strikers had abandoned the picket lines and were desperately seeking jobs to replace their lost earnings. The following winter, the NFLU renewed the strike, but despite favorable court injunctions barring *bracero* employment, the union failed to clear the fields of *braceros* and illegals (Galarza 1971, Mitchell 1980).

The NFLU had been politically overwhelmed. Growers had imported *braceros* and illegals. Local courts had issued court injunctions, barring picket lines and boycotts. Local police had escorted strikebreakers, illegals and *braceros* as well as domestic workers, through the picket lines. In addition, the NFLU had failed to sustain participation, in part because of the social fragmentation of the farmworkers and in part because the initial strategy of recruitment had offered few incentives independent of union contracts. Only in the last rounds did the organizers begin to focus on broader social issues that sustained participation, such as citizenship and political rights. Even then, the Union confronted the problem of repression, an insoluble problem as long as insurgents lacked strong allies.

THE FAILURE OF STRATEGY: THE AGRICULTURAL WORKERS ORGANIZING COMMITTEE

If the NFLU had demonstrated that an effective challenge could not be mounted by a powerless group in the face of extensive political repression and weak outside support, then the Agricultural Workers Organizing Committee demonstrated that strategic considerations can play a decisive role in the collapse of insurgency. Over a four-year period, the AWOC received massive support from organized labor—over $1 million in direct financial aid and considerable political protection—but failed to develop an effective strategy of recruitment. The principal problem was the decision to focus exclusively on migrant workers, especially the rapidly declining body of Anglo migrants. Even more than the NFLU, the AWOC ignored incentives for participation beyond union contracts. Despite extensive organizing resources, the challenge was even less successful than the NFLU in recruiting a membership. The only success was the accidental mobilization of several crews of Filipino migrants, later to form a base for the United Farm Workers.

The AWOC was launched in the fall of 1959 by the AFL-CIO under the leadership of Norman Smith, a veteran UAW organizer. With an annual budget of $250,000, the AWOC fielded a team of fifteen full-time organizers. Rejecting the advice of veteran farmworker organizers, Smith instructed the organizers to concentrate on the 4 a.m. "shape-ups" at which day haul crews of farmworkers, mostly Anglos, were recruited. These shape-ups counted for less than 5 percent of the harvest workers, however, and were attended largely by drifters, alcoholics, and workers seeking only a single day's wages. Despite the ample AFL-CIO support, the organizing campaign produced few results. Throughout 1960, crews of local workers organized a series of "job actions"— Stockton cherries, DiGiorgio again, and Corchoran tomatoes—but failed to produce a stable membership. Without an organized base, wage gains were promptly rescinded.

The AWOC's major target quickly became the *braceros*. The California Federation of Labor had played a key role in the election of Governor Edmund Brown in 1958, and he had promised to enforce federal statutes prohibiting *bracero* employment in strikes. Smith then teamed up with the United Packinghouse Workers, which had lost several contracts to *braceros*, to attack the program in the Imperial Valley where the labor force was almost entirely *bracero*. Their strategy was to organize the few domestics workers with the promise that a strike would force a withdrawal of the *braceros*. If, as the organizers expected, Governor Brown failed to follow up his commitment, their plan was to attack the *bracero* camps in hopes that the conflagration would compel the Mexican government to end the program. On February 2, 1960, a handful of local workers marched out. The California Conciliation Service certified the strikes and, predictably, *bracero* officials rejected union petitions for removal on the specious grounds that the Imperial Valley Farmers Association, not the individual growers, was the legal employer. The growers moved the *braceros* from field to field under police protection, harvesting as normal. A local judge issued an injunction barring picketing, and the unions responded with a mass demonstration at two *bracero* camps, burning buildings and manhandling several *braceros*. The police promptly arrested the entire organizing staff of both unions. The AFL-CIO, informed that the AWOC leaders were in jail, promptly cut off its support and instructed Smith to turn over all union records. By the time that Governor Brown ordered removal of the *braceros*, the issue was mute (London and Anderson 1970).

The AWOC remained dormant for the next two years. In the winter of 1962, pressure from Walter Reuther and an impassioned speech by farmworker representatives convinced the AFL-CIO Executive Council to renew support. Unfortunately, the new organizers adopted the same strategy. The only new element was the decision to enlist the support of labor contractors to serve as the "grass roots" leadership that would collect dues from crew members and coordinate strike actions. While labor contractors favored higher wages which would increase their commissions, they were determined to block centralized union controls over hiring. Moreover, intense rivalries among contractors and their personal ties to growers consistently undermined contractor cooperation. The tactic did, however, generate a more stable income of union dues and the illusion of successful recruitment. Contractors simply ordered crew members to pay the union dues or get off the bus.

The few strikes in which the new AWOC became involved were inadvertent. The only workers actually organized were a few crews of Filipino migrants, later to be the initiators of the Delano grape strike. The strong ethnic and personal ties between Filipino contractors and their crew members led these contractors to support genuine unionization efforts. This success, however, was inadvertent. C. Al Green, the new AWOC director, had instructed organizers to ignore Filipinos and concentrate on the handful of Anglo contractors. Green's only success was in maintaining Governor Brown's cooperation in restricting *bracero* employment. This was quite limited, however, for in 1964 Brown reneged on a campaign commitment to oppose renewal of the *bracero* program and flew to Washington to lobby for an extension (London and Anderson 1970).

The AWOC, then, had demonstrated that serious flaws in the mobilization strategy could produce failure. Despite lavish sponsorship, the AWOC focused on the least promising segment of the workers, ignored ethnic cleavages, refused to offer incentives beyond narrow economic gains, and, at the end, attempted to build an organization of labor contractors rather than farmworkers.

THE PROBLEM OF MOBILIZATION

Before looking at the United Farm Workers challenge, we should consider why the economic benefits of a union contract were insufficient to mobilize and sustain farmworkers' participation in the strikes. One answer is given by Mancur Olson in his seminal work *The Logic of Collective Action*. Olson argues that individuals rationally pursuing their self-interest will not participate in collective action because they stand to gain whether or not they participate. All workers benefit from a union contract, but only those who strike pay for this benefit. Thus, according to Olson, the most rational course of action for any individual member of a group is to try to be a "free rider" on the efforts of others. Of course, if all individuals acted this rationally, there would be no collective action, and no one would benefit. Thus, Olson argues, organizers of collective action must provide "selective incentives" to those, and only those, who pay the cost of the collective action.

This is not easy. Even when unions provide strike funds, they are insufficient to compensate strikers for lost wages, let alone provide additional incentives for striking. One reason unions seek "union shops" is so that contributions of dues and participation are a prerequisite to the benefits of a union contract. It is also why unionizing groups on strike try to muscle "scabs" off their jobs. Such coercion is a selective disincentive to support the strike even if one does not actually join the union.

For most of their history, farmworkers were such a socially fragmented and economically deprived group that they could not afford to pay the certain short-range costs of a sustained strike for the uncertain possibility of long-range gains. It was only the infusion of massive resources from outside, to at least pay for organizers and provide a small strike fund, that made their sporadic challenges possible. Yet these resources were also uncertain, and, at least until the 1960s, inadequate.

By the 1960s, outside support for farmworkers organizing became more available due to the generally liberalizing climate of public opinion and the greater public realization of the dismal economic condition of farmworkers. Yet AWOC's use of this outside support was not successful because it could not translate it into effective incentives for farmworkers' support. The resources available were for paid organizers and strike funds, and these were only sufficient for an occasional action, not the creation of a sustained challenge. It took an organizer—Cesar Chavez—with a background in community, not union, organizing, and with a source of funds not dependent on classical unionization efforts, to realize that a different kind of incentives were necessary, and to forge these incentives out of the farmworker community itself.

The incentives Chavez employs, in fact the incentives most social movements must employ, are not material but "social." Such incentives provide the connecting link between the needs of individuals and the needs of a group, and when skillfully used, solve the problem of mobilizing rational self-interested individuals for collective action.

"Social" incentives are at the same time individual (i.e., experienced by single individuals) and collective (i.e., dependent upon experiences shared with other individuals). The rewards entailed by "social" incentives are either intrinsic to participation in collective actions or tightly tied to such actions. In a way not possible for material incentives, "social" incentives resolve the problem of "free riders" (those who refuse to contribute to the collective good but would receive it anyway) by restoring the link between individual incentives and social movement goals.

"Social" incentives are best described by James Q. Wilson in *Political Organization* as *solidary incentives* (individual and collective) and *purposive incentives*. Solidary incentives rest on emotional commitments; their receipt, on the maintenance of valued relations. They can be experienced only in the process of collective action, either as the major aim or as a by-product. Individual solidary incentives (Wilson's "specific solidary incentives"), such as special honors and recognition, are handed out to single individuals who contribute significantly to group endeavors. Such honors are an important incentive for movement activists and cadres who invest large amounts of time and energy in movement activities.

Individual solidary incentives, though, possess the drawback of being inherently scarce. Only a limited amount of honor can be bestowed upon individuals before its value declines. Nor, as Wilson (1973) points out, are such incentives wholly controllable by movement leaders. Honors have a tendency to become fixed benefits, not readily transferred to new individuals or to motivate old honored figures toward renewed efforts.

Consequently, movement organizations tend to emphasize collective solidary incentives. Raising the societal prestige of the group as a whole and enjoying the sociability of collective actions become key in creating the loyalties or attachments that mobilize a constituency into a movement. Like individual solidary incentives collective solidary incentives are intrinsically social, but they are even more tightly tied to collective actions per se.* One cannot have the experience of attending exhilarating demonstrations without actually participating in the collective action itself. In effect, participation in collective action becomes its own reward.

Nevertheless, groups held together primarily by solidary incentives are not social movements but social clubs. Such groups tend to be relatively flexible about their goals because it is not the goals but the process that is of importance. While movements do degenerate into social clubs when their incentives become exclusively solidary (e.g., the Townsend movement; see Messinger 1955), for active movements the primary incentives to participation are purposive: commitment to the goals of the movement for their own sake. Purposive incentives depend on a deep commitment to a high purpose—on an internalized moral code adhered to by the individual. The "coin" is the satisfaction received from having contributed to a worthwhile cause: a coin that is available only by acting on one's beliefs. When organizers provide such opportunities, participation in collective action again becomes its own reward.

In sum, movements resolve the problem of "collective goods" by leaning

---

* Collective solidary incentives are thus not "selective" incentives in Olson's sense, that is, benefits accruing to individuals that are distinct from collective goods. As Fireman and Gamson (1979) have argued, the collective nature of these social incentives requires a broader theoretical framework than the utilitarian model used by Olson.

heavily on solidarity and purposive commitments to pave the way for collective action. "Social" incentives tie individual and collective benefits together, or at least make them closely interdependent. Mobilization, then, is the process of creating social loyalties and self-images dependent on membership in the movement organization. In the process the boundary between individual and collective action becomes blurred. Individual benefits become intrinsic to collective goods.

The implications of this argument for farmworker mobilization can be spelled out by looking at the two poles of the mobilization process—the broad group or constituency possessing a need for social change and the movement organizers attempting to galvanize this potential membership into action. The social characteristics of the group—cohesion, cultural commitments, social ties to the opposition—determine its structural potential for mobilization. The organizers' recruitment program—their focus on certain subgroup segments and the incentives for participation—define the extent to which potential members are recruited.

Recruitment occurs either by the "bloc recruitment" (Oberschall 1973, p. 117) of preexisting groups or by individual recruitment through one-on-one solicitation and the use of conversion techniques to resocialize recruits. In both, the building of group solidarity and commitment to movement goals are central. In bloc recruitment, "natural" loyalties to work and neighborhood, ethnic and fraternal affiliations, are reinforced and transferred to the movement organization. The social infrastructure of a movement relying heavily on bloc recruitment will resemble that of a federation of small "cells" or informal cliques. This provides the advantages of a small-scale group in creating and sustaining participation and simultaneously allowing mass membership. Individual recruitment requires intensive effort and considerable one-to-one interaction. It is more typical of cadre recruitment and of small person-changing movements such as sects and communes.

Bloc recruitment is feasible only when there are cohesive small groups, optimally linked together by a complex network of informal social ties. If, in addition, vertical ties to the opponents of insurgency are weak or nonexistent, mobilization will be rapid and will require minimal investment of organizing resources. The social fragmentation of the farmworker community has discouraged bloc recruitment. The chaotic, seasonal character of farmwork has militated against strong solidary groups defined by work and community. Migrancy—coupled with short-term immigration, intensive competition for jobs, ethnic discrimination, and grower manipulations—has generated intense ethnic and occupational rivalries. On top of this, growers have erected paternalistic controls and informal cooptation devices. Thus, farmworker insurgencies have had only limited success, generally mobilizing only the more cohesive subgroups within the farmworker community.

As we shall see, farmworker organizing did not succeed until efforts were focused on local workers and attention paid to broader social incentives. In addition, farmworker unions did not bring about major changes until this mobilization strategy was combined with significant outside contributions.

THE "DUAL" STRATEGY: THE UNITED FARM WORKERS

The United Farm Worker story properly begins in the early 1960s with a dramatic shift in the temper of national politics. In 1960 John Kennedy slipped into the White House on a narrow margin provided by increasingly volatile black voters. In 1962 Congress underwent a major reapportionment that significantly weakened the power of the conservative "farm bloc." The civil rights movement had already mounted a campaign of mass action to dismantle racist institutions and by 1963 was organizing southern blacks into a voter bloc. Sensing the need to mobilize blacks and other minorities around a national program of social reform, Kennedy began laying the plans for a "war on poverty" and national civil rights legislation. One of the prices for the Mexican American and labor vote was a promise to terminate the *bracero* program,* a price that had been politically cheapened by congressional reapportionment. In the wake of Lyndon Johnson's landslide victory in 1964, congressional liberals pushed through the Civil Rights Act, the War on Poverty legislation, and a vote bringing the *bracero* program to an end. Over the next two years the central insurgency of the period—the civil rights movement— expanded and then collapsed into warring factions, leaving behind a model of protest action that the UFW borrowed and an expanding liberal constituency convinced of the necessity for profound social changes, a sentiment the UFW tapped.

In the winter of 1962 Cesar Chavez resigned as director of the Community Service Organization, an organization of urban Mexican Americans initially sponsored by Saul Alinsky, and set out to organize Mexican farmworkers into a union. Rather than build a union directly, Chavez chose the indirect route of community organizing. Recruitment focused on Mexican grape workers, the majority of whom were local workers residing in small rural towns in the southern San Joaquin Valley. The program centered on individual benefits, such as a credit union, a consumer coop, welfare and citizenship counseling, and on community issues such as racism in the local schools and exorbitant rent hikes. In other words, mobilization initially centered on two incentives: selective material benefits that provided the initial contacts around which a movement would later be built, and social incentives tied to existing solidary groupings (London and Anderson 1970, Levy 1975).

Drawing upon the contacts he had developed as a community organizer, Chavez secured the financial support of several small foundations and church groups. His main sponsor was the Migrant Ministry, a mission agency of the National Council of Churches that had decided that the unionization of farmworkers was the most effective avenue of "Christian service" to its farmworker clientele. In June 1964 the Migrant Ministry fully merged its California program with Chavez's National Farm Worker Association, providing the NFWA with the resources to field five full-time organizers. By the winter of 1965 the ranks of the NFWA had swollen to over a thousand active members.

* Thus the UFW built upon the meager gains of the AWOC period, though it was the AWOC's liberal allies, not the insurgents, that actually brought about Congressional termination of the *bracero* program.

In the spring of 1965 several Filipino crews nominally organized by the AWOC called strikes in the grape harvest. On September 8, when the Filipinos struck the Delano grape harvest, the home base of the NFWA, the NFWA was faced with a difficult decision. Chavez had not planned to openly transform the NFWA into a union for several years, but the Filipino strike forced the timetable. NFWA members worked in the same fields as the Filipinos and had to join the strike or break it. Despite on enthusiastic strike vote at a rally on Mexican independence day, September 16, the joint NFWA-Filipino picket lines held for less than a week. Though growers were inconvenienced by loss of the *braceros*, they quickly dispatched contractors to round up crews of strikebreakers from across the border. The problem of strikebreaking continued.

As the strike collapsed, Chavez embarked on a speaking tour of universities, church gatherings, and union meetings to mobilize outside support. The response was overwhelming. Student organizations and churches held benefit rallies. Student civil rights activists journeyed to Delano, offering their services as full-time volunteers. Unions collected strike funds and organized car caravans to bring food and clothing to strikers. At the San Francisco docks, members of the Longshoremens and Teamsters Unions refused to load "scab" grapes. In December, Walter Reuther, then president of the United Auto Workers, brought national attention to the strike by defying the Delano police and marching through the streets of Delano with the strikers. By pledging $5,000 monthly, to be split equally between the NFWA and the AWOC Filipinos, Reuther pressured the AFL-CIO to reconsider its exclusive support for Al Green's faltering AWOC (London and Anderson 1970).

Despite this support, the NFWA lacked the membership to mount strikes the following spring. Amid this collapse, Chavez pressed the adoption of a new strategy. Protest in the past had been designed to elicit contributions of organizing resources. The new protests would instead focus on creating external leverage through boycotts to compensate for strike failures. The first step was to capture popular attention through the mass media. With Reuther's prodding, Senator Robert Kennedy brought the Senate Subcommittee on Migratory Labor to Delano for public hearings. On March 17, 1966, while the television crews were still in town, the NFWA embarked on a 230-mile protest march to Sacramento that remained on the evening news for twenty-five consecutive days. En route, NFWA marchers carried signs proclaiming a consumer boycott against Schenley Industries, a mammoth liquor corporation that owned a ranch in the strike zone. Though the NFWA had organized boycott committees in December, the media coverage created the first genuine threat. Sympathetic Teamsters blocked Schenley's main warehouse, and the San Francisco Bartenders Union threatened to pull all Schenley liquors from their shelves. Since the grape ranch represented less than 1 percent of Schenley's operations, the corporation offered to sign the first union contract in the long history of farmworker insurgency.

The following day, the marchers repainted their signs: *Boycott DiGiorgio*. DiGiorgio Corporation owned a small grape ranch in the strike zone, but its profits depended primarily on processed fruits and marketing. The corporation immediately offered to hold a union recognition election. Over the next six months the NFWA battled company harassment, a "company union" set up by DiGiorgio, and the Teamsters, who held contracts on the farm's truck drivers. Chavez went on a fast to mobilize followers and control violence. When it appeared that the NFWA and AWOC would split the farmworker vote, the AFL-CIO forced a merger on the AWOC, placing Chavez in charge of the United Farm Workers Organizing Committee (UFWOC). After DiGiorgio held a rigged election, the UFWOC and its allies pressured Governor Brown to appoint an arbitrator for a new election, with the UFWOC promptly won, cementing its second contract (London and Anderson 1970).

In the spring of 1967 the UFWOC launched a series of strikes in the table grape harvest. Despite support for fifty organizers, the strikes failed. While the union could pull its members out of the fields, crippling injunctions weakened the pickets and the growers were able to recruit crews of migrant workers, many of whom were "green carders" and illegals. In the spring of 1967, again in desperation, Chavez dispatched the boycott teams. This time, the boycott was to be nationwide. More than sixty boycotters were sent to over fifteen cities to organize boycotts against the entire table grape industry.

The table grape boycott caused a major shift in the cadre's strategic thinking. While boycotts had been key, the leaders had assumed that a massive recruitment effort would eventually succeed on its own. The collapse of the table grape strikes convinced the union that boycotts were the key to power (Levy 1975).

Over the next two years the UFW conducted a nationwide boycott of California table grapes through committees set up in almost every major city in the United States. Truck drivers, longshoremen, and grocery clerks furnished the backbone of the boycott, conducting "hot cargo" actions by refusing to handle "scab" grapes; students and clergy marched through grocery stores, harrassing store managers, conducting "shop-ins," and closing off entrances; liberal politicians, including two presidential candidates (Senators Kennedy and McGovern), joined prominent celebrities in endorsing the boycott; liberal clerics sermonized their congregatations on the boycott; universities and Catholic schools cut off standing orders to grocers that continued to handle "scab" grapes; and millions of consumers shunned grapes and the grocery chains that continued to handle them. By the summer of 1970 the grape growers faced a closed marketplace. While they were able to recruit enough workers to harvest the crop, half of their 1969 crop remained in cold storage. By May, four of the largest growers in the Coachella and San Joaquin valleys offered contracts, one after a landslide election, which the UFW won 152–2. In late July, the Delano growers finally conceded defeat. By the end of August 1970, the UFW held contracts on 150 ranches, representing 20,000 jobs and over 10,000 members (Taylor 1975).

Nevertheless, the UFW's future was far from secure. The union was still vulnerable if the growers could break the boycott. The grape contracts had not even been signed before the growers counterattacked by signing "back door" contracts with the Teamsters Union. Teamster contracts were clearly preferable because, despite wage gains and fringe benefits, they left hiring and supervision in the hands of growers and labor contractors. Restrictions on arbitary firings and pesticides were eliminated, and growers could count on the businesslike Teamsters to ignore farmworker grievances. Most important, Teamster contracts threatened the UFW's most potent weapon—the boycotts. Growers could claim a union label, switching the public definition of the conflict from a moral cause to a union jurisdictional dispute. Teamster labels also meant that the UFW would secure less labor support, especially "hot cargo" actions when freight handlers refused to move shipments of boycotted (or "hot") products. The contracts constituted a windfall for the Teamsters. Without investing in organizing, the Teamsters skimmed off the union dues and shored their hold over the critical packing sheds (Meister and Loftis 1977).

The lettuce workers, mostly Mexican migrants who had been the target of recruitment efforts over the past two years, were outraged by the "sweetheart" contracts and spontaneously formed strike committees, phoning the UFW for instructions. The workers refused to sign Teamster authorization cards, attacked the Teamster organizers, and carried out spontaneous "job actions." In support, the UFW organized a mass march on Salinas, and on August 24 called the largest agricultural strike since the 1930s. Over 6,000 workers from 150 farms marched out, creating turmoil throughout the Salinas and Santa Maria valleys. Teamster guards, imported to protect strikebreakers, attacked UFW pickets. For a week, the strikers closed the packing sheds and shipping terminals. But by the third week, the growers and their Teamster allies had regained the edge by importing strikebreakers. The less committed UFW members, concerned about their lost earnings, began slipping back into the fields. When a judge barred strike and boycott activity on the grounds that the growers were the innocent victims of a jurisdictional dispute, the UFW defied the injunction, called a national boycott, and filed countersuits. Two lettuce growers vulnerable to a boycott hastily signed contracts. But the rest of the growers, representing over 70 percent of California and Arizona head lettuce, kept their Teamster contracts (Taylor 1975).

Over the next four years the UFW suffered a series of major setbacks. Off-and-on boycotts of head lettuce cut into grower profits but failed to produce contracts because of the disorganization and vulnerability of lettuce workers. Moreover, the political strength of the union's liberal and labor allies was declining, and their support for the boycott was on the wane. The Teamsters pressured other unions that had been key supporters, especially the Retail Clerks and the Butchers Union, to withdraw support. The boycott teams had to revert to organizing consumers, always the least effective method. Public support declined because of confusion about the Teamster contracts and because lettuce was a staple, not a luxury. The UFW added to this confusion by twice calling off the boycott when the Teamsters pledged to withdraw and then renewing the call when the Teamsters backed away.

Strikes and boycotts against nonunion wineries were also unsuccessful and further alienated labor supporters, especially the Distillery Workers and the Glassblowers Unions. Then the Nixon administration, strengthened by the landslide reelection in 1972, "packed" the National Labor Relations Board and threatened an injunction against the boycott. Though the boycott was clearly legal, the UFW backed down, accepted a single contract with the Heublein winery, and called off the boycott in exchange for a withdrawal of the injunction threat.

At the same time that external support dropped off, the recruitment campaign stalled. Ethnic symbolism had proven an effective rallying point for Mexican migrants, but it deeply offended Filipino, Portuguese, and Anglo workers. In the midst of an escalating ethnic conflict, Larry Itliong, the main organizer of the AWOC Filipinos and vice president of the UFW, resigned in protest (Meister and Loftis 1977). Shortly afterward, the UFW lost its first representation election because of Filipino defections to the Teamsters. In addition, the union confronted an administrative crisis traceable in part to the boycotts. With the leadership and core of loyal members working on the boycott, the administration of the grape contracts had fallen to inexperienced and occasionally disloyal hands. In addition, a rift developed among Mexican workers between locals, who preferred an annual base for dues and benefits, and migrants, who preferred a monthly base. The leadership tried to ignore this issue and alienated many migrant workers.

The UFW's vulnerability became fully apparent in the loss of the Schenley contract in June 1972 when Schenley sold the ranch to Buttes Land & Oil. After extensive but fruitless negotiations, the UFW called a strike, which Buttes overrode with strikebreakers. This prompted the grape growers to open secret negotiations with the Teamsters, and by July 1973, 78 grape growers had signed with the Teamsters. The UFW called mass strikes, but the growers dispatched labor contractors, and by claiming a jurisdiction dispute, secured 63 injunctions barring virtually every conceivable form of strike activity. In Coachella, the Teamsters shipped in 400 guards, who attacked UFW strikers. The UFW defied the injunctions, packing the jails for publicity and to secure a legal basis to contest the injunctions. But despite strong worker support, the strikers failed to halt the harvest because of the contractor-imported strikebreakers, many of whom were illegals. Amid escalating violence that claimed two lives, the UFW called off the strike and announced a boycott. By late August the UFW was a shrunken version of its former self, reduced to 12 contracts covering around 6,500 jobs and 12,000 members (Meister and Loftis 1977).

The extent to which political support had declined was graphically illustrated by the UFW's failure to rekindle the boycott. Despite greater resources, the renewed grape boycott was unable to force growers to renege on Teamster contracts. The key element, again, was the weakness of labor support. The Teamsters pressured former supporters to ignore the boycott teams. In addition, the AFL-CIO leadership despaired of the UFW's failure to hold solid picket lines, and pressured by several affiliates, refused to endorse the secondary boycott against Safeway Stores and the consumer boycott against Gallo wines. Nor were the boycotters able to build, as they had in the late 1960s, off other movements. The antiwar, student, and civil rights movements that had supported the grape boycott had collapsed, and after McGovern's crushing defeat in 1972, liberal politicians were in retreat. Though the boycott still had some impact—sales of Gallo wines dropped 9 percent and Safeway suffered declining sales—the pressure was insufficient to force a settlement (Meister and Loftis 1977).

The UFW was far from defeated, however, as it had cultivated other allies than labor. In the 1968 California Democratic primary Chavez had forged a key political alliance with Robert Kennedy by mobilizing the urban Chicano and middle-class vote behind liberal Democrats. In 1972 the UFW used this alliance with the Democratic party to defeat Proposition 22, a Farm Bureau initiative designed to outlaw harvest strikes and boycotts. In 1974 the UFW again mobilized key support behind Jerry Brown's successful bid for governor of California. Simultaneously, the UFW intensified farmworker organizing, mounting a challenge to the Teamsters by conducting "wildcat" strikes in Teamster ranches and infiltrating the Teamster structure to encourage workers to demand full Teamster enforcement of their contracts. Softened by the continued boycott and strike pressure, by the spring of 1975 the growers were finally prepared to reach a settlement. Under Governor Brown's diplomatic handling, the Democratic-controlled California legislature finally enacted the Agricultural Labor Relations Act, creating a system of union recognition elections and instituting legal protections on union organizing while preserving the right to boycott if a grower refused to sign a contract after a union election (Meister and Loftis 1977).

The UFW's dual strategy of simultaneously organizing farmworkers by emphasizing solidarity and commitment to "*la causa*" and mobilizing external support through boycotts provided the basis for consolidating a position. After a lengthy series of battles, the UFW won the majority of the union elections, losing on the few ranches such as the Gallo Vineyards and several Delano grape ranches where the ethnic conflicts and grower patronage had generated support for the Teamsters. By the fall of 1975, the UFW managed to win almost two-thirds of the elections, boosting its membership to over 30,000 workers (Meister and Loftis, 1977).

The string of contracts secured by the UFW since 1975 has solidified its position. Though UFW strikes have continued to be hampered by the fragmentation and poverty of farmworkers, the growers and the Teamsters have conceded that the UFW will represent the majority of farmworkers. Farmworker wages have more than doubled in the past decade; worker-controlled grievance committees on UFW ranches are able to halt grower harrassment, dangerous pesticide use, and irregular firings; work hours beyond a forty-hour week are optional and are paid as overtime; seniority rules encourage a more stable if not year-round employment pattern. In 1978 and 1979 the UFW organized a series of strikes in areas that had largely been left untouched, such as the Imperial Valley and southern Arizona vegetable farms where illegals constitute virtually the entire work force and along the coastal regions neighboring the Salinas Valley.

The picture is still not entirely rosy. Unionization has forced a speed-up in the rate of agricultural mechanization, thereby reducing the number of jobs. Moreover, the Teamsters have managed to hold on to 60 percent of their contracts, and despite promises to relinquish them when they expire in 1982, whether they will do so remains unclear. Most damaging, the UFW has been forced in several recent lettuce contracts to recant one of its major gains—the union-controlled hiring hall—that strengthens worker cohesion and thereby union organization. If this becomes a trend, the union will be seriously weakened.

Despite these setbacks, the situation is profoundly different from that in 1970. The union is no longer dependent on the support of outsiders to exercise power against the growers. The organizational effort and the contracts have provided a sufficient membership base to organize powerful harvest strikes, as those in the Salinas Valley in the fall of 1979 demonstrated. The time is past when growers can unilaterally control farmworkers, playing on their cooptative controls, labor contractors, the Teamsters, and the local police to break farmworker insurgency.

A STRATEGY FOR SUCCESS?

Does the UFW's dual strategy offer a model for successful insurgency elsewhere, especially among the poor and disorganized? The UFW's strategy of mobilization ultimately proved effective in a situation that had stymied virtually every other approach. If the UFW had not mobilized a solid farmworker base, it would not have survived the repression in the early 1970s, much less exerted sufficient leverage to force the growers to accept the passage of collective bargaining legislation. This required the distinctive community organizing approach developed by Cesar Chavez. By focusing on cohesive subgroups, by building on existing cultural commitments, and by offering a set of incentives that emphasized solidarity and moral commitments, the UFW was able to sustain participation even in the most desperate of circumstances. At the same time, if the UFW had not mobilized external support, this participation would not have generated sufficient power for the farmworkers to get the necessary union contracts. It was the combination of these two thrusts that was crucial. Unfortunately, the use of protest to mobilize outside support does not guarantee success. Because protest actions ultimately depend on the responsiveness of potential allies, it is a strategy that is only available occasionally. It takes skilled organizers to recognize these times and take advantage of them.

REFERENCES

California State Assembly, Committee on Agriculture
  1969 *The California Farm Labor Force: A Profile.* Sacramento: State of California.
Craig, Richard
  1971 *The Bracero Program.* Austin: University of Texas Press.
Dunbar, Anthony, and Linda Kravitz
  1976 *Hard Traveling: Migrant Farm Workers in America.* Cambridge, Mass.: Ballinger.
Fireman, Bruce, and William Gamson
  1979 "Utilitarian Logic in the Resource Mobilization Perspective." Pp. 8–44 in
       Mayer Zald and John McCarthy, eds., *The Dynamics of Social Movements.* Cambridge, Mass.: Winthrop.
Galarzo, Ernesto
  1964 *The Merchants of Labor.* Santa Barbara, Calif.: McNally and Loftin.

1970   *Spiders in the House and Workers in the Field.* South Bend, Ind.: University of Notre Dame Press.

1977   *Farm Workers and Agribusiness in California, 1947–1960.* South Bend, Ind.: University of Notre Dame Press.

Levy, Jacques
  1975   *Cesar Chavez: An Autobiography of La Causa.* New York: Norton.

London, Joan, and Henry Anderson
  1970   *So Shall Ye Reap: The Story of Cesar Chavez and the Farm Workers' Movement.* New York: Crowell.

Meister, Dick, and Anne Loftis
  1977   *A Long Time Coming: The Struggle to Unionize America's Farm Workers.* New York: Macmillan.

Messinger, Sheldon L.
  1955   "Organizational Transformation: A Case Study in a Declining Social Movement." *American Sociological Review* 20: 3–10

Metzler, William
  1964   *The Farm Worker in a Changing Agriculture.* Giannini Foundation Report No. 277. Davis, Calif.: University of California Press.

Metzler, William, and Afife Sayin
  1948   *The Agricultural Labor Force in the San Joaquin Valley, California, 1948.* Washington, D.C.: U.S. Department of Agriculture.

Mitchell, H. L.
  1980   *Mean Things Happening in This Land.* New York: Allanheld Osmun.

Olson, Mancur
  1969   *The Logic of Collective Action.* Cambridge, Mass.: Harvard University Press.

Sosnick, Stephen
  1978   *Hired Hands: Seasonal Farm Workers in the United States.* Santa Barbara, Calif.: McNally and Loftin.

Stein, Walter J.
  1973   *California and the Dust Bowl Migration.* Westport, Conn.: Greenwood Press.

Taylor, Ronald B.
  1975   *Chavez and the Farm Workers.* Boston: Beacon Press.

Wilson, James Q.
  1973   *Political Organizations.* New York: Basic Books.

4

The Men's Movement: Personal Versus Political

Alan E. Gross,
Ronald Smith, and
Barbara Strudler Wallston

In the early seventies, some men, especially those who were aware of the changes in male-female relationships that the new feminism promised and threatened, began to feel uneasy with the traditional male role. Some of them attended talks and meetings where the sanctity of the male role was questioned and on occasion ridiculed or assaulted. A few men formed themselves into small groups that met regularly to discuss their lives and form bonds around their common male experiences. Even fewer attended national conferences, and at some of these meetings there were rumblings about the need for a permanent national organization.

During the past decade, largely through these meetings and a few publications, books, and media appearances, the national network of people we call the men's movement has influenced the lives of several thousand men. But it has not succeeded in significantly challenging traditional ideas about the male sex role, in suggesting new legislation, in creating alternative career and family models, or even in providing relief for the personal frustrations of millions of American men. In fact, we may be stretching the concept of "social movement" to apply it to the informal network of people interested in men's

We appreciate the helpful comments of Robert Brannon, Peter Levison, and Joseph Pleck on an earlier version of this paper. Jo Freeman's editorial skills are largely responsible for overhauling and abridging the more than forty pages we originally submitted.

issues. Nonetheless, something did happen in the mid-seventies that contains many elements of a social movement, something that has neither died nor achieved national influence.

This chapter examines two key factors: motives for participation, and the structure that serves as a vehicle for that participation. These may explain why the men's movement could begin but not expand to a mass movement, and how, unlike similar movements, it continues without contracting. We begin with a brief analysis of why people join and participate in social movements, and the men's movement in particular, and then we examine these motives in the context of the organization and structure of the movement including the roles of local groups, national meetings, and communications networks.

Two major motivations—political/instrumental and personal/social—predominate in discussions of why people participate in social movements. The former are those that prompt people to pursue the articulated goals of a movement as expressed in its public purposes and rallying cries. Typically, these are the only reasons openly offered by individuals to explain their participation. But swift attainment of instrumental goals is relatively rare for most causes and therefore these goals are usually insufficient to sustain participation over the course of an arduous, uphill struggle.

Most participants need something more, and often that something is the unstated satisfaction that comes from the pleasure of associating with like-minded people, opportunities to assume new roles, or the status of holding an office. These personal rewards balance the costs of working, usually without immediate payoffs, toward long-term goals. Thus, those movements that survive their formative stage are those that satisfy both political/instrumental and personal/social needs. These two kinds of needs are not always compatible, however. The exclusive pursuit of one may interfere with the achievement of the other.

In addition to successfully meeting these needs, the growth of a social movement is influenced by its structure, and by the attitudes of its members about what structure is appropriate. Because structure provides the vehicle through which personal and political needs are met, it often affects how well they are satisfied. For most people, social needs are best met in small groups of people meeting in relatively unstructured, informal settings. In contrast, many political goals are best served by more tightly organized institutions, with centralization of decision making and a stable division of labor.[1] It is in part because structures best for facilitating personal/social needs are so different from structures best for achieving political/instrumental needs that the mutual satisfaction of both creates conflicts for social movements.

Before applying these general concepts to our analysis of the men's movement, we present a brief historical description.

AN OVERVIEW OF THE MEN'S MOVEMENT

The beginnings of the United States men's movement were very tenuous. Local meetings were held in such places as Des Moines, New York City, and Oberlin as early as 1973 and 1974, and a manifesto was published by the Berkeley's Men's Center in 1973. While a national organization is still in formation, seven national conferences have been convened since the first one in 1975 in the unlikely city of Knoxville, Tennessee. But since only a few hundred people ever attended these conferences, information has spread primarily through publications, books, and personal appearances by a few public figures, most notably Warren Farrell, Mark Fasteau, and Herb Goldberg.[2]

These public figures and others who identified themselves as leaders have never been able to attract a substantial following. Instead, many of the thirty men's centers listed in a national newsletter started at the 1975 conference have disappeared, and the newsletter itself ceased publication in 1978. The Male Box, a shoestring mail-order operation for the distribution of literature, posters, and other movement memorabilia was born at the third national conference in 1977 and announced its demise at the sixth national conference only two years later. On the other hand, a new movement magazine debuted in 1979, and in its spring 1981 issue listed approximately thirty men's centers and a few service projects involved with the prevention of rape and battering.

Throughout this checkered history, the most visible portion of the national movement has been the national conferences. It is at these conferences that the tension between the personal and political has been most evident. The first conference at Knoxville consciously emphasized the personal. Titled "A Playshop," all but one session were on such topics as men's theater, men's poetry, and men and dance, in an attempt to move beyond the instrumental, intellectual, and political spheres traditionally considered appropriate to men. The second conference eighteen months later in Pennsylvania continued this emphasis with its theme of "men supporting men," but almost a third of the sessions included a political focus.

At the third conference in 1977 it was evident that a major shift had occurred, though it was not clear whether this shift reflected the desires of the organizers or the wishes of the participants. Titled "Straight/White/Male: Struggling with the Master Culture," the Des Moines meeting stimulated heated discussion over the propriety of personal goals versus political ones. Some participants complained that their sessions focusing on "important" political activity were poorly attended, while personal growth sessions were filled.

This debate paralleled an equally acrimonious conflict in the early days of the younger branch of the women's liberation movement. Having roots in the

CATHY   by Cathy Guisewite

social movements of the sixties, women initially met together to develop a political analysis of their condition. But their small groups repeatedly turned to personal experiences and feelings. Initially leftist women in these groups, and the new left men they were associated with, denounced such discussions as hen parties and bitch sessions. It was only after introspection was legitimated as consciousness raising in some widely circulated papers that radical feminists began to assert that "the personal is political."[3]

The political emphasis continued through the fourth and fifth conferences. But it became more and more evident that there was a serious split as the majority of participants ignored workshops and activities with a political thrust. Perhaps as a response to this split and to some lengthy and sometimes unproductive attempts at political discussion, organizers of the sixth and seventh conferences in 1979 and 1981 attempted to join the goals of political action and personal change. For example, the theme for the sixth meeting was "The Men's Movement: A Loving Revolution," and a keynote address exhorted participants "to express our love through political and social action." As we shall see, the shift back toward the personal in part resulted from a separation of political activities from the conference mainstream.

The national conferences made it clear that those who were willing to organize them and those who wanted to attend did not always share identical purposes. The volunteers who planned the themes were generally more politically aware than the participants. In addition, some of the organizers and public figures who keynoted the conferences wanted to create a national organization, despite a notable lack of support and even some opposition from their potential constituents. For example, Sam Julty, in a 1977 keynote address at St. Louis, argued that the "gestation" of the men's movement was at an end and that "our history prompts us to prepare for our own birth as a movement." Many of the two hundred people scattered in the large theater auditorium must have realized that any movement "birth" at that time would most likely have resulted in a premature organization that would need artificial support to survive. In any event, Julty's attempt to induce labor failed.

At the 1978 Los Angeles conference, two days were devoted to a national organization ambitiously named the Men's Alliance for Liberation and Equality (MALE). However, MALE never actually functioned. Frustrated by the lack of progress in Los Angeles, a group of twenty-five politically active men met the following year in Madison, Wisconsin, and agreed that a national umbrella organization was desirable. The meeting concluded with a list of organizing principles and the impetus for a new men's magazine, but still no operational organization. Late in 1979 a version of the Madison organizational statement was distributed at the Milwaukee national conference, but for the first time, efforts toward national organizing were clearly separated from other more personal conference activities, and no formal endorsement for these principles was requested.

At the 1981 Boston conference these principles were adopted by a subgroup of twenty people as a basis for a proposed national dues-paying organization. Flyers were distributed at the conference and solicitation letters were mailed a few months later. Several of the Boston organizers argued that a national organization could counter or balance publicity that identified the men's movement primarily with backlash to women's liberation.[4]

PARTICIPATION IN THE MEN'S MOVEMENT

WHO JOINS AND WHY

Most people who join social movements admit their political motives but are unwilling to freely acknowledge their personal ones. Perhaps because personal benefits have been so important at men's conferences, those attending are much more willing to stress the role of the personal. At the 1979 Milwaukee conference we distributed a brief questionnaire that was returned by 39 of the 300-plus participants. Asked their reasons for attending, 62 percent of our respondents said their primary reasons were personal. However, only 13 percent listed reasons coded as purely personal, compared with 23 percent whose motives were coded as purely political and 64 percent who listed both.[5]

On the same questionnaire, 87 percent of the respondents indicated they had participated in a small support group. These responses fit with the possibility that the men's movement attracts many nonpolitical men whose main interest is personal growth rather than politics. For men who have been socialized to remain strong and independent, joining a growth or therapy group may connote weakness and dependency. It is more legitimate and "male" to report attendance at a men's group with its somewhat vague purposes of achieving freedom from restrictive male roles than to seek more formal help and support.

These personal motivations are consistent with our observation that many of the early men's support groups were organized by heterosexual men whose relationships with women had become more strained as women became more dissatisfied with traditional relationships. Joining men's groups was one response to relationship stress that often threatened to destabilize marriages and other primary relationships. Some joined seeking support during crises such as loss of child custody. Others wanted the benefits obtained by women from their support groups, which offered meaningful friendships not readily accessible to men.

This analysis is akin to Merton's[6] concept of manifest and latent functions. For example, it is easier to admit going into a bar manifestly to have a drink than it is to admit the latent function of seeking social contact. The men's group may have provided a means for fulfilling needs for therapy, affiliation, and support without the participants having to admit it to themselves and others. Traditionally these needs have been met by families and such institutions as men's clubs. But these traditional institutions have been declining, first with the virtual disappearance of the extended family and more recently with the isolation and decline of the nuclear family. For younger men team sports and for older men work groups and fraternal organizations have provided for some affiliative needs, but many of these groups are limited to special interests and in only a few cases provide even the intimacy and friendship of traditional women's clubs and social gatherings. Nor are exclusive men's clubs an available option. The typical participant in the men's movement is a youngish, college-educated, middle-class, straight, white male who is sympathetic to feminist demands to eliminate male dominance. Such men are not likely to join traditional men's organizations that discriminate against women.

For many men, small male support groups allowed for discussions of personally meaningful issues that could eventually lead to trusting and intimate friendship bonds. Support from other men who openly disclosed their feelings and vulnerabilities were often a welcomed palliative from the alienation and competitive rigors of the male world. These groups allowed men to experience new roles as well as new feelings. A man with little power or authority at work or in his family could assume a leadership role in a group; a man with overbearing responsibility at home or office could allow others to take responsibility for a men's group.

Although the participants have been mostly heterosexual, a significant minority have been gay. Since gays have their own movement, why do they join the men's movement? We have no data that would give clear answers, but our observations suggest two possible reasons. Individuals just beginning to question their sexual identity are reluctant to "come out" to the extent required by open participation in the gay movement. The men's movement may provide a vehicle that permits some men to express themselves in a safe environment while remaining undetected as gay in other contexts.

Another attraction may be the feminist ideology that predominates in the men's movement. Feminism criticizes the sex-role boundaries that are one of the aspects of gay oppression. Because the gay movement has not explicitly embraced feminism, gays for whom appropriate sex roles are a major concern may find they have more in common with straight feminist men than with gay men.[7]

This deliberate feminism is also an attraction to women, who have provided a strong but diminishing presence. While women are not typically found in the small groups or service projects, they have comprised from 5 to 50 percent of the conference attendance. The female participants tend to be heterosexual feminist women who perceive the men's movement as a beginning of rapprochement with men—a step beyond the separatism found in some segments of the women's movement. The presence of women and the predominance of feminism has created some tension, which is most clearly reflected at national conferences. Issues arise over women's presence, their role at the conferences, and the extent to which they should influence or dictate men's movement policies and ideology.

The presence at conferences of several nonfeminist or antifeminist factions has added to the tension. Several sessions sponsored by these factions have been viewed as antiwomen and rejected by conference organizers. Their prototype group, Free Men, a Maryland group claiming to be the only national men's organization,[8] bases its philosophy largely on the writings of Herb Goldberg, who focuses on man as victim of the stressful and limiting male sex role. Feminist men have little argument with Goldberg's description of sex-role limitations, but they call for a broader perspective. For example, Robert Brannon, a spokesperson for the feminist men's movement writes about male responsiveness to injustice, sometimes self-perpetrated: "Perhaps a men's movement motivated only by male self-interest might...encourage men to overcome their restrictive masculine programming and nothing more. A movement this narrow in vision would lack any broader legitimacy...to the other more serious victims of sexual oppression, it would be part of the problem rather than part of the solution."[9]

In contrast, a Free Men spokesman[10] views male feminists as "largely men filled with self-loathing who expiate their guilt through the worship of a goddess who gets her kicks out of dumping on men." Apparently Haddad does not see the possibility that men can act both to free themselves from destructive sex roles and to care about those who have been historically less powerful. Free Men and associated groups are small relative to the feminist men's movement, yet they have sustained a small-circulation national magazine, have received a disproportionate share of media publicity, and have been involved in a 1981 "Congress of Men" in Houston.[11]

PERSONAL VERSUS POLITICAL GOALS

The heightened importance of personal motives in the men's movement may be partially due to the vagueness or absence of specific political goals. For example, the Statement of Principles formulated at the 1979 conference is little more than a collection of values and ideals: "We are a group of men and women who support men through constructive lifestyle changes they want or need in these rapidly changing times.... We pledge to find ways to share power equitably...." Such vagueness is a consequence of the fact that the typical straight white man is not underpaid or underprivileged. He usually joins a men's group in response to disequilibrium in his personal life and, in some cases, to seek escape from the traditional male sex role.

Because such goals make specific aims difficult to identify, the movement has frequently assumed a supportive posture for the goals of others who suffer oppression. These vicarious goals are evident in virtually all the formal resolutions at recent national conferences, which were on such general issues as nuclear energy, racism, rape, violence against women, and the Equal Rights Amendment.

The men's movement has also legitimated personal intimacy and togetherness as desirable ends in themselves. Precisely because the movement has made men aware that they have been unwilling or unable to form and

HELLO CAROL
by B. Johnson

© 1981, Los Angeles Times Syndicate. Reprinted with permission.

maintain close or intimate relationships with each other, it may be uniquely able to acknowledge the importance of social interaction as a goal.

The activities of many local men's groups and the national meetings demonstrates the importance of social gathering as a legitimate end in itself. It is a rare men's gathering that doesn't include some music, camaraderie, and parties. At the national conventions, play is given equal priority with political activity. For men, it is not diverting or time-wasting to have fun with each other; it is an acknowledged achievement in a society that has kept men away from one other, except in traditional male activities such as business, sport, or womanizing.

Essentially, the men's movement offers to teach men how to give up positions of advantage in exchange for the long-range and intangible goals of a more humane and less sex-typed existence. Acting out these long-range objectives has few immediate benefits and many immediate costs such as career interruption and loss of social status. Unfortunately, the knowledge that someday one's actions will lead to a better world is insufficient to sustain most people. They need more immediate rewards. In the men's movement these can come from the small groups and the personal interactions at national conferences.

STRUCTURE OF THE MEN'S MOVEMENT

The men's movement operates on two levels that are largely independent of each other. On one level are the frequent national conferences where the personal and political mix and occasionally conflict. These attract between 300 and 800 participants. Locally there are the small support groups. There are several hundred around the country, each composed of 5 to 15 men, and approximately 30 to 40 men's centers and service projects. There is little networking among the support groups or between the groups and the national conferences. What communication there is, is supplied by various low-budget, sporadic newsletters and magazines. Among the more important periodicals have been *Brother*, the first nationally distributed "new" men's magazine staffed essentially by one man for several years; *Changing Men*, distributed by a men's group in Portland, Oregon, and now apparently defunct; and most recently *M*, a quarterly magazine founded at the 1979 Madison meeting.

The lack of connection between the two levels is illustrated by an experience of the first author (A.G.). A member of a small support group in a large metropolitan area, he went to the 1975 Knoxville conference on Men and Masculinity. When he reported on the conference to his group there was some polite attention, but a frankly stated disinterest in becoming actively involved. It was clear that the priority for those men was improving their own lives and developing a support network. National men's issues were of little or no importance. A.G. continued to attend both national meetings and his group, but except for an occasional report or notice that he would be absent from a local meeting, there was virtually no overlap. He was neither a representative nor a communication link for his group.

This divorce of the national movement from its grass-roots constituency is less complete in some locations, especially those with active men's centers, service projects, or phone numbers, but it is not atypical. It is reflected in a concomitant reluctance of many men who become involved in support groups to organize at even the community level. For example, after A.G.'s support group had met for several months, it became aware of ten to twelve other men's groups meeting regularly in the same region. One member tried to organize a regional representative group to serve as a clearinghouse for men who wished to be referred to support groups, host speakers, show films, and generally increase community awareness of the men's movement and its ideals. This group faded from lack of attendance after four of five meetings.

The lack of interest in consciously expanding the movement is a result not only of the many apolitical participants and the lack of short-range instrumental activities but of the supportive function of the small groups. The personal gains of friendship, intimacy, and self-validation are best obtained in an ongoing, stable group of like-minded people. Adding new members, especially ones who do not share the characteristics and problems of the old ones, reduces the benefits to the old members. Consequently, local groups do not seek to replicate themselves, inadequate political incentives do not stimulate old members to proselytize, and the lack of a national organization means there is no entity that takes responsibility to set up new groups.

This inertia was experienced by the women's movement, but it was countered by several other factors. First, the early participants were often politically oriented and were driven by an almost missionary zeal to share their experiences and insights. Second, most early feminists were enmeshed within a community of people who shared their basic values and politics. The cooptable communications network that Freeman postulates in Chapter 1 as crucial to movement formation simply does not exist for men. Most men find it difficult to broach "men's issues" to acquaintances or strangers out of concern that they will be viewed as weird or even gay. Third, the national media very quickly focused on the emerging feminist movement as an entertaining event. This publicity, ridiculing though it was, attracted the attention of sympathizers, who flocked to join. The men's movement has had only limited success in obtaining press coverage, and much of that has focused on antifeminist men.

Another impediment to an effective national men's organization is related paradoxically to political ideology and rhetoric endemic to the men's movement. Most of the hesitations about organizing revolve around fears that a national group might organize in a centralized or hierarchical manner typical of the traditional patriarchal structure that is anathema to most movement men. On the other hand, men who have been impatient with delays in forming a national movement have dismissed these fears as unreasonable organophobia.

SUMMARY AND CONCLUSION

Both political/instrumental and social/personal motives are important to attract and maintain participation in social movements. Participants usually acknowledge the former but not the latter. In the men's movement, personal/

social goals have been established as desirable ends in themselves. These goals have been strongly emphasized in the men's movement because (1) specific political goals have been absent, vague, or borrowed from other groups; and (2) achieving intimacy, viewed as a spinoff effect in many movements, has acquired the status of a legitimate political goal in the men's movement.

The emphasis on the personal and political/personal conflict are related to movement structure. The men's movement operates on at least two levels: the local support group and national meetings. Participants on different levels do not always share common purposes, and communication links between levels are not strong. Local members find that their personal needs are best met by retaining closed homogeneous groups; most of these men have shown only minimal interest in national meetings. Those men who participate nationally disagree on emphases and form for these activities; some favor a social and personal growth format, and others prefer to mix the personal with an explicitly political movement including a national organization.

Thus the feminist men's movement continues to exist but fails to achieve the impact of a mass movement. As long as support groups and national meetings continue to satisfy some personal needs, the movement is likely to continue, but until one or more national organizations or communications networks are effectively developed, the movement is unlikely to grow in numbers or influence.

NOTES

1. William A. Gamson, *The Strategy of Social Protest* (Homewood, Ill.: Dorsey Press, 1975), pp. 92ff.
2. In addition to their appearances, these men have authored three of the most influential men's books: W. Farrell, *The Liberated Man: Beyond Masculinity: Freeing Men and Their Relationships with Women* (New York: Random House, 1975); M. Fasteau, *The Male Machine* (New York: McGraw-Hill, 1974); and H. Goldberg, *The Hazards of Being Male*, (Plainview, N.Y.: Nash Publishing, 1976). A number of other more scholarly publications have been influential, e.g., D. S. David and R. Brannon, eds., *The Forty-nine Percent Majority: The Male Sex Role* (Reading, Mass.; Addison Wesley, 1976) is a popular reader/text at the college level; and J. H. Pleck, *The Myth of Masculinity* (Cambridge, Mass.: MIT Press, 1981) promises to become the major intellectual work on male role and male development growing out of the men's movement.
3. Jo Freeman, *The Politics of Women's Liberation* (New York: Longman, 1975), pp. 139ff.
4. See, for example, "Battle of the Sexes: Men Fight Back," *U.S. News and World Reports* 23 (8 December 1980): 50–54.
5. The following are typical of responses: "personal uplift and support: contact with like-minded people; political network contacts"; "continue growing, share support, develop our politics and our power to work together"; "finding resources and men's groups to tap into for support in my growth and struggle."
6. R. Merton, *Social Theory and Social Structure*, rev. ed. (Glencoe: Free Press, 1957), pp. 19–84.
7. See S. F. Morin and E. M. Garfinkle, "Male Homophobia," *Journal of Social Issues* 34, no. 1 (1978): 29–47; or G. K. Lehne, "Homophobia among Men," in *The Forty-*

nine Percent Majority: The Male Sex Role, ed. D. S. David and R. Brannon (Reading, Mass.: Addison-Wesley, 1976), pp. 66–88.

8. R. Haddad, *The Men's Liberation Movement: A Perspective* (Columbia, Md.: Free Men, 1979).

9. R. Brannon, "Changing Men, Changing Women" (unpublished ms., Department of Psychology, Brooklyn College, 1980).

10. Haddad, *The Men's Liberation Movement*, p. 7.

11. The Houston conference, which attracted less than 150 men, was organized primarily by groups such as Fathers United that are concerned with "male rights" issues especially in the areas of child custody and visitation. The men's movement groups we described have tended to view such groups as non- or antifeminist and sometimes as homophobic. See Robert Brannon, "Are Free Men Part of the Men's Movement?" (unpublished ms. Psychology Department, Brooklyn College, 1981). It is likely that press attention (e.g., *New York Times*, 15 June 1981, "A Congress of Men Ask Equality for Both Sexes") given the Houston meeting was at least in part a stimulus for the attempt to operationalize a profeminist national organization at the Boston conference during the same week.

5

Mobilizing the Disabled

Roberta Ann Johnson

There have always been large numbers of people with disabilities living in the United States. At present, it is estimated that there are approximately 30 million.[1] There have always been some charitable and service organizations to meet some of the needs of some disabled people, and particularly during the last decades, the number of disabled organizations has grown rapidly as the bureaucracy of government service agencies has expanded. But until very recently there had never been a large and effective social movement that bridged the gap between different disabilities, spanned the coasts, and continually spawned groups who prodded for disabled rights and services—what Jenkins and Perrow call groups acting in "insurgent" fashion.[2] With so many disabled people, why was there no social movement of the disabled?

To understand the long-time absence of a general social movement we must look to the one area in the United States where a social movement of the disabled was most visible and strong: Berkeley, California. This chapter focuses on what was unique in the Berkeley experience, as well as on more general factors that work to encourage the mobilization of the disabled.

This chapter was written by Dr. Roberta Ann Johnson in her private capacity. No official support or endorsement by the Office for Civil Rights or the Department of Education is intended or should be inferred.

Judith Bell, a student at the University of California, Santa Cruz, provided research assistance for this chapter.

LEGISLATIVE BACKGROUND

That there has not been a general social movement of the disabled does not mean there has not been legislation to provide "services for the handicapped." There has. The main thrust of the congressional acts, however, was not civil rights but vocational rehabilitation; and judging from the dates of the major acts, the congressional aim seems to have been largely one of accommodating returning wounded GIs. In fact, accommodating the returning soldier was the specific purpose of the first bills introduced in Congress in 1917 and 1918 and the Smith-Sears Act (P.L. 178), which passed and was signed by President Woodrow Wilson in 1918. The first of a series of rehabilitation acts, Smith-Sears included provisions for the industrially handicapped as well. Each client was eligible for training, counseling, and placement services. In 1935 the program became permanent with the passage of the Social Security Act.

World War II brought the next major changes in the rehabilitation program (P.L. 73–113). Medical, surgical, and other restorative services were authorized, and for the first time, the bill included the mentally ill and mentally retarded.

During the Korean peace talks, Congress passed P.L. 83–565, which improved the financial arrangements of matching monies to induce states to improve their programs. And in 1968, as the Vietnam war escalated, Congress passed P.L. 89–333, which was designed to expand and enlarge public programs for the handicapped. Services were again expanded in 1967 and 1968 (P.L. 90–341), but it was not until the 1973 Vocational Rehabilitation Act (P.L. 93–112) that there was a major change in legislative philosophy.

The major achievement of this act was not more vocational rehabilitation, although an important feature of the act included services for the severely handicapped, but that it included a significant, far-reaching, and potentially revolutionary commitment to the rights of the disabled. The revolution was wrought in a one-sentence-long section of the bill, Section 504, which read: "No otherwise qualified handicapped individual in the United States, shall solely by reason of his handicap, be excluded from the participation in, be denied the benefits of, or be subjected to discrimination under any program or activity receiving Federal financial assistance."

The wording of Section 504 paralleled the language of Section 601 of Title VI of the 1964 Civil Rights Act and Title IX of the 1972 Education Amendments Act. And like these sections, its passage did not guarantee implementation and compliance.

It is important to note that Section 504 was not heralded as groundbreaking civil rights legislation. In fact, congressional supporters avoided such a focus for fear it would turn the more conservative members of Congress against the bill. All the press attention and debate seemed to be riveted on the struggle between the Nixon White House and Congress over spending. In fact, Nixon vetoed the bill twice (Congress passed the third, cut version), and a *Washington Post* editorial characterized its unfortunate history by saying, "All in all this appears to be a meritorious bill which has become a pawn in the bitter struggle between an obstinate Congress and an equally stubborn President."[3]

The small part of the news coverage which focused on the bill's content, rather than on its political or financial aspects, was generally condescending in tone and not infused at all with a civil rights perspective. For example, Senator Hubert Humphrey reacted to the Nixon veto with, "It's just a goddamn outrage. It's a day of infamy for the White House. It's an example of the President ganging up on the lame, the sick, the blind and the retarded."[4] And Representative John Brademas, House manager of the bill, said about the impending vote to override the presidential veto that he didn't believe that there were many congress-people who "would want to vote *against the crippled* more than once in a session."[5]

That is not to say that there was no lobbying pressure from the physically disabled and their supporters. Thirty-five organizations lobbied to override Nixon's veto including the AFL/CIO, UAW, Easter Seals, and State Mental Health Departments.[6] There were some demonstrations in New York City and in The District of Columbia, more than two hundred people with disabilities, most of them from the annual meeting of the President's Committee on Employment of the Handicapped and the United Cerebral Palsy Association, held a day-long protest ending with a candlelight vigil at the Lincoln Memorial.[7] And although there was a *Washington Post* article that in passing touched on the "rights" of the disabled by warning that it was "time to stop treating the disabled as 'second rate citizens,'"[8] civil rights was not part of the congressional debates and was never raised as an issue during the hearings.[9] At this time, although some of the disabled saw their cause as a civil rights one, most people did not.

During 1975 and 1976, the Office for Civil Rights of the Department of Health, Education, and Welfare delayed implementing Section 504 regulations, first with an inflationary impact study and then with countless meetings with groups across the country including ten town meetings held in May and June 1976.[10] Even after HEW composed a final form for Section 504 "regs" (as they were later called), the secretary of HEW did not sign them, ignoring a federal court order to do so.[11]

Under the Carter administration, HEW did not move any faster. HEW Secretary Joseph Califano delayed signing the implementing regulations so that his staff could rewrite them.[12] In February and March 1977, when it became clear that more than cosmetic changes were being considered by HEW, disabled groups started to plan action[13] to prevent Califano from building "loopholes, waivers and exemptions"[14] into the regulations.

THE TAKEOVER

The American Coalition of Citizens with Disabilities (ACCD), an umbrella lobbying group representing forty-five groups and based in Washington, D.C., was created in 1974 by people attending the annual meeting in Washington of the President's Committee on Employment of the Handicapped. The American Council of the Blind, the National Association of the Deaf, Paralyzed Veterans of America, the Center for Independent Living, the National Paraplegic Foundation, and disabled student programs of colleges and universities from across the country were some of the early groups affiliated with ACCD.[15] The American Council of the Blind had a particularly important role to play in the beginning, at times even representing ACCD.

It was not until October 1975 that there was enough money collected from the membership to pay for a director. Frank Bowe, the first director, thought it was of primary importance to establish ACCD's presence in Washington. Until 1977, the organization's primary goals were to seek funding by applying for federal contracts and grants, to appear before congressional committees to testify on legislation, and to develop membership by recruiting organizations to join.

In March 1977 ACCD threatened political activities nationwide in a letter to President Carter. In the letter ACCD gave Secretary Califano a deadline of April 4, 1977, to sign the regulations "to bring his line agencies on-board and to begin preparation of an extensive compliance/enforcement program" [16] Groups of disabled people across the country were asked to prepare for protest demonstrations.

The Berkeley Center for Independent Living (CIL) spearheaded the creation of a "504 Coalition" in the Bay Area, which included the Independent Living Project in San Francisco and thirty or so disabled and supporting groups. By late March the northern California emergency coalition was already explicitly threatening protest demonstrations and sit-ins.[17]

Demonstrations were scheduled to take place on April 5 at HEW buildings in ten different cities. The demonstrations either failed (like the one in New York where only six people showed up to demonstrate) or were small and short-lived. The sit-ins held in Washington, D.C. and Denver lasted one day; the one in Los Angeles had very few participants, but lasted three.

In Washington, D.C., 300 disabled people, most of them from the immediate area, demonstrated, and 50 to 75 people (estimates vary) remained overnight in HEW offices on the sixth floor where Secretary Califano's office was located.[18] The General Service Administration wanted to oust the Washington demonstrators, but Califano and other HEW officials insisted that "no force" be used. Instead, the demonstrators were starved out.[19] The next day, having been allowed only one cup of coffee and a doughnut, those who sat-in decided to leave as a group rather than trickle out, and a "band of blind, deaf or otherwise disabled" demonstrators left the HEW building after twenty-eight hours of occupation.[20] The Washington demonstrators had neither community support nor support from government officials.

In Denver, 150 people showed up to demonstrate, while others blocked the intersection at 18th and Stack streets to coincide with the demonstration. Coverage on the noon news encouraged more people to join. Taking their directions from the Washington-based ACCD, when the Denver demonstrators heard that San Franciscans and Washington, D.C. demonstrators were planning to stay overnight, the Denver folks got bedding and medication, and 52 stayed. At 9 p.m. they let the news media into the building, and the 10 p.m. news included coverage of the sit-in.

The next morning, the Denver group left the building at about the same time the Washington demonstrators did. In Denver they called their demonstration a success because, according to one of the more active participants, Janet Dorsey, the sit-in had opened up important communication lines with regional HEW officials. When the demonstrators left the building, they held a press conference and then attended debates in the state Legislature on a disabled civil rights bill that just happened to be scheduled for that day.[21]

The Los Angeles sit-in lasted three days. Preparation began in March at meetings attended by a handful of people and held at the Westside Center for Independent Living. On April 5, between 40 and 50 demonstrators showed up for a scheduled rally outside the HEW building, and approximately 15 disabled people entered the building for a sit-in. The demonstrations had some support from local church groups, and food was provided by friends of those who were sitting-in. They had some political support as well. The second night, before the federal employees left the building, officials threatened that the disabled demonstrators would be removed by police. Congressman Tony Bielensen, of the 23rd Congressional District, gave the demonstrators a haven in his office in HEW, preventing any police action. Ed Roberts, director of California's Rehabilitation Department, was also there, giving support. Nevertheless, the Los Angeles demonstrators did not have general community support, nor did they have complete support from disabled groups. The California Association of Physically Handicapped, for example, refused to get involved in the struggle. During the week, no new people joined the sit-in, no new community support was forthcoming, and the sit-in did not generate a growing momentum.[22] They left the building on Friday, April 8, announcing:

> When we left the demonstration, we did not have the organizational support to provide food and medical supplies over the weekend, when the doors would be closed to all people coming in and out. Friday afternoon all disabled people and supporters were denied access to the building. There were no attendants for the severely disabled demonstrators, and at that time we could get none into the building for the weekend. These restrictions, imposed on us suddenly, were a complete policy reversal by the Federal Security Officers.[23]

In San Francisco, the experience of the demonstrators was quite different. Strategy meetings were held in March at Berkeley's Center for Independent Living. Numerous northern California organizations of disabled persons were represented in their coalition,[24] and the demonstrators had the support of important community groups and businesses as well. Flyers went out, with the CIL logo prominent at the top, advertising a noontime demonstration to be held at the San Francisco HEW building "to demand signing of Federal anti-discrimination regulations for the disabled." Hundreds of the disabled and their supporters demonstrated outside, and hundreds entered the building. Approximately 150 did not leave when the building officially closed at 5 p.m.

The Salvation Army was there with food, coffee, and blankets for the first night. The Delancy Street Foundation, a well-established, politically important ex-prisoner organization, knew in advance about the San Francisco takeover and was also there providing food on the first day of the sit-in.[25] By the third day, the Black Panthers were providing food and endorsing the demonstrators' goals in their newspaper; the local Safeway was supplying food and medicine;[26] and a Hispanic group, the Mission Rebels, was providing hot breakfasts. Labor organizations, including many AFL/CIO affiliated unions—in particular, the International Association of Machinists, the Teamsters, and the International Longshoremens Association—gave their support to the demonstration. The Federal Workers Union, including many employees in the HEW building, gave support and assistance, as did Werner Erhard of est, who visited and contributed money. Gay groups, like the Butterfly Brigade, assisted the demonstrators by smuggling in walkie talkies and toiletries. As one demonstrator put it, "The thing that was neat was it was disabled folks from all over working together and it was also nondisabled support up the kazoo."[27]

The demonstrators at first planned only to stay overnight, then only over the weekend, but plans can change. The San Francisco demonstrators vowed that they would not leave HEW until Califano signed the Section 504 regulations. Judy Heumann, one of the demonstration leaders, remembers the decision to stay:

> I think what was the deciding factor for us staying in the building was the fact that the other demonstrations were failing and that the group in Washington was starved out and so a lot of us here began to feel like we had the strongest base and that we wanted to continue what was going and that we were the only ones left to do it. So it wasn't like a frolicksome, you know . . . it's OK so we'll stay, it was much more strategy of why are we staying. . . .[28]

California officials and politicians spoke out in behalf of the demonstrators. On April 8 Joe Maldonado, the HEW regional director, called Califano to urge him to sign the regulations. On April 9 Ed Roberts, director of the state's Rehabilitation Department, urged approval. California's secretary of health, Mario Obledo, followed suit on April 10.[29]

By April 12, Congressman Phillip Burton expressed his support for the 150 demonstrators who remained at HEW. Burton openly criticized Califano, and on April 15, Burton and Representative George Miller arranged to hold congressional hearings on the proposed regulations right there at the site of the sit-in.[30]

Attention and political support grew. California Congressman Tom Bates of Berkeley sent Califano a letter with the signatures of forty-six state assembly people supporting the demonstrators' demands; and endorsements came from Assemblyman Willie Brown, Mayor George Moscone, and the San Francisco Board of Supervisors. The *San Francisco Chronicle* carried at least one story a day about the demonstration, as did the television news.

By April 18, San Francisco Mayor Moscone had obtained hoses to rig up showers at the city's expense, as well as mats, towels, soap, and cream for chair sores at the city's expense, and while HEW Commissioner Maldonado caused some delays—at one point saying, "We're not running a hotel here," and warning he'd have Moscone arrested—by the second week of the demonstration the city had even installed showers.[31]

As the sit-in continued the San Francisco demonstrators selected a group of eighteen (mostly the CIL leadership), who went to Washington on April 19 to lobby in person. They brought with them more endorsements, including a San Francisco Board of Supervisors' resolution urging Califano to sign and the "official" endorsement of Mario Obledo, California's Secretary of Health.[32]

The demonstrators carried with them other Bay Area support. The ABC-TV San Francisco affiliate, KGO, sent a reporter and photographer to Washington to accompany the group. The International Association of Machinists organized a banquet at its Washington headquarters, provided the demonstrators with drivers, and rented a Hertz truck to transport the disabled around Washington. In fact, the union attached a "504" sign to the truck, and when Hertz people saw the logo on the truck on a television program, they asked for the truck back. The Machinists refused.[33]

The San Francisco representatives were not allowed into the HEW building. "Two dozen deaf, blind, and mentally retarded demonstrators," the *Washington Post* wrote, "many of them in wheelchairs, turned away from HEW by armed guards, were demanding to see Califano."[34] Instead, they continued their demonstrations outside, including an all-night vigil and candlelight prayer service in front of Califano's home.[35]

The demonstrators never spoke personally with either Califano or Carter, but they did have two meetings with Stuart Eizenstat, assistant to the President in domestic affairs.[36] They also persuaded Senator Alan Cranston to write Califano urging him to sign the regulations.[37] When the demonstration was over, the protestors called their attempts to contact the administration "a tremendous success." Said one of the leaders, "We raised a lot of consciousness back in Washington. We got the support of more than thirty Congresspersons. We were able to talk to all kinds of people."[38]

Finally, on Thursday, April 28, 1977, day 24 of the San Francisco sit in, Secretary Joseph A. Califano, Jr., signed "the regs." He issued an eleven-page announcement for immediate release. It began,

> For decades, handicapped Americans have been an oppressed and, all too often, a hidden minority, subjected to unconscionable discrimination, beset by demoralizing indignities, detoured out of the mainstream of American life and unable to secure their rightful role as full and independent citizens.
>
> Today I am issuing a regulation, pursuant to Section 504 of the Rehabilitation Act of 1973, that will open a new world of equal opportunity for more than 35 million handicapped Americans—the blind, the deaf, persons confined to wheelchairs, the mentally ill or retarded, and those with other handicaps.[39]

Jubilant, the demonstrators went home to California. Two days later, all the demonstrators left the San Francisco HEW building, flanked by politicians, friends, and supporters, feeling victorious. They held a well-publicized rally attended by hundreds. Said Kitty Cone, "What we have done is shown this country that disabled people can carry on a fight—to the highest levels of government. In the process we have gained a whole lot of self-respect."[40]

THE PROTEST

Michael Lipsky defines "protest activity . . . as a mode of political action oriented toward objection to one or more policies or conditions, characterized by showmanship or display of an unconventional nature, and undertaken to obtain rewards from political or economic systems while working within the systems."[41] Since so few disabled people were involved in the "protest activity" just described, it seems, in retrospect, a great miracle that they achieved their goal. One factor was that the goal was specific and "achievable." Another was that they "successfully activated," to use Lipsky's model, "third parties," creating bargaining resources.

But there is a more fundamental issue to be addressed here. The real question is how and why, in 1977, Bay Area disabled people seemed to suddenly burst on to the public arena so much more effectively than in any other area, with a well-articulated collective goal and with a vision larger than that of their disability-specific organizations. Their protest did not succeed because of shared interest or "potential" shared interest. As Jenkins so aptly puts it, "common interests do not collective action make."[42] The protest was just the tip of the iceberg. A social movement had already been congealing in the Bay Area, and thus the events of April 1977 were merely a catalyst to protest activity.

What laid the foundation for a social movement of the disabled was the development of an independent living philosophy—a consequence of independent living programs (ILP) that had developed and grown in California. The programs consisted of "non residential service centers controlled by disabled individuals that enable persons with diversified disabilities to live in integrated settings within their own communities . . . independence [did] not mean doing things physically alone. It mean[t] being able to make independent decisions. It is a mind process not contingent on a 'normal' body."[43] The movement for independence was called unique. One journalist described it as a search "for the means to give each person not only equality but as much control as possible over his or her life."[44] Judy Heumann candidly described the importance of ILP in her life when she spoke to congresspeople holding hearings in 1978 on the Vocational Rehabilitation Act:

> I had polio when I was 1½ years old, and I am a severely disabled individual. I grew up in New York City, and I lived there for 25 years. I liked New York but the environment there demanded a lifestyle of dependency. In order for me to make the advances that I wanted to with my life, I learned to manipulate my environment to the best of my ability. There was no formal support system.
>
> In 1973, I was contacted in New York by Ed Roberts and urged to apply to graduate school at the University of California, Berkeley, and to get involved in a program he called CIL. . . . I decided that I would come out for one week as an experiment to see the situation for myself. I was what people in California might describe as "blown away."
>
> I came to Berkeley, was met at the airport by a disabled friend, driving a van with a hydraulic lift. I stayed in a home that was accessible and was given a loaner electric wheelchair to use, and I was assisted with personal care needs by a paid attendant.
>
> My life quickly began to change. I was in charge of my own activities, getting up when I wanted, going to bed when I wanted, taking a shower when I wanted and the like. All these things may appear small to you, but for me it was the first time that my handicap did not completely control my life. I decided to stay in California.[45]

During the 1970s, the Bay Area became "the nation's capital for the handicapped" with proportionately more severely disabled people than anywhere else in the country. Berkeley became the "unwilling" center of the disabled movement with the establishment of the Center for Independent Living in 1972.[46] CIL grew "from a staff of eleven, working in a two bedroom apartment, funded by one federal grant, to an organization staffed by 117 people, supported by more than 21 different contracts with an annual budget of around $900,000."[47] The development of an independent living philosophy was essential for birthing a social movement of the disabled—not only because of its emphasis on pride and autonomy for the disabled but because it took disabled people out of their isolation and brought them together in large numbers.

Three elements were required for a social movement of the disabled, and these were prevalent in Berkeley, California, in quantities and forms not available elsewhere: (1) a change of consciousness, (2) preexisting social networks, and (3) legitimation and facilitation by political elites.

A CHANGE OF CONSCIOUSNESS

A change of consciousness was the biggest hurdle for the disabled. What was required for the disabled to become a social movement was nothing short of a redefinition of themselves. Traditionally they had been dealt with in a paternalistic way and had accepted gratefully bureaucratic gifts coming from "on high." They were seen as unfortunate people—"poor crips," as some of the demonstrators mockingly described it. Disability was stigmatized as shameful; the disabled were seen, and felt themselves to be, dependents on a charitable society. With this self-image, there could never be a social movement, for the felt dependency inhibited the sense of efficacy a movement required, and the stigmatized view of self discouraged identification with other disabled people. A change of consciousness was necessary. There were three parts to the change of consciousness necessary for a disabled social movement: (1) destigmatization, (2) group identification, and (3) the development of feelings of efficacy.

Destigmatization was a vital first step. A new self-image required feeling pride about a condition seen as shameful and often ugly. The following description of a disabled children's summer camp illustrates vividly the abhorrent qualities attached to the disabled:

> The woods and paths of Camp Wiggin were accustomed to troops of running feet and the noise of children at play. With these children there was only silence. Parents unfolded wheelchairs, and carefully lifted their children into them. In procession, they wheeled the children—about 120 in all—toward us waiting counselors. They would be under our care for the next two weeks.
>
> What do you say to a parade of children who move toward you only by the energy of their parents: children with swollen heads, or sightless eyes, or bodies without arms or legs; children drained of expression, pallid in color and spirit. They seemed old for their age, yet without visible life, crumbled and stuffed into wheelchairs, covered with blankets to ward off, not the cold, but the sight of disfigurement.[48]

Not only did the disabled have to develop a positive self-image but they had to identify with others who were disabled. This second shift in consciousness, group identification, was also difficult because there is a psychic cost in identifying with crippled people in a culture that emphasizes youth and beauty and allows some disabled to blend in and "mainstream." The problem of group identification existed for other social movements based on an immutable characteristic. But disability is more stigmatizing than any other characteristic, even race.[49] Demonstrations have functioned for stigmatized groups to reduce the felt differences between members. For example, Alice Walker remembers the 1963 black Civil Rights March on Washington in the following way: "...I felt my soul rising from the sheer force of Martin King's eloquent goodness...whatever the Kennedy Administration may have done, or not done, had nothing to do with the closeness I felt that day to my own people."[50] In much the same way, for many disabled people, the persistent San Francisco sit-in and its success in 1977 marked a change in their consciousness of group identification, or as one woman put it, "started her awareness."[51]

Connection with others was not only psychologically harder but was physically more difficult than with other groups. In general they experienced more isolation than the suburban housewife separated from other women or the closeted homosexual in smalltown America. Not only did they rarely come in contact with other disabled people but many of the disabled had less contact with *anyone* because of their disabilities. Exceptions, like the deaf community, were people who had so much contact with each other that they knew no one else. This ingrown contact tended to prevent their wholesale participation in and identification with a general disability movement. The deaf, for example, were used to identifying with their group alone, and many did not see themselves as "physically disabled."[52]

Additionally, many of the disabled "subcultures," as the demonstrators called them, had made advances on their own. Organizations such as the National Federation of the Blind were not enthusiastic about coalescing with others because they had their own history of accommodating legislation.[53] Gary Gill is most candid about how his identification as a blind person was transformed to identification with the disabled movement at the 504 takeover:

> For me [the takeover] was great. Up to that point, I was working somewhat in the blind community...but when I got in the building...slowly, you know how realizations climb up from the gut to the brain, slowly I had to realize that hey, there's some other stuff going on here...I saw all these folks in chairs and I learned a little finger spelling and started working with deaf folks and it was just neat to see that *as a group* we could do stuff.[54]

Another way in which consciousness was changed was by labeling the disabled demands as a civil rights struggle. Although not originally seen as civil rights legislation, implementation of 504 was portrayed by the ACCD as a civil rights issue, and the leaflets disseminated by CIL for the San Francisco demonstration demanded "equal rights for the disabled."

After the Bay Area sit-in started, the disabled protesters repeatedly connected their struggle to other civil rights struggles. At one of their early meetings with the press the demonstrators focused on the tone of media coverage and expressed their concern that the event be covered as a civil rights issue "to get them to stop focusing on 'this is how so and so gets put to bed'" coverage, according to Heumann.[55] "This is the age of civil rights and liberation," one demonstrator declared. "We have had the black man's [*sic*] rights, gay rights, women's rights and now it is disabled rights."[56] Another demonstrator, referring to Rosa Parks and the black civil rights movement, said, "I don't want to move to the front of the bus, I just want to be able to get on it."[57] During the sit-in, supporting organizations like the Black Panthers and politicians like Congressman Phillip Burton also used the civil rights perspective in their endorsements. Some, like Assemblyman Willy Brown, even referred to the 1970s as the "era" for "the rights of the handicapped and the disabled."[58] The press quickly picked up the connection.[59]

The disabled used more than civil rights rhetoric. They used its *method*— the sit-in—and its *chant*—"We shall overcome."[60] Not surprisingly, the press was soon referring to disabled leaders as "the new militants,"[61] their demonstration as a "most poignant civil rights demonstration,"[62] and the 1973 Vocational Rehabilitation Act as their "first major Civil Rights Act."[63] Even Califano, when he finally signed the regulations, referred to then as opening "a new era of civil rights in America,"[64] and President Carter one month later vowed that "we are committed to guaranteeing the civil rights of the disabled."[65]

Thus the civil rights perspective provided a philosophical basis for the takeover. By linking the disabled with other civil rights movements it also helped legitimize their demands as well as normalizing and dignifying a stigmatized group. Most important, the civil rights perspective created a unifying theme that all the distinct and separate disabled people could rally round.

The third prerequisite for a change in consciousness was the development of feelings of efficacy. Piven and Cloward call efficacy the essential transformation of consciousness. It is required before people who are ordinarily fatalistic can assert their rights.[66] The idea of independent living was a key to the development of feelings of efficacy.

The idea of independence and self-help was romanticized by the press during the San Francisco sit-in. One journalist described day three, "Amid the chanting and singing there were touching scenes of wheelchair demonstrators who still had the use of their arms feeding those who were too disabled to help themselves"[67] and the new philosophy connected with the est.vision of Werner Erhard who said, when he visited the protestors, "It's moving and inspiring to see these people take charge of their own lives."[68]

When the disabled began to feel more self-sufficient, it enabled them to move from a recipient role to that of actor. This was clearly illustrated during the sit-in. As one paraplegic protestor proclaimed, "I slept on the floor last night and I'll stay here until the bill is law. It's hard for people like us to do something like this. But we believe enough in our cause to put up with inconvenience."[69] Another boasted, "The movement was begun by the disabled and run by and for the disabled."[70] It was only in Berkeley where all three changes of consciousness—destigmatization, group identification, sense of self-efficacy—were occurring in a large-scale way.

PREEXISTING SOCIAL NETWORKS

It was also only in Berkeley that social networks were well enough developed to make a strong, autonomous, community-based movement of disabled people possible. Many social scientists have described the importance to social movements of already existing social networks.[71] Among the disabled, the primary social networks were within their own disabilities. Gary Gill's candid description of his involvement in the sit-in illustrates the importance of, and his dependence on, his own social network: the blind community. For him, the patronizing local coverage of the sit-in got him to act and activate his network:

> That night I watched the news . . . it was the Channel 2 News . . . they were particularly not good this night . . . the guy comes on and says . . . these blind so and so's, these crippled up so and so's, what are they trying to do, they already got welfare, I mean, are they asking for more charity, they already got rehabilitation. . . . Well, I had a quantum reaction to that, kinda' like a bad smallpox vaccination . . . so my wife and I started gathering blind folks because we're tied in, somewhat, to the blind network at that time, and a bunch of us went over.[72]

It was a spontaneous reaction, but it would have died in the bud without the already existing social network to activate.

In no other city was there such a large proportion of disabled residents visible and interfacing with each other and with other members of the community. In no other city did you have so many disabled people living, not isolated in their parents' homes or rest homes, but living in the community and connected to organizations for service as well as for social life.

The importance of Berkeley's networks is illustrated by contrasting it with other cities. A civil rights-oriented disabled group had formed in New York City in 1970 when Judy Heumann was denied the right to teach in public school. It had sponsored demonstrations in support of the passage of the Vocational Rehabilitation Act. Yet in 1977 disabled people were not mobilized. Heumann suggests it was because the activists of the early seventies had left and the organizations were only "political" organizations without a service component,[73] which, for a disabled person, makes the ties to the organization much stronger. The service component generated social connections. In 1977 the disabled in New York City were not sufficiently socially connected with one another or with the greater community to have a successful sit-in. Consciousness may have been there, but social networks were not.

In Los Angeles, two Independent Living Centers and a fairly large number of deaf people participated in the HEW sit-in. Yet there wasn't a large range of disabled organizations involved in the demonstration and sit-in, and although there was some local church support, there wasn't the range of community support the Berkeley disabled experienced. Food in Los Angeles was supplied by supportive friends, not by supportive organizations. For Doug

Martin, who was then head of the Northside Independence Center, the most crucial difference between L.A. and the Bay Area was geography. The sheer size of L.A. prevented physical connections among L.A.'s disabled; Berkeley's small size and street use made such connections possible.[74]

There were social networks among the disabled in Denver, but they lacked a history of aggressive autonomous activity, and they lacked the ability, in 1977, to act independent of ACCD directives. The coalition of demonstrators was described by one of its members as "loose and informal." It was made up of people from the Cerebral Palsy Center, members of the Commission on the Disabled, the Governor's Council on the Disabled, Atlantis Community (a CIL-type group started in 1974), and others.

In Washington, the home of ACCD, there was nowhere near the same level of networking with the community that there was even in Denver. Although large numbers of the disabled participated in the District demonstration and sit-in, the demonstrators had not created the necessary bonds with community groups so that they could be nurtured by their community's food and supplies and bolstered by their community's encouragement, support, and political endorsements.

There is another factor which contributed to the disabled as a social movement and that is elite legitimation and facilitation.

ELITE LEGITIMATION AND FACILITATION

The prime example of elite legitimation was the passage of the 1973 Vocational Rehabilitation Act itself. The inclusion of Title V and especially the development of the 504 section, had a profound effect on the goals and aspirations of disabled people.

It was precisely what Piven and Cloward describe happened with the passage of section 7a of the 1933 National Industrial Recovery Act which provided employees the right to organize and bargain collectively. This gave the workers "an elán, a righteousness that they had not had before."

> The impact on workers was electrifying. It was as if incipient struggles had now been crowned with an aura of what Rudé called 'natural justice.' Felt grievances became public grievances, for the federal government itself had declared the workers cause to be just.[75]

Likewise, the federal government facilitated the movement when it declared the disabled cause to be a just one in 1973.

What was different for the disabled was that the passage of the 1973 law was a cause and not a consequence of a general disabled movement and struggle. As Judy Heumann describes it:

> The '64 Civil Rights Act was the culmination of years and years of work. Striving towards the '64 civil rights act was also an organizing tool, for the movement. Now, with the '73 act substantially the work, in my opinion, that was done on it was done by the key legislators themselves. There was ... no street action, there was no national uniform letter-writing campaign ... so it was put through so you kind of picked up ownership of it after it was through ... I think that has been

detrimental . . . in as much as you've had to give it to the disabled population and make them own it and accept pride in what it is and then fight for it.[76]

The real danger was that the government's generosity would work against a social movement, for paternalistic welfare feeds a welfare mentality and militates against a move from recipient to actor. As Turner suggests, "Individuals and groups who are totally dependent upon a dominant group are those least likely to challenge the propriety of their situation."[77] Thus, the government's paternalistic generosity might have *undermined* a social movement of the disabled had there been no four year delay in the signing of the "regs". Instead, the government legitimized a goal and then ignored it, thus forcing the disabled to struggle, and the struggle created consciousness. (This is analogous to the effect the sex provision of Title VII had on the women's movement.)

The Bay Area was the only place in which elite legitimation happened on a grand scale. Public officials seemed to be tripping over one another in the rush to endorse the disabled cause. However, the government not only helped legitimize a social movement of the disabled,[78] it also facilitated its development. It provided numerous town meetings and conferences,[79] recruited supporters, developed leaders, facilitated corporate action, gave information, and provided funding. In fact, the federal government played the facilitator role even *before* the 1973 act was passed. The 1973 Washington vigil held in support of the bill was made up mainly of participants from a federally sponsored annual conference, the President's Committee on Employment of the Handicapped.

After the 504 regulations were signed in 1977, the federal government continued to facilitate the movement. First, the law gives the movement focus; as one participant candidly admits, "The direction of the movement is overseeing that laws are enforced."[80] Second, the federal government funds the movement. A nationwide 504 training program, designed to teach disabled people their rights under 504, has reached five thousand disabled people in the West and Midwest and eight thousand in the rest of the country.[81] In fact, the 504 training workshops have become a means of movement recruitment. As one 504 training participant describes it,

> One of the big things now is getting disabled folks to know they have these rights
> . . . all these 504 trainings all over the country . . . we teach them what their rights
> are, we also teach them how to organize and become radical. That's the hidden
> agenda. We teach them how to do coalition work which means to coalesce with
> other folks with other disabilities.[82]

Furthermore, in 1978, a year after the 504 regulations were signed by Secretary Califano, amendments to the 1973 Rehabilitation Act were passed. They provided for the establishment of Independent Living Programs throughout the country, as well as for the strengthening of state protection and advocacy systems for disabled individuals.

The federal government legitimizes and facilitates the social movement of the disabled, but the government did not cause the movement. The movement blossomed in the Bay area because of the aggressive support of local officials against a backdrop of independent living ideology that was vital for a change of consciousness and because an extensive communication network was strongly in place and ready to be activated. The Federal Government merely contributed to the development of a social movement but the contribution was important.

The Vocational Rehabilitation Act of 1973 legitimized a vision of social integration for the disabled. The government's delay in implementing the law stimulated the demonstrations and sit in and helped integrate the disabled into the tradition of civil rights struggles. Standing out as a measure of that success is the fact that today in Berkeley and the surrounding Bay Area, police paddy wagons are wheelchair accessible.

NOTES

1. Steven V. Roberts, "Putting a Price Tag on Equality," *New York Times*, 25 June 1978, p. 1.
2. J. Craig Jenkins and Charles Perrow, "The Insurgency of the Powerless: Farm Worker Movements (1946–1972)," *American Sociological Review* 42 (April 1977): 249.
3. Caspar W. Weinberger, "The Rehabilitation Veto: An Administrative View," *Washington Post*, 4 April 1973, p. A19; confirmed by Reese Robrahn, executive director of American Coalition of Citizens with Disabilities, telephone interview, 10 March 1981.
4. Spencer Rich, "Senate Fails by Four Votes to Kill Veto," *Washington Post*, 4 April 1973, p. A1.
5. Richard L. Lyons, "Hill Again Passes Pocket-Vetoed Bill," *Washington Post*, 16 March 1973. Italics added.
6. Rowland Evans and Robert Novak, "They've Given Up on Mr. Gray," *Washington Post*, 25 March 1973, sect. C, p. 7.
7. "Vigil Ends Protest by Handicapped," *Washington Post*, 4 May 1973, p. C2.
8. Ralph Craib, "PUC Member Tells of Her Outrage: HEW Protesters Talk about It," *San Francisco Chronicle*, 15 April 1977, p. 10.
9. According to the executive director of American Coalition of Citizens with Disabilities, Reese Robrahn, the civil rights issue was avoided by the bill's sponsors so as not to alienate the more conservative but supportive members of Congress.
10. For a list of the meetings, see "Twenty-two Meetings Set on Proposed Bias Ruling," *Washington Post*, 16 July 1976, p. A10.
11. "Mathews Hesitates at Order for Rules to Aid Handicapped," *Washington Post*, 19 January 1977, p. C12; according to Reese Robrahn, executive director of American Coalition of Citizens with Disabilities, colleges and universities spearheaded the opposition to implementation using the cost issue.
12. James D. Whitaker, "Carter Broke Promises Say Handicapped," *Washington Post*, 8 January 1977, p. 43.
13. In their call for action, the Northern California Emergency Coalition wrote: ". . . it is now more than one month since the Secretary's announcement and we have now been informed that the task force review will not be completed for another few weeks. Furthermore, it is now clear that many of the substantive provisions in the regulations that were developed after exhaustive negotiations by HEW with beneficiaries and recipients of federal fund alike, are being reconsidered for purposes of major revision. We are dismayed by this apparent breach of faith and feel the time may have come for us to begin to take action." Frank C. Bowe, executive

director ACCD, Center for Independent Living, Inc., letter announcing the 5 April noontime demonstration at San Francisco HEW, p. 3.

14. Joseph Whitaker, "Handicapped Gather at HEW to Agitate for Rights Enforcement," *Washington Post*, 6 April 1977, p. B8.

15. Joyce Jackson, "History of ACCD," to Board of Directors, ACCD (unpublished paper), June 1981.

16. Frank G. Bowe, letter to President Jimmy Carter from American Coalition of Citizens with Disabilities, Inc.

17. The ten cities were Washington, D.C., Boston, Seattle, New York, Atlanta, Philadelphia, Chicago, Dallas, San Francisco, and Denver. Joseph Whitaker, "Handicapped Plan Protest at HEW Offices in Ten Cities," *Washington Post*, 30 March 1977, p. AC.

18. Whitaker, "Handicapped Gather." Estimates of numbers vary. See also "SF Demonstration: HEW Protest by Handicapped," *San Francisco Chronicle*, 7 April 1977, p. 9.

19. According to Reese Robrahn, present director of ACCD, based on the advice given to them by the NAACP and other groups, the demonstrators simply didn't anticipate that they would be denied food. Telephone interview, July 1981.

20. Michael Grieg, "Disabled Protestors Continue Sit-In at HEW Office Here," *San Francisco Chronicle*, 7 April 1977, p. 9.

21. Interview with Janet Dorsey, Denver disabled activist and demonstrator, 26 March 1981.

22. Telephone interview with Doug Martin, former director of the Westside Center for Independent Living, 12 August 1980.

23. Quoted in the San Francisco 504 Coalition news release of 9 April 1977.

24. The following, from Bowe's letter to Jimmy Carter (n. 16), is a partial list of organizations and their representatives making up the 504 Emergency Coalition:

   Paralyzed Veterans of America
   Gray Panthers
   American Council of the Blind of California
   AID Retarded Citizens
   Catholic Social Services Hearing Impaired Program
   Silent Strength
   Center for Independent Living
   Lighthouse for the Blind
   Community Arthritis Project
   Diane Schechter of the Committee for Equal Access to Parks and Forests
   United Cerebral Palsy
   Margaret Emory of the Mental Health Consumer Concerns of Alameda County
   Association of the Physically Handicapped, California
   Senior Citizens Centers
   Physically Disabled Students Program
   Mark Randol, Secretary, Hemophilia Foundation of Northern California
   Adult Independence Development Center
   Jim Pechin, Coordinator, Disabled Paralegal Advocate Program
   Swords to Plowshares Veterans Organization
   Herbert Levine, Director, Employment Project for the Physically Handicapped
   John King, Director, United Cerebral Palsy Foundation
   Coalition of Veterans for Human Rights
   Flower of the Dragon Veterans Rights Organization

Disabled People's Legal Resource Center

United Paraplegics of Berkeley

25. Delancy Street was involved with CIL in the planning of the demonstration and sit-in because Delancy Street was a substance-abuse organization (alcohol, narcotics) and the 504 regulations included in their list of disabilities, drug abusers and alcoholics. There were rumors that a revised version of the regulations might exclude these groups so it was in Delancy Street's interest to keep up the pressure on Califano against major revisions. Interview with Karen Parker, consultant, Center for Independent Living, Berkeley, and former San Francisco Aid for Retarded Citizens, 1 August 1980.

26. "Panthers Back Handicapped Demonstrators," *San Francisco Chronicle*, 8 April 1977, p. 38.

27. Interview with Gary Gill, 504 consumer advocate trainer, Berkeley, California, 9 May 1980.

28. Interview with Judy Heumann, senior deputy director, Center for Independent Living, Berkeley, California, 1 August 1980.

29. "Panthers Back Handicapped"; "Handicapped Rights Plea," *San Francisco Chronicle*, 9 April 1977, p. 38; A. Fumiko Nakao, "State Rehab Chief Joins the Protest," *San Francisco Chronicle*, 10 April 1977, sect. A, p. 7.

30. "Phillip Burton Backs HEW Protestors," *San Francisco Chronicle*, 12 April 1977, p. 5.

31. Alex Abella, "Mayor Blasts HEW on Sit-in," *San Francisco Chronicle*, 18 April 1977, p. 9.

32. "Handicapped Spurn Offer by HEW Chief," *San Francisco Chronicle*, 19 April 1977, p. 7.

33. Interview with Karen Parker, consultant at Center for Independent Living, Berkeley, California, and former San Francisco Aid for Retarded Citizens, 1 August 1980.

34. "Handicapped Take Protest to Washington," *San Francisco Chronicle*, 20 April 1977, p. 6.

35. Ibid.

36. Carol Pogaser, "The Disabled: Through with Silence and Shame," *San Francisco Chronicle*, 24 April 1977, p. A1.

37. "Handicapped Take Protest"; Joseph Whitaker, "Handicapped Protest Turned Away at HEW," *Washington Post*, 23 April 1977, p. B5.

38. "Kitty Cone, quoted in "Handicapped Return from Washington," *San Francisco Chronicle*, 28 April 1977, p. 3.

39. Joseph A. Califano, Jr., *HEW NEWS*, 28 April 1977.

40. "The Handicapped Will End Their Sit-in at Noon," *San Francisco Chronicle*, 30 April 1977, p. 2.

41. Michael Lipsky, "Protest as a Political Resource," *American Political Science Review*, December 1968, p. 1145.

42. J. Craig Jenkins, "The Dynamics of Mobilization: The Transformation of a Constituency into a Movement" (paper presented at the annual meeting of Society for the Study of Social Problems, Chicago, 4 September 1977), p. 5.

43. Judy Heumann, senior deputy director, Center for Independent Living, Berkeley, California, statement, *Hearings Before the Subcommittee on Select Education of the Committee on Education and Labor*, House of Representatives, 95th Cong., 2nd sess., April 1978, p. 78.

44. Georgie Anne Geyer, "Moving Back into Society," *Washington Post*, 25 July 1977, p. A21.

45. Heumann, *Hearings*, p. 77.

46. Geyer, "Moving Back into Society."
47. Phil Draper, executive director, Center for Independent Living, Berkeley, California, statement in *Hearings*, p. 214; also see *New York Times*, 17 April 1977 for a description of CIL.
48. Ron Jones, "The Acorn People," *Psychology Today*, June 1977, p. 70.
49. John Gliedman, "The Wheelchair Rebellion," *Psychology Today*, August 1979, p. 99.
50. Alice Walker, "Ten Years After the March on Washington: Staying Home in Mississippi," *New York Times Magazine*, 26 August 1973, p. 9.
51. Interview with Joyce Jackson, counseling coordinator, Community Resources for Independent Living, Hayward, California, 30 May 1980.
52. Ibid.
53. The American Council of the Blind was one of the founding organizations of ACCD. Examples of disability-distinct legislation are the Randolph-Sheppard vending stands for the blind enacted in 1936 and the 1938 Wagner O'Day Act for federal government purchase of blind-made products. Also, see note 12 for the large number of organizations that represent particular kinds of disabilities as an illustration of the degree of separation between the disabilities.
54. Gill interview (n. 27). Italics added.
55. Heumann interview (n. 28).
56. Steven Handler Klein, quoted in Craib, "PUC Member Tells of Her Outrage."
57. Pogaser, "The Disabled: Through with Silence and Shame."
58. Assemblyman Willy Brown, "The Disabled in the 70s," *Phoenix*, 12 May 1977, p. 6 (San Francisco State University).
59. *New York Times*, 17 April 1977.
60. Pogaser, "The Disabled: Through with Silence and Shame."
61. Myra MacPherson, "Newly Militant Disabled Waging War on Discrimination," *Washington Post*, 9 May 1977, p. A2.
62. Ralph Craib, "Emotional Plea for Handicapped, Hearing at Protest Site," *San Francisco Chronicle*, 16 April 1977, p. 5.
63. Myra MacPherson and Joseph D. Whitaker, "Handicapped Rights Rules Is Signed," *Washington Post*, 29 April 1977, p. A1.
64. Ibid.
65. "Carter's Promise to Disabled," *San Francisco Chronicle*, 24 May 1977.
66. Frances Fox Piven and Richard A. Cloward, *Poor People's Movements* (New York: Vintage Books, 1979), pp. 3–4.
67. Michael Grieg, "S. F. Handicapped Sit-In Grows", *San Francisco Chronicle*, April 8, 1977, p. 6.
68. Nakao, "State Rehab Chief Joins the Protest," op. cit. (fn. 29).
69. Grieg, "Disabled Protestors Continue."
70. Pogaser, "The Disabled: Through with Silence and Shame."
71. Jo Freeman; See Chapter 1 of this book.
72. Gill interview (n. 27).
73. Heumann interview (n. 28).
74. Martin interview (n. 22).
75. Piven and Cloward, *Poor People's Movements*, p. 113. I am grateful to Professor G. William Domhoff, University of California, Santa Cruz, for pointing out the similarity with the industrial workers example.
76. Heumann Interview, *op. cit.* (fn. 29).
77. Ralph H. Turner, "The Sense of Injustice in Social Movements," *Proceedings of the South Western Sociological Association*, Dallas, Texas, April 11–13, 1968, p. 124.
78. See Gary T. Marx, "External Efforts to Damage or Facilitate Social Movements:

Some Patterns, Explanations, Outcomes, and Complications," in *The Dynamics of Social Movements*, ed. Mayer N. Zald and John D. McCarthy (Cambridge, Mass: Winthrop 1979), p. 96.

79. The following is a list of town meetings held in 1976:

August 3	Newark and Albuquerque
August 5	Richmond and Denver
August 10	Pittsburgh and Syracuse N.Y.
August 13	Manchester N.H. and Raleigh N.C.
August 17	Portland Ore. and Anchorage
August 24	Little Rock Ark. and Honolulu
August 26	Los Angeles, Phoenix and Birmingham Ala.
August 31	Miami, Kansas City and Salt Lake City
September 2	Detroit and San Antonio Texas

80. Jackson interview (n. 51).
81. Heumann interview (n. 28).
82. Interview with Linda Gill, consultant, Center for Independent Living, Berkeley, California, 9 May 1980.

6

Protest and the Problem of Credibility: Uses of Knowledge and Risk Taking in the Draft Resistance Movement of the 1960s

Barrie Thorne

How do protest movements, which lack the legitimacy of existing institutions and whose purpose is to challenge law and tradition, establish a claim to authority? This is a problem movements confront, for to be successful—to create political resources by gaining sympathetic public attention, recruiting new members, and mobilizing third parties as movement allies (Lipsky, 1968)—protest groups must establish credibility with various outsiders.

The issue of how movements expand their base in society is often studied by asking who is recruited (e.g., the literature on origins of student activists reviewed by Keniston [1973]), or by examining social conditions that favor or discourage movement mobilization (e.g., Oberschall 1973, Smelser 1962). This case study does not ask who is recruited, but rather how recruitment is done. The focus is on movement strategies for approaching outsiders and persuading them to join or be sympathetic to a protest cause.

Social movements have used a variety of means to make contact with outsiders: staging public meetings and demonstrations; mass media reports and advertisements; circulating movement literature; approaching people on the

This chapter is dedicated to Kurt H. Wolff. In addition, I would like to thank Everett C. Hughes, Michael Useem and Rachel Kahn-Hut for their comments and suggestions.

street, at doorsteps, or at places of work; making personal contact with relatives, friends, and associates (Wilson 1973). Lofland (1966) divides this range of proselytizing efforts into two "strategies of access": "embodied," or face-to-face contact between movement partisans and outsiders; and "disembodied," or use of media, leaflets, public meetings, and other means of mediated access.* These categories refer to *forms of contact* between a movement and potential recruits or sympathizers. Gaining access, however, is only the first step of successful proselytizing. Movements must also be *persuasive*; they must devise techniques for establishing credibility with those who might otherwise be indifferent or hostile to the protest cause. This study shows how central protest strategies are geared not only to challenge or influence the protest target (Turner and Killian 1972) but also to establish legitimacy with outsiders.

This is a comparison of different strategies of persuasion used by groups within the same movement. In Boston there were two organizations that were part of the Resistance, the nationwide movement that, from 1967 to 1969, protested the draft, and the Vietnam war (on the history of the Resistance, see Ferber and Lynd 1971, Useem 1973, Thorne 1971). The groups shared a common origin and ideology but differed in strategies and tactics. The Boston Draft Resistance Group used draft counseling (the offering of expert knowledge), and the New England Resistance used noncooperation with the draft (encouraging risk taking) to confront the federal government (the protest target), to mobilize participants, and —the focus of this analysis—to seek attention and credibility with outsiders.

This study is based on active participation, and observation, in the draft resistance movement in Boston between March 1968, when the movement was building toward its peak, and July 1969, when the Resistance was very much on the decline. I took an active role in both movement groups and did not disguise the fact that I was doing research in addition to being a participant committed to the goals of the movement (for a discussion of the ethical and political problems involved, see Thorne 1979).

DESCRIPTION OF THE TWO STRATEGIES

DRAFT COUNSELING: THE USES OF KNOWLEDGE

The Boston Draft Resistance Group (BDRG) grew out of the New Left philosophy of community organizing, previously tried in southern civil rights work and among the urban poor. BDRG organizers hoped to reach poor and working-class people, especially the draft eligible, and to use the draft issue to draw them into opposition to the Vietnam war, imperialism, and the structure of American society. To make contact with Selective Service registrants, BDRG workers canvassed from lists of 1-As (a draft classification meaning "available

---

* There is evidence from a variety of movements (Gerlach and Hine 1970, Oberschall 1973, Freeman 1975) that recruits are more often made through preexisting relationships between movement members and outsiders, than through disembodied means alone. Recruiting through preexisting networks of friendship, family, work, or other associations is the most intense type of embodied access.

for induction") and at preinduction physicals, and—the central tactic—provided draft counseling.

Draft counseling involved compiling and disseminating extensive knowledge about Selective Service rules, regulations, and informal operating procedures—information of great practical value to those "uptight with the draft" and hoping somehow to evade or resist conscription. BDRG expertise included knowledge of official regulations and the accumulated wisdom of actual experience, gleaned from thousands of individual cases handled by the counseling group. For example, BDRG counselors knew if a given local draft board was easy or tough on conscientious objector applications or what sort of evidence was most effective in getting a physical deferment. They offered practical tips that one could never learn from official sources, for. example, "If you can get a peek at the form the last doctor fills out at the pre-induction physical, here's how you can tell if you flunked. . . ."

Offering this information through formal and informal draft counseling was a way of demystifying the Selective Service. It also provided the "bait" for bringing registrants to the BDRG office and into contact with the movement. In counseling sessions, BDRG workers combined technical information with political education, trying to "radicalize" those they talked with and to persuade them—however their individual draft situations turned out—actively to oppose the draft and the war. BDRG workers saw themselves primarily as political organizers, but technical expertise was essential in establishing their initial credibility with potential recruits and sympathizers.

NONCOOPERATION: THE USES OF RISK TAKING

The guiding vision of the early New England Resistance (NER) and other noncooperation groups around the country was both simple and powerful: What if they gave a war and nobody came? If enough draft-age men refused to serve, the war and the draft would end. Even if they didn't get enough noncooperators directly to stop the war, Resistance leaders hoped that by acting in a public and dramatic way, noncooperators would embarrass the government and create a wave of national indignation. They provoked public confrontation with the government in order to spur more and more people into protest.

The taking of risks was essential to this strategy. The acts of noncooperation—refusal to register, to carry a draft card, or to accept induction—carry a penalty of up to 5 years in prison and a $10,000 fine. The NER sought to increase the number and visibility of noncooperators and to draw individual risk takers into a community of support. This was partly done by staging public events built around these acts of risk: a series of draft card turn-ins, demonstrations for those refusing induction and coming to trial, and "symbolic sanctuaries" for indicted draft resisters and AWOL soldiers. The NER worked to mobilize large groups and to attract extensive media coverage for these events. Acts of risk were used to challenge the Selective Service System, to draw attention to the movement, and to claim legitimacy for organized opposition to the war and the draft.

THE PROCESS OF PERSUASION

One of the central goals of the Resistance was to reach outside audiences: to make new, active recruits to the movement (especially from among the draft-eligible); to gain political, financial, and other kinds of support from sympathetic third parties; to become widely publicized as a movement; and to persuade more and more people to oppose the war, the draft, and their underlying causes. The BDRG and the NER shared these goals, but their styles of proselytizing differed in ways closely tied to their different protest strategies.

GAINING ACCESS TO OUTSIDERS

The first step of persuasion is to gain the attention of outsiders who might otherwise be apathetic, indifferent, or hostile to one's message. This is the process Lofland (1966) conceptualizes in terms of embodied and disembodied strategies of access.

Although members of both Resistance groups made personal, or embodied, contact with outsiders, this style of proselytizing was more strongly emphasized by the Boston Draft Resistance Group. The central BDRG activities—draft counseling, canvassing from lists of 1-As, and talking with registrants at preinduction physicals—all facilitated personal contact with outsiders. The New England Resistance emphasis on staging large, well-publicized events (demonstrations, draft card turn-ins, sanctuaries), replete with extensive leafletting and media coverage, entailed a more indirect, or disembodied, form of contact with the public. Around Resistance circles it was often said that the NER was "media-oriented" and geared to creating "spectacles." In contrast, the BDRG was more low-key, routine, and workaday.

THE USE OF KNOWLEDGE TO GAIN ACCESS

To make personal contact with outsiders, BDRG organizers devised ways to accost strangers and solicit encounters that could be turned to proselytizing purposes. BDRG workers regularly showed up at local draft boards on days when preinduction physicals were scheduled, to talk with registrants waiting for the bus that would take them to the army base where physicals were held (this project was known as the "Early Morning Show"). The organizers capitalized on the fact that most registrants were anxious, curious, and uncertain about what to expect; they were in an exposed position, relatively open to being approached by strangers (Goffman 1963). Posing as preinductees, male BDRG workers would accost waiting registrants and engage them in what initially sounded like idle talk ("Goin' for your physical today? Think you can get out?"), but that could be turned into a proselytizing chat. Mutual accessibility was facilitated by the appearance of being in the same boat, of both being in a cohort going through a preinduction physical. Female BDRG workers were more visibly outsiders, since women (except for draft board clerks) are rarely present at any stage of the preinduction physical. Women organizers usually began encounters with preinductees by explaining their presence and implicitly offering help ("I'm from a group that does draft counseling."), but, not infrequently, the registrants they accosted implied that the encounter had the sexual overtones that seem to go with women soliciting in public places. Female activists often found themselves in a marginal and ambiguous position (Thorne 1975).

Goffman (1963, p. 127) points to the special accessibility of an individual who is in "patent need of help." Registrants obviously vulnerable to the draft had anxieties that the BDRG equipped itself to meet, and by eliciting problems and offering services, organizers found a way to establish contact with strangers. The typical Early Morning Show pitch involved bringing out a problem ("Are you 1-A?" "Do you have any physical conditions that might get you out?") and then suggesting that the movement could provide solutions ("If you come to our office, we can tell you how to appeal a 1-A" ...). By being knowledgeable about the Selective Service and the special dilemmas of draft-age men, Resistance organizers found a way to accost outsiders and engage their interests.

These proselytizing expeditions met with mixed success. Some registrants ignored or rejected the overtures of BDRG organizers; conversations sometimes developed into heated arguments about the Vietnam war or the antiwar movement. Even if a friendly conversation ensued, it was never clear if one's efforts had made an impact.

THE USE OF RISK TAKING TO GAIN ACCESS

In contrast with the person-to-person approach of the BDRG, the New England Resistance used strategies of access that were more colorful, spectacular, and theatric. Demonstrations, marches, and sanctuaries drew attention to the Resistance movement and helped publicize its issues. These events, in contrast with the more muted and less newsworthy style of draft counseling, often drew media coverage, which brought antidraft protest to the attention of mass audiences, as well as physical onlookers.

Risk taking enhanced the dramatic appeal of NER events and helped draw the attention of outsiders. Acts of noncooperation were unexpected, fateful, and to many, inexplicable. When the risk was assumed voluntarily, and by people whom it was difficult to discredit on other grounds, the acts assumed even greater significance. During a meeting to plan support for indicted men, a resister spoke of the "shock value" of noncooperation:

> Here us straight, middle-class guys from the suburbs are getting ready to go to prison, to become felons, to wear uniforms and be known by a number, it surprises people.... When we talk to student audiences, it gives them pause to realize that several years ago we were also neatly secured with 2-S [student] deferments, and here we are.

Acts of risk taking raise the implicit question: "Why would a person do a thing like that?" This curiosity became a foot in the door, a point of initial contact between the NER and outsiders. Risk helped create a platform for resisters to explain their motives, describe their intentions, and present the Resistance message. In the same meeting, a resister spoke of the access to outsiders his jeopardy provided:

You can really use your situation to rap to people. Like back in my hometown I'll go into a grocery store and be rapping with Mrs. Jones. She'll say, "What are you doing these days?" And I'll say, "Getting ready to go to trial on May 3rd." It really blows their minds, and we have great discussions.

ESTABLISHING CREDIBILITY

Gaining access to outside parties is only the first step in the process of persuasion; access and attention are not equivalent to agreement, sympathy, or even to being taken seriously. The next step of persuasion involves establishing credibility and gaining a respectful hearing, instead of being rejected, ridiculed, or quickly ignored.

Other parties—Selective Service and court officials, political antagonists, and hostile outsiders—were quick to impute discrediting motives to opponents of the war and the draft. Outsiders referred to noncooperators as "cowards," "draft dodgers," "draft evaders," "criminals," "communists," and "fools." The Resistance continually sought to counter these discrediting labels, to persuade outsiders that opposition to the war and the draft was a just, a rightful position, and that those who protested and resisted conscription were heroes rather than cowards or criminals.

KNOWLEDGE AND CREDIBILITY

The Boston Draft Resistance Group used expertise to claim credibility in the eyes of the public. BDRG organizers "knew what they were talking about"; they often excelled even Selective Service officials in their detailed, technical knowledge about the draft; they were also well informed about the history of American involvement in the Vietnam war.

Draft counselors sought to establish legitimacy and gain a clientele, which was also a potential constituency, through devices that many professions have used in gaining a special niche in society (see Hughes 1971, Freidson 1970). They claimed a special body of expert knowledge and skill, gained through a period of formal training (the BDRG ran regular training sessions and informal apprenticeships for new draft counselors). Of course, draft counselors lacked formal certification or license, and their training period was brief; they did not call themselves "professionals" ("professionalism" was a pejorative term around the movement); their services were free; and being a draft counselor was rarely a central or prolonged source of personal identity. But draft counselors did develop a strong sense of being experts, of developing and offering skilled knowledge, and of taking responsibility for individual cases much as professionals take on clients.

BDRG expertise was widely acknowledged in the Boston area. On busy days as many as thirty draft registrants would come in person to the BDRG office for information, and numerous others telephoned for advice. A major Boston newspaper ran a column of draft information and advice written by two BDRG counselors; it was seen as a coup for the Resistance that the newspaper asked the antidraft movement, rather than Selective Service officials, to write the column.

RISK TAKING AND CREDIBILITY

While the BDRG used knowledge to establish legitimacy with outsiders, the NER relied more on risk taking. Many draft resisters assumed risk voluntarily by giving up or refusing to seek deferments. This voluntary assumption of risk expressed strong individual commitment to opposing the war and the draft (the rhetoric of noncooperation included phrases like "show the sincerity of our beliefs" and "this movement is worth my life"). Noncooperators were intent on explaining and justifying their acts, on showing the public that they protested the war and the draft on moral and political grounds, not out of private or selfish motives.

Resisters used every occasion to put forward their statements of motive, their reasons for refusing to cooperate with the draft. Draft card turn-ins, induction refusal demonstrations, and trials gave resisters public forums for explaining and justifying their acts and elaborating the Resistance perspective.

The fact of risk became a way of claiming legitimacy, of giving weight to "raps" against the war and the draft, since "communications media and potential allies will consider more soberly the complaints of people who are understood to be placing themselves in jeopardy" (Lipsky 1968, p. 1150).* One of the founders of the NER expressed a belief held by many resisters: "Turning in my card put me in a position to organize other guys, to talk to people from my own situation of jeopardy." Another resister talked about the persuasive impact of his position of risk:

> I do a lot of public speaking for the Resistance, and sometimes there are hecklers there. But it's the hecklers who often stay around the longest afterwards, and we've had some incredibly good talks. My having turned in my card gives credibility to what I say. They see that I'm willing to jeopardize myself. I could have a deferment, probably two deferments: I'm legally deaf in one ear, which is an automatic 4-F, and as a Quaker and a pacifist, I could probably get a C.O.

It was often claimed that being in jeopardy was of special value in reaching those groups (such as soldiers, and working-class registrants with limited access to deferments) who themselves ran unusual risks because of the war and the draft.

CONTRASTING SYTLES OF PERSUASION

To be most effective in persuading outsiders to join or become sympathetic with a movement, should the proselytizers minimize differences between themselves and those they hope to reach? Or should they set themselves apart, establishing a visible alternative and evoking a partisan response? This debate dominated many tactical discussions within the antiwar movement and was a point of tension within the Resistance. The protest strategies of the BDRG and the NER involved contrasting styles of persuasion. Draft counseling, or the

---

* For the same reason—the fact that they made personal sacrifices in relation to the issue—the opinion of Vietnam veterans, both for and against the war, held more weight than opinions of nonveterans. In the antiwar movement, the fact of military service gave Vietnam Veterans Against the War credibility with the public that went far beyond that of other demonstrators.

offering of expert service on a person-to-person basis, involved minimizing differences and bridging the gap between BDRG organizers and those they sought to reach. In contrast, the acts of risk that were central to the large, media-oriented events of the NER tended to set noncooperators apart and encourage a more polarizing style of persuasion.

Implicit in the BDRG strategy was an assumption that persuasion is most effective when there is a common ground, a basis for identification, between proselytizers and their audience.* The BDRG sought especially to reach draft registrants from working-class communities who, ineligible for many special deferments and lacking middle-class know-how to evade the draft, carried a disproportionate burden of the draft and the war. Realizing that these groups were often alienated by long hair and other symbols of the counterculture, BDRG workers avoided flamboyant styles of appearance and manner. They talked about the importance of "learning to speak the idiom of those we are trying to reach." With relatively short hair and a generally "straight" appearance, BDRG workers could pose as preinductees and more easily make contact with registrants at draft boards and at the army base.

In proselytizing expeditions, BDRG organizers often used what Lofland (1966) calls "covert presentations." The message was muted, and various phrases (such as "draft resistance") were withheld to avoid alienating the listener before contact had been established. Those who went on Early Morning Show expeditions or canvassed registrants often presented themselves as draft counselors, as technical specialists in the problems of draft-age men. Expertise provided entrée. The political pitch, the Resistance message, came later.

In contrast, New England Resistance presentations were typically more overt, involving sharp differentiation from outsiders. Some referred to the "shock tactics" of the NER, whose members were set apart from other draft registrants by the fact of being noncooperators, of having violated the law. They also tended to dress and live in the ways of the counterculture; being "hip" was a subtle but important criterion for acceptance in the central core of the NER. The NER mode of dress tended to long hair and scruffy clothes, with touches of flair and self-expression, and ever-present political buttons. Buttons (the omega, the national symbol of draft resistance, and special buttons issued for demonstrations) became a form of mobile political advertising, raising questions ("What does the omega mean?" "Why does that say April 3rd?"), and provoking response ("You're a resister are you? Well, I'm with you!"; "Why don't you go back to Russia where you belong!").

---

* The literature on rhetoric, especially the writing of Kenneth Burke, is suggestive for the sociological study of persuasion. Burke (1950, p. 56) emphasizes the role of identification and compromise in rhetoric: "The rhetorician may have to change an audience's opinion in one respect, but he can succeed only insofar as he yields to that audience's opinions in other respects." A number of recent writers have begun to question the traditional view of persuasion through identification; this model, they suggest, does not adequately account for the confrontational style of many of the movements of the 1960s. For example, in his analysis of the student rebellion at Columbia University, Klumpp (1973) notes tension between the traditional model of persuasion through identification and an approach—close to that of the NER and typical of many of the radical movements of the 1960s—stressing confrontation and polarization as techniques of persuasion. Also see Scott and Smith (1969), Simons (1972), a Bowers and Ochs (1971).

NER events tended to force partisanship. Demonstrations, draft card turn-ins, marches, and sanctuaries were public events that set participants (who in a sense became performers) apart from onlookers or media audiences. These events were not intended to be passively watched or consumed; they were partly staged for persuasive effect, to force people to take sides and thereby enlist them in the protest cause.

While BDRG members muted differences between themselves and those they hoped to reach, NER activists "testified in and out of season,"* provoking a partisan response. Two events, where people from both Resistance groups were present, illustrate these contrasting ways of approaching third parties and potential recruits. One was a fancy cocktail party given in a suburban home to raise money for the legal defense of draft resisters. People from both the BDRG and NER were invited, free, although the other guests paid for admission and drinks as part of the fund raising. These guests ("rich liberals from the suburbs," they were typed in Resistance circles) were important allies for the movement, although they were sometimes regarded with cynicism. The BDRG contingent arrived on time and in apparel presentable in the straight world: The women wore dresses, and the men wore suits, or at least a spruced-up demeanor. NER people came late, wearing their usual scruffy clothes and looking haggard and preoccupied. The Arlington Street Church sanctuary was in process, and they made it clear that the cocktail party was a brief interlude, a Movement duty before returning to the scene of the action. While the BDRG group mingled, making polite conversation with the guests, NER people brought Resistance literature, leaflets, and political buttons to sell and hand around.

The other incident took place at the army base, in an early joint effort to infiltrate and reach registrants going through preinduction physicals. A report of this event in the October, 1967 NER newsletter acknowledged the contrasting styles of the two groups:

> Unblessed, as an organization, with respectable and/or officious looking guys, we [the NER] did not manage to get anybody inside the Army Base. They asked for our papers when the bus stopped at the gates. We showed them our drivers' licenses, high school honor society cards, etc., but this is not what they had in mind. We got thrown off the bus. The BDRG got lots of people on, being blessed with a number of respectable, officious, etc., guys. Like Roger King, who dressed up in a khaki shirt and made it past 12 guards by explaining to each in a loud military voice that he was going in to inquire about his "reserve points." We were jealous. But we got good publicity. Of the 173 pictures taken of the demonstration outside the gates, most showed the "October 16" button worn by people from the [NER. The button advertised the first draft card turn-in] ... One of these appeared in the Boston Globe on September 13th, page 24. The rest were taken by Army Base security officers, and will not immediately be made available to the general public.

In short, in contacts with outsiders BDRG workers sought to blend in, to proselytize in an unobtrusive, person-to-person manner. NER workers were more visible. They sought to polarize rather than build identification through

* A phrase suggested by Everett C. Hughes.

compromise, and they were more oriented to the media. The demands of the media for events that were unusual, dramatic, and visually interesting helped shape the differentiating style of the NER.

HOW THE STRATEGIES WORKED OUT OVER TIME

How successful were these various tactics for gaining attention, establishing credibility, and making converts? Part of the frustration of the movement was that it was difficult to determine success. Through Early Morning Shows, draft counseling, and other projects, the BDRG made contact with thousands of registrants. But few became active BDRG members, and it was difficult to know how many others were politicized or drawn into even partial sympathy with the movement point of view. During its peak of activity, the NER achieved media coverage and became widely known. But publicity must be distinguished from persuasion, and it was impossible to gauge the impact of the Resistance on mass audiences. Each strategy had built-in strains that became apparent over time; the strategies inevitably fell short of the original visions behind them. All of this contributed to the eventual demise of the movement.

PROBLEMS WITH THE STRATEGY OF DRAFT COUNSELING

Draft counseling, the core activity of the BDRG, was supposed to combine technical information with a political message. The service aspect of counseling involved drawing on expert knowledge to help registrants with their individual draft problems. The counseling also had a political purpose: to persuade counselees to protest the war and the draft.

BDRG counselors sought ways to give a political thrust to their conversations with registrants, by relating specific anxieties to their institutional causes and by turning the conversation to topics like the Vietnam war and American imperialism. But BDRG counselors often found that this kind of talk came across as forced, artificial, and manipulative, and that counselees were unresponsive. Counseling sessions vacillated between technical and political content, and less politically committed counselors often avoided the political side. It was difficult to be a technical expert and a missionary at the same time, especially when one's clients wanted technical advice but not a radical testimony.

It was the political side of BDRG draft counseling that justified the activity in the eyes of the radical movement. It was the service, the technical expertise, that most counselees valued and sought, and that was the basis of much of the legitimacy of the BDRG in the eyes of outsiders. Some counselors complained (usually outside the BDRG office) that they got a "heavy political rap" and not enough technical help. Movement critics were prone to voice the opposite complaint: that the BDRG was merely providing "service counseling" and "had no politics." One leader of the New England Resistance sarcastically referred to the organization as "BDR and G., Counselors."

Draft counselors themselves vacillated between the dual, not always harmonious goals of providing service and proselytizing for a political movement. Some counselors kept score on how many registrants they had helped avoid induction; "I've kept 80 percent of my counselees out!" was a typical proud announcement, which reflected one way of measuring success. But the more seasoned political activists emphasized the goal of radicalizing counselees and noted that getting someone a deferment is not equivalent to making a radical. In those terms, success meant that a counselee was moved towards active opposition to the war and had come to identify with the radical movement— whether or not he received a desired deferment. Although it was difficult to measure political impact, over time more and more people in the BDRG and other New Left groups began to believe that the BDRG was primarily a service organization and did not live up to its radical claims.

This opinion was strengthened by the fact that although the group set out to reach working-class and poor communities, in fact most of the BDRG constituency was middle class. Estimates varied, but anyone familiar with the BDRG would admit that at least two-thirds and perhaps as many as 90 percent of all counselees were white, middle-class college students. This fact undercut an early BDRG rationale: that the organization would spread knowledge about the Selective Service and an antiwar perspective into communities that lacked the tools to avoid being drafted. In the eyes of many radicals, the BDRG ended up an adjunct to an already privileged social class. This disillusionment—the sense that the BDRG reached the wrong audience and for the wrong reasons—contributed to the eventual decline of the movement organization.

PROBLEMS WITH NONCOOPERATION

The noncooperation strategy also fell short of the original vision. It did not have the direct and immediate impact on the draft that the NER founders had envisaged. The estimated 4,000 noncooperators nationwide (the NER claimed around 700 noncooperators in the Boston area) had no apparent effect on the government; the war and the draft continued, with no hint of a manpower shortage. In many ways, the noncooperation branch of the Resistance resembled a millenarian movement, looking ahead to a moment of great transformation, investing present actions in a hoped-for future hour. But the hour didn't come, and when even the most optimistic had to admit that the draft was in no danger of crumbling, morale collapsed.

Furthermore, for many, perhaps the majority, of those who turned in draft cards, the act did not make a significant personal difference. Many were not heard from again after their initial acts of risk taking, and there was strong indication that the majority of resisters did not stick with noncooperation (by asking for a new draft card, accepting a deferment, fleeing to Canada, or submitting to induction). Although the NER called itself a "club of resisters," most resisters did not opt for full-time movement activity; some seemed to feel that by turning in their draft cards, they had "done their thing to end the war" and were absolved from any further political activity. Gradually NER leaders began to reconsider the strategy of voluntarily sending large numbers of men to prison, and to wonder if they wouldn't have more political effect by staying out.

The NER was not always satisfied with its approach to outside audiences. From the beginning, there were those who disagreed with the claim that being a noncooperator was in itself a persuasive stance. Those concerned with recruiting in nonmiddle-class communities argued that noncooperation had limited appeal; they claimed that, more often than not, working-class and black registrants thought resisters foolish to volunteer for jail. Critics of noncooperation argued that the strategy was moralistic and elitist and that it thwarted, rather than facilitated, reaching outsiders with a political message.

Around Boston movement circles, people often described the NER as "fixed on staging spectacles," "apocalyptic," and "crisis-oriented." This group seemed always to be "where it's at," in the center of crisis, risk, and the 6 o'clock news. In its efforts to stay newsworthy, the NER adopted a theatric style of protest and shifted rapidly from one type of event to another. After a few draft card turn-ins, the event lost its novelty; the NER then began to stage sanctuaries, which in turn ceased to get media coverage after a few months. The NER sought publicity, exposure, and confrontation; it moved from crisis to crisis with little follow-through or routinization. As a result, it had an unstable relationship to its constituency.

Taken as a whole, the draft resistance movement had difficulty mobilizing individual registrants into a lasting collectivity and building cohesive and growing protest organizations with committed membership. The separate histories of the Boston Draft Resistance Group and the New England Resistance can be analyzed in terms of their central strategies, the problems and strains involved, and gradual moves to disenchantment.

CONCLUSION

This comparison of two groups within the same protest movement—one based on a strategy of risk taking and the other on disseminating expert knowledge—has shown different methods of approaching outside audiences and trying to persuade them to support the movement. In its bid for credibility the Boston Draft Resistance Group used person-to-person persuasion, relying on expertise to gain attention and legitimacy. This strategy involved a strain between the offering of technical advice (which was seen as a means to reach outsiders, but which often became the only connection with them) and the protest goal of spreading radical opposition to the war and the draft. In the end, many activists concluded that political purposes had been unduly compromised by efforts to gain credibility.

In contrast, the New England Resistance developed around a strategy that visibly set it apart from outsiders. Noncooperation with the draft entailed serious personal risks, and the demeanor of resisters, and the large dramatic events that were their forte, conveyed a strongly partisan stance. The noncooperation strategy succeeded in making the movement visible and in attracting media attention; as an approach to persuasion, it involved forcing choices rather than making compromises. However, some began to conclude that the choice was too often against the Resistance, that noncooperation set the group too far apart and was not sufficiently persuasive to potential recruits and allies.

Comparison of these two strategies and their implicit strains highlights a dilemma many protest movements have experienced: To gain legitimacy involves the risk of compromising the movement's beliefs and political goals— but to stay apart, to be true to the group's differences with the existing culture, may limit the movement's effectiveness. Wilson (1973, pp. 167–68) alludes to the same dilemma:

> Organizing collective effort to change the world demands acceptance of part of that world as a constraint upon one's own behavior, especially if one belongs to a minority. Social movements are forced to adapt themselves to present social norms and institutions in the ambient society, and yet they must maintain their own sense of apartness and purity, their own distinct identity, to retain membership commitment and avoid the dilution of co-optation.

This analysis may be extended to other movements with strategies based on the use of expert knowledge, or on risk taking. Draft counselling is one example of what appears to be a trend: A number of recent social movements have developed forms of counseling, turning a quasi-professional activity toward political objectives. For example, women's liberation groups have established abortion counseling and rape counseling as service activities with a proselytizing dimension, and the National Welfare Rights Organizations has counseled those on welfare about ways to work the system (Piven and Cloward 1971). This trend seems worthy of further analysis.

Organized protest has often involved risk, especially when movement activities have run counter to the law, or become a focus of social control (Wilson 1974). There are parallels between the strategic use of risk taking in the draft resistance movement, the civil rights movement (the jeopardy of early Freedom Riders in the South, for example), and the United Farm Workers movement (the risks undertaken by striking members of the UFW). This deliberate use of risk as part of protest strategies could be compared with the impact of risks unanticipated by movement groups (e.g., the killings at Kent State).

Whatever the chosen strategy, protest movements are up against great odds. They typically confront powerful institutions (in the case of the Resistance, nothing less than the federal government, the military, and the law). The success of protest often depends on gaining recruits and sympathizers from an indifferent or even antagonistic outside world. Yet protest movements do have effects that reach beyond themselves, and in tracing the history of particular protest strategies, one can better understand both social change, and resistance to change.

REFERENCES

Bowers, John Waite, and Donovan J. Ochs
1971 *The Rhetoric of Agitation and Control.* Reading, Mass.: Addison-Wesley.
Burke, Kenneth
1950 *A Rhetoric of Motives.* Englewood Cliffs, N. J.: Prentice-Hall.

Ferber, Michael, and Staughton Lynd
    1971 *The Resistance*. Boston: Beacon Press.
Freeman, Jo
    1975 *The Politics of Women's Liberation*. New York: Longman.
Freidson, Eliot
    1970 *Profession of Medicine*. New York: Dodd, Mead.
Gerlach, Luther P. and Virginia H. Hine
    1970 *People, Power, Change: Movements of Social Transformation*. Indianapolis: Bobbs-
        Merrill.
Goffman, Erving
    1963 *Behavior in Public Places*. New York: Free Press.
Hughes, Everett C.
    1971 *The Sociological Eye: Selected Papers*. Chicago: Aldine-Atherton.
Keniston, Kenneth
    1973 *Radicals and Militants: An Annotated Bibliography of Empirical Research on Campus
        Unrest*. Lexington, Mass.: Lexington Books.
Klumpp, James F.
    1973 "Challenge of Radical Rhetoric: Radicalization at Columbia." *Western Speech*
        37 (Summer): 146–56.
Lipsky, Michael
    1968 "Protest as a Political Resource." *American Political Science Review* 62 (Decem-
        ber): 1144–58.
Lofland, John
    1966 *Doomsday Cult*. Englewood Cliffs, N. J.: Prentice-Hall.
Oberschall, Anthony
    1973 *Social Conflict and Social Movements*. Englewood Cliffs, N. J.: Prentice-Hall.
Piven, Frances Fox, and Richard A. Cloward
    1971 *Regulating the Poor: The Functions of Public Welfare*. New York: Pantheon.
Scott, Robert L., and Donald K. Smith
    1969 "The Rhetoric of Confrontation." *Quarterly Journal of Speech* 55 (February): 1–8.
Simons, Herbert W.
    1972 "Persuasion in Social Conflicts: A Critique of Prevailing Conceptions and a
        Framework for Future Research." *Speech Monographs* 39 (November): 227–47.
Smelser, Neil J.
    1962 *Theory of Collective Behavior*. New York: Free Press.
Thorne, Barrie
    1971 Resisting the Draft: An Ethnography of the Draft Resistance Movement."
        Ph.D. dissertation, Brandeis University.
    1975 "Women in the Draft Resistance Movement: A Case Study of Sex Roles and
        Social Movements." *Sex Roles* 1 (June): 179–95.
    1979 "Political Activist as Participant-Observer: Conflicts of Commitment in a
        Study of the Draft Resistance Movement of the 1960's." *Symbolic Interaction* 2
        (Spring): 73–88.
Turner, Ralph H. and Lewis M. Killian
    1972 *Collective Behavior*. 2nd ed. Englewood Cliffs, N. J.: Prentice-Hall.
Useem, Michael
    1973 *Conscription, Protest, and Social Conflict: The Life and Death of a Draft Resistance
        Movement*. New York: Wiley-Interscience.
Wilson, John
    1973 *Introduction to Social Movements*. New York: Basic Books.
    1974 "The Effects of Social Control on Social Movements." Paper presented at
        69th annual meeting of American Sociological Association, Montreal, Canada.

McCarthy for President Demonstration, Democratic National Convention, Chicago, 1968.

NOW ERA Demonstration at the Republican Convention, 1976.

Part 3
Organization

All movements have some structure, but not all movements have major formal organizations that dominate and direct movement activity. For decades it was assumed that the ideal movement structure was one that applied the principles of bureaucracy, with centralization of decision making, a specific division of labor, and rewards based on merit and expertise. Movements lacking these elements were viewed as defective. In 1970 Luther Gerlach, in collaboration with Virginia Hine, made a major challenge to this view. The essence of their analysis appears in Gerlach's article comparing the black, Pentecostal, and environmental movements. He points out that a movement structure that is segmentary, polycephalous, and reticulate has several significant advantages over a centralized and bureaucratic organization or a movement dominated by one. These advantages include resistance to suppression; the possibility of multipenetration; and an increase in adaptive variation, system reliability, and competition.

Lawson argues that this structure also has some disadvantages. He feels the structure of the tenant movement, which has three distinct levels of organization, combines the best of both models by providing the flexibility of the "spr" structure with the ability of traditional organizations to focus their energies and concentrate expertise where it is most needed.

The antinuclear movement Dwyer analyzes is complex in organization. Dwyer uses Gerlach's spr framework to look at the interaction of structure and strategy. Although the antinuke movement, like the tenant movement, has several levels, they are not as well linked. Perhaps that is why the antinuke movement has had more success in attracting attention and recruiting participants than in achieving permanent gains.

Davidson and Ross turn their attention to internal problems of movement organization rather than overall movement structure. Davidson analyzes the consequences of applying the participatory principles of the counterculture to actual service projects. He shows that there is an essential conflict between task efficiency and organizational stability and creating a sense of community and commitment.

Ross illustrates how this sense of community can create factionalism in a social movement by causing distinct cohorts to become cliques. When new cohorts are not integrated into already existing primary groups, they will form their own groups and eventually challenge the 'old guard." A lack of proper integration is more common among movements that are inclusive—movements that anyone can join—and that also draw from a heterogeneous population. Inclusive movements drawing from a homogeneous population can generally rely on common cultural values and experiences to prevent cohort formation. Exclusive movements either restrict recruitment to homogeneous groups or actually socialize new participants into the movements' particular ideas.

All the chapters in this section illustrate that a movement's structure makes a great deal of difference in its success. It determines its ability to deal with its environment, to mobilize members, to formulate goals, to focus its energies, and to deal with internal problems. None of these chapters clarifies, however, what the ideal structure ought to be. Perhaps there is no ideal structure, but a series of conflicting options whose costs and rewards vary with the circumstances.

7

A Decentralized but Moving Pyramid: The Evolution and Consequences of the Structure of the Tenant Movement

Ronald Lawson

The literature on social movements is noticeably deficient on the subject of the structure of movements and the consequences of structure for movement growth, survival, effectiveness, or other behavior. Structure is ignored or treated only implicitly or in passing in many theoretical books on social movements (e.g., Smelser 1962, Oberschall 1973, Tilly 1978). Yet the structural forms taken have important repercussions for movements.

Two questions are addressed by this paper. First, what structural forms do social movements take? And second, what is the significance to a movement of the forms taken? In order to answer these questions, an array of theoretical generalizations concerning movement structure is first examined. Then the structure of the tenant movement in New York City and in the State of New York is explored and used as an example to test the theoretical views and pull their insights together more coherently.

THEORETICAL VIEWS OF MOVEMENT STRUCTURE

Until the mid-1970s the dominant approach to social movements interpreted them in terms of collective behavior theory. For example, Herbert Blumer saw a social movement as growing out of uncoordinated pieces of collective behavior such as riots and other forms of impulsive protest. He characterized this initial phase as a "general social movement." With time this evolved into a "specific social movement" with organization and structure, as well as a well-defined goal, accepted leadership, and a definite membership characterized by "we-consciousness" (1974, pp. 5–7):

> In its beginning, a social movement is amorphous, poorly organized, and without form; the collective behavior is on the primitive level, ... and the mechanisms of interaction are the elementary, spontaneous mechanisms. ... As a social movement develops, it takes on the character of a society. It acquires organization and form, a body of customs and traditions, established leadership, an enduring division of labor, social rules and social values—in short, a culture, a social organization, and a new scheme of life. (Ibid., p. 4)

Blumer borrowed an outline of four stages through which a movement evolves during its career from a textbook by Dawson and Gettys (1935) The first stage, "social unrest," is characterized by impulsive behavior. Each succeeding phase—the stages of "popular excitement," "formalization," and "institutionalization"—is more organized and centralized than its predecessor until, at the last, "the movement has crystallized into a fixed organization with ... a structure to carry into execution the purposes of the movement" (ibid., p. 7). Blumer makes no suggestion that such a movement has component parts.

Turner and Killian (1972) are also influenced by the collective behavior tradition. They consider social movements as intermediate forms of social organization between randomly structured outbursts of collective behavior and formally structured organizations. They differentiate social movements from panics or riots because of their "considerable organization, emergence of rules and traditions, and stability and continuity in time" (p. 245). While rejecting the strict four-phase life-cycle held to by Blumer and others, they nevertheless espouse an evolutionary view: "The longer the life of a social movement and the larger and more powerful it is, the more it takes on the characteristics of an association rather than a collectivity" (ibid.). In this view they are deeply indebted to such sociologists of religion as H. Richard Niebuhr (1957), who depicted religious "sects" and movements as evolving over time into "churches" or "denominations" (Turner and Killian 1972, pp. 333, 405). Partly because at any time the array of movements within a society will be at different stages of "development from sect to institution," and partly because each movement has a "unique mission and setting," movements show diversity of organizational form: "Some movements practice highly centralized decision-making but others are loose clusters of relatively autonomous units" (ibid., p. 397).

Turner and Killian did little to develop this insight. They did not elaborate further on the actual forms taken, on why and when they vary, or on the implications of the structural forms taken for particular movements. Instead, these two contrasting types of movement structure were elaborated on separately by other theorists without, however, systematically comparing their advantages and disadvantages.

Two anthropologists, Gerlach and Hine, published a study focusing on two movements, Pentecostalism and Black Power, in 1970, although the study did not become well known among sociologists working in the field until after mid-decade. Their view of movement structure as segmentary, decentralized, and reticulate is considerably different from that of the collective behavior sociologists. *Segmentary* has to do with a movement being composed of many local cells that, instead of being arranged hierarchically, maintain a great deal of autonomy. There is considerable fission and fusion among the local organizations. Movements are also *decentralized*, or without central control or direction. Leaders may be powerful, and even dictatorial, within their local groups, but their dominance extends no farther. Movement leadership is therefore "polycephalous," or many headed. Moreover, there is no membership in the movement as a whole, but only in its constituent organizations. Finally, a movement is *reticulate*, or networklike. The cells "are tied together, not through any central point, but rather through intersecting sets of personal relationships and other inter-group linkages" (ibid., p. 55).

Gerlach and Hine mention various hierarchically organized Pentecostal denominations, and civil rights organizations such as the NAACP and the Urban League, which they compare to the denominations. They describe them as "super-cells in the body of the movement": "All members of these bodies are members of a local church in that one denomination" (ibid., pp. 59, 60). They also refer to temporary and permanent associations with cross-cutting memberships. But they fail to integrate these into their segmented structure model, and they do not explain how these accord with local autonomy or why the power of leaders is limited to local groups. Moreover, their model, as presented, is static: They do not consider what structural changes may occur over time. However, Gerlach and Hine do argue that a segmented structure promotes both rapid growth (especially across class and cultural boundaries) and the achievement of the social changes sought.

During the 1970s the collective behavior approach to social movements, with its emphasis upon initially impulsive and irrational action, was superseded as the dominant viewpoint among sociologists by what has become known as the *resource mobilization* approach. This regards movements as rationally created to pursue certain group and/or individual goals, to which ends resources, especially both labor and capital, are mobilized.

Perrow (1979) divides the resource mobilization theorists into two schools, "RM1" and "RM2" (pp. 199–200). RM2 stresses (often individual) economic motivation and rationality and is associated with the work of McCarthy and Zald (1977). These theorists, like Gerlach and Hine, view social movements as typically represented by multiple social movement organizations (SMOs). As they endeavor to aggregate resources, SMOs compete and cooperate like formal organizations. They are themselves centralized, although they may, from the top down, develop federated local chapters in order to organize constituents into small local units. SMOs form coalitions with each other when the realization of their goals is close.

RM1 is associated in the first instance with the work of Gamson, Tilly, and to some extent, Oberschall. Rather than stress individual motivation, as does RM2, it assumes that groups of people with joint political goals can act together rationally to pursue them. Both Tilly and Oberschall neglect movement structure. Gamson's (1975) discussion of structure focuses not on movements as a whole but on their component SMOs—for the 53 "challenging groups" that make up his sample are in fact mostly SMOs, such as individual labor unions or minor organizations within the movement for women's suffrage (although he does generalize illegitimately from these to movements as a whole in his conclusion). Gamson classifies his sample organizations according to whether or not they have a centralized power structure. His finding that a majority of his organizations, 28 of 53, have a single center of power, and that in 19 of these cases this is associated with the personal leadership of a central figure, is congruent with the views of both McCarthy and Zald and Gerlach and Hine. On the other hand, almost half the groups are decentralized. Typically these have "chapters or divisions . . . that maintain substantial autonomy and the freedom to decide whether or not to support the collective action of the group as a whole" (Garnson 1975, p. 93). In assessing whether a challenging group is successful in attaining its goals, Gamson considers two kinds of achievements: gaining acceptance by the group's antagonists "as a valid spokesman for a legitimate set of interests," and winning new advantages for the beneficiary of the group (ibid., pp. 28–29). He argues that centralization is associated with goal attainment, although more strongly with gaining new advantages than with winning acceptance for the organization. It also has much to do with preventing factionalism, which in turn is strongly related to winning both new advantages and acceptance. However, since his data are based on SMOs rather than whole movements, and the winning of new advantages, in particular, must surely be related to the efforts of all constituent SMOs, the validity of his findings must be questioned.

In general, then, the various theories concerning movement structure are at best sketchily developed. Moreover, they disagree on such important factors as whether movements are centralized or decentralized, and whether they normally have subdivisions, and, if they do, how subdivisions are organized and how the various parts relate to each other and to the movement as a whole. There is no discussion of the significance of one structural form compared to another.

RESEARCH METHODS

The vehicle for analysis in this chapter is the tenant movement, the crusade for the recognition of tenants' rights to security within well-maintained housing at reasonable rents, in New York City and New York State from the first major rent strikes in 1904 until 1981. Data were collected using a combination of three main methods. Historical research on the period from 1890 to 1974 drew on city and local press, city and state government archives, tenant organization records as available, and extensive oral history. Fieldwork covered the three main federations extensively from 1973 to 1981, the other three in less detail; and 25 neighborhood and 40 building organizations during 1973–75.* There was considerable follow-up of these organizations and extension

* Federations and neighborhood and building organizations are defined below.

of fieldwork to others newly important after the initial period. Surveys in 1975–76 broadened coverage to the leaders and key activists of 129 neighborhood organizations, and to leaders, members, and nonmembers within 108 organized buildings, together with their landlords; the leaders of 99 other buildings were added later. This sample represents almost all the neighborhood groups active in 1975–76 whose central purpose was to organize tenants, together with a sample of 36 OEO-funded housing agencies, most of which mainly serviced tenants rather than organized them. The leaders of all organizations were reinterviewed in 1980–81 in order to check the outcome of their actions and their organization survival rates.

THE STRUCTURE OF THE TENANT MOVEMENT

Three-quarters of the residents of New York City are tenants, but while sharing this status they are otherwise far from uniform. For example, they are drawn from all socioeconomic strata and differ considerably in their housing problems. Among tenants who live in privately owned housing, some are concerned about building security and amenities but do not have serious problems of building maintenance. Several groups of tenants living on such boulevards as Park Avenue and West End Avenue, for example, founded organizations to protest the replacement of elevator operators by automated elevators because they felt that this would result in a deterioration of building security. Such tenants tend to be from high-income groups and are overwhelmingly white. Another source of tenant dissatisfaction concerns rent levels. Of course, the amount paid for rent is a concern for all but the wealthy tenant, but in New York City rent levels are particularly an issue for tenants whose rents are kept below "market levels" by rent regulations. These tenants are often also concerned about the quality of maintenance and services in their buildings, but their central concern is rising rents. These are mainly moderate and middle-income tenants and are predominantly white.* Mitchell-Lama tenants, who live in buildings constructed with public subsidies, and are drawn from similar strata, have a similar concern with escalating rent levels. Still other tenants (mostly middle-income), have been threatened with eviction when landlords have attempted to convert their buildings into cooperatives or condominiums, or (mostly moderate and low-income tenants) to demolish them in order to construct new, high-rent luxury apartment buildings.

The largest grouping consists of tenants whose housing lacks essential services or is in serious need of repair. For example, many tenants suffer from a lack of heat and hot water during the winter because old boilers break down or landlords neglect to provide fuel. Many of their apartments require painting and new plaster or have plumbing leaks, unsafe electrical sytems, and roach and rodent infestations. Moreover, these buildings are often crime-ridden and

---

* Poor tenants are much less likely to have their rents kept below "market levels" by rent regulations than are tenants with middle and moderate incomes for two reasons: (1) Poor tenants move much more frequently on the average, and rent regulations provide for steeper increases upon vacancy; (2) market rents in poor neighborhoods tend to be lower because of the inability of poor tenants to pay more and because decay and abandonment have often led to a slackening of the demand for apartments there as compared with other neighborhoods.

prone to fires. Vacant apartments frequently become havens for drifters and drug addicts who may set fires, rip out wiring and pipes to sell as junk, and otherwise terrorize the remaining tenants until the building is rendered uninhabitable. The end result of this process is vacant, abandoned buildings. Tenants who must cope with these problems are mainly poor blacks and Hispanics.

Given the heterogeneous composition of the tenant population of New York City and the variety of problems faced, it is not surprising that the tenant movement is now far from monolithic. But the movement's structure was not always so complex; it has evolved over time.

The two initial major episodes of tenant activism in New York City, in 1904 and 1907–8, began when residents of one building (or perhaps a few buildings) on Manhattan's Lower East Side protested against sharply increasing rents by forming organizations in their buildings (building organizations, or BOs) and withholding their rents in a rent strike. Both actions spread rapidly, led by women organizers who relied on networks among women in this heavily Jewish community. On both occasions, once the potential for mobilization around tenant issues was demonstrated, men associated with the Socialist party moved in and founded short-lived umbrella organizations (neighborhood organizations, or NOs), which attempted to coordinate and channel the activity (Lawson and Barton, 1980).

In 1917, when another acute housing shortage stimulated sharply escalating rent levels, action was initiated at the neighborhood level. The Socialists formed neighborhood "tenant leagues" (NOs), which then reached out to organize BOs. As the leagues spread rapidly through the neighborhoods where tenements were concentrated, rival neighborhood "tenant associations," with ties to established political parties, were founded. These continued till the close of the 1920s, helping tenants use the complex state rent control laws enacted in 1920 (Spencer, forthcoming).

Numerous NOs reemerged in the wake of the Great Depression as attention shifted to the housing decay that accompanied a period of high vacancy rates and landlord neglect. In 1936, in an attempt to bolster political influence, a number of NOs joined together in the first federation, the City-Wide Tenants' Council. The movement's third structural level was in place. Although federations have changed their names and leaders several times, the three-decker structure has remained intact since 1936, except for the years 1952–59 when the federations collapsed following both their success in winning state rent controls and the onset of McCarthyite repression (Schwartz, forthcoming).

Tenant action in New York City swelled considerably after 1971. Virtually every neighborhood now has at least one NO, and tenants in thousands of buildings have taken joint action. The spectrum of socioeconomic status represented within the movement has also broadened considerably, and the range of tenant strategies has diversified. Even the traditional rent strike now has several forms (Lawson 1981), and to it have been added a lobbying presence in the state legislature; tenant initiated court cases; the direct expenditure of rent monies on repairs; the management and moderate rehabilitation of buildings abandoned by their landlords; the gut rehabilitation of totally abandoned buildings through "sweat equity" by would-be tenants; and the fostering of cooperative ownership of their buildings by low-income tenants (Lawson, forthcoming). The highest level of the movement structure has also developed commensurately: There are now one statewide, four citywide, and one borough-wide federations. They represent tenants with different housing problems and of differing socioeconomic status; they also stress somewhat distinct strategies.*

The structure of the tenant movement in New York has thus evolved a pyramidal shape, with three levels or kinds of organizations most easily distinguished from one another by the size of the geographical area and the number of tenants they attempt to serve. Thus, a BO is composed of tenants from one building and serves only the tenants of that building. An NO serves tenants from a number of different buildings and usually defines its territory as coterminous with the boundaries of an existing neighborhood or perhaps a large housing development; it sees itself as serving only the tenants of that neighborhood or development. At the highest level, a federation groups NOs from a large geographical area and sets out to speak for the tenants of that area.

The functions of the organizations at the three levels are also different. BOs exist to deal with the particular problems of a building. They unite the tenants of a building in order to increase their bargaining power with a landlord or, if the landlord has abandoned a building, to unite the tenants in order to keep it habitable. NOs are formed in order to serve BOs, and in many cases they also organize buildings and help create new BOs. They provide technical assistance to BOs, advising them on tactics and supplying the expertise on tenant and housing matters gained through helping other buildings. They also support the activities of the federations and are the links between the federations and the tenants in their BOs. Federations, for their part, represent the interests of tenants in relations with authorities and powerful resource providers, especially city and state governments. They undertake activities designed to alter rules, practices, and decisions that work to the disadvantage of tenants. In some cases this may mean attempting to change laws that define tenant rights through established political processes or it may involve demonstrations or disruptive actions designed to force authorities to act in favor of tenants. Federations also attempt to educate the general public and authorities about the goals of the tenant movement.

Linkages between the various levels of the movement may be tenuous. Some buildings (a small minority of the total) organize without the help of an NO and then remain isolated thereafter.[†] This may occur for a number of reasons: because no NO exists in the area; because the BO and the NO are unaware of each other; or because there is an ethnic, socioeconomic, or ideological difference between the building tenants and the NO. In addition, BOs

---

* Moreover, just as the first BOs preceded NOs but later NOs initiated BO organizing, history has recently repeated itself at the next level: The first federation has been formed in advance of the NOs it later stimulated, and older federations are setting out to create NOs where they see the need and the possibility.

[†] Since these "egocentric" BOs are the most difficult to locate, it is not possible to be more precise concerning their number.

may not join or ask for assistance from an NO if they feel they have adequate expertise available among their own members. This situation is most prevalent in buildings occupied by middle- and upper-income, college-educated and professional tenants.

The nature of the interaction between NOs and BOs is primarily a downward, one-way flow of services and information. Although NOs may be established through the efforts of tenants from one or a few BOs, in most cases their objectives become to help as many other tenants as possible and build among them a loyal support base. The assistance provided varies greatly, depending on the kind of housing problem that is most prevalent in an area and the philosophy and expertise of the local organization. For example, while some NOs insist on helping tenants who came to them for aid to organize BOs, others are more likely to try to ease their access to government agencies. Strategically, an NO may teach tenants how to run a rent strike, manage their abandoned building, or organize against an unwanted conversion. The degree to which a BO becomes involved in the activities of an NO also varies greatly; in general, however, with the exception of the involvement of a few individuals who may become interested in broader issues of tenant rights, BOs contribute little more than some funds to the NO. Only rarely is an NO built upon a stable base of organized buildings because BOs tend to be active only when confronting a crisis and to lapse into inactivity at other times; other BOs sever meaningful contact with an NO after an initial "how to" meeting. BOs receiving help in managing their buildings from an NO are much more likely to remain in contact with it because their need is ongoing.

At the next level up the pyramid, relations between NOs and federations are of a reciprocal, interdependent nature. Most NOs have at least intermittent contact with a federation; a few are formal members of more than one. But again, not all organizations are affiliated with the next level. NOs that remain unaffiliated do so because they have developed political expertise internally and thus feel no need to rely on federations to provide this service; or because their primary purpose is to provide a base of popular support for an aspiring political entrepreneur who is more interested in a personal following than a tenant movement; or because their leaders are unwilling to devote the extra time participation in a federation would require.

Federations serve NOs in several ways. First, they help unify the movement by bringing the independent local organizations together into constellations pursuing common goals. This function not only increases the political strength of each local group and of the movement but it also can lift morale and have a positive effect on NOs that were unaware of the existence of other NOs or unaware that other tenants have the same problems they do. Second, federations aid NOs by serving as a communication link between them: Linkages between NOs are rarely established except through contact and participation at the federation level. Even after contact has been established, NOs often communicate with one another only through the leaders of a federation or through contact at federation meetings. Federation networks allow NOs to learn of and benefit from the experience of others. The third and most distinctive function of federations is to act as representatives of NOs and to articulate their demands to governmental authorities and other organizations outside the movement, such as the media. This role is vital since NOs seldom have the time, expertise, or resources needed to be effective in the political arena.

NOs, in turn, perform several functions that are vital to the effectiveness of federations. In some federations they provide the funds and personnel without which the federation could not exist. In almost all cases the NOs have sole responsibility for the recruitment of new movement participants. The distinctive role and contribution of NOs lie in their contact with individual tenants and BOs. Federations, in general, have little contact with tenants, but it is crucial for their political effectiveness to be able to claim a large and organized constituency and be able to show a mass following. It is the task of the NO to provide the linkage between the tenant and the federation. The NOs, therefore, are the key to the movement's success, because they are responsible for educating, organizing, and mobilizing tenants, and integrating them into the broader movement.

Because of their geographic and functional differentiation, NOs coexist with little lateral competition or conflict. Even when they share the same territory, they usually appeal to constituencies that differ according to their housing problems, socioeconomic status, and/or desired strategies. Moreover, housing problems are normally so endemic that there are more than enough buildings for each NO to handle. Competition and conflict seem to occur only among NOs in which the leaders of neighboring groups are both trying to build political careers and/or when they fall out personally to a severe degree.

There is even less conflict and competition among BOs because their territories—their own buildings—are normally discrete. It is only on those rare occasions when there are rival organizations with opposing goals within the same building that conflict erupts and then it is bitter indeed: For example, in the wake of a landlord's proposal to convert a building into a cooperative, tenants may divide between one group wishing to win the best deal possible and another implacably opposed to any conversion.

It is between federations that most conflict occurs—mainly for symbolic leadership of the movement.

Federations form coalitions and NOs create ad hoc associations with cross-cutting memberships when a previously enjoyed right comes under attack; then likely losses produce like minds. Thus, when an important rent law was threatened in 1977, the New York State Tenant and Neighborhoods Coalition and the Metropolitan Council on Housing were able to shelve their antipathies in order to work together defensively (Lawson 1980).

The three-tier functional division of labor within the movement took time to evolve. Theoretically there is a fourth structural level, a national level, which seems to be emerging for the first time among tenants of private housing. (The short-lived National Tenants Organization filled this position for public housing tenants during the early 1970s). Three constraints delayed the emergence of this level of organization. Washington, D.C., is not the *immediate* site of the tenant battle, except in public housing; most housing issues are decided at the state and local levels. State-level organizations, the most logical member units of a national federation, have emerged only in a few states.

And the distance to Washington and scale of organization necessary make it extremely difficult for a largely voluntary, local crisis-oriented movement to support such an enterprise without direct external funding for it. Nevertheless, the felt need for representation in Washington increased during the late 1970s as federal funds and work programs became important to the movement, as the widespread thrust for rent regulations encouraged the formation of state federations, and as the real estate industry expanded its lobbying presence in Washington. The Earl Warren Legal Institute in Berkeley, California; *Shelterforce*, a national tenant newspaper published in New Jersey; and a series of conferences on rent regulation strategies sponsored jointly by *Shelterforce* and the New York State Tenants and Neighborhoods Coalition had already begun to create networks and fill some coordinating functions. Finally, in the summer of 1980 representatives from over 50 tenant organizations from 25 states met in Cleveland and formed a National Tenant Union, a loose organization without headquarters, to assemble and share relevant information. In 1981 its second national meeting, in Washington, D.C., featured lobbying on Capitol Hill and plans for closer coordination of information and joint activities by member organizations, and for a continuing presence in Washington to monitor and lobby for or against relevant legislation.

The structure of the tenant movement as it has evolved over three-quarters of a century is thus much more complex than the passing references of the theorists would have led us to expect. It has three functionally differentiated levels of organization (and a nascent fourth level), each with multiple component parts. Yet, in spite of the hierarchical order of the structural levels, there is considerable organizational autonomy with usually no chain of command from top to bottom. Indeed, federations were typically formed by groups of NOs to perform certain specialized functions. However, the oldest of the currently existing federations, the Metropolitan Council on Housing, which dates from 1959, has in recent years adopted a centralized structure that is the envy of some other federations because of its success in mobilizing monetary resources from the grass roots to the center. This may indicate that a thrust toward hierarchical centralization is likely over time.

THE SIGNIFICANCE OF STRUCTURAL FORMS

The complex structure of the tenant movement has important repercussions for the rest of the movement. First, the existence of BOs and NOs makes it easier to mobilize the tenant constituency. BOs act as "locals" organized around the immediate needs of tenants who, as neighbors, are likely to be linked in networks. Because of this and their relatively small size (Olson 1965), BOs are likely to maximize participation levels. Thus the typical BO is formed in response to inadequate heating during winter by women who know one other from contact in the laundry room, from supervising the children at play, or from seeking relief from the summer heat on the stoop of the building. These factors also make it easier to retain members and the commitment of their resources, at least while the housing problems in a given building continue and the tenants retain their faith in the program suggested to them by NO leaders. That is, participants in the tenant movement are not isolates who are likely to disappear after a mass mobilization such as a March on Washington; movement leaders know where to find them, clustered in their building locals.

The availability of many autonomous, varied NOs also facilitates recruitment. NOs can shape themselves to deal with the particular problems and ideological and stylistic preferences of their constituency. Thus the movement may spread more readily across cultural and class boundaries. One result of this is that the movement encompasses many unexpected bedfellows—middle class and poor (troubled respectively by threats of conversion and abandonment), radical and relatively conservative, timid and daring—each protected from disquiet through membership and activity located in more homogeneous local organizations. Moreover, because the NO is also local, it is easier for it to gain the participation of members, to give them social rewards, and to keep them involved.

Second, multiple levels of organization facilitate the emergence of leaders. Tenants who show enthusiasm and leadership skills in a BO can be urged to participate in an NO, and ultimately in a federation. Or, alternatively, a person interested in broader tenant issues, such as rent regulations, may enter the movement at a higher level (Lawson and Barton 1980). This structure also facilitates an appropriate marshaling of expertise, for example, of organizers in NOs and political tacticians in federations. It also singles out certain leaders in the federations who can act as spokespersons for the movement.

Third, functional specialization by level facilitates the adoption of positions and strategies that suit each level. Thus federations may choose to work within the political system while, concurrently, affiliated NOs may be using unorthodox or extralegal strategies such as taking control of certain buildings as they combat encroaching abandonment or uncooperative landlords. A corollary of this is that multiple structural levels and organizations ease strategic experimentation. For example, in the early 1970s rent strikers in a few BOs in badly deteriorated neighborhoods became impatient when their landlords failed to make the repairs they demanded, and began to make repairs and buy oil themselves with the rent monies they had accumulated. In this way they demonstrated the effectiveness of a new strategy to movement leaders who had reacted negatively when such action had been suggested, fearing that it was likely to result in the eviction of the tenants involved (Lawson 1981). Again, the success of one or two NOs in managing local buildings that landlords had abandoned to city ownership led the city to develop a Community Management Program involving up to twenty NOs and hundreds of buildings.

Fourth, there are advantages in having multiple federations instead of always presenting a monolithic political face. The more radical federations are able to raise the consciousness of the membership and help formulate long-term goals for the movement; they also, by voicing seemingly "extreme" demands (such as for socialized housing or rigid statewide rent regulations), make the more moderate federations seem so much more "reasonable" to authorities. This enhances the impact of the latter on movement targets (Lawson 1980).

The structural form of the tenant movement also has dysfunctional elements. The indirect links between grass-roots members and the issues embraced by higher-level organizations may make the activities of the latter seem more remote, especially when compared to the immediate relevance of issues espoused by their BOs. The further the action gets from individual buildings (i.e., the higher the structural level), the more difficult it is to involve tenants. There is a precipitous decline in the proportion of tenants consistently involved at each higher level. Moreover, members mobilized solely around problems in their own buildings are likely to become inactive when these problems pass and their BOs lapse into latency.

That is, the structure of a movement may have repercussions on the mobilization of participants and the ability to retain their loyalty, the emergence of leadership, strategy options, and the impact of the movement. Since structure evolves, it is important to analyze movements in dynamic terms.

CONCLUSION

The literature dealing with social movements has burgeoned following the proliferation of movement activity during the 1960s. Nevertheless, to the extent that movement structure has been considered by theorists, it has been seen either as basically monolithic and centralized or as a decentralized network of equal organizations. This is surprising since the multiple level/many SMO examples of civil rights, antiwar and feminist movements are readily available.

I would argue, then, that multiple levels are typical of the structure of movements mobilizing grass-roots participants. It is more usual for local SMOs to join together in federations so that the structure is, initially at least, decentralized. The reverse is also possible, however, especially when the movement is dominated early by a strong personality.

On the other hand, if a movement is primarily mobilizing its resources either through mass mailings to sympathizers or external funding, it may have no need of local organizations. It may then be a single-level, centralized movement. If it does then develop local branches, power is still likely to reside at the apex, especially if funds are normally channeled there.

The tenant movement is distinct in the way its lowest-level unit is so close to home. This structure parallels the workplace local within the labor movement. To date the tenant movement's structure of locals has not been as great a source of strength as that of the labor movement. It needs to battle to institutionalize the BO as permanently in control of buildings or at least as having regular input to their operations. If such BOs then normally channeled a portion of their dues to higher-level organizations, the seeming remoteness from home of the broader issues that the movement faces would be less troubling.

It has been argued that theorists writing about social movements have largely ignored the structures of movements and that their comments made in passing have missed both the complexity and significance of movement structures. While a multiple level/many SMO structure, as found in the tenant movement, seems common, many variations seem both possible and likely. Since the structure of the tenant movement has proved to be significant for many other aspects of the movement, it would seem worth exploring the structures of other movements and their implications. This exploration should also delineate the various structural patterns possible, and when and why each is likely to occur.

REFERENCES

Blumer, Herbert
(1939) "Social Movements." Pp. 4–20 in S. Denisoff, *The Sociology of Dissent*. New
1974 York: Harcourt Brace Jovanovich.
Dawson, C. A., and W.E. Gettys
1935 *Introduction to Sociology*. Rev. ed. New York: Ronald Press.
Gamson, William A.
1975 *The Strategy of Social Protest*. Homewood, Il: Dorsey Press.
Gerlach, Luther P., and Virginia H. Hine
1970 *People, Power, Change: Movements of Social Transformation*. Indianapolis: Bobbs-
Merrill.
Lawson, Ronald
1980 "Tenant Mobilization in New York." *Social Policy*, March/April, pp. 30–40.
1981 "The Origins, Evolution and Transformation of a Social Movement Strategy:
The Rent Strike in New York, 1904–1980." Paper read at the meeting of the
American Sociological Association, Toronto, August.
forthcoming *Rent Strikes and Tenant Takeovers: Tenant Action and the Urban Housing Crisis
in New York*.
Lawson, Ronald, and Stephen Barton
1980 "Sex Roles in Social Movements: A Case Study of the Tenant Movement in
New York City." *Signs: Journal of Women in Culture and Society*, pp. 230–47.
McCarthy, John D., and Mayer N. Zald
1977 "Resource Mobilization and Social Movements: A Partial Theory." *American
Journal of Sociology*, pp. 1212–41.
Michels, Robert
(1911) *Political Parties: A Sociological Study of the Oligarchical Tendencies of Modern
1962 Democracy*. New York: Free Press.
Niebuhr, H. Richard
(1929) *The Social Sources of Denominationalism*. New York: Meridian Books.
1957
Oberschall, Anthony
1973 *Social Conflict and Social Movements*. Englewood Cliffs, N. J.: Prentice-Hall.
Olson, Mancus, Jr.
1965 *The Logic of Collective Action*. Cambridge, Mass.: Harvard University Press.
Perrow, Charles
1979 "The Sixties Observed." In Mayer N. Zald and John D. McCarthy, *The
Dynamics of Social Movements*. Cambridge, Mass.: Winthrop.
Smelser, Neil
1962 *Theory of Collective Behavior*. New York: Free Press.
Schwartz, Joel, and Bonnie Fox Schwartz
forthcoming "1943–1971: Tenants, Landlords and Planners in the Rent Control
Era." In Ronald Lawson, *From "Tenant Rebellion" to Tenant Management:
The Evolution of the Tenant Movement in New York, 1904–1981*.

Spencer, Joseph
forthcoming "1915–1943: Mass Action, Legislative Gains and Organizational Development." In Ronald Lawson, *From "Tenant Rebellion" to Tenant Management: The Evolution of the Tenant Movement in New York, 1904–1981.*

Tilly, Charles
1978 *From Mobilization to Revolution.* Reading, Mass.: Addison-Wesley.

Turner, Ralph H. and Louis M. Killian
1972 *Collective Behavior.* 2nd ed. Englewood Cliffs, N.J.: Prentice-Hall.

8

Movements of Revolutionary Change: Some Structural Characteristics

Luther P. Gerlach

Much of the discussion about movements has focused on their organizational efficiency or seeming lack of it. In time it became clear to all but the most devoted conspiracy thinker that these movements were composed of essentially autonomous, often competing segments, each of which seemed to follow the oft-repeated injunction to "do its own thing." True, at times these segments did seem to pull together in a kind of concerted action and often enough a large number of segments acted in the same ways, and their participants said the same things. But always there was a basic pattern of schism, factionalism, and ongoing segmentation that led movement foes, friends, and participants alike to characterize these movements as disorganized or at least inefficient.

Wherever we examine evaluations of organizational efficiency we find the same bias against segmented structure. According to this powerful bias, centralized, bureaucratic organization with a pyramidal chain of command is efficient, rational, proper, and a sign that the organization is mature and effectively able to mobilize its members and accomplish its objectives. Even if the evaluator dislikes the organization in question, he respects it if is centralized and bureaucratic and can ridicule it if it does not have these qualities. A movement, or a collectivity that does not have such central structure, is either considered unqualified as an organization at all, or, perhaps if the analyst is charitable, it is described as an "organization in embryo" or a "rapidly emergent institution" (Kopytoff 1964).

The sentiment against segmentation is nothing new. Preserved Smith, a historian writing some five decades ago (1920) looks upon the Reformation in the sixteenth century as a movement that transformed the Western world and ushered in a "new season in the worlds great year" (Smith 1962). But he finds great fault in the "lack of organization and division into many mutually hostile sects" (ibid., '115), sects that compete with each other for leadership and power. What, we can wonder, did Preserved Smith think that the Protestant cause could have achieved had it been centralized? Can we not say instead that segmentation into competing sects contributed to the very real success of the Protestant movement? Far from being fatal to its cause, segmentation and competition were probably the key to the overall Protestant triumph—just as they are the key to the success of all movements of change. Let us briefly summarize opinions. Some people suspect that movements are injected into our society from the outside and do have a kind of secret command structure stretching back perhaps to Moscow or Peking. Others see such movements as a natural and spontaneous explosion whose very presence proves that all is not right in the land. In time it does become rather obvious to all but the most conspiracy-minded person that movements are not centralized but are segmented and have many leaders. As people have done over the ages and in respect to many movements, most Americans find this segmented structure quite defective. They deplore movement segmentation, factionalism, and schism as weakness; they call ideological diversity and competition divisive; and denigrate undirected proliferation of movement groups or segments as a wasteful duplication of effort.

We find much that is faulty and misleading in such analysis. Our research* leads us to say that a movement is neither a centralized conspiracy nor an amorphous collectivity, a spontaneous mass eruption. Instead, it has a definiable structure that we term "segmentary, polycephalous, and reticulate" in structure. Such structure is not inefficient but rather is highly effective and adaptive in innovating and producing social change and in surviving in the face of established order opposition.

DESCRIPTION AND ANALYSIS

In the balance of this essay let me describe and analyze the main organizational characteristics of social movements as we have studied them primarily in Black Power, environmental activism which we call participatory ecology, and in the new-Pentecostal religious movement, which some call the charismatic renewal. We regard such movements as examples of a class of events we call movements of personal transformation and revolutionary social change. The organizational characteristics we discuss interrelate dynamically in mutual causation of the type described by Maruyama (1965) with four

* Research began in 1965. Research methods have included participant observation, interview, questionnaire, and media survey. Research has been funded by grants from: Hill Family Foundation; Rockefeller Foundation; Office of Water Resources Research, Department of Interior; University of Minnesota Graduate School; and Ferndale Foundation.

other characteristics of such movements. These include their means of *recruitment*, the process by which they enculturate and *commit* new participants, their *ideology*, and their perception of and response to *opposition*. Our focus here is on movement organization or structure which we describe as "segmentary, polycentric, and reticulate."

We describe their structure as "segmentary, polycephalous, and reticulate."

1. *Segmentary*: A movement is composed of a range of diverse groups, or cells, which grow and die, divide and fuse, proliferate and contract.
2. *Polycephalous*: This movement organization does not have a central command or decision-making structure; rather, it has many leaders or rivals for leadership, not only within the movement as a whole, but within each movement cell.
3. *Reticulate*: These diverse groups do not constitute simply an amorphous collection; rather, they are organized into a network, or reticulate structure through cross-cutting links, "traveling evangelists" or spokesmen, overlapping participation, joint activities, and the sharing of common objectives and opposition.

Let us now examine each of these in turn.

DESCRIPTION OF SPECTRUM OF SEGMENTS

Observation of any of the movements we have studied in detail (i.e., Black Power, participatory ecology, the charismatic renewal), shows them each to be made up of organizationally distinct, often rival, units that tend to proliferate by setting up "daughter cells." Still other segments in a movement are large bureaucratically organized national groups that have predated the emergence of the movement but identify with it (or in some cases, claim to have initiated it). All movements have expanded suddenly, proliferating exponentially from a core or base that has long been present in this country. One is tempted to see this core as a kind of persistent mutation from which exponential growth then took place under a set of appropriate conditions and selective pressures.

It is possible to range the various groups in any movement along a continuum of conservative to radical according to means and goals, or according to degree of institutionalization. Simply stated, there is more obvious growth and agitation at the radical end. This action is often deplored by older, more conservative cells who characteristically have ambivalent feelings about all of the attention paid to the "impetuous newcomers." Participants in the conservative groups claim that the radical activists will "ruin all of the things that we have accomplished and lose us the good will of the public we have so painstakingly cultivated." But, characteristically, the more middle-range and conservative groups, either purposely or inadvertently, use this radical action to spearhead their own drives and make their own demands and actions seem *comparatively* reasonable.

In the cities where we have conducted field research in 1967–68, Black Power ranges from such groups as the NAACP and the Urban League–by 1968 considered conservative—through a middle spectrum of church-based and community centers, parapolice patrols, campus black student groups, to radical and militant groups such as the Black Panthers, and various segments trained in guerrilla warfare.

Similarly, the participatory ecology movement as we studied it in several cities in 1969–70 ranges from such essentially conservative organizations as the Audubon Society, the Conservation Foundation and the Sierra Club, through such middle-spectrum segments as Friends of the Earth, and the John Muir Institute, which evolved through a 1968 split in the West Coast Sierra Club. These latter were once considered radical deviations from the established conservation groups, but since 1970 there have sprung up many activist segments calling themselves such names as the Peoples Architects, the Food Conspiracy, Ecology Action, Ecology Freaks, and Ecology Commandos.

In the ecology movement conservatives and radicals are divided primarily over their view of the established order or "the system" and the ability of this established system to change its course and save itself from ecocatastrophe. Radicals believe that one cannot work within the system to change it since it is, by its very nature, responsible for not only pollution but also the major ills of poverty, racism, and war making.

Similarly, Pentecostals can be ranged along a continuum reflecting intensity of involvement in personal religious experience and degree of institutionalization. As a basic distinguishing characteristic Pentecostals seek to receive the "gifts of the spirit" recorded in the New Testament as fundamental to first-century Christianity. These include such ecstatic manifestations as tongue speaking, prophecy, and interpretation. Assemblies of God represent the conservative, institutional end of the Pentecostal spectrum. Many are literally and figuratively the grandchildren of those who participated in an earlier wave of Pentecostal revivals that did appeal primarily to blue-collar workers. The opposite, cutting, growing edge of the movement is composed of small home-meeting groups of "underground" or "hidden" church-types, attracting primarily new converts from middle- and upper-middle-class Americans. Between these polar segments range a variety of independent churches and storefront groups of varying sizes.

SEGMENTATION PROCESS

Observation of the segmentary nature of movement organization suggests four basic ways in which cells split, merge, or proliferate:

1. Movements characteristically include in their ideology a concept of personal power. In religious movements, this involves beliefs concerning the direct access to God from whom power is derived. In the Black Power movement, this concept is expressed in terms of "doing your own thing." Each individual as well as each small group is credited with and encouraged to "do his own thing" and to take initative in acting to

promote movement goals he considers important. This results in organizational splits over ideological or methodological approach and stimulates the gathering of new recruits to support each new venture.

2. Preexisting socioeconomic cleavages, factionalisms, and personal conflicts are carried over into the movement and increase the so-called fissiparous, or splitting nature, of the movement organization.

3. Movement members, especially those with leadership capabilities, compete for a broad range of economic, political, social and psychological rewards. For example, Black Power leaders are continually vying with one another for funds that whites contribute through fear, guilt, or a genuine desire for social change. Similarly, Pentecostal evangelists compete for the honor of leading a large revival and ecology spokesmen contend for media and student attention. This personal competition leads to continual splitting of cells, realignment of followers, and intensified efforts to recruit new participants and broaden bases of support.

4. Segmentation of movement organization occurs over ideological differences. As we have pointed out in other papers, a truly committed movement participant experiences an intensity of involvement over ideological differences that the ordinary person feels only for events which threaten his immediate well-being, his family, or home. For instance, we indicated above how differences in opinion about the "system" and its ability to change are a basis for significant organizational fission in the ecology movement.

DECENTRALIZATION AND POLYCEPHALOUS STRUCTURE

Leadership in the movements we have studied, in Weberian terms, is charismatic more than bureaucratic. Power and authority tend to be distributed among several of the most able and dedicated members of a group, of which one is recognized as *primus inter pares*, the "first among equals." This is similar to the pattern of leadership in various African, Asian, and Middle Eastern societies that anthropologists have characteristically called segmentary and *acephalous*. The term acephalous, or "headless," indicates the strong bias scholars have had against such noncentralized organization. If the tribal organization has many leaders, Western observers call it headless. We prefer the term polycephalous. A typical leader in a polycephalous tribe or in a movement achieves his status by building a personal following and displaying abilities and characteristics pertinent to situational needs and the expectations of his adherents and potential recruits. He must prove and continue to demonstrate his worth to maintain his position.

In his study of segmentary lineage systems, Sahlins (1961) points out that leadership in such systems is often situation specific and hence ephemeral. A man who proves himself as a war leader over a confederation of segments fighting a common foe is not necessarily able to work as a leader of this confederation or of its components in peace.

This situational aspect of leadership is characteristic of the movements we have studied, especially Black Power. Those qualities that enhance the leader's reputation in some types of militant and action-oriented operations may not be pertinent to assure maintenance of leadership under different conditions. A person may secure leadership over a group or collection of groups by his ability to "sock it to Whitey," or mobilize and lead a short-run militant operation and obtain concessions from the establishment. But he may not have the ability to lead these groups in the more routine consolidation of gains, and hence might fade, at least for a time, into the background while persons with more pertinent organizational skills assume control.

Even where leaders have both charismatic-action and bureaucratic-administrative capabilities most will find it difficult to employ both at one time. Administering the ordinary activities of many of the Black Power groups often implies working to some degree with whites, taking their advice and funds (often with some strings attached or implied) and reducing overt manifestations of militancy. This leads other blacks to brand such leaders as Uncle Toms and accuse them of being coopted by the system. Similarly, some environmental activists wind up working with government or industry and experience similar problems of identity. Of course, a few gifted individuals will actually thrive in such situations, and will switch back and forth from administrative to militant role, playing one off against the other with deceptive ease.

Although certain particularly charismatic and able leaders, such as Stokely Carmichael, H. Rap Brown, Dick Gregory, Eldridge Cleaver for Black Power, or Paul Ehrlich for ecology activism, or David Wilkerson for Pentecostalism, may be highly revered and widely influential at any moment, the newest convert to the movement can perceive them more as "soul brothers" than as "commanders of the faithful." Each has organizational power only over his own segment of the movement, and this only for a limited time. To outsiders, such men often appear to be the key individuals without whom the movement would grind to a halt. But not one of them could be called the leader of the movement as a whole, because:

1. They quite clearly disagree upon such crucial matters as the goals of the movement and the means by which these goals should be achieved.
2. Not one of these leaders has a roster, or even knows about all of the groups that consider themselves participants in the movement.
3. They can make no decisions that are binding on all or even a majority of the participants in the movement.
4. This is most frustrating for representatives of the established order: None of these leaders has regulatory powers over the movement. In the case of Black Power, city officials are often upset when well-known leaders whom they assume to have incited a riot cannot control it, even when they are obviously working tirelessly to do so. Officials then conclude either that the leader is not sincere in his efforts to stop the riots or that it got out of hand and beyond his original orders. In one riot in Miami in 1968, city and state officials called in a well-known Black Power leader, who had been speaking in the area, to plead for an end to the violence. Local black leaders said afterward that they felt this only made

the situation worse. The assumption that local groups were under his control angered them. In environmental issues established authorities frequently want the ecology protesters to centralize, hire a lawyer to represent them, and negotiate.

5. Another manifestation of the polycephalous, segmentary nature of the movement is that there is no such thing as a card-carrying member of the movement. That is, there are no objective requirements to qualify a person as a movement member, although some groups do have such membership requirements. Participants in the movement share a common history and experience and recognize each other through bonds of objectively perceived commitment. This means that there is no leader who can determine objectively who is or is not a member of the movement, let alone direct, regulate, or speak for the movement as a whole.

RETICULATION

The decentralized, segmentary, organizational structure of a movement owes its cohesion to linkages among the autonomous cells. Through these linkages the various cells intermesh to form a network which, following Mayer (1966), we regard as essentially "unbounded." That is, the network ramifies extensively throughout society and there are no well-defined limits to such extension. We identify five types of such linkages:

1. Lines of kinship, friendship, and other forms of close association between individual members of different local groups. Often a single individual will be an active participant in more than one group as well. Even after an organizational split over some issue, previous ties of friendship tend to form loose linkages between the resulting splinter groups. Such ties form the basis for potential cooperative action in the face of future large-scale opposition.

2. Personal, kinship, or social ties between leaders and other participants in autonomous cells form networks that sometimes extend beyond the local community and tie together independent groups in distant cities. Such ties are extended and facilitated by telephone and letter. Circulating newsletters play such a role in Pentecostal and ecology movements.

3 Every movement has its traveling evangelists who crisscross the country as living links in the reticulate network. When such an evangelist-organizer comes to town, members of many different local segments bury the hatchet temporarily to hear him speak and often act in concert under his ad hoc leadership in a specific activity such as a demonstration or march. Ordinary movement participants can also travel along the movement network. For example, a university student and ecology activist from Minneapolis traveled along such an ecology network up and down the West Coast. Everywhere his ecology contacts gave him housing and food, shared ideas about ecology and change with him, and sent him on to new contacts in his next stopping-off place. As he traveled, he disseminated his growing information, like Johnny Appleseed, sowing seeds to bear tomorrow's fruit.

4. Closely related to the rally or the revival meeting of the traveling evangelist are the more permanent cross-cutting activities of the areawide, regional, or national "in-gathering." One example of the regional and national in-gathering for Black Power was the Poor People's March. Another, somewhat earlier example, was the open housing demonstration of Father Groppi and the "Commandoes" in Milwaukee. For the ecology movement the April 1970 Teach-Ins not only helped to bring ecology and related counterculture groups together but also generated new awareness and poured it out across the land.

5. A crucial cross-cutting linkage providing movement unity are those basic beliefs shared by all segments of the movement, no matter how disparate their views on other matters. All movement ideologies are split in the sense that there are a few basic themes and an infinite variety of interpretations and emphases. The variety of interpretation is the ideological basis for fusion, enabling members of warring factions to conceptualize themselves as participants in a single movement or revolution. Sometimes these unifying tenets spread as powerful integrating concepts, such as the concepts of ecosystem, interdependence, limited resource base, spaceship earth, no-growth economy. Sometimes such concepts become slogans that transcend initial meaning and epitomize the movement. The term "ecology" is one example of this. Black Power gives us a splendid instance of the condensation of ideology into battle cry and unifying slogans: Black Power, Black is Beautiful, Racism is Whitey's Hang-up. Green Power through Black Power, and the like. The concepts of ecology, system, interdependence, limited resource base, spaceship earth, have interpenetrated the ecology movement. Such statements express the core beliefs which make possible the system of intercell leadership exchange, temporary coalition on specific actions, a flow of financial and other material resource through nonbureaucratic channels, and an often surprising presentation of a united front in the face of external opposition.

EXTRAMOVEMENT LINKAGES

This movement structure articulates and gains strength from various significant extramovement linkages. We can identify two such linkages to groups, organizations, and persons in the established order, and linkages to other movements. Here, again, those links ramify in an essentially unbounded, expanding web. For example, participants in the Black Power movement will have various white or black friends, associates, and other contacts who are not involved in the movement. These relationships may have been established through or quite independently of Black Power activities. A participant in any one movement cell may prevail upon his extramovement friends and associates to aid him in ways which directly or indirectly help the movement locally or nationally. Through their relationship with any one participant, or cell, nonparticipants may be influenced to support the movement by word or deed. In turn, many such nonparticipants will use their own networks of friends, relatives, or associates either directly or indirectly to help them provide such support. As an example of these extramovement linkages, we can note that personal associations of varying intensity among several dynamic black militant spokesmen and various white churchmen, community leaders, students, and university faculty members in one urban center provided the primary and initial channels through which these black leaders were able to obtain financial and political support to establish a unique and controversial community center in one city where we conducted research.

ADAPTIVE FUNCTIONS

As we have noted, there is a popular bias, often shared by movement participants, against such a segmented, polycephalous structure as inherently weak. We have found, however, that these characteristics of segmentation, ideological diversity, and proliferation of cells are highly adaptive in situations of social change. Bureaucratic centralization, while efficient, is not noted for producing rapid organizational growth, for inspiring depth of personal commitment, or for flexible-adaptation to rapidly changing conditions. All of these are necessary to a successful movement aimed at implementing personal and social change. A decentralized, segmented, reticulate social structure is adaptive for seven major reasons:

First, it prevents effective suppression by the opposition. Multiplicity of leadership and lack of centralized control ensures the survival of the movement even if leaders are jailed or otherwise removed. In fact, such action stimulates emergence of new leadership because of heightened commitment in the face of opposition. Autonomy and self-sufficiency of local cells make effective suppression of the movement extremely difficult. For every cell coopted into the establishment it can indeed appear like the hydra of mythology. Also, the behavior of the movement cannot easily be predicted. We can hypothesize that in response to the polycephalous, segmental nature of movements the established order would find it necessary to seek to penetrate almost every movement segment, and indeed, in some cases, even to establish cells of its own. In short, the intelligence agencies of the established order will respond to a polycephalous, segmented structure by establishing a polycephalous, segmental counterintelligence structure. This will lead to the same characteristics of factionalism and competition for which movements are noted. It could be expected that interagency rivalry and factors of security would prevent such segments from cooperating in an effective network or under a central administration even though intelligence data are centrally collected. Perhaps the proliferation of army intelligence activities within the United States is a response to such movement segmentation.

The second function of such organization we call multipenetration. Factionalism and schism facilitate penetration of the movement into a variety of social niches. Factionalism along lines of preexisting socioeconomic cleavages provides recruits from a wide range of socioeconomic and educational backgrounds with a type of Black Power group with which they can identify. The variety of ideological emphases and types of organizational structures produces an organizational smörgasbord that has something for everyone, no matter what his taste in goals or methods might be. A segmented social structure is designed for multipenetration of all sociological levels and psychological types.

Third, the resultant multiplicity of cell types maximizes adaptive variation during a time of marked environmental change. As each cell does its "own thing" in its own way, each contributes synergistically to the success of the whole. While it is popular to stress the need for centralized unity in Black Power, some astute black spokesmen and movement participants note the advantages derived from segmentation. Nathan Hare (1968), a militant black sociologist, takes a somewhat Machiavellian approach to diversity and argues in a *Negro Digest* article that Black Power can utilize "even Uncle Toms" to accomplish Black Power goals. A young black community organizer in Miami explains that some blacks who superficially appear to be "Uncle Toms" may in fact be what he terms "Uncle Bobs"; that is, persons who pretend to play the white man's game while in reality working for the black cause. "They all play their part," he says.

A special issue of *Ebony* (1969) emphasized the synergistic unity that exists among blacks, irrespective of their diverse approaches to the black revolution. For example, they explained that while the Black Panthers may seem poles apart from members of the Urban League and the NAACP, they are bound together in common cause, drawing from a common heritage of blackness, of white oppression and discrimination. They constitute, in fact, complementary, mutually enhancing, components of one movement.

The fourth function of such organization is that it contributes to system reliability. While diversity of function produced by multiplicity of cell types is an obvious and adaptive characteristic of movement organization, it is also significant that some groups duplicate and overlap the functions of others. While this duplication is often seen as inefficient by the many exponents of movement centralization, it in fact helps assure that one group is available to accomplish necessary tasks even if another falters or fails. For example, when one community center retires from its role as the spearhead of militant protest, another group is there to move in and quickly take its place. When tensions and conflict potential were high, more than one group existed to serve as community parapolice, and more than one organization was available to isolate and counter dangerous rumours. However, we would state that the factors of redundancy, duplication, and overlap are adaptive only in a segmentary, polycephalous, and reticulate structure, in which the failure of one part does not harm the other parts. A centralized bureaucracy would seem to link the duplicated parts in such a way that the liabilities of each are maximized. If one part of a bureaucracy is faulty, this impairs all parts either laterally or through the center.

A fifth function of such a decentralized structure is what we have called the escalation of effort. This sometimes, but not always, involves personal competition between leaders. When a militant segment of a movement acts, a host of more moderate groups benefit. On the grounds that they agree with the goals but not the means of the militants, representatives of the affected established order make concessions. In the end, overall movement goals are achieved. This inspires a sort of escalating dynamism. Today's radical is tomorrow's Uncle Tom, no matter what the movement. As one segment of a movement goes militant and attracts public attention, other segments are motivated to step out and upstage it. Thus, demands or concepts once viewed as outrageous soon appear as relatively moderate and reasonable. Gains for the whole movement are thus consolidated. For example, establishment whites contribute money to a radical Black Power community center because they are warned that if this center is not funded angry militants will become even more radical and join ever more threatening groups such as the Black Panthers.

In the case of ecology, a leader of the Isaac Walton League urges legislators to pass a bill that will protect the wilderness by saying that if the "kids" do not see that they can save the environment by working within the system, they will lose faith and will join really radical groups that "act only on emotion." A leader of an old established conservation group was amazed when he heard a young ecology activist call him an Uncle Tom on conservation efforts. His initial reaction was to say that he and his association were saving the environment when the young radicals were still in diapers. But he is spurred on to greater effort by this accusation to prove that he and his colleagues are as active as anyone.

Similarly, different Pentecostal evangelists from the United States and Latin America compete for the honor and challenge of controlling large revival meetings in Bogotá, Columbia just as North American Pentecostal evangelists in Haiti compete with each other for funds from the Pentecostal contributors to support "their fight against Voodoo." As each seeks to outperform the other, the Pentecostal movement presses forward.

The dynamics of small-group structure also contribute to the escalation of effort. Most movement segments are small enough to permit fact-to-face interaction among participants in it. Participants can observe, evaluate, praise, or condemn the contributions of other participants to the operations of their small group. Participants can also observe how their own activities help or hinder these operations. This contributes to the striving of each segment, which in turn carries the whole movement forward as segments and leaders compete. Our findings here corroborate Mancur Olson's (1965) observation that small groups are more effective in mobilizing energies of members to achieve shared objectives than large collectivities within which individual efforts or lack of effort can go unnoticed. Furthermore, our concept of movement network or reticulate structure explains how these individual energized segments combine in a large-scale effort.

It promotes innovation in the design and implementation of social, economic, and political change. This, from the standpoint of society at large, is the most significant and the most broadly adaptive function of segmentation and decentralized control. The climate of such a social structure fosters entrepreneurial experimentation. For example, Black Power sensitivity-training groups are using innovative techniques in communicating the need for change across previously formidable barriers. As noted above, black action has stimulated the development of a multitude of white or interracial "positive response groups," which are experimenting with ways to make adaptive social change and facilitate face-to-face interracial communication. These efforts require social innovation, for existing institutions have not provided channels through which these people ordinarily meet on a face-to-face, talk-it-over basis.

Black groups are experimenting with communal ownership of businesses, with tutorial programs in schools, and with the use of extraparty political organizations in certain localities. Parapolice forces of black youth are springing up with varying degrees of success in many cities. The trial-and-error approach to social change facilitated by the segmented social structure of the Black Power movement has inspired a similar type of social innovation among white positive-response groups. All such innovators are finding that it must be a grass-roots attempt; using one-to-one communication and personal initative not normally found through bureaucratic channels.

Similarly, ecology groups have generated important new ideas about resource use, about interdependence, and about the concept of ecosystem. They have promoted a range of new approaches to teaching about ecology and total systems, and have involved Americans in various attempts to recycle goods, to reduce population, and to control energy consumption. They have pushed some industries to seek less polluting technologies and have led some economists and government representatives to reevaluate conventional priorities and question even established worship of growth.

The seventh feature of such a social structure is closely related to the fourth. Innovation through trial and error results in a variety of adaptive and successful social "mutations." It also results in many failures. In fact, if social processes are at all analogous to natural processes, there are a good many more failures than successes. Under the pressure of selective adaptation, the maladaptive variant simply passes out of existence. This can only occur on the social level, however, within a decentralized, segmented social structure where the errors of one group have little if any effect on another. Members of a group who failed to find a viable answer to a problem can disband, reform under new leadership, or simply be absorbed into another group. The life of the movement continues unabated. A social innovation that fails affects only those closely associated with it, and may indeed benefit others by showing them what will not work. Information about success and failure of such experiments flows rapidly through the reticulate network of a movement and across extra-movement linkages to other movements and established orders.

SUMMARY

Social movements are characteristically *segmentary*; that is, they are composed of many groups of varying sizes and scope. And they are *polycephalous*; that is, their varied groups have many competing leaders. Popular opinion has it that such organization is at best inefficient—at worst it is no organization at all, but an amorphous collectivity. But the diverse cells which and the many leaders who compose a movement in fact weave together to form a network or *reticulate* structure. In short, movements are well described as segmentary, polycephalous, and reticulate.

Segmentation and proliferation of groups within a movement occur because of a belief in personal access to power, because of preexisting social cleavages, because of personal competition, and because of ideological differences.

Leadership is ephemeral and weakly developed above a local group level just as organized activity above this level is ephemeral. As in polycephalous, segmentary societies, leaders "build a name" and establish a following on the basis of personal qualities and skills and personally established social links and bonds. In spite of these centrifugal characteristics, these varying groups manifest sufficient cohesion and ideological unity to be perceived as a large-scale movement. Such cohesion is obtained through a range of integrating, cross-cutting links, bonds, and operations, including ties between members and group leaders, by the activities of traveling evangelists, or spokesmen, large-scale demonstrations and "ingatherings," sharing of basic ideological themes, and collective perception of, and action against, a common opposition.

Such organization is adaptive in implementing social change and helping the movement survive. It makes the movement difficult to suppress; it affords maximum penetration of and recruitment from different socioeconomic and subcultural groups; it maximizes adaptive variation through diversity; it contributes to system reliability through redundancy, duplication, and overlap; and, finally, it encourages social innovation and problem solving. Such organization appears to generate countermovement intelligence activity of a segmentary, polycephalous nature.

REFERENCES

Bennis, W. G., and P. E. Slater
  1968   *The Temporary Society.* New York: Harper & Row.
Bohannan, L.
  1958   "Political Aspects of Tiv Social Organization." In J. Middleton and D. Tait, eds., *Tribes Without Rulers*. London: Routledge and Kegan Paul.
Bohannan, P.
  1954   "The Migration and Expansion of the Tiv." *Africa* 24, no. 1: 2–16.
  1969   "The Unity of Blackness." 24 (August): 42.
Eisenstadt, S. N.
  1959   "Primitive Political Systems: A Preliminary Analysis." *American Anthropologist* 61, no. 2: 200–20.
Evans-Pritchard, E. E.
  1940   *The Nuer.* Oxford: Clarendon Press.
Fortes, M.
  1963   "The Political Systems of the Tallensi of the Northern Territories of the Gold Coast." Pp. 239–71 in M. Fortes and E. E. Evans-Pritchard, eds., *African Political Systems*. London: Oxford University Press.
Gerlach. L. P.
  1968   *People, Power, Change.* A 16-mm sound/color film. University of Minnesota. Audiovisual.
  1970a   *People Eco-action.* A 16-mm sound/color film. University of Minnesota. Audiovisual.

1970*b* "Corporate Groups and Movement Networks in Urban America." *Anthropological Quarterly* 43 (October): 123–45.

1970*c* "Eco-Gemini." *Natural History*, May.

Gerlach, L. P., and V. H. Hine

1969 "Five Factors Crucial to the Growth and Spread of a Modern Religious Movement." *Journal for the Scientific Study of Religion* 7, no. 1: 23–40.

1970*a* "The Social Organization of a Movement of Revolutionary Change: Case Study Black Power." In N. Whitten, Jr., and J. Szwed, eds., *Afro-American Anthropology: Contemporary Perspectives*. New York: Free Press.

1970*b* *People, Power, Change: Movements of Social Transformation*. Indianapolis: Bobbs-Merrill.

1970*c* "You and the Ecology Movement." *Natural History*, June/July, pp. 27–29.

1970*d* "Wit, Wisdom, and Woe." *Natural History*, October, pp. 8ff.

Gluckman, M.

1959 *Political Institutions: The Institutions of Primitive Society*. Glencoe, Ill.: Free Press.

Hare, N.

1968 "New Role for Uncle Toms." *Negro Digest* 18, no. 10: 14–19.

Hine, V. H., and L. P. Gerlach

1969 "Pentecostal Glossolalia: Toward a Functional Interpretation." *Journal of the Scientific Study of Religion* 8: 211–26.

1970 "Many Concerned, Few Committed." *Natural History*, December.

Jackson, J.

1969 Interview. *Playboy* 16: 85ff.

Kahn, R.

1969 "The Collapse of the SDS . . . Spectator's Guide to Warring Factions." *Esquire* 72 (October): 140ff.

Kasdan, L., and R. F. Murphy

1959 "The Structure of Parallel Cousin Marriage." *American Anthropologist* 61, no. 1: 17–29.

Kopytoff, I.

1964 "Classifications of Religious Movements: Analytical and Synthetic." *Proceedings of the 1964 Annual Spring Meeting of the American Ethnological Society*. Seattle: University of Washington Press.

Landau, M.

1969 "Redundancy, Rationality, and the Problems of Duplication and Overlap." *Public Administration Review* 24 (July/August): 346–58.

Lewis, I. M.

1961 *A Pastoral Democracy: A Study of Pastoralism and Politics Among the Northern Somali of the Horn of Africa*. London: Oxford University Press.

Life

1971 "Persons of Interest." 70 (26 March): 21–27.

Maruyama, M.

1965 "The Second Cybernetics: Deviation Amplifying Mutual Causal Processes." *American Scientist* 51, no. 2: 164–79.

Mayer, A.

1966 "The Significance of Quasi-Groups in the Study of Complex Societies: The Social Anthropology of Complex Societies." In M. Banton, ed., *Association of Social Anthropologists Monograph*. New York: Praeger.

Mecklin, J. M.

1970 *Fire and Steel for Palestine* 82 (July): 84ff.

Middleton, J., and D. Tait, eds.
  1958   "Introduction." *Tribes Without Rulers*. London: Routledge and Kegan Paul.
Newsweek
  1970   "The FBI's Toughest Foe: The Kids." 76 (2b October): 22–23.
  1971   "The Decline and Fall of the Panthers." 22 March, pp. 26–28.
Olson, M.
  1965   *The Logic of Collective Action*. Cambridge, Mass.: Harvard University Press.
Sahlins, M. D.
  1961   "The Segmentary Lineage: An Organization of Predatory Expansion." *American Anthropologist* 63: 322–45.
Smith, P.
  1962   *The Age of the Reformation*, vol. 1. New York: Collier.
  1966   *The Age of the Reformation*, vol. 2. New York: Collier.
Time
  1968   "Rhetoric into Relevance." 92 (9 August): 21.
  1970   "Jordan: The King Takes on the Guerrillas." September, pp. 16–25.
  1971   "Radicals: Destroying the Panther Myth." 22 March, pp. 19–20.
Von Neumann, J.
  1956   Probabilistic Logics and the Synthesis of Reliable Organizations from Unreliable Components." In C. E. Shannon and J. McCarthy, eds., *Automata Studies*. Princeton: Princeton University Press.

9

Structure and Strategy
in the Antinuclear Movement

Lynn E. Dwyer

There has been much debate among social movement scholars about which organizational form is the most effective for movements to reach their goals. The traditional view is that bureaucracies are the most rational form of organization, whether for traditional institutions in society or for social movements that are trying to change it. Those who advocate centralized, and/or bureaucratic* movements feel that they are more efficient and waste little time and effort on duplication and decision making. They can place the qualified person in the most appropriate position, or they can recruit someone who has the needed expertise. This bias for formal organizations stems from Max Weber's prediction that social movements and other organizations will gradually rationalize their structures to efficiently meet their member's needs and movement goals.[1] Movements have often been criticized for being disorganized and inefficient when they do not have centralized organizations with identifiable leaders and a well-defined division of labor. Gamson,[2] among others, has argued that organizations that are both bureaucratic and centralized are most likely to succeed.

---

* Centralized organizations are ruled by one leader or one decision-making committee. A bureaucracy has explicit rules and a hierarchy of command; its employees have specific duties, and their selection is based on their qualifications and their promotion on the quality of their work.

In the last ten years this view has been challenged by Gerlach and Hine.[3] They argue that movements that are segmented, polycephalous, and reticulate are far more effective and longer lasting than those which follow the traditional pattern. In this chapter we apply that model to the antinuclear movement to examine the association between structure and strategy and ascertain how each contributes to overall effectiveness.

STRUCTURE OF THE ANTINUCLEAR MOVEMENT

A movement's structure is the pattern of relationships between individuals and organizations within and among the movement's constituent groups. These groups in turn have their own distinct organizational forms. The antinuclear movement as a whole fits the segmentary, polycephalous, reticulate model, but some of the organizations within it are more traditionally bureaucratic. Segmentary movements are "composed of a great variety of localized groups or cells which are essentially independent, but which can combine to form larger configurations or divide to form smaller units."[4]

While the antinuclear movement has a wide variety of groups, most are local. They are formed when a utility announces that it proposes to build a nuclear power plant nearby. They are usually composed of rural men and women whose land borders or is on the proposed site, though some groups are situated in nearby cities. Other groups are centered on college campuses. Some groups last only a year or two, as they may become discouraged or run out of money. Others have bursts of activity over a five- to ten-year period in response to actions by the utilities, the Nuclear Regulatory Commission (NRC), or other parts of the movement. The groups maintain their autonomy even when they join together to file interventions* against the construction and operation of nuclear power plants before the NRC. Thus the failure of a

---

* Interventions result when the U.S. Nuclear Regulatory Commission or other regulatory body, such as a state water commission or a local zoning board, allows a citizen or group of citizens to argue for or against the request of the utility to build or operate a nuclear plant. While these are not tried before a court, their procedures are much like those of the courts, and many citizens' groups have had to hire an attorney to argue their case against the plants before the hearing panels of the local, state, or federal boards.

The privilege of intervening against (or for) the construction of nuclear plants was granted by the passage of the National Environmental Policy Act in 1969. In this act, public hearings and proof that such construction or operation will not harm the social or natural environment must be provided by the utility. It is because the federal NRC licenses the plants that NEPA applies. Therefore, the Congress and courts of the United States have given citizens the opportunity to argue for or against the plants. While most citizens' groups agree that such a right is desirable and while they are against efforts by utilities to bar citizen hearings and interventions from licensing proceedings, most citizens' groups opposed to nuclear power plants do not look on the interventions as a realistic way to stop the plants. This is because the NRC appoints the hearing panels (the equivalent of the judges in court trials), and those panels are usually composed of two nuclear experts and one attorney. Generally, the nuclear experts have worked for many years in the nuclear industry either for the federal government or for the companies that build the plants.

Citizens' groups are at an additional disadvantage in these proceedings. As in a court, evidence and cross-examinations are used. Because the citizens' groups work with limited budgets, usually they cannot hire expert witnesses whose reputations and educations are comparable to those the utilities can muster. Therefore, they are at a decided disadvantage before the hearing boards.

single group does not necessarily result in the abandonment of an intervention, as other groups may still pursue it.

Local groups and coalitions that file interventions are often advised by the National Intervenors. Composed of attorneys and other people who have participated in interventions, it is an informal organization that shares its expertise in administrative litigation on request. It does not initiate actions. National Intervenors is publicized in movement newsletters and member attorneys give intervention advice at talks before antinuclear meetings.

Besides these groups, urban areas often have chapters of the larger national environmental organizations like the Sierra Club, the Friends of the Earth (FOE), the Audubon Society, the Izaak Walton League, and some hiking and wilderness societies. Some of these organizations are large with thousands of members. Both local chapters and the national organizations are often rather formal with short chains of command and at least some explicit rules. The majority of the members are middle class, often working in the professions.[5]

The national organizations often publish newsletters that alert members to events and facts in the areas of the organization's concern. To belong to the organization, one has only to pay a membership fee. Attending local meetings is not necessary for membership in the national organizations, but it is usually mandatory for local chapters. These voluntary associations are interested in many environmentally related issues in addition to the nuclear controversy. Their newsletters, especially FOE's, play an important part of the antinuclear movement's information network. Additionally, FOE has served as a coordinating structure, ensuring that the small local groups all receive instructions about mass meetings, dates and activities planned for simultaneous nationwide and local demonstrations, and letter-writing and telephoning campaigns on particular congressional bills.

There are a few national antinuclear groups. The major two are the publishers of the newspaper *Nuclear Opponents*, and Critical Mass, which organizes national meetings and publishes a newsletter by the same name. This organization is affiliated with Ralph Nader's environmental and political investigation network, the Public Interest Research Groups. Critical Mass's staff organization has some formal characteristics with an explicit division of labor of people possessing the appropriate skills for the jobs they occupy, and a short chain of command. Ralph Nader is the group's leader. *Nuclear Opponent's* structure is less formal, but is somewhat centralized around its leader, Lawrence Bogart. These groups have no members—just 1,000 to 4,000 subscribers to their newsletters, most of whom also belong to local antinuclear groups.

Another group of national environmental organizations allied with the antinuclear movement specializes in using legal procedures to fight actions they feel endanger the natural environment. These multiissue groups include the Natural Resource Defense Council, the Environmental Defense Fund, and the Union of Concerned Scientists. While many people contribute to these groups' expenses, they have staff but no members and do not publish newsletters or magazines. They have conducted several of the most effective administrative legal battles against nuclear power.

Many large and formally organized groups, such as the United Mine Workers, the United Auto Workers, the Oil, Chemical, and Atomic Workers Union, Common Cause, and Church Women United participate in the antinuclear movement, even though their primary interest is in nonenvironmental matters. They became interested in the antinuclear cause either because prominent members are antinuclear or because the nuclear issue has touched many of the members' lives. For example, Walter Reuther, president of the United Auto Workers, spearheaded an intervention against the construction of the proposed Fermi breeder reactor because he felt that it was too near Detroit where many of the union's members work and live. He expressed the fear that the reactor might explode, killing and injuring millions.[6]

All the above groups cooperate in coalitions to mount interventions and court suits, to put together large demonstrations, or to campaign for referenda to ban nuclear power plants in a number of western states. The number of people who meet together to coordinate the various groups' efforts is usually quite small, although the number of participants in the overall activity may be large. These coalitions last two years, at most.

The composition of groups in the antinuclear movement constantly changes through fission of groups, as well as their fusion and allying. When cell members disagree about the best strategies to use in opposing nuclear plant construction, the groups often split permanently. For example, one group in middle Tennessee was interested in opposing all nuclear plants by fighting the construction of the proposed breeder reactor that would create fuel for all other commercial reactors. Other groups wished to narrow their opposition to the nearest proposed nuclear plant. Their leader asked, "How can I spend my energy and money on your plant when I've got one being built in my front yard?" This goal difference eventually caused a schism so wide that the leaders could not talk to one another and the groups' members could not participate in the same events because the leaders would accuse them of helping the other's cause. In this case the leaders' incompatibility prevented their followers from contacting one another. The reverse is often true—when leaders are friends, their followers often cooperate and form new relationships.

The antinuclear movement is polycephalous. This means that the "... movement organization does not have a central command or decision-making structure; rather, it has many leaders or rivals for leadership, not only within the movement as a whole, but within each movement cell."[7] National leaders include Ralph Nader, Lawrence Bogart, attorney Myron Cherry, and Drs. Tamplin, Goffman, and Sternglass. They travel about the nation speaking before many different audiences, and help form the movement's ideology. Bogart's newsletter, *Nuclear Opponents*, publishes his views favoring fusion energy and linking the Rockefeller family with the nuclear industry. He also helps lead the New England region, which is now partially organized into the Clamshell Alliance. Attorney Cherry and Drs. Tamplin, Goffman, and Sternglass are hired often by antinuclear groups to testify in legal and administrative procedures and to speak to audiences. Thus the movement has chosen them as spokesmen. A regional leader is Ed Koupal, who helped organize the "western bloc" states to hold referenda on building nuclear plants. Local groups may have more than one leader, or one leader may head more than one group, usually in different towns.

Local leaders are usually not regional or national leaders, but the latter are often influential on the local level. National leaders are often not well known outside movement circles. Some antinuclear activists, such as Robert Redford, Jane Fonda, and Jack Lemmon, are movement media stars, but they were chosen by the press, not antinuclear organizations. Since they have contributed their names and time to getting publicity for the movement and have raised money for the cause, their support is appreciated by movement personnel.

The antinuclear movement is reticulate. "... (T)hese diverse groups... are organized into a network, or reticulate structure through cross-cutting links, 'travelling evangelists' or spokesmen, overlapping participation, joint activities, and the sharing of common objectives and opposition."[8] The antinuclear movement demonstrates all these forms of reticulation. Members move from one group to another frequently. "Evangelists" spread the word through speaking engagements and informal meetings. Joint meetings and mass demonstrations such as Critical Mass '74 and the May 1979 demonstration in Washington, D.C., occur regularly. Friendships made at these events are often kept alive by telephone and letters. Another source of intercell connections is family relationships. One family member may persuade others to join resistance to the plants.

When people have similar beliefs and experiences, they generally work together more easily. While they may have never met, many movement members have participated in local versions of national antinuclear celebrations. Often a national publication such as the FOE newsletter or *Critical Mass* will propose that on the same day members all over the United States do such things as loose tagged balloons announcing that the balloon's finder is in the wind pattern from a nuclear plant.

The connections between the cells of the antinuclear movement spread by the formation of ever-larger coalitions. Many early alliances were formed by small groups to file interventions. The Environmental Coalition on Nuclear Power was formed by thirteen environmental groups from Pennsylvania and New Jersey to oppose further nuclear plant construction in the two states; three Vermont groups argued before the state Public Service Board that the Vermont Yankee plant should be built only by obeying very strict state environmental standards; seven groups fought the Bell Station plant in New York; and at least eight intervened against the Midland (Michigan) plant. A large alliance of sixty groups from all over the nation united to oppose the nuclear industry's arguments in the 1972 NRC Emergency Core Cooling System hearings.[9]

Beginning in 1971 and accelerating in 1973, the movement formed alliances with already existing groups not previously antinuclear, such as the Audubon Society, the National Wildlife Federation, the United Auto Workers of America, Common Cause, Another Mother for Peace, workers for McCarthy and McGovern, the Federation of American Scientists, the Sierra Club, the Izaak Walton League, the Friends of the Earth, the United Mine Workers, and the Americans for Democratic Action.[10]

An organizational leap was made when Ralph Nader called a national convention of nuclear opponents in 1974. Named Critical Mass '74, it formed a coordinating organization that publishes a newspaper by the same name and has a small staff to do legislative lobbying. While there were already coalitions of people in limited geographical areas, this organization sought to coordinate the activities of antinuclear people throughout the nation. During the meeting, Ed Koupal pulled together leaders of local organizations in twenty western states and assembled the "western bloc," whose activities were similar to those promoting the California Nuclear Safeguards referendum.[11]

After two years of collecting signatures to put the issue on the ballot and educating voters in California, Oregon, Maine, Missouri, Arizona, Washington, Montana, Colorado, and Ohio, only the efforts in Missouri and Montana were successful. Most movement sources attribute the loss of the referenda to the small amounts of money they had to spend to buy media time for advertising. By a 2 to 1 margin, Missouri voters banned the use of the Construction Work in Progress plan that allowed utilities to bill their customers for nuclear plant construction while the plant was being built. The result was the cancellation of at least one plant. In Montana, voters required that each nuclear plant win a referendum plus meet certain safety and insurance standards before construction.[12]

In 1974 and 1975 groups in several states with no initiative or recall provisions tried to push nuclear moratorium bills through their legislatures. The bills said that no new nuclear plants were to be built in those states until certain conditions were met.[13]

In the summer of 1975 in Wyhl, West Germany, about 28,000 protestors occupied a nuclear plant site to stop its construction. They remained on the site for about a year, though police tried to clear them away with water cannons and other forceful tactics.[14] Inspired by their example, about 40 people from New Hampshire and Massachusetts decided to engage in similar civil disobedience on August 1, 1976, at the Seabrook, New Hampshire, nuclear plant site. Eighteen protestors were arrested when they walked onto the Seabrook site, and 600 rallied in sympathy. They chose civil disobedience because interventions, referenda, petitions, and public education efforts had failed to halt nuclear plant construction. They formed the Clamshell Alliance, a regional coalition of New England groups. On August 22, 180 people entered the site, and 179 were arrested. They were backed by a 1,200-person rally.[15]

A major organizational change resulted from the Clamshell Alliance's decision to use civil disobedience to oppose the construction of the Seabrook plant. To prepare for their protest activities, some Clamshell members formed "affinity groups." These small groups intensively train in nonviolence. Through their training they become acquainted and can be confident of one another's loyalty to the groups and the cause. Their nonviolent emphasis comes from two sources—many were Quakers and many more came from the antiwar and antinuclear weapons movements. In the affinity groups decisions are reached by consensus. Alliance business is done by a committee composed of representatives of each member group.[16]

During the next winter, the Clamshell Alliance added many member groups. Thirty-five New England groups organized 2,000 people to occupy the construction site parking lot at Seabrook for twenty-four hours on April 22. On May 1, 4,000 protestors rallied nearby. These actions resulted in 1,414 arrests with extensive media coverage; more than half refused bond and spent two weeks in National Guard armories.[17]

The Clamshell actions and their resulting publicity inspired other areas to form regional coalitions and use similar sit-in techniques. Missouri groups formed the Great Plains Alliance and 400 to 500 people attended their April 30, 1977, demonstrations. In 1977, 9 groups united into the Great Plains Federation of Nuclear Opponents and Safe Energy Proponents.[18]

Finally, in 1979 the largest antinuclear demonstration ever held was organized by Critical Mass in Washington, D.C. Over 90 groups participated and between 75,000 and 125,000 people marched. Such groups as the Union of Concerned Scientists, the Women's Strike for Peace, the Amalgamated Meat Cutters, the National Council of Senior Citizens, and the Sierra Club urged their members to participate.[19]

These data show that the movement became more complex organizationally as its ideas changed on what the most effective strategy would be. Interventions required only small coalitions; congressional lobbying, participation in complex and expensive NRC generic hearings and the need for more money and personnel led to coalitions with other already existing organizations; the growth of Critical Mass, a national coordinating group, allowed regional strategic planning and simultaneous actions nationwide. The use of civil disobedience brought another structural change—affinity groups. They were necessary for security and for training.

THE EFFECTS OF STRATEGY ON STRUCTURE

Strategy can create structure, and it can change it. New structures are occasionally created in order to make new strategies possible. When the Clamshell Alliance sought to engage in mass civil disobedience, it drew on already existing local groups but required that they re-form themselves into closely knit, small, and specially trained affinity groups to illegally occupy the plant site. Those groups that engaged only in legal demonstrations—and maintained the movement's activities while affinity group members were in jail— retained their previous form of organization.

A particular strategy may also foster a greater division of labor. In coalitions that file interventions, local groups frequently specialize in particular tasks. One may raise money, while another reads the nuclear scientific literature, and still another publicizes discoveries made during the intervention proceedings.

Repeated use of existing structures may strengthen them because participants become accustomed to working together and may compromise to facilitate their efforts. Student antinuclear groups often groomed themselves more conservatively to work with groups composed of middle-age, middle-class members.

THE EFFECTS OF STRUCTURE ON STRATEGY

The varied structure of the antinuclear movement gives it great strategic flexibility. Local groups may spontaneously engage in local actions without waiting for authorization from a central authority, and national groups may draw upon local members when they are needed for national actions. Formal organizations have established membership lists, funding sources, offices, and staffs with specialized expertise to facilitate long-range planning. Informal organizations are able to easily recruit people into them and offer the kind of working environment conducive to contributions of time and energy. One group within the movement can engage in spectacular and threatening tactics without all the others losing legitimacy. More conservative groups can use their access to decision makers and their knowledge of legal and lobbying tactics to achieve incremental gains without thereby compromising the ability of the other groups to use coercive means.

Not all movements are as fortunate as this one. Movements with little money or access to professional skills cannot file legal actions, nor can they easily generate publicity. Very small movements cannot draw on membership time necessary to run a boycott or a referendum. Movements with esoteric or only locally significant issues cannot attract the attention of decision makers without using tactics so threatening that the retaliation might well destroy the movement.

Movements with only one national organization or one type of group are limited in their options by the structure of that organization(s). If the national organization is centralized and hierarchical, good ideas developed at the grassroots level might die by the time they are approved (or not) by the national authority. Or they might fail to be implemented because no one is assigned that task. Their proponents within the organization are often accused of disloyalty or of undermining the movement organization if they pursue their ideas without central approval.

On the other hand, movements composed solely of small informal groups are limited to actions that can be performed by only a few people. Many local cells in the antinuclear movement can engage in educational campaigns, petitioning, local lobbying, or occasionally court battles; but they cannot organize national demonstrations or congressional lobbying. These can be coordinated only by national groups.

When these groups also have a bias against formal decision-making rules, they may be stymied by their inability to reach a consensus. Barkan[20] feels that the affinity groups used by the Clamshell Alliance, which made decisions by consensus, were unable to decide whether or not to make bail after being arrested at Seabrook.

Another problem with the small-group structure is that there is no way to prevent many groups from forming in the same locality, nor is there any way they can be forced to resolve differences between themselves. When there are several antinuclear groups in one area, each must compete with the others for the resources necessary to maintain the group—money, members, media time, legitimacy, community goodwill. If the groups are compatible, they can pool their resources and efforts. If not, these resources are split and the future of all the groups is made more tenuous. It is much more difficult to raise the people and goods necessary to successfully stage an action if groups are trying to discredit one another. In Nashville, Tennessee, in the mid-1970s when two major leaders could not agree on the proper goal, the Middle Tennessee movement was split. While the leaders managed to cooperate in some of their strategies, once their disagreement grew more heated, they halved the money, people, time, and goodwill available to each. Furthermore, their disagreement lost the movement many potential recruits because they were alienated by the acrimonious debate.

STRATEGIC SUCCESS AND STRUCTURE

Of course, strategies are seldom used simply to influence movement structure. Rather, they are performed to reach a goal. Therefore, the most often asked question of a strategy is "Does it work?" A strategy's success or failure not only affects the next strategic move but the life of the group sponsoring it. An important, visible failure can kill a whole movement;[21] a conspicuous success can recruit new members and move it toward long-run success in meeting its goals.

There is a debate among movement scholars about the most effective form of social movement structure. Some movement theorists say that formal organizations are most effective, or that movement organizations are formal, effective or not. Later movement thinkers, such as those using the natural history approach, agree.[22] Many modern movement scholars have taken the same position. For example, Killian says, "...it is more accurate to think...of a group of leaders, often a hierarchy, which plays a major part in guiding the movement from its inception." He further states that the "...lack of a unified structure can be a source of weakness."[23] Wilson[24] feels that a movement seeking efficiency will routinize its procedures, differentiate its subparts by function, and develop a hierarchy. McCarthy and Zald[25] add that movements with routinized resource flows tend to become oligarchic and bureaucratic. Turner and Killian[26] state that highly centralized, hierarchical, and disciplined structures are best in conflict situations.

The most thorough attempt to empirically verify this view was by Gamson,[27] who statistically compared fifty-three "change organizations" to determine the characteristics associated with success. He found that bureaucracies and centralized organizations were more successful than non-bureaucratic or uncentralized structures. Organizations that were both bureaucratic and centralized were most often successful; those with neither feature were seldom successful. He also observed that centralized structures are seldom factionalized. Bureaucratic organizations are more likely to be factionalized than centralized. Factionalized movements are associated with failure.

Jack Goldstone reexamined Gamson's data statistically. "When data on the rates of protest group success are reanalyzed, no effect of organizational or tactical parameters is evident." Rather, he finds that the timing of movement successes in relation to national crises is more important, but timing is "independent of the organization and tactics of the protest group."[28] Gamson disagrees, saying that Goldstone is unnecessarily quibbling about the definitions of the terms used as a basis for the analysis. Gamson also points out that he, too, examined the timing of movement challenges and successes, finding that challenges made during wars were more likely to yield new advantages, though this was not true for the 1930s depression, an economic emergency.[29]

Since the antinuclear movement has a varied structure, we can compare its components to see which organizational form was more successful. One of the first extensively used strategies was interventions before local, state, and federal hearing boards and suits against utilities' condemning land for plant sites. Almost none[30] of these actions stopped plant construction or operation more than temporarily. A few suits caused the designs of the plants to be changed to enhance safety, some plants were delayed, and the Natural Resources Defense Council pressured the federal government to study the problem of nuclear waste disposal. Because of the high failure rate of interventions, many of the small organizations that sponsored them died, exhausted and impoverished by their efforts.

The small local groups also collected signatures on petitions opposing nuclear plants and promoting solar energy development. These were computerized by congressional district by a Washington office allied with the Nader organizations in 1973 and sent to state and national representatives to persuade them to shift money from nuclear development to solar energy research. The Taskforce Against Nuclear Pollution also wanted a federal law banning nuclear plant construction.[31] These efforts generated more federal money for solar research efforts and hampered governmental promotion of nuclear plant construction. However, many nuclear opponents think that the decline in the number of nuclear plants utilities planned to build was due more to the price and scarcity of loan money and the unwillingness of stockholders to sink large sums into plants whose efficiency and cost were being strongly questioned than to the efforts of the antinuclear movement.

The two strategies discussed above were often used by small local groups, and by small national* organizations. Generally, the latter groups were more successful at legal procedures than the local ones. This is probably because the national structures could command better-qualified and experienced scientific and legal experts than could the local cells. While petitions to local zoning boards, county courts, or state water quality commissions had been used by local groups since their beginnings, it was not until the national efforts and statewide referendum votes were used that the federal bureaucracy began to soften its previously favorable estimations of nuclear power plants. Referenda and recall votes failed in most states, however, and efforts to convert legisla-

---

* "National" antinuclear organizations are actually small staffs supported by people from all over the United States. These organizations plan nationwide activities and run a national information network (i.e., they serve the local groups). Only occasionally do they act independently of the local cells.

tures to the antinuclear view were generally unsuccessful. And the Reagan administration is enthusiastic about nuclear energy. Thus, efforts to change the political climate from pronuclear to antinuclear have failed in most cases and have worked only temporarily on the national political level.

The last major strategy used by the antinuclear movement is demonstrations. They have been used since the movement's beginning, but early protest rallies were small and local. Later ones have been large with considerable media attention, but their effect on public opinion has been slight.[32]

The movement itself is still strong. While it has been infiltrated and spied upon,[33] it has not stopped. And while there has been some loss of leaders and followers, more people have been recruited. Indeed, if there is one thing in which small local cells excel, it is recruiting. Despite a fairly high dropout rate, the movement has managed to grow through the years, though individuals tend to alternate active with passive periods.

The movement has demonstrated innovation in strategy and organizational form. When court suits and interventions did not work, some groups turned the proceedings into guerrilla theater by making speeches before judges or hearing panels, mocking them, bringing people dressed as cows to testify before the hearings, and recruiting brass band parades to make it impossible for the hearings to continue. One opponent even tore down a utility weather tower and converted his trial for vandalism into a forum to express his antinuclear opinions,[34] becoming a movement hero. In addition, if a strategy or structure works in one place, other groups elsewhere are likely to adopt it. The Clamshell Alliance's use of civil disobedience has inspired others to do so, and their idea of affinity groups has also spread.

But the widespread use of affinity groups and civil disobedience may have become maladaptive. While the New England groups did stage a number of protests after the Three Mile Island nuclear plant accident, only one (at Shoreham, New York) attracted as many as twenty thousand people. The others drew only two or three thousand spectators. This is probably because the public associates civil disobedience with "hippies" and others they consider undersirable. Additionally, repetition has made the media tired of antinuclear demonstrations so that they have stopped reporting the reasons for the protests and limited themselves to the number of arrests and to violent episodes.[35] When affinity groups are not engaged in civil disobedience, they have often stagnated. Because they became bored and disillusioned by the lack of movement success, many members dropped out, and individuals who stayed became leaders by default. Thus their dependence on civil disobedience and demonstrations has stalled the New England groups.[36]

Is the movement hampered by its lack of a central decision-making body and by having no universal set of decision-making rules? Probably. This is because it cannot act rapidly as a whole; no one can legitimately speak for the whole movement, nor can anyone effectively decide what all movement groups should do. Therefore, the movement's reaction to such potential bonanzas as the Three Mile Island accident is often slow.[37] Unlike the mass student strikes and demonstrations organized in a week for most U.S. college campuses following President Nixon's announcement of the Cambodian invasion in 1970, the large demonstrations following the Three Mile Island accident were slowly organized and were not staged nationwide. Rather, in the antinuclear movement large protests against continued use of nuclear reactors for power generation were concentrated in the Northeast, with people coming from all over the East to attend. The first large demonstration occurred over a month after the accident.

The antinuclear movement's lack of growth in 1981 may also be due to a slowdown in the construction of nuclear plants resulting from a lessened demand for electricity in the United States and the skepticism of utility stockholders about the plants' reliability. Ironically, the antinuclear movement appears stymied because its issue is disappearing!

NOTES

1. Max Weber, *The Theory of Social and Economic Organization*, edited and introduced by Talcott Parsons (New York: Free Press, 1947) pp. 364–72.
2. William Gamson, *The Strategy of Social Protest* (Homewood Ill.: Dorsey Press, 1975), pp. 91–93, 105.
3. Luther Gerlach and Virgina Hine, *People, Power, Change* (Indianapolis: Bobbs-Merrill, 1970).
4. Ibid., p. 41.
5. Virginia Hine and Luther Gerlach, "Many Concernerd, Few Committed," *Natural History* 79 (1970): 16.
6. Anna Gyorgy and Friends, *No Nukes: Everyone's Guide to Nuclear Power* (Boston: South End Press, 1979), pp. 14–15.
7. Luther Gerlach, "Movements of Revolutionary Change," Chapter 8 in the volume.
8. Ibid.
9. "Group Formed to Fight Nuclear Power Stations," *Philadelphia Inquirer*, 6 December 1970; *People and Power/Watch on the AEC*, November 1973, p. 3; "More Conservation Units Join Yankee Control Fight," *Burlington Free Press*, 14 September 1970; Dorothy Nelkin, *Nuclear Power and Its Critics: The Cayuga Lake Controversy* (Ithaca: Cornell University Press, 1971), Chap. 3. Steve Ebbin and Raphael Kasper, *Citizen Groups and the Nuclear Power Controversy: Uses of Scientific and Technological Information* (Cambridge, Mass.: MIT Press, 1974), pp. 59–65, 293.
10. "Maine A-Plant Capacity Limit Pressed," *Boston Globe*, 6 July 1972; Ebbin and Kasper, *Citizen Groups*, pp. 98–107, 59–65; 293; *Nuclear Opponents*, Winter 1973, p. 2; and *Nuclear Opponents*, March/April 1975, p. 5.
11. *Critical Mass*, April 1975, p. 12.
12. *Nuclear Opponents*, March/April 1975, p. 5; *St. Louis Post-Dispatch*, 7 August 1973.
13. Gyorgy, *No Nukes*, pp. 384–385. The states included Iowa, Vermont, New York, Pennsylvania, Nebraska, Kansas, and Missouri. *Watch on the AEC*, 8 February 1974, p. 1.
14. Gyorgy, *No Nukes*, pp. 324–325.
15. Ibid., p. 397.
16. Ibid.
17. Ibid. Two to three thousand protestors, organized in affinity groups by the Abalone Alliance in California, are using civil disobedience to protest the anticipated licencing to operate the Diablo Canyon nuclear plant at San Luis Obispo. Almost 300 were arrested on 15 September 1981. Thus this form of organization continues to be used for mass civil disobedience in the United State.

18. Ibid.

19. Anthony Ladd, Thomas Hood, and Kent Van Lierre, "Ideological Strands in the Anti-Nuclear Movement: Consensus and Diversity" (paper given at the meetings of the Popular Culture Association, April 1980), note 4.

20. Steve Barkan, "Strategic, Tactical and Organizational Dilemmas of the Protest Movement against Nuclear Power," *Social Problems* 27 (1979): 27.

21. Maurice Jackson *et al.* "The Failure of an Incipient Social Movement," *Pacific Sociological Review* 3 (1960): 35–40.

22. The natural history approach involves the identification of stages of movement growth and the factors necessary for a movement to go from stage to stage. These are determined by examining the histories of social movements. Examples of authors using this approach are Carl Dawson and Warner Gettys, *Introduction to Sociology* (New York: Ronald Press, 1935); Rex Hopper, "Revolutionary Process: A Frame of Reference for the Study of Revolutionary Movements," *Social Forces* 28 (1950): 272–79; and Theodore J. Lowi, *The Politics of Disorder* (New York: Basic Books, 1971).

23. Lewis Killian, "Social Movements: A Review of the Field," in *Social Movements: A Reader and Source Book*, ed. Robert Evans, (Chicago: Rand McNally, 1973), p. 30.

24. John Wilson, *Introduction to Social Movements* (New York: Basic Books, 1973), p. 334.

25. John McCarthy and Mayer Zald, "Toward a Resource Mobilization Theory of Social Movement Organization" (paper delivered to the Southern Sociological Society, April 1973), p. 36.

26. Ralph Turner and Lewis Killian, *Collective Behavior* (Englewood Cliffs, N.J.: Prentice-Hall, 1972), p. 398.

27. William Gamson, *The Strategy of Social Protest* (Homewood, Ill.: Dorsey Press 1975), pp. 91–93, 105.

28. Jack Goldstone, "The Weakness of Organization: A New Look at Gamson's *The Strategy of Social Protest*," *American Journal of Sociology* 85 (1980): 1017.

29. William Gamson, "Understanding the Careers of Challenging Groups: A Commentary on Goldstone," *American Journal of Sociology* 85 (1980): 1017.

30. Two plants have been stopped by interventions—the Indian Head plant in New York and Bodega Head in California. Gyorgy *No Nukes*, p. 16.

31. Ralph Nader, "Franklin Gage, A Tough Kid, Fighting Atoms," *The Tennessean*, 30 April 1975, p. 9.

32. In the 1976 Gallup poll, 71 percent of those asked wanted more nuclear plants built to ensure adequate electricity supplies for the United States; the April 1979 poll (done less than a month after the Three Mile Island accident) showed that 63 percent wanted them. In 1976, 40 percent wanted a cutback in nuclear plant operations until safer standards of operation were adopted; in the 1979 poll, 66 percent of the sample wanted the same thing. The January 1980 Gallup poll showed that 55 percent of those asked felt "nuclear operations should be cut back until stricter regulations can be put into effect," and 30 percent felt that nuclear plants were "safe enough with present safety regulations." *The Gallup Opinion Index*, no. 134 (1976): 14; *The Gallup Opinion Index*, no. 165 (1979): 1–2; *The Gallup Opinion Index*, no. 174 (1980): 21–22.

Harris polls show a slowly declining support for nuclear plants from the 60 percent level in March 1975 to a low of just over 40 percent in October 1979. By January 1980 the poll showed the support level at about 50 percent. Harris asked, "In general, do you favor or oppose the building of more nuclear power plants in the United States?" See Morris W. Firebaugh, "Public Attitudes and Information on the Nuclear Option," *Oak Ridge Associated Universities Institute for Energy Analysis Report*, no. 80–6(M) (May 1980): 3.

33. Barkan, "Strategic, Tactical, and Organizational Dilemmas," p. 34; Mark Dowie, "Atomic Psyche Out," *Mother Jones* 6 (1981): 54.
34. Gyorgy, *No Nukes*, pp. 393–94.
35. Stephen Vogel, "The Limits of Protest: A Critique of the Anti-Nuclear Movement," *Socialist Review* 10 (1980): 125.
36. Ibid., pp. 130–31.
37. In March 1979, the Three Mile Island nuclear power plant had a severe accident: ". . . the cooling water system . . . went awry, the fuel rods blistered, a hydrogen bubble began to form, radioactive steam began to escape, infants and pregnant women were evacuated from the area . . ." See Lloyd Shearer, "Credibility Crisis," *Parade*, 3 June 1979, p. 15.

10

Countercultural Organizations and Bureaucracy: Limits on the Revolution

Leonard Davidson

Between 9:30 and 10:30 on a Monday morning, eight young men and women walk into an old frame house near downtown Boston. When the last person arrives, the group members—looking like a noisy bunch of camp counselors reunited after a winter apart—arrange themselves in a circle on the floor to begin their weekly "organizational meeting." One woman, who happens to be sitting closest to the blackboard, gets up to record agenda items for the meeting: "OK, what should we talk about?" About ten items, such as "funding," "new members," and "radio show appearances" are suggested by the eight participants. But before getting to the agenda, someone suggests, "Preprocessing." The group acknowledges the idea, quiets down, and a man in a short beard brightens up, a big smile on his face. "I'll go first," he beams. "Well, I finally did it. I saw Susan again and she was glad to see me! I feel really on a cloud today."

"OK!" "Yeah!" and "All right!" resound from the other group members, all obviously familiar with Susan and glad she and Larry are together again.

A small woman speaks up. "I just feel sort of here today—no really strong feelings."

"I finally wrote that article about the commune near Rockport," adds the next person.

The author wishes to thank the many members of the alternative organizations who contributed to this endeavor, the researchers who collaborated in this investigation, and John Van Maanen, Dennis Bumstead, and Rosabeth Moss Kanter, who commented on earlier drafts of this article.

"I feel sexy today."

"I worked on my bike over the weekend." ...

The members of Alternative Living Service (ALS) have begun their workday.

ALS facilitates the operation of New England communes and might be called a countercultural organization. Its goals revolve around social change and actualization of members and do not focus on profit. Further, its internal structure is set up to avoid bureaucracy and foster community. As can be seen in the introductory narrative, at a work meeting specialized roles are avoided, time schedules are flexible, and a sincere personal concern for other members is apparent.

These and other aspects of work life at ALS are different from the workings of "traditional" organizations. In fact, the term *counterculture* implies a way of life different or even opposite from that of the mainstream culture. But are countercultural organizations such as ALS as revolutionary as they are portrayed in media? What problems do such organizations face in posing an alternative to mainstream institutional settings?

These broad questions were addressed by examining ALS and seven other alternative organizations. These organizations, which consisted of free schools and alternative counseling, employment, housing, and neighborhood planning centers, were studied by a group of six graduate students in a course led by the author. (A brief description of the organizations studied appears at the end of the chapter.) Members of our research team involved themselves in these organizations as participant-observers or as periodic outside observers for periods ranging from three months to two years. Our research was exploratory in nature and aimed at drawing inductive generalization about the defining characteristics and functioning of alternative organizations.

In defining these organizations as countercultural we were able to elaborate a set of organizational goals and values and a philosophy of organization structure that were consistently demonstrated across all eight organizations. The goals involved social change, member actualization, and sense of community; the structure was one that attempted to be nonbureaucratic.

This set of goals and structure stands in contrast to the goals and structural elements of traditional work organizations. In this sense they are the aspects of organizational life that constitute a revolutionary alternative to mainstream organizations. Many participants expressed this desire to present an option to organizations in the wider society. This was illustrated by a member of Employment Information Service, (EIS) who stated:

> About 75 to 100 people come into EIS weekly—mostly college people. We've thought about getting to others [noncollege] but haven't yet. We want to show people that there's something else they can do besides regular jobs.

The sentiment was also reflected by a member of Alternative Living Service, who claimed, "A really good part of the counterculture is expanding out and serving, and bringing other people in."

In providing services, these eight organizations could thus be seen as rivals to traditional organizations: To look for a job a person could go to Snelling and Snelling or to Employment Information Service; City Hospital or Group

Center (GC) offered encounter group experiences; housing could be obtained through a realty firm or Alternative Living Service; children could be educated in the public school system or the Community Free School (CFS).

FORCES TOWARD EMERGENCE: REACTION AGAINST BUREAUCRACY

The forces leading to the emergence of these alternative organizations can be better understood by examining member accounts of why the organizations were formed and theorists' statements about the origination of the counterculture.

In most cases, members claimed that the organizations emerged from traditional organizations as a reaction against existing organizational goals and structures. Four organizations originated, at least in part, from churches and religious organizations (ALS, CS, CFS, EIS); two from universities (Free Form Free School [FFFS], Community Action Experiment [CAE]; and one from a hospital (GC). Artistic Free School didn't originate from a particular organization but as a reaction against a group of organizations—booking agencies and agents. AFS was set up by artists who were unhappy with employment procedures in obtaining bookings.

A dominant reason for starting most of the organizations was a member desire to satisfy needs for actualization and social change that could not be met within the original structure. Thus, participants in Group Center and Counseling Service noted:

> Group Center was started by some friends who didn't like mental health work as practiced in hospitals. They were aides at Central Hospital who weren't given a chance to use their skills. They didn't have M.D.'s or Ph.D.'s.

> Counseling Service was started when two guys who ran coffee houses funded by the Diocese wanted to do more.

These comments reflect a common countercultural theme: the reaction against bureaucratic organization structures that limit human expression and relationships. The hospital aides and administrators of a church youth program felt constrained by hierarchically imposed role requirements that limited their organizational contributions. While such constraints are the foundations of bureaucratic organizational functioning, they are also a prime reason for the emergence of countercultural organizations. Many members expressed this point of view in discussing their reasons for joining alternative organizations.

This reaction against inhuman bureaucratic structures and movement toward actualization and community permeates writing on the counterculture. It is clearly seen, for example, in the work of Roszak (1969) and Reich (1970), who euphemistically discuss youth's alienation from the "technocracy," the "machine," and the "corporate state" that control American life. Slater (1970) also describes the cultural malaise that stems from our existence in work and home environments that stifle community, human engagement, and interdependence. According to Roberts (1971), the disaffection of the young from such bureaucratic environments has led to the growth of communal ventures—societies that are "consciously antibureaucractic in structure" (p. 13).

Thus, in both the theorists' writings and in our present definitional efforts, there appears to be some consistency in the alternative goals and structures proposed. But in exploring what is new and unique in countercultural organizations we also discovered an organizational characteristic that is very old. This organizational property often conflicted with the goals and structural elements that made the countercultural organizations revolutionary. The characteristic is the pressure toward bureaucracy that is inherent in any formal organization.

AN INCESSANT TREND TOWARD BUREAUCRACY?

The predominant form of organization structure found in traditional organizations can be identified as bureaucratic. Though organizational officials often profess an attempt to get away from bureaucratic structures, and organizations theorists and change agents frequently advocate the movement toward nonbureaucratic forms (e.g., Bennis 1966,[*] Argyris 1964, Myers 1970, Likert 1967, Herzberg 1966), a body of sociological evidence argues that bureaucracy is inevitable. For instance, Perrow (1970) claims that there is an "incessant trend toward bureaucracy":

> Nonbureaucratic organizations which are successful grow in size and stability; introduce economies of scale and complex control devices; reduce the skill level or introduce ever more laborsaving, efficient machinery; attempt to manage demand through advertising, monopoly, and collusion to stabilize their environment; and eventually they become profitable and bureaucratic. . . . Thus, the thrust is to routinize, limit uncertainty, increase predictability, and centralize functions and controls. Whether the lure is security, power, growth, or profits, and whether the field is government, industry, culture, or welfare, bureaucratization proceeds apace (pp. 66–67).

The idea of an incessant trend toward bureaucracy is not new, of course. In 1915 Michels presented the now classic "iron law of oligarchy"; that is, leaders in large-scale organizations inevitably coopt the democratic structures and revolutionary zeal that characterize organizational origination. An oligarchy eventually forms, more dedicated to maintenance of leader power and organizational survival than to the original organizational mission. Such dynamics of formalization and displacement of mission to organizational survival have been noted in a literature review on voluntary organizations (Smith and Freedman 1971).

Because countercultural organizations are not as geared toward the goals Perrow and other theorists mention—security, power, growth, profits—it is possible that they provide an exception to the incessant trend. In fact, they often define themselves as countercultural simply because they are trying to

---

* Though Bennis originally viewed democratic organization structures as inevitable, he later reconsidered these views in a most interesting article, "A Funny Thing Happened on the Way to the Future" (Bennis 1970).

avoid bureaucracy. This is by no means an easy task, and in many ways the attempt to stay nonbureaucratic is the key developmental problem these organizations face.

Some of the central elements of the bureaucratic form of organization structure include selection of members via technical competence, impersonality of interpersonal relations, division of labor, hierarchy of authority, and increasing size. Examining how the alternative organizations dealt with these issues should be instructive on two levels; theoretically, to elaborate bureaucracy theory, and practically, to understand the operational problems of countercultural organizations.

SELECTION OF MEMBERS BY TECHNICAL COMPETENCE

While traditional organizations openly stress their desire for increasing levels of member technical expertise (as seen in typical recruitment, selection, and training procedures), alternative organizations seemed to experience conflict on this issue. This was apparent in the heated discussions often engaged in concerning professionalism. Professionalism can be seen as a licensing procedure to ensure human competence. Most of the organizations respected the notion of competence but rebelled against mainstream standards and procedures in its measurement and development.

The four organizations that required some competence in group dynamics and counseling originally accepted members on an informal basis. They took people with whom they had personal ties ("at first it grew by people coming in who knew someone else") and/or who earned acceptance by involving themselves in the organization's activities. These informal mechanisms were depended on while the organizations were small or when everyone entering was of the minimum competence level. In time, however, the two largest organizations adopted "intricate selection procedures" (Counseling Service) and "controls" (Group Center). The development of these mechanisms partially supports the hypothesis of an incessant trend toward bureaucracy. Such mechanisms were seen as necessary to organizational survival: "There are controls in Group Center. Drop-In and People Center [other group centers] fell apart because there were not good controls. We're not nonselective. There are bylaws which we've recently changed."

In effect, these organizations became their own licensing institutions. Nevertheless, they differed from professional licensing in an important respect, since they usually felt that organizational evaluations of experience or motivation were more important than formal outside certification. Along these lines they claimed:

Degrees aren't needed to lead a group [Group Center].
Our message is you don't need a degree to relate to people. Most people at Counseling Service have degrees but our feeling is "so what!" They'd have to show why that degree is of value rather than just having it . . . . We don't feel that a degree is important and we bill ourselves as paraprofessionals.

In principle, the mechanism used instead of degrees for establishing competence was open communication and feedback. In practice this was often difficult to carry out. If communication was not sufficient, problems could develop, as when part-time volunteers did not receive enough information to know where they stood. For instance, in one organization the staff did not approve of a volunteer's work but had difficulty getting that across. The volunteer eventually left, resolving the problem.

In any case, technical competence was not the most strongly held value in counterculture. One organization member told how competence conflicted with the value of community when the organization selected an outside person over a volunteer for a paid position:

> At the Friday meeting I said that's putting organizational values above individual values—we weren't rewarding a loyal part of the community [the volunteer]. They wanted to get someone who would be more competent. Phil [the volunteer] could have been good if you worked with him, but Jim wanted someone with quality. For me it's not competence but being capable of growing into the job. *We'd be slower in going on as an organization, but we'd be together as a group* [italics added].

Thus it appears that the organizations experienced problems because they had difficulty coming to terms with the "technical competence" element of organization structure. Though some members were selected and evaluated on a competence basis, the selection standards and evaluation procedures were less formalized than in traditional organizations. Further, though all organizations relied on professionals, professional techniques, and/or professionally developed information to some extent, there was great ambivalence toward the selection of "experts." Often the ambivalence was founded in the view that expertise was inconsistent with community and personal relationships. This desire for personal relations contrasts with the second key element of bureaucracy: impersonality.

IMPERSONALITY OF INTERPERSONAL RELATIONS

A common value in alternative organizations was that people rather than things had prime importance and that people should be dealt with in a personal way. Professional relationships were often seen as violating these norms, lowering the person being served into an object—a subject, client, or patient. Moreover, it was felt that by giving one's intellectual or technical self, but withholding his emotional self, the professional was a model of detachment. Thus a member of Employment Information Service revealed conflicts about using professional techniques in the organization:

> There is some resistance in EIS to technique, professional counseling methods like fantasy trips, though Ellen and I want to use some. Some members criticize professionalism and the detachment that results between client and counselor.

Another illustration of this concern for personal relationships was the resistance we met from a few organizations when we proposed doing "research"—something that is typically done in a very detached, professional way. We were often able to interact with the organizations, however, because we weren't detached—at least one of us had close ties with four of the organizations.

In addition, we offered feedback so that we would not be obtaining all the benefit of the relationship.

Nevertheless, the resistance to uninvolved outsiders was strong, and was shown by the answer we got from a Community Action Experiment member about attending a future meeting:

> No—not really. We made a policy that you must ask a week in advance to attend the next week's meeting. We all agreed in the beginning that this wouldn't be for studying the community like some sociologists do.

Personal interaction was not only important in relationships with outsiders; the focus on personal relations was an essential part of internal organizational functioning. This was made explicit by many organization members who described "sense of community," "friendship," or "I liked the people" as their most important reasons for joining the organizations. In fact, as already noted, community involvement was an important organizational goal—often as important as the more obvious 'task" of the organization. The balance between these two goals was precarious, however. Bureaucracy was a condition in which the balance was destroyed—the task overwhelming the members' personal relationships.

To maintain the close relations in a large alternative organization, a great deal of personal communication was required, so much that the task sometimes suffered. Counseling Service described the problem as follows:

> We resolve conflicts by talking them out. So far it has always been equitable. If a person is upset he can get it out. He can say, "I don't like the way you said that." However this is very time-consuming and *there's always a pull to do the work versus talking and analyzing* [italics added].

In smaller organizations, instead of a task orientation dominating, the balance was sometimes tipped in favor of personal involvement. Thus a member of Employment Information Service revealed, "It sometimes seems like we talk more to each other than to outsiders [i.e., clients]."

The most extreme example of an organization with a dominant interpersonal orientation was Free Form Free School. In FFFS, schedules and rules were often ignored, classes were frequently canceled, turnover of leaders was rapid, and the task part of meetings would often be neglected as jugs of wine were passed around. Nevertheless (or because of this), the organization was loved by its members and was successful for a time: "Free Form was so mystical just that it existed, that it's hard to believe it really happened sometimes."

Organizations that were larger than FFFS tried many other mechanisms to maintain personal relations. Both Alternative Living Service and Counseling Service used decentralization to set up separate autonomous departments. Decentralization allowed interaction in the small group, though involvement with the rest of the organization decreased. Sitting in the tiny office of the Education Division, a member of CS described this as follows:

> Most people in Counseling Service say there are serious problems in how much bureaucracy is needed, how to select people, who should make decisions. These

things are thought of often. In the Education Division we only have four people and can always make consensus decisions.

In addition to decentralization, a few organizations would foster interpersonal involvement by setting up "community days" in which the whole organization would go away for a weekend of recreation. Sensitivity training techniques were sometimes used at these weekend retreats. Other organizations obtained a balance in task and interpersonal involvement by holding separate task and interpersonal meetings each week, organizing cooperative living arrangements for members, and sponsoring open houses, rent strikes, potluck suppers, health care services, and other activities.

All these mechanisms were geared toward a major purpose: the avoidance of the impersonality aspect of bureaucracy. The organizations were largely successful in this regard, but the personal emphasis often was obtained at a cost of decreased time for the major organizational task. Still other elements of bureaucracy that were generally overcome at the price of task efficiency were division of labor and hierarchy of authority.

DIVISION OF LABOR AND HIERARCHY OF AUTHORITY

While traditional organizations divide jobs via specialized roles, job descriptions, and areas of responsibility, the alternative organizations tried very hard to do the work in as equally shared a manner as possible. They generally tried to avoid the typical pyramidical distribution of authority in dividing up activities. "The problem with large organizations is staying nonhierarchical" was a typical member comment heard along these lines. Illustrations of this desire for egalitarian work structures were readily observed in Community Free School and Group Center, where the entire group of parents (CFS) and group leaders (GC) acted as the final decision-making bodies. In fact, most organizations spoke of "consensus" as the preferred mode of decision making. In addition, pay rates were usually equal for all permanent (nonvolunteer) organization members, further promoting egalitarianism.

The concern for a structure free of hierarchy and specialization was well illustrated in Employment Information Service's literature on their operation:

> In the same (collective) way decisions are made, so should the work be done, right? Pretty close. When EIS first formed, we had specialists!! Each person would pretty much handle one aspect of the office work. This wasn't real great, because sometimes a person would split, and no one left would be able to pick up on his/her work. We have since (partly from trying to break down female/male roles) moved toward sharing of all routine office work. The only exceptions to this deal mostly with work requiring some temporary continuity (from doing rough drafts of articles to taking care of the books) where it's very hard to work with more than one person at a time—in this case we try to rotate the responsibility.

Despite using numerous methods aimed at equality in work, some hierarchy and specialization of task inevitably took place. An EIS member indicated, almost in a confessional tone, "We try not to, but we get into roles—

one person takes care of funding more than others. But generally it's a collective decision-making process."

In a few cases, the organizations developed somewhat specialized roles of coordinators, supervisors, and directors. Counseling Service had a formal organization chart, and Community Action Experiment often found students and neighborhood residents divided into roles according to skills—students doing data analysis and residents canvassing. These divisions of the work were usually met with ambivalence even when it was clear that tasks were better accomplished with some specialization and hierarchy. The case of Free Form Free School was illustrative. With their system of volunteer teachers and students attending on an irregular basis, it was apparent that a centralized structure worked better for getting daily tasks accomplished. Yet they tried to decentralize to avoid "elitism":

> When one or two or four tight people ran Free Form it was OK. But when we tried to decentralize it was poor. The teachers and students worked full time and came here just for classes. It was supposed to be that the teachers and students would do the work of cleaning, paying rent, running the library, answering the phone. Unfortunately we learned that people do things only when they're told. The people at the core of Free Form didn't do work besides Free Form, but found ways to survive. It was an elite core and we used to talk about elitism.

This concern with elitism prevented the leadership from stabilizing, and Free Form went through many cycles as leaders and structures changed. Organizational activity was erratic and frequently nonexistent during the low periods of the cycles. While a traditional organization would have cemented some structure to obtain stability and continuity, Free Form was less concerned with permanence. The organization dissipated after two-and-a-half erratic but enjoyable years.

The distaste for centralized, specialized, elitist structures was also reflected in the previously mentioned ambivalence toward professionalism. Professionals could cause clients and nonprofessional organization members to feel dependent and powerless. This issue was especially relevant to working-class organizations where "being against professionals is a matter of power since an articulate person can shut us up."

Thus in Community Free School the principal and nonparent teachers were *not* given a vote on the board that controlled the school. The board was composed of parents only. One parent described how this policy was established: "The parents said we, and not the educators, will run the school, and three quarters of the educators who were at the meeting left. In this way we eliminated people who wanted to be researchers, consultants, and so on."

Similarly, over the years Community Action Experiment redefined the roles of its professional community planners from decision makers to advisers. Techniques of doing the work changed so that community members had more control of the neighborhood planning activities. With the changed techniques and roles, it was reported that the professionals also changed personally. They changed their assumptions about the community people, organizational allegiances, and manner of talking. In these ways the working-class organizations partially avoided hierarchies in which the best educated resided at the top.

Ironically, if the organization was successful at developing an egalitarian structure and accomplishing its task, it met further problems. With success came pressures toward increasing size, the final element of bureaucracy.

SIZE AND GROWTH

As has been shown, these organizations saw themselves as work alternatives, and thus in a broad sense they wanted to change society. To reach more people and provide more services, however, it was generally required that the organizations grow. Because organizational growth was inevitably coordinated via bureaucratic mechanisms such as rules, hierarchy, and departmentalization, members of the organizations were wary of increases in size as they became well known and successful. As a result, many organizations grew cautiously if at all. For instance, a member felt that Employment Information Service should not grow any more due to increasing bureaucracy:

> When this organization grew from just four to eight I saw differences in staff meetings, and I don't feel positively about EIS growing more. Growth would bring more committees, less interpersonal involvement, and separate decentralized organizations.

A cautious attitude toward growth was also expressed at Group Center: "There has been a great deal of growth since September and we don't know if we want to grow. Now we have committees to make decisions that were previously done by the whole community."

Only Artistic Free School clearly wanted to expand. They had a more centralized structure in which five coordinators made decisions, and growth would not have introduced more impersonal and bureaucratic mechanisms into their organization structure. Therefore it was not growth per se but the bureaucratic forms that growth inevitably introduced that were seen as undesirable.

The ambivalence toward growth put the organizations in an unstable position. With expansion would come specialized positions for directors, fund raisers, and others who could attempt some control over the environment. But the costs of such stability appeared great to organization members, who suspected that stabilization would bring cooptation of mission and structure. Most organizations instead lived with instability and ambivalence. A member of Counseling Service described this problem of organizational instability when he reflected: "We think about whether we should be a demonstration project or ongoing, and if so, where the funds would come from. It's foolish to think of careers here right now."

CONCLUSIONS

Growth was one of the key political enigmas that countercultural organizations faced: To change society required expansion and some stabilization of organizational activities, but such expansion might change the nonbureaucratic character of the alternative organizations. The problems of growth, hierarchy, specialization, impersonality, and technical competence were not black-and-white issues, however—they were problems of degree. While organization members varied in their tolerance for bureaucracy, they resisted these structural features when they reached a subjective point—a point where the organization began to look and feel like a traditional organization.

In general, it must be concluded that on most dimensions, this sample of eight organizations was successful in containing the growth of bureaucratic structures. Thus they provide an exception to the "incessant trend" noted in the literature.* Limited task accomplishment, a precarious existence, and the diversion of a great deal of organizational resources to internal maintenance were the costs of this exceptional status.

It may be inappropriate to refer to these outcomes as "costs" because task accomplishment, permanence, and efficiency were not necessarily key goals for these organizations. I am suggesting that this analysis of bureaucracy uncovers a dilemma basic to countercultural organizations. It is this: Can an organization be set up to efficiently provide goods and services *and* serve as a setting that fosters values of community and personal growth? In the early 1900s, Weber portrayed bureaucracy as the most efficient form of organization ever devised; he has yet to be proven wrong. In this light, the alternative organizations that moved toward formalization were succeeding as organizations in the usual sense—that is, they were becoming more efficient producers of goods and services. Nevertheless a formalized organization was viewed derisively in the counterculture. Because of its impersonality and specialization, it had failed as a dispenser of new human values.

This dilemma is not new. In analyzing nineteenth-century utopian communities, Kanter (1972) pointed out that

> they attempted both to express values and to implement practical concerns in a single social unit. Criticisms have been leveled at utopian communities to the effect that social life cannot be both "human" and "efficient," that brotherhood and economics do not mix, that it is impossible both to satisfy individual needs and to work toward the collective good, and that value expression is incompatible with pragmatism. (p. 148)

Thus today's countercultural organizations find themselves in an ambiguous position similar to that experienced by utopian communities over a hundred years ago. It is interesting to note that the cultural forces stimulating these alternative ventures may be more powerful today. Before the birth of nineteenth-century utopias, preindustrial America contained family and neighborhood units that shared in both community and economic life. Over the centuries there has been a progressive segmentation of these social realms. Due to such recent developments as bureaucracy, nuclear families, and suburbia, the segmentation of community and work in modern America has become extremely severe. Countercultural organizations not only attempt to provide products and services but they attempt to rectify this split. This is an important factor differentiating them from modern business organizations.

In fact, referring to these social units as "organizations" may be a misnomer. Schein (1970) provides an elementary definition of an organization as

---

* For a portrait of an exception among labor unions, see Lipset's (1952) discussion of the International Typographical Union.

172

"the rational coordination of the activities of a number of people for the achievement of some common explicit purpose or goal, through division of labor and function, and through a hierarchy of authority and responsibility."

Even this basic definition fails to fit alternative organizations in important ways. Their avoidance of division of labor and their nonhierarchical distribution of authority set them apart from traditional organizations and generate the important norms of community and equality so central to their character. Thus, in trying to understand and evaluate these social units, new criteria may be necessary. Typical evaluations of organizational effectiveness such as stability, productivity, and adaptability to external environments are only partially applicable to social units emphasizing social change, individual actualization, and community.

Though they play the organization game by new rules, the alternatives interact with traditional organizations, which do not. Thus the alternatives often find themselves literally and figuratively in the shadow of more powerful traditional organizations, and they face problems in determining how independent they might be of this external environment. For instance, since the eight organizations studied were typically born as outgrowths of traditional organizations, the parent organization often had an immediate influence on member composition, organizational policies, and funding.

Though the influence of parent organizations lessened over time, funding remained a particularly difficult issue for the alternatives. Years after origination, most organizations were forced to continue their reliance on outside institutions for support, and this dependence left them in a vulnerable position. Organizational activity fluctuated greatly as the availability of funding changed, and even when support was obtained, it usually came at a cost of purity of activities or conscience.

Another problem in dealing with the environment concerned the recruitment of committed members. Most members—particularly volunteers— divided their time between the countercultural organizations and traditional employment. The reason in almost all cases revolved around inadequate funding and the resultant minimal pay available in the alternative setting. Though members claimed a strong preference for their alternative employment, most found it economically impossible to avoid traditional employment completely.

A last environmental problem arose as the alternatives tried to interact with consumers of their products and services who did not identify with the counterculture. In offering drug education to teachers, recreational activities to neighborhood residents, mental health services to hospital patients, and educational programs to working-class families, the organizations frequently had difficulty meeting their aims because of suspicions of the counterculture that members of the "straight" society held.

Thus relations with the external environment— with funding institutions, the labor force, and consumers—posed serious problems for the alternatives. As with increases in bureaucracy, added interaction with the external environment usually increased task efficiency and organizational stability by regularizing inputs of money and labor and stabilizing a market for output. However, as with increased bureaucracy, increased environmental interaction lessened sense of community, member satisfaction, and psychological commitment. Members experienced a gradual loss of community as task accomplishment became more important than intraorganizational relations, and as the kind of work and style of doing work changed to meet funding agency and consumer demands. Organizations were faced with the dilemma of tailoring their activities toward the wider society and sacrificing their alternative character, or withdrawing into themselves and sacrificing task accomplishment and stability.*

FUTURE PATHS FOR ALTERNATIVE ORGANIZATIONS

How can the organizations deal with these dilemmas? Where will these social experiments lead? Based on the previous analysis, four possible paths for countercultural organizations can be suggested. First, the individual organizations can resist formalization toward bureaucratic structures and interaction with the wider society. Such organizations will develop few formal coordination devices and will of necessity be small. Generally they will manage themselves via informal interaction and consensus. Though an organization of five to ten members may be able to effectively provide a service, such an organization will be able to influence relatively few clients or customers. Further, it will lack the adaptive subsystems to ensure some permanence in its operation. Overall, such an organization, taken individually, will be ineffectual in influencing the wider society and will often dissipate in a short time.† Free Form Free School provides an example of such an organization.

At present, most countercultural ventures I have studied appear quite limited in scope and stability. In fact, many observers view all countercultural organizations this way, and with some reason. I recall an interaction I had with Saul Alinsky that is illustrative. At a lecture he gave, I responded to his discussion of community organizing against supermarkets by suggesting the countercultural alternative: Avoid the supermarket completely and start a food coop. Alinsky's reaction was that such actions are "small time"; substantially more people could benefit from a change in a supermarket's policies than from the formation of a coop.

---

* These findings parallel Kanter's (1972) analysis of nineteenth century utopian communities with an important exception. Kanter also found that increased interaction with the environment fostered production goals, lessened community feeling, and led to the dissolution of the utopias. Alternately, during the few years of the present study, countercultural organizations became *more stable* as they interacted with their environments. That is, as they more closely adjusted to the demands of funding agencies, consumers, and the labor market they became more stable as service and production *organizations*, but they too began to dissolve as value-oriented community settings. A similar example among the early utopias was the Oneida Community, which ceased to exist as a commune but became an enduring business organization.

One reason why countercultural organizations, unlike utopias, could not exist in isolation and poverty was that they were all located in cities and could not depend on farming for survival. Thus it is interesting to note that Free Form Free School, the organization that attempted to be most independent of the wider society, unsuccessfully tried to grow subsistence crops on a small plot of land next to their storefront center. FFFS was the only organization that dissolved during this investigation.

† Evidence indicates that the organizations with a total lack of structure will be the least stable. For instance, though speaking of communities and not work organizations, Kanter (1970) concludes that "the prospects for most of today's anarchistic communes are dim" (p. 78).

Alinsky's point is well taken—but leads to a second possible path. Just as in the first option, the organizations can resist formalization and internal growth but can become involved in an organizational growth of a new sort. Instead of expanding internally, these small organizations might aid *each other* and multiply through mechanisms such as associations, networks, and newsletters. A past member of Free Form Free School, the organization now defunct, expressed this poem of the 1960s. Sadly, but with a glimmer of excitement still in his voice, he reminisced:

> I guess at a high, bullshit level, if everyone did what we did there'd be a revolution. We'd get letters from people saying can I teach in your school or be a student in your school. We'd say, "Start your own Free School."

It appears that the second path has not yet become reality—not to the extent predicted by authors such as Charles Reich, who saw an expanding counterculture as inevitable. A third path has materialized, however, and was clearly observed in our sample of organizations. These are the organizations like Counseling Center, Group Center, and Alternative Living Service, which walked a fine line. Such organizations moved toward enough formalization of structure and linkage to the external environment to effectively accomplish their task and maintain their operation, but did not go so far that their alternative climate, goals, or structures were coopted. These are the organizations that rely on community days, potluck dinners, and other techniques to maintain their task/community balance.

A last path is that of cooptation—fulfilling Perrow's and Michel's predictions of the iron law of oligarchy and the death of revolutionary zeal. None of the organizations in the present sample reached this state, though I am aware of others that have. One such organization evolved to having a budget (mainly provided by city government) in excess of a million dollars, a large technically selected staff, specific roles, and hierarchy. They now appear to be a city agency with a flower-covered van.

THE ORGANIZATIONS STUDIED IN THIS CHAPTER

A brief description of each organization follows: *Alternative Living Service* (ALS) provided services to facilitate the development of communes. Activities involved meetings, files, courses, consulting, and counseling. The paid staff of less than 10 was supplemented by about 30 part-time volunteers. *Artistic Free School* (AFS) had a cooperative of musicians at its core along with a free school. A wide variety of topics was taught in the school. A playground for children was also run within the building facility. *Community Action Experiment* (CAE) was an organization of 60 members that fostered neighborhood development in a working-class community. The organization was founded by two professional planners who maintained involvement in the organization along with students and community residents. *Community Free School* (CFS) was run by the parents of about 150 children in a low-income neighborhood. Both professional teachers and community residents taught the classes. Member families were also involved in community housing and health care issues. *Counseling Service* (CS) was divided into four groups: Administration, Research, Counseling (of runaways) and Education (mostly drug education for people not in the counterculture). CS also published books on these topics and had a membership of 22. *Employment Information Service* (EIS) provided job information and job counseling to people looking for alternative employment opportunities. EIS also provided information on the counterculture in general through its publications and through files of information kept in its storefront office. EIS was a group of less than 10. *Free Form Free School* (FFFS) provided classes on varied topics such as pottery, mechanics, and massage. Students and teachers put up signs in the storefront asking for people to join free classes on any topic of interest. FFFS was also a community center for dinners, activities, and entertainment. *Group Center* (GC) provided group interaction services by means of personal growth groups, group leader training, and consulting to outside organizations. A paid staff of less than 10 handled administrative work, while about 30 part-time volunteers did committee and group work.

REFERENCES

Argyris, C.
    1964   *Integrating the Individual and the Organization.* New York: Wiley.
Bennis, W. G.
    1966   *Beyond Bureaucracy.* New York: McGraw-Hill.
    1970   "A Funny Thing Happened on the Way to the Future." *American Psychologist* 25: 595–608.
Herzberg, F.
    1966   *Work and the Nature of Man.* Cleveland: World.
Kanter, R. M.
    1970   "Communes." *Psychology Today* 4: 53–57.
    1972   *Committment and Community.* Cambridge, Mass.: Harvard University Press.
Likert, R.
    1967   *The Human Organization: Its Management and Value.* New York: McGraw-Hill.
Lipset, S. M.
    1952   "Democracy in Private Government." *British Journal of Sociology* 3: 47–63.
Michels, R.
    1915   *Political Parties.* New York: Hearst's International Libary.
Myers, M. S.
    1970   *Every Employee a Manager.* New York: McGraw-Hill.
Perrow, C.
    1970   *Organizational Analysis: A Sociological View.* Belmont, Calif.: Wadsworth.
Reich, C. A.
    1970   *The Greening of America.* New York: Random House.
Roberts, R. E.
    1971   *The New Communes.* Englewood Cliffs, N.J.: Prentice-Hall.
Roszak, T.
    1969   *The Making of a Counter Culture.* New York: Doubleday.
Schein, E. H.
    1970   *Organizational Psychology.* Englewood Cliffs, N.J.: Prentice-Hall.
Slater, P.
    1970   *The Pursuit of Loneliness.* Boston: Beacon Press.
Smith, C., and Freedman A.
    1971   *Voluntary Associations: Perspectives on the Literature.* Cambridge, Mass.: Harvard University Press.

11

Generational Change and Primary Groups in a Social Movement

Robert J. Ross

      The role of face-to-face personal relationships within larger impersonal structures has been a persistent theme in the social science analysis of public and business bureaucracies. It is not surprising that such relationships should also be of importance in the development of social movements. This chapter proposes that these relationships, in the form of clique and friendship networks, contribute significantly to the formation of political generations within a social movement and that these generations in turn are sources of social change in a movement. As will be shown, the consequences of friendship networks were particularly evident in Students for a Democratic Society (SDS) and in the New Left, a movement with which the author has extensive personal experience.

MOVEMENT GENERATIONS

      The political importance of generationally based historical experience has been widely recognized (Mannheim 1952; Eisenstaedt 1965, 1971; Feuer 1969; Turner and Killian 1972, pp. 286–87). Because a political or social movement generation is not the same as a biological one, some have urged that *cohort* be used instead. Regardless of the term preferred, Ryder's definition is still applicable. He defines a cohort as "the aggregate of individuals (within some population definition) who experienced the same event within the same time interval" (1965, p. 845).

A cohort may be defined in terms of age—a birth cohort—but this is not necessary. We are using the defining experience of a given cohort as the time of and stimulus to subjective entrance to a social movement. An example of such a cohort was the earliest group of recruits and founders of SDS. Their common and characteristic experience was the phase of the civil rights movement initiated by the lunch counter sit-ins of 1960. These were supported by white college students in the North through picketing and boycotts of Woolworth and Kresge stores. These persons came to the New Left under different conditions from those, five years later, who were mobilized by opposition to the Vietnam war.

When such cohorts in a movement and its organizations have, in Blumer's terms, a sense of common identity or *esprit de corps*, we will call them a movement generation, thereby implying the intellectual continuity of cohort with classical generational analysis (cf. Bengston, Furlong, and Laufer 1974; Bass 1974) Such generations are always potential carriers of change in a social movement. "Each new cohort," explains Ryder, "makes fresh contact with the contemporary social heritage and carries the impress of the encounter through life" (1965; p. 844). If this be true for a society, it may also be true for a movement organization.

For example, while analyzing the evolution of strategy in the Women's Christian Temperance Union, Gusfield (1957) discovered two "generations." One, which was "conviction oriented," had entered the WCTU before the repeal of Prohibition, and held the key offices in the organization. This group was older than other members and held a righteous and uncompromising view negative to all alcohol use. The other group was characterized by Gusfield as "public-oriented." This group was younger, had been recruited after the repeal of Prohibition, and was (in the fifties) still excluded from powerful office incumbencies. The "public-oriented" generation advocated more compromise and the projection of an image less eccentric and more realistic about alcohol use than its organizational elders.

While different movement generations may be separate birth cohorts and therefore may be characterized by age homogeneity, as in the WCTU, the swift pace of events in a turbulent period may produce more rapidly discontinuous waves of new movement entrants (cf. Turner and Killian 1972). Thus, rapid creation of more or less distinct movement cohorts may have only a general relationship to biological age. In the New Left and SDS observers and participants (see below) generally agree that a new generation appeared within the movement and SDS in the 1965–66 period. Nevertheless, Carl Oglesby, the SDS president whose election represented the beginning of this shift, was elected in 1965 when he was older than any of the candidates from the founding group. He had been an SDS member for less than a year (Sale 1973) and was thus a symbolic representation of "new members" who in turn began to identify as a distinctive cohort.

Though we refer to a movement generation when a cohort of new recruits develops *esprit de corps*, Blumer (1951) points out that such identity is not sufficient for a collectivity to sustain action. It must also develop morale (i.e., some sense of discipline and program). We hypothesize that the formation of such consciousness is negatively related to the degree to which a movement cohort becomes part of the circles of intimacy that already exist in the groups they join. Some general observations on the role of primary group ties in social movements may clarify this contention.

PRIMARY GROUPS IN SOCIAL MOVEMENT ORGANIZATIONS

The rewards of social movement participation, even in political or economic movements, are not all instrumental. Blumer referred to the function of movement participation as, in part, overcoming loneliness and isolation; Zald and Ash (1966) use the felicitous phrase "the joys of participation." Staughton Lynd, a historian and New Left participant, had this experience in mind when he referred to the movement as a "band of brothers in a circle of love" (Lynd 1966, p. 8–9). This rewarding experience, let us call it expressive, has one of its key origins in the primary groups that develop within organizations and among participants.

Kopkind (1973, p. 30) describes his first visit to an SDS organizing project in Newark:

> Their commitment to a common cause cut into the loneliness of work, which I had always assumed was inevitable.... In that intense mood, I fantasized an end to alienation, despair, emptiness.

Turner and Killian (1972, p. 366) refer in general to the 'ecstatic experience of membership in a cohesive, committed, like-minded group" becoming "an independent source of satisfaction."

RECRUITMENT AND SOCIAL MOVEMENT ORGANIZATION (SMO) CHANGE

If a movement organization grows in membership, it may incorporate potential change elements within it. Indeed, this is true for any voluntary association (cf. Schattschneider 1960, Killian 1964). As new members join, they may or may not be integrated into the lattice of primary groups which existed before their participation. Killian has implied that the size of an association is a relevant variable: "Involvement in informal fellowship associations is more feasible for the small elite than for the large number of adherents...." (ibid., p. 445). And in a societal context Ryder notes the same issue: "As the new cohort reaches each major juncture in the life cycle, the society has the problem of assimilating it" (1965, p. 845).

The new recruit who remains isolated from old movement hands may leave the organization. Such an exit is often the meaning of subjective reports by people who feel a given group is "cliquish," and unresponsive to the needs of new members.

In his analysis of the Boston area draft resistance, Useem (1972) reports a case of successful integration of new participants with older members through their inclusion in a web of friendship ties. The paradox is that these 1966–67 draft resisters were frequently those leaving or rejecting SDS, in part because they felt excluded from the dominant cliques (cf. Sale 1973). Lynd (1969, p. 11) attributes this to a developing ("generational") split between "political" vs. "moral" activists.

Many new members will stay in an organization, despite their unsuccessful primary integration, under a number of conditions. They will stay if their "political" (i.e., ideological or moral) commitment is high. Alternatively, newcomers will stay if they are in chapters or local groupings relatively homogeneous as a cohort thus, ipso, facto, becoming the local in-group (cf. Gerlach and Hine 1970). Or finally, they will stay if new member cliques develop and are sufficiently gratifying to hold them.

Tsouderos (1955) has concisely summarized what happens when new recruits stay despite the lack of primary-group integration into an old guard. Though based on a study of ten voluntary and civic associations in Minneapolis, his summary is similar to the hypothesis explored here:

> With an increased membership, however, there is a corresponding increase in the heterogeneity of the group in terms of sentiments, interests, dedication to the "cause," etc., and a corresponding decline in a feeling of intimacy and frequency of interaction. More specifically there is a decline of membership in meetings and volunteer work. As a consequence, the membership becomes extremely passive and increasingly removed from the leadership of the association. As the membership expands, the group as a whole is likely to lose its primary character. This is not to say, however, that the primary group disappears; certain clusters of individuals are found to interact with one another more frequently than they do with the rest of the membership. Sub-groups appear which retain the primary character previously extending over the entire membership. These sub-group clusters are integrated into the manifest social structure and the membership is organized in membership units. At the same time the need for control arises out of the fact that some of these membership units tend to become relatively autonomous from the rest of the organization. In varying degrees loyalty of the members is diverted from the association to the membership units so that the basis for a conflict within the organization has been laid. p. 209.

We are now prepared for a formal statement of our hypothesis:

1. New members of a social movement organization are potential change agents within it.
2. This change potential of a movement cohort is dampened and the appearance or impact of a movement generation is smoother when new members are integrated into the primary-group ties of the old guard.
3. If new members are not so integrated, but nevertheless remain in the organization, they will tend to form cliques and circles of their own.
4. New member cliques provide the opportunity for *esprit de corps* and morale to arise in a way that defines the movement cohort as a distinctive movement generation.
5. When a movement cohort feels itself to be a distinctive generation in a more or less democratic association, it will act politically to reject the leadership and thereby the definition of the situation it feels to be dis-

tinctive of the old guard. It will try to produce the appearance of a shift in the movement's goals and strategies; it will try to appear, in historical terms, as a new movement or "political" generation.

6. Members of a movement generation, even within a given SMO, may not necessarily agree with one another. "What they agree on is the identity of the adversaries" (Turner and Killian 1972, p. 287). The global identity thus shared, therefore, is apt to be as symbolic as it is programmatic; the new guard may suffer splits and factions similar to those it rode to power.

These propositions do not explain all rancorous or factional conflict within social movement organizations; they are specifically oriented to those events widely or popularly understood to be "generational." In the analysis of SDS and the New Left that follows, the focus is on hypotheses 1, 3, 4, and 5. Useem's (1972) work provides a case of the second hypothesis (successful integration), and the analysis of the final schisms of the New Left is left for another occasion.

GENERATIONS IN THE NEW LEFT AND SDS

Space does not permit a detailed case history of the New Left or SDS. But our hypothesis can be tested in three steps. The first entails documenting the existence of a marked change in the New Left in the post-1966 period; the second entails demonstrating the existence of this shift at first signaled in SDS in 1965–66; the third marshalls the evidence that assigns an important role to primary-group ties in the generational shift observed in SDS.

THE NEW LEFT

Among journalistic, scholarly, and participant observers, there is impressive unanimity that there was a rapid expansion of the New Left after 1965 and the appearance, after 1966, of a change in the New Left, both in the tone and content of its outlook and in the kinds of persons at the center of the movement.* The Berkeley Free Speech Movement and escalation of the Vietnam war are frequently mentioned as catalysts.

Flacks (1974, p. 30), a social scientist and early SDS participant, noted that the "optimism of the New Left founders" was systematically obliterated by a series of events during the mid-sixties. Skolnick (1969, pp. 99–100) discussed the post-1965 "phase" of the movement as one in which there was "progressive deterioration in . . . acceptance of authority." Lynd a historian and activist, discussed the "tendency in the second half of the 1960s . . . away from the distinctive atmosphere of humor, emotional expressiveness, experimentation, and (as it seemed to some), chaos, which had characterized the early years of the White New Left" (Lynd 1969, p. 10).

Unger (1973), a historian, observed a post-1965 split in the movement be-

---

* The present author was a national officer of SDS from 1960 to 1965 and in 1966–67. Unless otherwise noted, the sources cited below document his own observations.

tween political and counterculture activism. This is overly specified, but former SDS officer Booth (1974) notes more generally the post-1965 rise in anarchism within the movement. Lasch (1969, p. 183) locates the Vietnam war—the opposition to it—as the source of a "nihilism and despair"; he discusses this in the context of 1967.

Rothstein (1969, p. 282) a New Left organizer, however, observes that community organizers and projects loosely tied to SDS had, by winter 1965, already begun to perceive power structures as hopelessly "inflexible" and "unresponsive." He is supported by Gitlin (1975) who was SDS president in 1963–64. Teodori (1969, p. 56) dates the "radicalization" of the movement from the 1965 protests against the Vietnam war.

The consensus about the timing and tone of the shift in the New Left is an inferential but not a definitive basis for the emergence of a movement cohort. More direct evidence that the post-1965 shift was generational in that new cohorts brought distinctive styles and self-perceptions to the movement is provided by Mankoff and Flacks (1971). They report Mankoff's 1969 research on movement generations at the University of Wisconsin where they mailed a questionnaire to student sympathizers of demonstrators who had obstructed a Dow Chemical Company recruiter in 1967. Those who identified their politics as "radical" (i.e., either socialists, communists, anarchists, revolutionaries, or New Leftists) were labeled movement cadre. Over half of this group had engaged in some form of civil disobedience. Mankoff and Flacks call cadre members "veterans" if they had been active for three or more years prior to May 1968. They write:

> It was believed that this cutting point between veteran and non-veteran cadre would distinguish fairly accurately between those who were politically involved when the movement was small and isolated during the pre-1965 period and those who probably became involved after the bombing of North Vietnam in February, 1965. (1971, p. 55)

The veterans were more apt to be from big cities, to have college-educated fathers, to be Jewish or atheist, to have liberal or radical parents, and to read more political periodicals than the nonveterans. The authors interpret their data as due to a broader recruitment base over time, one more nearly resembling backgrounds of conventional college students. They speculated that a new consciousness, of a quasi-class character, had become widespread, despite its original location in the affluent and professional classes and that the new recruits had a less sophisticated political and intellectual culture. They suggest what was at stake in the generational shift when they conclude:

> It would seem clear that long-term viability of the movement depends, in part, on the capacity of those within it to synthesize the spontaneous, anti-political "gut" radicalism of the new recruits with the more systematically politicized and intellectual radicalism of the veterans. (Ibid. p. 67)

In effect, movement expansion was synchronous with internal change because the confrontation of generations failed to produce that synthesis. This was acted out most clearly in SDS.

SDS

As with the New Left in general, there is broad agreement about the shift in the tone and style of SDS in 1965–66. Though there is little doubt that spring 1965 through June 1966 was the period of transition, this author's experience and observation is that the winter of 1964–65 was the seed-time of the change.

In the fall of 1964, the Free Speech Movement at Berkeley mobilized thousands of students in protest and direct actions against restrictions on campus-based political activity. The response in SDS was immediate. Local chapters and officers, with national office encouragement, set up a nationwide tour for a number of Free Speech Movement leaders. It was clear as they traveled that a sympathetic response from SDS chapters and toward SDS chapters had been found. Throughout 1965–66, the militant on-campus confrontation of the Free Speech Movement acted as a kind of model for on-campus protests, but now they were focused on issues raised by the war and the draft.

In August 1964 the Tonkin Gulf incident revealed that the Johnson administration was willing to use direct American armed intervention in Vietnam. By December 1964, before the February 1965 bombing in Hanoi and the escalation of troop landings that followed it, there was a widespread perception in SDS circles that full-scale war was imminent. With much controversy, the National Council of SDS, meeting between Christmas 1964 and New Year's 1965, called for an April 1965 March on Washington to End the War in Vietnam. Despite opposition from the anticommunist Left, the march was a success, and SDS became, as its sponsor, the recipient of a large influx of new recruits.

The vote to hold the April 1965 march prefigured the later generational split in SDS. It was very close; indeed, the march was initially defeated and only narrowly passed on reconsideration. The most influential bloc opposed to holding the march was that part of the founding group—the most prestigious part—that had left college and was engaged in off-campus community organizing. They argued that the nationally focused activity of the march would take energy and resources from local grass-roots organizing. When the march took place, bringing with it a new wave of student members, the group that included most of the central old guard figures tended to withdraw from commitment to SDS inner organizational matters. One former officer has, in personal correspondence, referred to this withdrawal as "abdication."

Turner and Killian (1972, p. 284) have a nice formulation that, by analogy, was similar to the situation in which SDS subsequently found itself: "Publics typically ascribe unannounced broader goals to any movement that attracts attention, and the public definition affects the adherent's conceptions of their purposes in the movement."

Although SDS had always (since its manifesto of 1962, the Port Huron Statement) been *inclusive* in recruiting policy, it had remained a slowly growing, relatively small group. Face-to-face contacts and the use of intellectually oriented working papers were the way it spread its ideas. Now, in 1965, the mass media did the recruiting for SDS. One consequence of this was the transformation of the meaning of the phrase "participatory democracy." Coined in the Port Huron Statement, the phrase was interpreted, by some mass media and even friendly observers, to imply "consensus in group decision-making." To this author's knowledge, that meaning was not used at all at the Port Huron meeting in 1962, and rarely until 1965–66. The original use of a "participatory democracy" was essentially an expansion, to community and other politics, of the socialist idea of industrial democracy (i.e., workers' control of their places of work). But the new recruits (and later, scholars; cf. Turner and Killian 1972) came to SDS with this "procedural" impression, and they made it into a partial reality.

Beyond such specific transformations, all observers agree that the new recruits brought change in the tenor of the group. In Sale's (1973, p. 198) definitive history of the organization he shows that the number of chapters doubled from December 1964 (40) to June 1965 (80). "The new spirit in S.D.S. was the genie that April 17 (1965: The March) let out of the bottle." At 1965's June convention the president elected was the first from outside the founding group. Sale summarizes it this way:

> ...Now S.D.S. was starting to become the home for new breed of activist, a younger [sic] more alienated, more committed [sic] student.... They were new to national politics, had never before attended as S.D.S. convention, knew the organization essentially as the caller of the April March.... Much to the bewilderment of the older S.D.S.ers, now irrevocably christened "the old guard." For the first time at a convention most of the people were unknown to each other, the proceedings were out of the hands of a group of old friends, the Port Huronites no longer dominated. (Ibid., p. 204)

Participants shared Sales's sense of the change over that year. Haber (1969), the first president (1960–62) and most important single founder, noted that new recruits have "no time for educational work...because the urgency of direct moral expression outweighs for them all other considerations." On the other side of the developing generation gap, Shero, elected vice-president, claimed, "We were by instinct much more radical, much more willing to take risks...." (Sale 1972, p. 206). Shero, in fact, attributed his election to his disaffiliation, with the most prominent of the old guard, Tom Hayden: "I thought he was a great dude, but I wasn't in awe of him at all...I got a certain amount of respect...for taking him on" (Ibid., p. 209).

As 1965 wore on, the old guard realized SDS was changing. In December an "educational" conference was held. Sale comments:

> The December meetings were a touching symbol. Called by the old guard to reestablish the kind of S.D.S. they had known and loved, it actually served to indicate that, inevitably, the organization was headed in new directions, the clock could not be turned back. The S.D.S. that was family, that was shared assumptions and shared lives, was fading now, and something new and uncertain was growing in its place. (Ibid., p. 252)

By 1966 the change was complete. "A new group had taken over with no personal ties to the founders, indeed the new leadership was hardly acquainted with the old" (Flacks 1974, p. 36).

The small group of persons among the old guard who advocated coalitions with labor and liberals were now out altogether (Unger, 1974). The new guard, tremendously diverse, with views ranging from counterculture utopianism to a budding Marxism "had joined S.D.S. after the inception of its anti-Vietnam program, and...came from schools without much tradition of student activism" (Skolnick 1969, pp. 96–97).

Participant-journalist Kopkind (1973, p. 30), in fact, delimits the usage New Left to "a rather small group of white and black students and post-students committed to a Radical socialist reformism, who were working from about 1961–1966."

The evidence of the 1965–66 shift, seen in generational terms by its participants, is clear, and both participants and observers tend to define the cohort in terms of pre- or post-spring 1965 entry to SDS. By spring 1967, for example, a number of founding SDS members held a "Back-to-the Drawing Boards" conference that attempted, but failed, to create a post-student New Left organization. The usage "old New Left" as distinct from "new New Left" was semifacetiously used from that point on.

We have seen that expansion did bring change, including leadership turnover, and that the new leadership group defined itself in generational terms. What remains to be examined in the light of our hypotheses is the way in which clique, or primary-group, formation influenced that turnover.

PRIMARY GROUPS IN SDS

In the presentation of the "old guard-new guard" shift in SDS, observers and participants were struck by the absence of friendship and even acquaintance between the two leadership groups. Flacks (1974, p. 36) referred to "no personal ties to the founders"; Skolnick (1969) makes the same point.* Sale pointed out the "group of old friends" displaced in 1965 by conferees who were new to meetings (1973, p. 204). He describes the antipathy to the old guard as "based in part on nervousness, awe, and unfamiliarity, in part on the remoteness and inaccessibility of the old guard" (ibid., p. 206). By 1966, Sale says, "the SDS that was family" was gone (ibid., p. 252).

Organizational changes were also occurring. In the spring of 1966, before the vital 1966 convention, five new regional structures were formed in SDS. One of these (the Midwest: Ohio, Indiana, Michigan) was in an "old" area of SDS work, but chapters at heretofore unorganized campuses were brought in; another, the Niagara (upper New York State) was heavily infiltrated by the FBI, but also included chapters from new (to SDS) colleges (Rosenbaum 1971, as cited in Marx 1974).

The other three regions were the Plains States (Iowa, Kansas, Missouri, and Nebraska), and Mid-South (Texas, Oklahoma, Arkansas, Louisiana), and the Northwest (Oregon, Washington). At the 1966 convention, the acrimonious defeat of the "old guard" was referred to by the new guard as the victory of Prairie Power. And, indeed, the elected officers reflected this. The three

---

* It should be noted, however, that Flacks helped prepare Skolnick's chapter, so that this is not independent verification (Cf. Skolnick 1969, p. xvii).

most prominent figures at the convention were respectively from Texas, organizing in Nebraska, and attending Iowa State. Texas, Iowa, Los Angeles, Iowa again, Texas again: These were the homes or residences of members of the new National Council (NC). Every member of the NC except one, and the First Alternate, were identified with Prairie Power (Sale 1973).

The leadership of the new guard was largely drawn from regions without face-to-face contact with the old guard. Even within campus chapters where founders were present, new recruits and old hands would be socially segregated. But most of the important figures in the old guard had already left campuses (Sale 1973) and so, were hardly available to the bulk of new recruits. The new guard, complete with its diversity and ultimate internal contradictions, nevertheless felt itself arrayed against the most unifying of adversaries: strangers.

Sophisticated observers of SDS will note that the founding leaders of SDS almost unanimously believed in rotation of office and making way for new leadership. But *office turnover* by itself does not cause movement change. It is discontinuous waves of movement generations that create internal change. Flacks (1974, p. 36) put it well:

> In short, not only had the original new leftists given up their personal influence within the organization, but they failed to communicate their particular vision in such a way that it would be carried forward by any self-conscious group of successors.

Flacks's analysis implies that the socialization process bringing recruits into SDS broke down when the organization expanded rapidly. This is supported by the personal memoirs of older recruits that have recently appeared (Kopkind, 1973, Langor 1973, Potter 1971). For each, the original New Left vision became a "thematic heritage" (Kopkind 1973, p. 33), no longer attached to SDS as an organization.

The transformation of SDS in the mid-sixties fits the pattern anticipated by the hypotheses presented earlier: An influx of new members was not integrated into old-member primary group networks; new member cliques were most opposed to the old guard in new, geographically distant regions, and formed a consciousness akin to a generational one.

SUMMARY AND IMPLICATIONS

This chapter has examined four hypotheses that link the emergence of political or social movement generations to movement cohort formation. It showed, first, that a rapid period of expansion in the New Left and SDS was accompanied by a change in tone and content of the movement and its leading organization. That new members were a change element within the movement is related, second, to their distinctive experience, and third, to their lack of integration into previously existing primary-group networks. Both scholarly and participant accounts gave evidence of the generational consciousness of those changes, and also of the separate primary-group networks in which the different cohorts were involved. *Inclusive* organizations are obviously most vulnerable to this process in periods of rapid expansion; and democratic forms present critical opportunities for conflict and change in organizational direction. But a successful case (Useem 1972) was going on in the Boston region at the same time. The inclusion of new hands in friendship networks was analyzed by Useem as critical to that success.

A number of caveats to this analysis should be made explicit. First, the shift in SDS in 1965–66 cannot be solely traced to the creation of new member networks: Old hands were subject to similar historical circumstances, and in general became more thoroughly radical as the decade wore on. Second, regional variation was always present in SDS politics, and the cultural style of the organization tended to be more flamboyant west of the Mississippi. Finally, although the hypotheses are stated, and testable, in general terms, it may be that student movements are particularly vulnerable to the appearance of discontinuous cohorts of participants. These limitations, however, should not obscure the usefulness of the mode of analysis, nor hinder its wider application.

The practical implications are these: Ideology requires organized maintenance under conditions of expansion. But if an ideology derides "structure," as did that of the New Left, it will be difficult to maintain continuity within an organization. There may be functional equivalents to primary-group integration in an organization: formal internal education and organizational "schools"; rapid and complete information exchange; widespread physical presence (travel) by old hands. These can, perhaps, replace the informal socialization of peers. But when social movement organizations are both poor in resources and ambivalent about the internal use of authority, the central institutions to implement these programs will be weak or nonexistent. Organizers will need to balance the desirability of rapid expansion, the capacity to respond to changing circumstances, and low degrees of structure with a sense of organizational survival and continuity.

REFERENCES

Bengston, Vern L.; Michael J. Furlong; and Robert S. Laufer
    1974   "Time, Aging, and the Continuity of Social Structure: Themes and Issues in Generational Analysis." *Journal of Social Issues* 30, no 2: 1–30.

Blumer, Herbert
    1951   "Social Movements." Pp. 199–220 in Alfred McClung Lee, ed., *Principles of Sociology*. New York: Barnes and Noble.

Booth, Paul
    1974   "What Happened in the 60's and What That Means for the 70's." Midwest Academy, Chicago. Mimeographed.

Bass, Allan R.
    1974   "Generational Analysis: Description, Explanation and Theory." *Journal of Social Issues* 30, no. 2: 55–72.

Eisenstadt, S. N.
    1965   *From Generation to Generation*. Glencoe: Free Press.
    1971   "Generational Conflict and Intellectual Antinomianism." *Annals of the American Academy of Political and Social Science*, p. 395.

Feuer, Lewis
    1969   *The Conflict of Generations*. New York: Basic Books.

Flacks, Richard
    1974 "Making History vs. Making Life: Dilemmas of an American Left." *Working Papers* II (Summer): 56–71.

Freeman, Jo
    1975 *The Politics of Women's Liberation*. New York: Longman.

Gerlach, Luther P., and Virginia H. Hine
    1970 *People, Power, Change: Movements of Social Transformation*. Indianapolis: Bobbs-Merrill.

Gitlin, Todd
    1975 Personal interview, August 27.

Gusfield, Joseph
    1957 "The Problem of Generations in an Organizational Structure." *American Sociological Review* 35: 323–30.

Haber, Robert
    1969 "Nonexclusionism: The New Left and the Democratic Left." Pp. 218–28 in Massimo Teodori, *The New Left: A Documentary History*. Indianapolis: Bobbs-Merrill.

Killian, Lewis
    1964 "Social Movements." Pp. 426–55 in R. E. L. Faris, ed., *Handbook of Modern Sociology*. Chicago: Rand McNally.

Lasch, Christopher
    1969 *The Agony of the American Left*. New York: Knopf.

Lipset, S. M., and Everett C. Ladd, Jr.
    1971 "College Generations—from the 1930's to the 1960's." *Public Interest* 25: 99–113.

Kopkind, Andrew
    1973 "Looking Backward: The Sixties and the Movement." *Ramparts* 11: 29–34.

Langor, Elinor
    1973 "Notes for Next Time: A Memoir of the 1960's." *Working Papers* 1: 48–82.

Lynd, Staughton
    1966 In the *National Guardian*, 16 April 1966, pp. 8–9.
    1969 "Towards a History of the New Left." Pp. 10–13 in Priscilla Long, ed., *The New Left: A Collection of Essays*. Boston: Porter-Sargent.

McCarthy, John, and Mayer Zald
    1974 "Resource Mobilization and Social Movements." Unpublished manuscript, Vanderbilt University.

Mankoff, Milton, and Richard Flacks
    1971 "The Changing Base of the American Student Movement." *Annals of the American Academy of Political and Social Science* 395: 54–67.

Mannheim, Karl
    1952 "The Problem of Generations." In *Essays on the Sociology of Knowledge*. London: Routledge and Kegan Paul.

Marx, Gary T.
    1974 "Thoughts on a Neglected Category of Social Movement Participant: The Agent Provacateur and the Informant." *American Journal of Sociology* 80: 402–42.

Potter, Paul
    1971 *A Name for Ourselves: Feelings about Authentic Identity, Love, Intuitive Politics, U.S.* Boston: Little, Brown.

Rosenbaum, R.
    1971 "Run, Tommy, Run!" *Esquire* 76: 51–58.

Ross, Robert J.
  1975   "Primary Groups in the Biography of Social Movements." Unpublished
         paper, Department of Sociology, Clark University, Worcester, Mass.
Rothstein, Richard
  1969   "The Evolution of the ERAP Organizers." Pp. 272–88 in Priscilla Long, ed.,
         The New Left: A Collection of Essays. Boston: Porter-Sargent.
Ryder, Norman B.
  1965   "The Cohort as a Concept in the Study of Social Change." *American Sociologi-
         cal Review* 30, no. 6: 843–61.
Sale, Kirkpatrick
  1973   *SDS*. New York: Random House.
Schattsneider, E. E.
  1960   *The Semisovereign People*. New York: Holt, Rinehart and Winston.
Shils, Edward
  1970   "Center and Periphery." In *Selected Essays*. Chicago: Center for Social Organ-
         ization Studies, Department of Sociology, University of Chicago.
Skolnick, Jerome H.
  1969   *The Politics of Protest. A Report Submitted to the National Commission on the Causes
         and Prevention of Violence*. Washington, D.C.: G.P.O.
Starr, Jerold M.
  1974   "The Peace and Love Generation: Changing Attitudes Toward Sex and
         Violence Among College Youth." *Journal of Social Issues* 30, no. 2: 73–106.
Teodori, Massimo
  1969   *The New Left: A Documentary History*. Indianapolis: Bobbs-Merrill.
Tsouderos, John E.
  1955   "Organizational Change in Terms of a Series of Selected Variables." *Amer-
         ican Sociological Review* 20: 206–10.
Turner, Ralph, and Lewis Killian
  1972   *Collective Behavior*. Englewood Cliffs, N.J.: Prentice-Hall.
Unger, Irwin
  1974   *The Movement: A History of the American New Left 1959–1972*.
         New York: Dodd, Mead.
Useem, Michael
  1972   "Ideological and Interpersonal Change in Radical Protest Movement." *Social
         Problems* 19: 451–69.
Zald, Mayer, and Roberta Ash
  1966   "Social Movement Organizations: Growth, Decay and Change." *Social Forces*
         44: 327–40.

Mississippi, 1966.

Meredith, Mississippi March, Jackson, Miss., June 1966.

Part 4
Strategy

Probably the single most dominant concern of both movement participants and scholars is that of strategy. What works and what doesn't? But before one attempts to answer that question, one first has to ask: Works for what? Gamson identifies two kinds of success: the gaining of acceptance and the gaining of new advantages. But the goals of many movements are not that simple. Some have objectives so radical that it is unlikely that anything would successfully achieve them in the probable life of the movement. Some have goals that are neither acceptance nor new advantages (e.g., personal change). For some movements, merely to survive is success enough; for others, mere survival is failure.

The first chapter in this section answers none of our questions. Instead, it identifies four factors that affect strategic choices: resources, constraints on the use of those resources, the nature of the social movement organization, and expectations about potential targets. These factors can be used by participants to analyze strategic options, or they can be used by scholars to analyze decisions that were made.

However, strategy doesn't always involve choice. Sometimes it involves making do with what's available. LeVeen argues in her chapter on the Chicago Indian Village that Indians were so poor and so marginal to this society that their options were severly restricted. She sees their use of disruption as a creative use of their limited resources that had positive outcomes for the participants, if not for their goals.

Geschwender, in contrast, describes a successful use of disruption by a group of farmers in Hawaii and their supporters. Nevertheless, he points out that the disruption was successful in part because more respectable tactics earlier in the movement had gained it a good deal of respectability. Thus, when the movement turned to disruption, public sentiment was inclined to be sympathetic, and the politicians who decided the ultimate outcome were inclined to be sympathetic to public sentiment.

Evans takes a more historical perspective on the most extreme form of disruption—terrorism—by analyzing when it has been successful and when it hasn't. He notes that only right-wing movements have used terrorism without being subject to severe repression, and identifies this as a result of the historical reality that only right-wing movements have ever had the necessary mass base. Even this is not enough. In addition, the successful use of terrorism requires the connivance or neutrality of the authorities. Evans asserts that the failure of the Ku Klux Klan to suppress the civil rights movement was due to the success of the FBI's counterintelligence program in disrupting the Klan.

Despite the strong evidence Evans supplies for his position, it is unlikely that any group seriously considering violence would systematically research the possible outcomes before making a decision. The use of violence is more often the result of internal pressures and a perception that more conservative measures will not work. Nonetheless, some movements have researched the possible outcomes of their available strategies to identify the ones most suitable for their purposes. One such group was the Madison Tenant Union, which carefully analyzed the consequences of tenant activities in two other cities before organizing its own. Gillespie describes this rare phenomenon and how well it succeeded. He concludes that the avoidance of unnecessary conflict can preclude many problems.

12

A Model for Analyzing the Strategic Options of Social Movement Organizations

Jo Freeman

One of the many topics that has not been treated systematically by students of social movements is "the question of how a movement acts upon the larger society to promote changes with which it is identified."[1] Decisions about how a movement will act are not always made by a leader, or even by a small committee of strategic experts, because many movements are not subject to that kind of hierarchical control. Often, major strategic decisions flow from circumstances or are made and executed by an otherwise insignificant group of protestors whose success is then emulated by others.

For example, the first sit-in of the sixties was accomplished by some college students in North Carolina; it was not decided upon by the leaders of the major civil rights organizations of that year. While these leaders were quick to see its uses, the idea of sitting-in spread largely through the media and informal communications networks of students. On the other hand, the earlier Montgomery bus boycott was a decision made by the black community leaders of that city and organized through the churches. Many other examples could be given. I would like to offer a model within which strategic considerations, both planned and spontaneous, leader-directed and grass-roots, can be analyzed. This model highlights the resources available to a social movement organization at a given time, the limitations on the use of these resources, and how the resources can potentially be deployed.

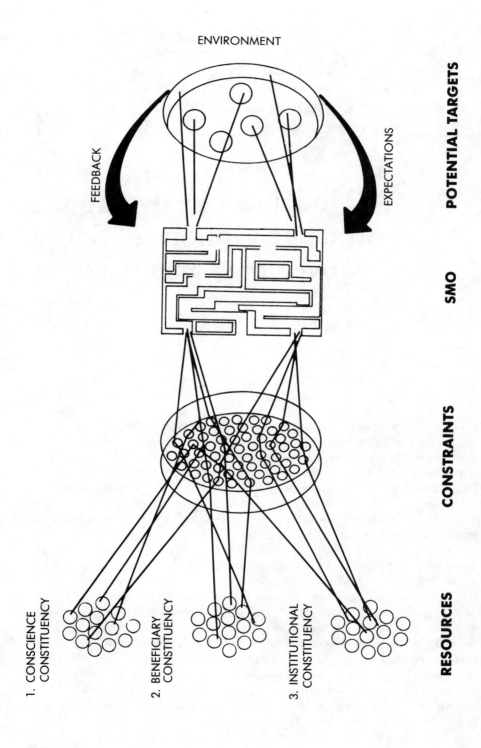

ENVIRONMENT

FEEDBACK

EXPECTATIONS

POTENTIAL TARGETS

SMO

CONSTRAINTS

1. CONSCIENCE CONSTITUENCY

2. BENEFICIARY CONSTITUENCY

3. INSTITUTIONAL CONSTITUENCY

RESOURCES

My model of strategic decision making (see page 194) by social move-ment organizations has four major elements and lots of components. The ele-ments are mobilizable resources, constraints on these resources, SMO struc-ture and internal environment, and expectations about potential targets. Each of these is deserving of a chapter in its own right. Since this is not feasible, only the major points of each component are touched on; less attention is paid to those questions or typologies adequately covered elsewhere.

MOBILIZABLE RESOURCES[2]

The most obvious distinction among the varieties of resources available to organizers is that between the tangible and the intangible. Virtually every so-cial movement must have some tangible resources, primarily money, space, and a means of publicizing the movement's existence and ideas. These re-sources are interchangeable, but only up to a point. Money can buy space, but not always vice versa. On the other hand, money can be used to publicize the movement, most of the time, and publicizing the movement can be used to raise money.

It is a mistake to judge the affluence of the movement by its monetary contributions. A primary reason many new movements emerge out of older ones is not only that the older movement provides a cooptable communications network[3] but that it also provides some very valuable resources that would be at best expensive, and at worst unattainable, if the older movement did not exist.

Both branches of the women's movement relied on space donated by others during their early days. The younger branch used a room and mimeo-graph temporarily contributed by the radical Institute for Policy Studies in Washington, D.C., to organize its first national conference in 1968. The National Organization for Women (NOW) initially was organized out of the Extension Division of the University of Wisconsin and then out of the United Auto Workers Women's Committee office in Detroit. When this was lost in 1967, due to the UAW's dismay at NOW's support for the Equal Rights Amendment, NOW was forced to divert precious funds to renting an office in Washington, D.C., which it had trouble womanning.

The younger branch had something more important than space—access to the network of underground newspapers and numerous New Left confer-ences held every year. Had this branch of the movement emerged five years earlier (or later), when such resources were minimal, it would have had a much harder time getting off the ground. The value of this particular resource for publicizing the new movement among potential adherents was so great that it is practically impossible to translate it into monetary terms. NOW did not have access to such a resource, and although it had more money than the younger branch, it did not have the enormous amount of money that would have been necessary to achieve the equivalent amount of press coverage. It took NOW years longer to achieve the numbers of the younger branch. Thus, movements that seem to be poor, that draw from seriously deprived consti-tuencies, may in fact be rich in some less obvious, but still tangible, resources.

People are the primary intangible resource of a movement, and movements rely heavily on them. In fact, one could say that a major distinguishing factor between a social movement and an organizing interest group is the particular mix of resources each relies on. Interest groups tend to mobilize tangible resources, some of which are used to hire professional staff to translate the rest of the resources into political pressure. Social movements are low on tangible resources, especially money, but strong on people resources. Such resources are harder to convert into political pressure, let alone social change, in part because they are not very liquid, but for many activities they are more valuable. The civil rights movement recruited many young people to spend dangerous summers in the South registering blacks to vote. Even had enough money been available, it is doubtful that this resource could have been bought. It is also questionable whether it would have been as effective. An analysis of the Southern Christian Leadership Conference's summer 1965 voter registration projects showed that those that registered the most voters tended to have the least money. In effect, lack of money forced the "outside agitators" to live in and depend on the local community, and this in turn facilitated registration.

Not all people can make the same contribution to a movement. The many different resources people can contribute can be divided into three categories. The first I call "specialized" resources. Their essential characteristic is that they are possessed by only a few participants—and only a few really need to possess them, for the point of diminishing returns is reached very quickly. These resources include expertise of various sorts, access to networks through which other resources can be mobilized, access to decision makers relevant to the movement, and status, whether within the movement's constituencies or within the polity the movement is trying to influence.

The other two categories are unspecialized in that any participant could contribute them if so inclined. These are time, primarily to perform necessary labor and/or sit through meetings; and commitment. Commitment is not dedication. Commitment is the willingness to take risks or entertain inconvenience. Whenever a deprived group triumphs over a more privileged one without major outside interference, it is because their constituencies have compensated with a great deal of time and commitment. As a member of President Ford's staff told me during the 1976 Republican convention when I asked her why the Reagan supporters were so close to victory, although they started so far behind: "They're willing to get up at six a.m. to go to a delegate caucus; we aren't."[4]

Since a movement relies so heavily on people resources, most activities involve their deployment. If a lot of time is demanded to attend meetings, there may be a lot less time available to do work. If the standard of commitment requires acts subject to felony arrest, movement resources may be quickly diverted to fighting legal battles. Groups that have little access to specialized resources through their own constituencies must frequently spend other resources developing conscience constituencies to supply their specialized needs. Even this can backfire. The southern civil rights movement effectively mobilized young white students to supply specialized resources, especially northern public attention. But within two years the movement decided that the whites'

TABLE 12.1/Resources Mobilized by the Early Feminist Movement

Resources	Younger Branch	Older Branch
Tangible		
Money	little	some
Space	people's homes; IPS	various offices
Publicity	underground papers; New Left conferences	committees on the status of women; lists; limited access to establishment papers
Specialized		
Expertise	community organizing; pamphleteering	public relations; lobbying
Access to networks	"radical community"; students	Committees on Status of Women; professional groups
Access to decision makers	none	some in government; media and unions
Status in polity	none	little
Status in group	only in the "movement"	little
Unspecialized		
Time	a great deal	little
Commitment	a great deal	some

value had been expended and that their presence interfered with local people developing organizing skills.

Table 12.1 compares the resources available to the younger and older branches of the women's movement at their beginnings (of course this has changed over time). But having categorized resources, we are still not finished with them. We next have to ask where they come from, and what are the costs of mobilizing them.

There are three major sources of mobilizable resources: the beneficiary constituency, any conscience constituencies, and nonconstituency institutions. Following Zald and McCarthy, the beneficiary constituency consists of political beneficiaries of the movement who also supply it with resources, and the conscience constituency are those sympathizers who provide resources "but are not part of the beneficiary base."[5] Institutional resources are those that are available independent of the movement's existence, which can potentially be coopted by it. For example, if a law exists prohibiting discrimination, the power of the state to enforce this law can theoretically be coopted to help a movement eradicate discrimination.

Before Title VII of the 1964 civil rights act was passed, the civil rights movement occasionally employed sit-ins to force employers to hire more blacks. Afterward, the movement encouraged individuals to file complaints with the relevant government agency and helped many to go to court to compel employers to end discrimination. By coopting the institutional resource of the court, through the passage of Title VII, the civil rights movement acquired legitimacy for its fight against employment discrimination and was able to have an impact on far more employers and far more jobs.

The primary distinction between a conscience constituency and a coopted institution is that one has a theoretical *right* to the resources of the latter. That is, access is *institutionalized*. The most obvious source of cooptable institutional resources is the government, but it is not the only source. When the YWCA made the ending of racism its "one imperative," it was in effect saying that the black movement had a *right* to the "Y"'s resources for that end.

Regardless of the origin or kind of resource, resources are not just there for the asking. They have to be mobilized, and this in turn takes resources, which a particular SMO may not always have in abundance. Before Title VII, the major resource the civil rights movement used to attack discrimination in employment was large numbers of individuals sufficiently committed to risk arrest in a sit-in. This resource was most frequently supplied by the Congress of Racial Equality (CORE), whose history of nonviolent action had attracted to it large numbers of individuals, black and white, who were willing to engage in these tactics. After Title VII, the major resource the civil rights movement needed was lawyers to argue cases in court. CORE had few of these, and its role in ending employment discrimination dissolved. Fortunately, the civil rights movement had another organization, the NAACP, well endowed with lawyers who could provide this now necessary resource.

Sometimes not having the resources necessary to take advantage of a particular opportunity can be disabling. The women's movement did not use court action as readily as the civil rights movement did—even though many of the same laws proscribed sex discrimination—because it had never organized legal resources adequately. Yet it could not use the sit-in against employment discrimination because the mere existence of a legal channel undermined any legitimacy of such a disruptive tactic. Fortunately the independent development of a "Title VII bar" has provided that resource, even though it is not under movement control. Similarly, the American Civil Liberties Union (ACLU) Women's Rights Project, under a Ford Foundation grant, now provides much of the legal planning and talent for the women's movement that the NAACP Legal Defense and Education Fund provided for the black movement. To a certain extent one could say the women's movement coopted the resources of the ACLU and/or the Ford Foundation to its ends.

A major factor affecting the costs of mobilizing resources is their density. Since campuses attract young people in large numbers, an SMO seeking to reach them can efficiently do so by going to the campus. Women are rather dispersed, however, so even with a mailing list of potential supporters, greater amounts of time and money must be spent to mobilize women for a particular activity than to mobilize students. Without such a list, the costs escalate.

Aggrieved groups that are atomized and scattered throughout the population require enormous resources to be reached, let alone mobilized. Those that are concentrated can be mobilized fairly readily, which is one reason why students are so readily available to so many movements. Groups that are scattered can be concentrated by being drawn together as part of the mobilization process of another movement or some other agency. For example, the Community Action Programs set up under the "war on poverty" became fertile grounds for welfare rights movement organizers. Without the government, the movement might not have been able to develop.

The reason many different movements tend to appear during the same historical period is not because different groups just happen to discover their grievances at the same time, or even because the example of one group alerts others to opportunities to alleviate their own grievances. Rather, it happens because the resources one movement generates can be used for cognate movements. Organizing or publicizing skills gained in one movement are readily transferable. One movement's conscience constituency can become the next movement's beneficiary constituency. The civil rights movement contributed significantly to the emergence of many other movements for just this reason.

CONSTRAINTS

It is easy to think of resources as abstract entities that, like money, can be used for most anything if enough is available. Unfortunately for most movement organizers, they aren't. Instead, all resources—even money—have constraints on their uses. These constraints differ, depending on the source, but their existence acts as a kind of filter between resources and SMOs. These filters are so important that they can totally redirect the resource of a movement, much as a prism does a beam of light. And it is these filtered resources that an SMO has to work with, not the raw product.

The two branches of the women's movement drew upon similar if not identical resources, in comparable if not identical amounts, from people with closely matched class and educational backgrounds. Yet one branch formed numerous national associations, many of which opened Washington offices to lobby the government; the other branch organized numerous small groups whose primary tasks were education, personal conversion, and service projects. The younger branch of the movement *could* have formed a national organization at its 1968 conference, yet it didn't even make plans for an annual conference. It *could* have used the IPS (Institute for Policy Studies) office in Washington as a base from which to put pressure on the government, but it never even discussed such a possibility. It *could* have organized mass demonstrations, like NOW did in 1970, but took to WITCH (Women's International Terrorist Conspiracy from Hell) hexes instead. Such divergence of energies cannot be explained unless one looks at the constraints, conscious and unconscious, on the resources available for action.

I have identified five different categories of constraints, and more could be found. Among these are values, past experiences, a constituency's reference group, expectations, and relations with target groups. The first and the last in the list have been identified by others,[6] while the middle three have either been overlooked or referred to vaguely.

Since these terms don't really require definitions, their filtering function can best be explored by applying them to the two branches of the women's liberation movement. Both the age difference and the political networks from which the two branches emerged provided their members with different values, experiences, reference groups, expectations, and relations with target groups. These differences strongly influenced the kind of SMOs created, and the SMO structure in turn joined with these filters in a synergistic effect that molded the strategic possibilities.

Early participants in the younger branch came largely from the radical community, and their values reflected that community's interpretation of basic American concerns.[7] The radical movement's concepts of participatory democracy, equality, liberty, and community emphasized that everyone should participate in the decisions that affected her life, and that everyone's contribution was equally valid.[8] These values led easily to the idea that hierarchy was bad because it gives some people power over others and does not allow everyone's talents to develop. The belief was that all people should be able to share, criticize, and learn from one another's ideas—equally. Any structure, or any leader who might influence this equal sharing, was automatically bad.[9] The logical conclusion to be drawn from this train of thought—that all structure and all leadership are intrinsically wrong—was not initially articulated. But the potential was clearly there, and it did not take long for the idea of leaderless, structureless groups to emerge and eventually dominate this branch of the movement.

The adherence to these values was premised on the assumption that all women were equally capable of making decisions, carrying out actions, performing tasks, and forming policy.[10] This assumption could be made because the women involved had little experience in democratic organizations other than those of the New Left where they saw dominance for its own sake, competition for positions in the leadership hierarchy, and "male ego tripping" rule the day.[11] They had felt similar domination and control for its own sake in social structures—primarily school and family—of which they had been part. The idea that there was some relationship between authority and responsibility, between organization and equal participation, and between leadership and self-government was not within their realm of experience.

The founders and early activists of NOW had gained their political experience in party politics, various bureaucracies, and the civil rights and labor movements. They felt structure in organizations was a help, not a hindrance; they were highly task oriented, found parliamentary procedure a convenience, were trained in public relations, and did not feel it necessary to live out egalitarian ideals in their own organization. Getting equality was more important than living it.

NOW's concept of a well-run organization was not one in which everyone participated, but one in which everyone contributed to the tasks of the movement. The concept of democracy was not one in which everyone had a say in all decisions, but one in which any who wanted to could have a say. Equality meant equal respect, not equal influence. Leadership was good, not bad.

The more immediate experiences of the early participants in the two branches also had an effect on their initial choice of tactics. Both had had experience with mass demonstrations, and both had had experience with the press. But radical women shared with radical men a certain jadedness about the value of mass demonstrations. They certainly hadn't ended the war, and they appeared to absorb enormous amounts of time and energy to proclaim messages that fell on deaf ears. Instead, what was needed were actions that would catch people's attention by challenging old ideas and raising new ones. The women in the younger branch did this creatively with WITCH hexes, zap actions, and a "freedom trash can" at the 1968 Miss America contest in which "instruments of female oppression" were tossed. Ironically, while women used these tactics to catch the eye of the public and press, they didn't want to talk to the press. Frankly, they were afraid of the press, and since they had access to the underground press, they didn't feel an acute need to appear in the established press. They had participated in so many demonstrations that were reported inaccurately that they did not feel their words would be reported the way they wanted them to be.

NOW women would have felt much too inhibited to engage in WITCH hexes (they thought they were silly) but felt no inhibitions about the press. Many were PR professionals and knew how to present their case, as well as not to expect too much. They were also willing to demonstrate, even though many knew the days of mass action were probably over. The first contemporary feminist picket line was organized by NOW in December 1967 to protest the Equal Employment Opportunity Commission's (EEOC) inaction on rewriting their want-ad guidelines.[12] NOW members had learned the uses of pickets and parades from the civil rights and union activities in which most had engaged. They did not give them up even when some of the their "more respectable" members left in disgust to form another organization, WEAL (Women's Equity Action League).

These direct-action tactics, and NOW's other activities, were aimed not merely at catching the public eye but, specifically, at pressuring the government. These tactics were part of an overall campaign that also used letter writing, court suits, and meetings with government officials. Many early NOW members had engaged in lobbying for other groups, and it seemed perfectly logical to continue their activities for a new movement. Besides, the initial impetus for NOW's formation had come because of the EEOC's reluctance to enforce the provision in Title VII prohibiting sex discrimination, so pressuring for equal enforcement clearly had to be a priority.

Another major difference between the women of the younger and older branches were their reference groups. Although a reference group is not always a group, it is a standard against which people compare themselves in order to judge their behavior and attitudes.[13] This well-established concept from social psychology is not one that has been used to analyze social movements, but it has a great deal of explanatory power. When I first watched and read about Weatherman's "Days of Rage" and other low-key terrorist tactics, I found myself puzzled by what seemed to be a totally unrealistic assessment of potential support from the American public. Only after I had read extensively in Weatherman literature and about the group[14] did they begin to make sense. I realized that many of them had spent the preceding years visiting international revolutionaries, largely Cubans and North Vietnamese, outside the United States or had talked to those who had. These revolutionaries in effect became their reference group. From them they acquired the idea that the true revolutionary is one who is not afraid to strike a blow in "the belly of the monster" (i.e., the United States), even if the blow was suicidal. I suspect that Weatherman tactics were calculated not to gain support, or even attention, from the American public but to gain a sense of having met revolutionary standards.

The standards new feminists wanted to meet were very different for the two branches. Women in the younger branch first and foremost considered themselves *radical* women. While women of both branches wanted to "start a mass movement of women to put an end to the barriers of segregation and discrimination based on sex,"[15] younger branch women felt this could be done only through "radical action and radical thinking." The desire to be radical virtually precluded any pressure-type activities. The greatest fear of radicals in the late sixties was that they would be "coopted" by the system into helping improve it through reform rather than destroy it through revolution. The idea that they could instead coopt institutional resources to their own aims was totally alien.

> Our role was not to be . . . a large "membership organization." What we were talking about being was . . . a "zap" action, political agitation and education group something like what the Student Non-Violet Coordinating Committee (S.N.C.C.) had been. We would be the first to dare to say and do the undareable, what women really felt and wanted.[16]

This kind of thinking meant actions that "blew people's minds" were OK, but picketing the EEOC to change its guidelines was not.

The movement's most prevalent activity and organization, the consciousness-raising rap group, also grew from this radical orientation. The women who developed this tactic felt "the first job now was to raise awareness and understanding, our own and others—awareness that would prompt people to organize and to act on a mass scale."

> Consciousness-raising—studying the whole gamut of women's lives, starting with the full reality of one's own—would also be a way of keeping the movement radical by preventing it from getting sidetracked into single issue reforms and single issue organizing. It would be a way of carrying theory about women further than it had ever been carried before, as the groundwork for achieving a radical solution for women as yet attained nowhere.[17]

While C-R, as it came to be called, started with one group, it quickly spread throughout the movement—for two reasons. First, many groups of women who met to discuss women's oppression and plan their strategy on how to change it found themselves talking more and more about their personal experiences. This was an activity for which they had ample resources. For those who had strong ties with the New Left, this was not an acceptable endeavor because it wasn't "political." When the women of New York presented consciousness raising as a form of radical action at the 1968 conference, it gave them a rationalization for what they were doing anyway. Second, there was extraordinary hostility and resistance by radical men to women's simply discussing their situation. Men dismissed the topics as petty and the process as therapy. Radical women took this resistance as a sign that they were on the right track.

> In the beginning we had set out to do our studying in order to take better action. We hadn't realized that just studying this subject and naming the problem and problems would be a radical action in itself, action so radical as to engender tremendous and persistent opposition . . . .[18]

Gerlach and Hine have emphasized the importance of opposition in maintaining movement cohesion.[19] The opposition of radical men to C-R not only created a high degree of group solidarity for the women engaged in it but strongly reinforced their belief that it was the way to be radical. As a result, C-R practically took over the younger branch of the movement as its sole *raison d'être*.

The women of NOW and the other national associations that began forming were not in the least concerned with being radical for the sake of being radical. Many felt that "equal rights" would take women only so far and that structural questions would have to be delt with, but they did not feel it necessary to provide an analysis and program for dealing with these issues. What they did feel was necessary was to be *effective*. Effectiveness was the standard they had acquired from the professional and political associations of which they had been members. Since the best way to be effective is to make demands for small changes, and to concentrate one's resources on a few specific areas, this is what they did. The most vulnerable areas were those where women could demand the same rights that blacks had already won. The immediate targets thus became attaining changes that would give women legal parity with blacks. Both their immediate goals and their tactics were borrowed directly from the civil rights movement. Only as these goals and tactics were exhausted did the movement begin to move in new directions.

The expectations of the women in the two branches were governed by their past experiences and the expectations of those they associated with. For young women, the goal was revolution, and the expectation was that it would come soon. Their job was not only to help bring it about but to prepare a plan for women's role in the revolutionary society. Consciousness raising and study groups were two ways of doing this. As the Left became more and more disillusioned with the idea that revolution was around the corner, attaining it could no longer be the primary goal. By then, however, the rap group had become the primary unit of the women's movement, and women were aware that these groups functioned not only to help women analyze their lives but to "change their heads." Just as important, these changes could be seen and felt within a short time. "People changing" consequently became the primary function of rap groups.

Older branch women expected to change institutions, not people. And they expected these changes to be slow and gradual. While younger women expected the revolution to come any month, those of the older branch debated whether the attaining of equal rights alone would take twenty years or a century. With a longer perspective, they could be content with imperceptible changes.

Analyzing the relations of feminists with their target groups is a little tricky, because first one has to decide what the targets were. For the women of NOW, WEAL, and similar organizations, the targets were concrete and identifiable. They were laws, institutions, discriminatory practices, and the people who could affect these things. In the younger branch, the first major debate was over just who the target was. Was it men or male-dominated institutions? Was it capitalism or patriarchy? Even when the women of a particular group knew which of these targets they wanted to attack, they were usually distant enough to raise some difficult strategic questions. For this reason, the usual targets became those much closer to home, the men in one's life and the women in one's group. And, contrary to Turner,[20] the fact that feminists had generally close and intimate relations to both these targets did not dissuade them from using some very coercive tactics.

SMO STRUCTURE

There are two heuristic models of SMO structure in the literature. One is the centralized, hierarchical organization with a well-developed division of labor.[21] The other model is the decentralized, segmented, reticulate movement with no real center and at best a simple division of labor.[22] Strategically, the former seems to be better for attaining short-range goals involving institutional change in which organizational survival is not the dominant concern. The latter appears better for attaining personal changes in orientation and attitude through recruitment and conversion in which organizational survival is a dominant concern.

The centralized movement devotes minimal resources to group maintenance needs, as it focuses them on goal attainment. However, this is somewhat reinforcing, for short-range goal attainment in turn becomes a means of maintaining group cohesion.[23] The decentralized movement, on the other hand, is compelled to devote major resources to group maintenance. As long as it defines its major task as "people changing," this too is reinforcing because maintaining a strong sense of group solidarity is the means through which personal changes are accomplished. These simple, heuristic relationships work out fine as long as a movement group is conscious of the way in which its structure limits its strategic possibilities. A source of problems for many movements is the frequent attempt to pursue strategies for which their structures are inappropriate.

As Zald and Ash,[24] among others, have pointed out, the most viable movement is one that has several organizations that can play different roles and pursue different strategic possibilities. Thus the growth, development, and demise of a movement are not the same as the growth, development, and demise of the individual organizations within it. Most contemporary movements in this country have had complex structures and consequently fit both heuristic models. For example, the younger branch of the women's liberation movement is almost a paradigmatic example of the decentralized model, as it has no national organizations and has consciously rejected hierarchy and a division of labor. The older branch has several national organizations that reticulate only slightly with one another. None fits the classic hierarchical model perfectly, but they are close enough for analytic purposes.

Neither branch of the movement deliberately created a structure specifically geared to accomplish its desired goals. Instead, the founders of both branches drew upon their previous political experience. Women of the older branch had been trained in and used the traditional forms of political action. They were familiar with national associations, and that is what they created. Women of the younger branch inherited the loose, flexible, person-oriented attitude of the youth and student movements, as well as these movements' disillusionment with traditional politics and traditional forms of political action. They strove for something new—and radical.

Once these different structures were created, they in turn molded the strategic possibilities—occasionally contrary to the professed desires of at least some of their members. Both branches have made some efforts to change their structures, yet both have remained essentially the same as they began. Organizational structure cannot be changed at will. What arises in response to one set of concerns in effect sets the agenda for what the movement can do next.

The younger branch provides an excellent example of this molding effect because the original intention of its founders was not consciousness raising but radical action. C-R was supposed to be a means to an end, not the major task of the movement. Nonetheless, the loose, fluid, supportive C-R group was so successful that it became the model for all other groups. People resisted the idea that different movement tasks required different structures, or for that matter any structure. Instead, they elevated the operating principles of the small group to the status of feminist ideology, making it virtually impossible to adopt any other structure.

I have discussed the problems derived from "the tyranny of structurelessness" elsewhere[25] and will not go into them here. Suffice it to say that the activities that could be developed by this branch of the movement were limited to those that could be performed by small homogeneous groups without major divisions of labor. These activities were primarily educational and/or service projects that could be set up on a local level. Consequently, the younger branch of the movement set up numerous women's centers, abortion counseling services, bookstores, liberation schools, day care centers, film and tape production units, research projects, and rock-and-roll bands. The production of a feminist publication was one of the most feasible projects for a small group to handle, and hundreds were developed. But there was never any national coordination of these projects; many were repetitive or competitive; and they frequently became closed, encapsulated units whose primary purpose was to provide a *raison d'être* for their members to stay together.

The molding effect is less obvious with older branch organizations because there was a greater congruence between strategic intentions and organizational structure, but it is there nonetheless. NOW and the National Women's Political Caucus (NWPC) provide an interesting study in contrasting problems. NOW was created to be a national lobbying organization, and initially that is what it was. From the beginning it required national dues be paid by all members, whether they were members of chapters or not. Chapters in turn, apart from paying dues, were largely autonomous units. After passage of the Equal Rights Amendment in 1972, it gradually became apparent that a mid-level structure of state organizations was necessary to press for ratification in the states. Neither individual chapters nor the national organization were capable of being effective on the state level. The creation of state organizations has proven to be a difficult, time-consuming task. In unratified states they facilitate lobbying efforts. But in ratified states they have generally undermined the autonomy of the local chapters by creating a new level of bureaucracy that makes it difficult for chapters to act.

The NWPC was created in 1972 in order to try to elect more women to office. Modeled on the American political party, it created state organizations from the beginning but did not require national dues. This hampered NWPC effectiveness on the national level, and it too has gone through a difficult period of trying to establish, and collect, national dues from recalcitrant chapters that prefer to concentrate their resources on state legislatures and local elections.

Ironically, a third organization, the Women's Equity Action League, has changed its strategy to fit its organization, instead of attempting the opposite. Founded in 1968 in Ohio as a split-off from NOW, WEAL was intended to be a small, powerful organization for professional, executive, and influential women around the country. Over time, it discovered that a significant percentage of its membership was in Washington, D.C., and that its members elsewhere had some influence on Washington politicians. Therefore, it came to redefine its primary purpose as that of a national lobbying organization whose primary resource was not numbers but expertise.

EXPECTATIONS ABOUT POTENTIAL TARGETS

As a SMO searches for effective actions there are three factors it must consider about potential targets and the external environment. They are (1) the structure of available opportunities for action, (2) social-control measures that might be taken and (3) the effect on bystander publics.

As Schattschneider has pointed out, "The function of institutions is to channel conflict; institutions do not treat all forms of conflict impartially, just as football rules do not treat all forms of violence with indiscriminate equality."[26] Nor do political institutions treat all demands from all groups impartially; instead, institutions and the "rules of the game" operate as a filter to eliminate some and redirect others. Because SMOs are generally dissident groups, they frequently lack the resources to exploit the "usual" opportunities for action. Thus the success of such a movement is often determined by its ingenuity at finding less obvious leverage points from which to pressure its targets, creating new avenues for action, and/or effectively substituting resources it has in abundance for those it does not have.

Finding leverage points within the political system generally requires some intimate knowledge of its workings and thus is an alternative available only to those not totally alienated from the system. Ralph Nader's "Raiders" have been every effective at finding leverage points. Affirmative action in higher education became a public issue when a faculty woman sought a remedy for her failure to get a particular job for which she was qualified and found that none of the antidiscrimination laws covered her situation.[27] Her discovery of Executive Order 11375, which required affirmative action for sex as well as race, is typical of the fact that such leverage points can be found as much through luck as through knowledge.

Creating new avenues is a far more common form of action for dissident movements, especially when they have minimal knowledge of or access to the political system. The civil rights and student movements very effectively attracted public attention to their causes through nonviolent demonstrations that prevented people from engaging in "business as usual" without so flagrantly violating norms of behavior that the demonstrators could be dismissed as pathological deviants. Unfortunately, such tactics are usually "creative" only when they are new; their effect wears off over time. Sometimes such tactics do become institutionalized, as did the strike and boycott, which were originally developed by the labor movement. But at other times they simply lose their impact. The arrest in 1977 of over a thousand people protesting at a nuclear plant at Seabrook, New Hampshire, made less of a public impression than the "freedom ride" buses of the fifties or the campus arrests of the sixties.

Resource substitution is a particularly common strategy for social movements that want to utilize institutional channels but do not possess the usual resources for their utilization. Groups that cannot command large voting blocks to elect favorable candidates can achieve equivalent access by supplying the time and commitment of their members as campaign workers. This has been successfully done by the gay rights movement to gain support from local politicians and other groups.

Not infrequently, the structure of available opportunities for action presents *no* feasible alternatives to some SMOs. This may be because a particular SMO constituency is too alienated or too ignorant to take advantage of what is available, as is the case with movements of the seriously deprived. It may also be because the particular resources of a movement do not fit the channels available for action, that the SMO's structure or values do not allow it to participate in those channels, or that the available channels are not capable of dealing with a movement's demands. In theory the younger branch of the women's liberation movement was just as capable as the older branch of mobilizing its supporters for lobbying activities, but the constraints on the uses of its people resources, as well as its small-group structure, made this opportunity for action unfeasible.

When there are no feasible opportunities, movements do not simply go away; instead, discontent takes forms other than political action. Many riots are now seen as a form of political activity. Withdrawal movements of varying kinds are common when dissident groups feel highly alienated. These withdrawal movements may be "apolitical" in the sense that their members identify their activities as spiritual or cultural. Yet many are political, but they redefine their politics in "alternative" forms. When the New Left turned to "alternative institutions," it saw these as a new means of pursuing its politics, not a rejection of politics. As has happened with communes and some other leftist activities, however, it is not uncommon for what began as an alternative political institution to become an apolitical one. In this way some movements can be "cooled out" so that what began as a means of making public demands becomes a refuge for seeking personal solutions.

When a movement does appear to find successful avenues for action, it generally encounters social control measures of one sort or other. These may suppress a movement, but not always so—direct opposition is a two-edged sword. As Gurr and Gerlach and Hine[28] have illustrated, some opposition is necessary to maintain movement viability. A solid opponent can do more to unify a group and heal its splits than any other factor. Many of the student sit-ins of the sixties would have never got off the ground if the university authorities hadn't brought in the police. But even if the enemy is not so blatant, it is the perceived and not the real opposition that is important. Movements that neither perceive nor experience opposition find it difficult to maintain the degree of commitment necessary for a viable, active organization. Often opposition will be blown up larger than life because to do so serves the needs of group cohesion.

Nevertheless, the relationship between opposition (real or perceived) and movement strength is not linear. Effective application of social control measures can kill a movement as well as completely ignore it. Similarly, a perceived opposition of great strength can effectively destroy a movement by convincing people that their actions are futile. For example, the many infiltration and conspiracy theories that leftist and feminist groups had developed to explain their internal problems had an initial effect of heightening commitment against a pernicious enemy. But if carried too far or too long, they served to undermine the mutual trust necessary for movement survival. Thus an opposition that contributes to trust and commitment in the short range can kill it in the long run.

The degree and success of opposition effects not only the movement but the relevant bystander publics. Bystander publics are not direct targets of a movement's actions, but they can affect the outcome of these actions. As a general rule, movements try to turn bystander publics into conscience constituencies that will supply the movement with additional resources and prevent them from becoming antagonists who will discourage targets from responding to movement demands.[29] Movements that cannot find leverage points are very dependent on the reactions of bystander publics, and it is not uncommon for demonstrations to be used, not to directly affect a particular target, but to gain sympathy and support from other parties. The southern civil rights movement's primary strategy was to use nonviolent demonstrations in expectation that an overly violent social control response would attract third-party support. When it brought these same tactics to the North where the bystander publics were the targets, it largely failed.

The civil rights movement's failure to appreciate that tactics viable in one arena wouldn't work in another is a common one. SMO's plan their actions on the basis of expectations about potential target and bystander public response. These expectations are initially derived from premovement experiences, or those of cognate groups. Once actions are initiated, direct feedback becomes relevant. When an activity proves successful, it is generally repeated without analyzing the context that permitted that success.

For reasons already discussed, the younger branch of the women's liberation movement was not interested in ordinary pressure tactics aimed at political institutions. Even if it had been, none of its participants had the experience in this kind of action necessary to provide a model of how to do it. They did have experience with zap actions, and several of these were executed during the first years of the movement's existence. While the actions were approved by other movement participants, they did not receive favorable feedback from the public at which they were aimed. Usually they were ignored; and when not ignored, they were ridiculed. Had this been the only available outlet for their energies, zap actions might have continued.

In the meantime, consciousness raising had been systemized and spread widely. Feedback from this process was immediate and favorable. Women recruited into C-R groups spoke frequently of the emotional release the groups sustained, and kept coming back. While not all women liked C-R, most did, and it became the prevalent activity. Because it was so successful, the movement's immediate targets changed from the general public to that of the women in the C-R groups with other younger branch activities serving less as a means of direct impact on the public than as a magnet by which to attract new recruits into C-R groups.

In the meantime, the older branch maintained its basic, successful strategy of institutional pressure, though it expanded its repertoire beyond the initial one of lobbying. While some organizations within the older branch, such as NOW, added C-R activities, they did so as a membership service and not as a basic strategic device. This branch of the movement has been very attuned to the structure of available opportunities for action. It has paid much less attention to actual and potential social control measures and bystander publics. Nonetheless, it is still affected by both these factors; its leaders are merely unaware of how.

In conclusion, some flaws in the model presented should be pointed out. The most glaring one is that it is not a dynamic model. It does not explain changes over time in any of its components or in strategic outcomes. Rather, it enables one to look at an SMO at one point in time to determine the resources available for mobilization and the potential ways in which these resources can be deployed. In addition, the model ignores fortuitous circumstances that might benefit a particular movement's goals and the accidents of history that are often so crucial in a movement's success or failure. Fortuitous resources, as well as accidents, certainly have an effect on final outcome, but unless their availability can be reasonably predicted or controlled by an SMO, they play little part in strategic decision making.

NOTES

1. Ralph H. Turner, "Determinants of Social Movement Strategies," in *Human Nature and Collective Behavior*, ed. Tamotsu Shibutani (Englewood Cliffs, N.J.: Prentice-Hall, 1970), p. 146.
2. John D. McCarthy and Mayer N. Zald, "Toward a Resource Mobilization Theory

of SMOs" (paper presented at the Southern Sociological Society, 12 April 1973), p. 17; William A. Gamson, *Power and Discontent* (Homewood, Ill.: Dorsey Press, 1968), pp. 100–105.

3. Chapter 1 of this book.

4. Interview with Bobbie Kilbourg, August 1976.

5. I borrowed the idea of beneficiary and conscience constituencies from McCarthy and Zald, and they in turn borrowed the latter from Michael Harrington, *Toward a Democratic Left: A Radical Program for a New Majority* (New York: Macmillan, 1968).

6. Turner, "Determinants of Social Movement Strategies," p. 151.

7. Daniel C. Kramer, *Participatory Democracy: Developing Ideals of the Political Left* (Cambridge, Mass.: Schenkman, 1972).

8. Linda Lewis and Sally Baideme, "The Women's Liberation Movement," in *New Left Thought: An Introduction*, ed. Lyman T. Sargent (Homewood, Ill.: Dorsey Press, 1972), p. 83.

9. Martha Shelly, "Subversion in the Women's Movement, What Is to Be Done," *Off Our Backs*, 8 November 1970, p. 7.

10. Lewis and Baideme, "The Women's Liberation Movement," p. 87.

11. Margo Piercy, "The Grand Coolie Damn," in *Sisterhood Is Powerful*, ed. Robin Morgan (New York: Random House, 1970); Robin Morgan, "Goodbye to All That," in *Voices from Women's Liberation*, ed. Leslie Tanner (New York: New American Library, 1970).

12. The EEOC had initially ruled that separate want-ad columns with racial labels were a violation of Title VII, but those with sex labels were not. NOW wanted the EEOC to "de-sexigate" the want-ads by ruling that all labels were illegal.

13. This term was first used in 1942 by H. H. Hyman, "The Psychology of Status," *Archives of Psychology*, no. 269 (1942), but the idea goes back much farther.

14. See especially the compilation *Weatherman*, ed. Harold Jacobs (San Francisco: Ramparts, 1971).

15. Kathie Sarachild, "Consciousness-Raising: A Radical Weapon," in *Feminist Revolution*, ed. Redstockings (New York: Redstockings, 1975), p. 131.

16. Ibid., p. 132.

17. Ibid.

18. Ibid.

19. Gerlach and Hine, *People, Power, Change*, chap. 7.

20. Turner, "Determinants of Social Movement Strategy," p. 153.

21. William Gamson most explicitly discusses the strategic possibilities of this model in his *Strategies for Social Protest* (Homewood, Ill.: Dorsey Press), p. 197.

22. Gerlach and Hine, *People, Power, Change*.

23. Freeman, *Politics of Women's Liberation*, pp. 100–102, 145–46, for further discussion of this point.

24. Mayer N. Zald and Roberta Ash, "Social Movement Organizations: Growth, Decay, and Change," *Social Forces* 44 (March 1966): 327–40.

25. Jo Freeman, "Tyranny of Structurelessness," *Ms.*, July 1973.

26. E. E. Schattschneider, *The Semi-Sovereign People* (New York: Holt, Rinehart and Winston, 1960), p. 72.

27. Freeman, *Politics of Women's Liberation*, pp. 191–209.

28. Gerlach and Hine, *People, Power, Change*, Chap. 8, Ted Robert Gurr, *Why Men Rebel* (Princeton, N.J.: Princeton University Press, 1970).

29. For further discussion of this point, see Turner, "Determinants of Social Movement Strategies," p. 152; and McCarthy and Zald, "Toward a Resource Mobilization Theory of SMOs."

13

Organization or Disruption? Strategic Options for Marginal Groups: The Case of the Chicago Indian Village

Deborah LeVeen

The nature of the political options available to the poor is a question that has generated significant controversy among political analysts and activists. No one disputes the political handicaps created by the absence of socioeconomic resources, but there is considerable disagreement about the most effective means to overcome those handicaps. Some argue that the poor should simply work harder at using the conventional political mechanisms of organizing, forming alliances, and electoral bargaining, thereby using organized numbers to compensate for their lack of socioeconomic resources and seeking to develop a stable position in the established political arena.[1] Others argue that poverty makes it impossible for the poor to use those conventional mechanisms, that the effort to develop stable positions of influence is not simply futile but counterproductive, and that as a consequence the poor have no recourse but to engage in sustained extralegal disruption.[2]

The issue is particularly significant for Indian people. They are not only institutionally marginal, like all poor people, but culturally marginal: that is, they not only lack stable positions within the central institutions of the dominant society, they do not share the values and aspirations of that society.[3] Thus they are hindered both by the absence of socioeconomic resources and also by the serious difficulty of trying to define goals that are both meaningful to them as Indian people and within the realm of political feasibility as defined

211

by the dominant society. Furthermore, their numerical weakness (there are just over 1 million Indian people in the United States[4]) further weakens the conventional argument regarding the use of organized numbers.

This chapter examines the experience of one Native American protest group, the Chicago Indian Village (CIV), which struggled for two years to generate influence and win benefits for Indian people in Chicago. It succeeded in creating new bargaining power and winning some gains for the Indian community, but in the end it was defeated. Because the CIV used a variety of strategies and tactics, it offers an opportunity to assess their relative value and thus to learn something about the broader question of strategic options for marginal groups. Before presenting the story of the CIV, however, we must look more closely at the theoretical issues.

THE THEORETICAL CONTROVERSY

The effort to develop political influence involves a number of stages including generating collective action; publicizing and legitimating one's demands; gaining access to the relevant authorities; creating and sustaining a bargaining process; and, ultimately, obtaining the desired response from the authorities and thereby, in a broad sense, shaping public policy. "Collective action" refers to any action undertaken by people acting as a group; it varies widely in terms of degree of organization, stability, common purposes, and so on. Influence and power are perhaps best thought of as degrees of effectiveness in the process of generating pressure, with influence referring to the capacity to force attention on the issues and force some negotiations, and power referring to the capacity to actually shape public policy.

Resources are critical to the process of developing power, for they are the basis of pressure; resources must be offered as an inducement to compliance or a threat against noncompliance with the demands being made. The most important resources are generally those associated with economic position and social status: economic control (control over employment, finance, essential goods, and so on); money and/or access to money; education; respectability. The key problem for the poor, then, is how to compensate for the absence of these resources.

The conventional answer, as noted, has been that organized numbers will compensate for the lack of resources. In a democratic system where votes determine electoral outcomes, groups of individuals acting in concert can create a collective resource of significant value in the bargaining process. However, the development of organized collective action is itself a major task. Simply generating the willingness to act collectively for some common good, as opposed to engaging in the pursuit of self-interest, is difficult.[5] Collective action requires resources—money, education, expertise, time—as well as some good reason to believe in the effectiveness of the effort. And it has been well documented that rates of political participation and levels of sense of efficacy are lower among those of lower socioeconomic status: Those who need it most, in other words, are least likely to believe in their political efficacy or engage in political action.[6]

This raises real questions as to whether the poor *can* use collective action to compensate for their absence of socioeconomic resources and, if so, what kind of collective action is most likely to be effective. These questions, in turn, raise critical questions about the viability and justice of the established political system. Can it be made to work for those without socioeconomic resources, or must they resort to extraordinary forms of political action, such as mass disruption, in an effort to generate political pressure?

These questions have given rise to an extended controversy, the key elements of which can be clearly seen in the views of the late Saul Alinsky, on the one hand, and Frances Piven and Richard Cloward, on the other.

THE ALINSKY POSITION

Saul Alinsky had enormous faith in the possibility of using organization to empower ordinary people for effective political action; indeed, he was the founder of the practice of community organization as a political strategy, and the methods he developed continue to provide the basis for organizing efforts across the country.[7]

The process begins when representatives of a community, preferably representatives of existing organizations within a community, such as churches, block clubs, and local businesses, solicit and raise funds for a staff of trained organizers. The staff familiarizes itself with the community and identifies potential issues around which to mobilize the community; then it arranges a variety of meetings with different groups within the community. Here the careful process of political education begins, as people discuss their common problems and plan strategic actions for dealing with them.

The issues selected for action, particularly at the outset, must be "specific, immediate, and realizable,"[8] for it is critical that the first actions be successful. Failure can devastate a fledgling organization; victories, no matter how small, provide incentives for continued participation and establish credibility with the authorities, thereby building the foundation for the pursuit of larger issues.

Alinsky had a clear sense of the problems faced by the poor. As he put it: "Power has always derived from two main sources, money and people. Lacking money, the Have-Nots must build power from their own flesh and blood.... Against the finesse and sophistication of the status quo, the Have-Nots have always had to club their way."[9] But he was confident that the poor could develop organizations, and through creative tactics—"doing what you can with what you have"[10]—could translate their "flesh and blood" into sustained political influence.

The central strategic principle governing the use of these organizations was what Alinsky called "jujitsu": using the strength of the opposition against itself. As he explained: "The opposition is always stronger than you are and so his own strength must be used against him. I have repeatedly said that the status quo is your best ally if properly goaded and guided."[11] In other words, the major source of strength for the poor lies in the enemy's reaction; and the poor must properly catalyze that reaction and then remain flexible and creative in moving with it so as to make it work for them.[12] And the most effective way to use the enemy's strength is to exploit its internal divisions, thereby "utilizing the power of one part of the power structure against another part."[13] By skillfully applying the principle of jujitsu to the use of organized collective action, the poor would be able to develop significant bargaining power.

Alinsky's optimism complements the view that the established processes can be made to work for the poor. And he has left a record of successful community organizations, which continues to grow. If one looks closely at this record, however, one finds much more evidence of success among working- and middle-class groups than among truly low-income or marginal groups.[14] This is one of the bases of the Piven and Cloward argument.

THE PIVEN AND CLOWARD POSITION

The core of the Piven and Cloward argument is that conditions associated with poverty prevent poor people from maintaining the kinds of organizations necessary to protect and advance their interests through the regular processes of the political system.[15] Poor people lack the resources, such as money and education, required even for Alinsky organizations, and organizations of poor people cannot aggregate enough of these resources to make them anything other than poor organizations. Even more important, poor people lack the kinds of institutional positions (e.g., as producers, property owners, or workers in the primary labor market[16]) that normally give rise to organizing efforts; instead, the poor are located in marginal institutions—the secondary labor market, unemployment office, welfare office—that do not provide the resources, the opportunities for regular interaction, or the possibilities for leverage necessary for the development of effective organizations. Finally, poor people have difficulty identifying "specific, immediate, and realizable" issues around which to organize. As Piven and Cloward said of the National Welfare Rights Organization: "...it was not clear how activists could, as a practical day-to-day matter of organizing, mount an attack on poverty by attacking its main cause—underemployment and unemployment."[17]

The only significant resource the poor do possess is the capacity to make trouble—to disrupt institutions of the established system and produce sufficient political reverberations so that the authorities are forced to respond. And when they are both forced to respond *and* reluctant to use force, as will be the case if the grievances of the protestors can be shown to be legitimate and can thus serve to generate public support, then the disruption may become the basis for political influence.

But disruption is a limited option. It is possible only under extraordinary historical circumstances, during times of social upheaval that give rise to new expectations and demands and allow new forms of behavior. And disruption is difficult to sustain. It is costly to participants, and because authorities are reluctant to reward disruptive organizations, it is difficult to obtain the benefits necessary to provide incentives for continued participation. Finally, authorities have a number of means of encouraging and/or compelling the poor to abandon their disruption and adopt the established procedures of the political system.

Thus the authorities will seek to placate and coopt the protestors by offering concessions as well as positions within the established institutions, thereby providing incentives for more cooperation and less threatening behavior. Then they will try to reduce public sympathy for the protestors by claiming that their needs have been met, thus reducing the legitimacy of further protest. Having done all this, if further action is necessary, the authorities may simply resort to repression.

Often this is not necessary, however, as protest leaders yield all too quickly, according to Piven and Cloward, to the offers of the authorities: accepting concessions, accepting positions in established institutions, and thereby deflating the momentum and support for further disruption. In doing this, they are guided by conventional beliefs regarding the necessity of developing stable, mass-based organizations as a means to power. This is a critical strategic error, not simply because of the near-impossibility of developing a permanent organization among very low-income people but, more important, because by blunting the disruptive impulse, the effort to develop a conventional organization critically undermines the most effective resource of the poor, namely, their capacity for disruption.

The crux of the Piven and Cloward argument, then, is to make the most of those rare occasions when collective defiance is possible—to push for maximum concessions in return for a restoration of quiescence.[18] For, although disruption is costly and ultimately limited, it is the most effective means to utilize those scarce resources available to the poor to win concessions that, bit by bit, may improve the conditions of their lives.

THE CHICAGO INDIAN VILLAGE EXPERIENCE

BACKGROUND

Like most poor communities, the Chicago Indian community was relatively powerless. There were about 16,000 Indian people in Chicago in 1970,[19] and most of them had come since the relocation policy initiated by the Bureau of Indian Affairs in 1953.[20] This policy was intended to bring Indians from reservations to selected urban areas for the purpose of improving their employment opportunities and thereby facilitating their assimilation into the larger society—the dominant society, as Indian people refer to it.

However, neither employment opportunities nor the broader processes of assimilation had changed significantly for Indian people in Chicago. According to some estimates, about three-fourths of the Indian population was either unemployed or employed in marginal jobs, often on a day-labor basis.[21] Only a tiny fraction of Indian children were in school.[22] And, although they were concentrated in Uptown, on Chicago's north side, most had not put down roots in the city; about half of them moved at least once a year, within the city or between the city and the reservation.[23] One study estimated that of the total population, 10 percent had been assimilated into the middle class of the larger society, 20 percent had become members of the stable working class, and the remaining 70 percent were essentially marginal to the larger society.[24]

This marginality was cultural as well as structural; that is, the Indian people did not share many of the values of the dominant society. Indian people are not motivated by the intense desire for material security, nor by the competitive striving for individual success that characterizes the dominant culture. Rather, Indian culture is more egalitarian and community oriented, emphasizing sharing and generosity rather than individual gain. At the same time, independence is more important than material security. Finally, Indian people remain fundamentally attached to their land: The reservation remains home. All these values conflict with the institutions of the dominant society and impede the assimilation of Indian people into those institutions. Thus Indian people will leave a job in order to return to the reservation, or refuse to apply for assistance from a social service agency because it is an admission of dependence.

In sum, then, most Indian people do not want assimilation into the dominant society. What they do want is accommodation on their own terms—that is, sufficient accommodation to allow them to obtain the resources necessary to their survival as Indian people. That such accommodation is not easy to achieve is evidenced by the extreme poverty that continues to characterize Indian communities.

There were several cultural and service organizations in the Chicago Indian community. The most important of these was the American Indian Center, which was founded in 1953 through the joint efforts of the Indian community, a group of anthropologists, and several private organizations. The status of its patrons quickly established the Center as the most legitimate and reliable organizational representative of the Indian community, and it was funded accordingly. Its stance was explicitly nonpolitical; given its connections, not only was political activity unnecessary but it might even have threatened the relationships on which its survival depended.[25]

By the late sixties, however, the broader changes that were politicizing minority communities across the country were beginning to permeate the Chicago Indian community. The year 1968 saw the formation of American Indians United (AIU), the first national Indian organization for urban Indians. Funded by the Ford Foundation, its roots as well as headquarters were in Chicago. AIU was short-lived, but it helped stimulate subsequent developments. And in December 1969, one month after the occupation of Alcatraz (the former federal penitentiary located on an island in San Francisco Bay) by a group of Indians, an Alinsky-style organization called the Native American Committee (NAC), was launched in Chicago.

NAC began with relatively significant resources: two Alinsky-trained organizers (a Sioux with a master's degree in social work and a Presbyterian minister who had also been instrumental in the founding of AIU), financial support from the church, and meeting space provided by the Indian Center. NAC's organizing strategy adhered closely to the Alinsky model of meetings, consciousness raising, and limited demonstrations, and it succeeded in generating new forms of political action in the Chicago Indian community and winning new recognition of the needs of the Indian community, as well as limited gains from various local agencies.

THE FOUNDING OF THE CHICAGO INDIAN VILLAGE[26]

Early in May 1970 NAC used the eviction of a Menominee woman from her apartment to launch a protest designed to dramatize the housing problem faced by Chicago Indians. The Indian Center's teepee was borrowed and set up in an empty lot across from the woman's apartment, which just happened to be next to Wrigley Field, the stadium used by one of Chicago's baseball teams. Additional pup tents were pitched, and a group of people moved in. Ideally suited to generate publicity, the tent village was conceived in good Alinsky fashion as an imaginative but limited demonstration intended to produce limited gains. As such, it had broad support in the Indian community.

However, when the predictably limited gains were offered—a list of vacancies in housing no better than that which had provoked the protest—support divided between those in favor of "consolidating their gains" no matter how limited (i.e., accepting the housing and disbanding the village) and those who wished to continue the protest in hopes of generating further support and pressure. A schism resulted, with the Center and some NAC members withdrawing their support from the village and the remaining people forming a new organization, the Chicago Indian Village (CIV).

The CIV continued the encampment through July. It was an excellent means of establishing a new organization, as it continued to generate publicity, participation, and a variety of official efforts to help (and relocate) the Indians. The most important of these was the decision by the Chicago school board to begin planning an all-Indian high school for the Indian community.[27] Eventually, however, both the attraction and the strategic value of the encampment began to wane, and so the tents were disbanded. The Village continued its activities as a community organization.

LEADERSHIP AND IDEOLOGY

Leadership in the Chicago Indian Village was concentrated in the hands of Mike Chosa, a Chippewa from Wisconsin, and Betty Jack, his older sister. Mike was an imaginative entrepreneur whose pride in being able to "make something out of nothing" was ideally suited to the effort to organize poor people. Educated in BIA schools and experienced in a wide variety of jobs, Mike had the resources and skills for success in the dominant society. His values and interests, however, were rooted in the Indian community. He traveled extensively and spent several years in California, organizing farmworkers and hustling pool. He returned to Chicago shortly before the formation of NAC and became one of its original leaders; when the first Indian organizer had to leave Chicago, Mike replaced him at the Alinsky training school for organizers. Mike thus brought a combination of education, experience, and entrepreneurial talent to his role as chief of the Village; he became its principal strategist and spokesman and earned profound respect and loyalty from his followers.

Betty was fearless, outspoken, and tough. She, too, had been educated in BIA schools and had come to the city in search of employment. Like so many

Indian people, however, she took to drinking and eventually ended up on skid row, where she spent the better part of ten years. She brought to the CIV the survival and leadership skills she had developed during those years, as well as a solid network of contacts among "street" Indians. Her capacity to mobilize and maintain a following, as well as the fact that she was still an alcoholic— capable of sustained periods of sobriety but also of heavy binges—were critical to the CIV.

The CIV developed a relatively coherent set of objectives. These included elements of the larger movements of the sixties, but at heart they were uniquely Indian, for underlying the usual demands for housing, schools, and jobs was the theme running throughout the contemporary Indian movement: the desire for cultural and material self-determination.[28] In the broadest sense, self-determination meant the revitalization of Indian culture and the development of the material bases—in employment, housing, schools, community services —for self-determining Indian communities. In the Chicago context, these goals came to focus upon the acquisition of a site *outside* the city (with all its problems) on which a comprehensive Indian center could be established—one that would offer housing, education, job training, jobs, and the rebuilding of a confident and informed Indian identity. It would be a sort of transition center, serving to orient newcomers to the city and rehabilitate those who had already been to the city and met defeat.

The CIV strategy for the pursuit of these objectives evolved slowly and experimentally. In line with the commitment to self-determination, the overall strategy included not simply an attempt to generate pressure for external assistance but also the attempt to establish Indian-owned businesses, which would provide both jobs and material support for other community efforts. Mike called it a two-pronged strategy, with community organizing to jar loose the external funding necessary for economic development and economic development to provide an independent basis for ongoing community activities.

STRATEGY: COMMUNITY ORGANIZATION

Following the disbanding of the tent village, the CIV moved into a storefront in Uptown, using the stipend Mike received as an Alinsky student to pay the rent and other basic expenses. For a while, Mike adhered relatively closely to the Alinsky model. Regular meetings were held, events (including large community feasts for Thanksgiving and Christmas) and demonstrations were sponsored, and cooperation with other neighborhood organizations, both Indian and non-Indian, was pursued. On the economic development "prong," the CIV obtained a contract with National Accelerator Laboratories and a loan from W. Clement Stone, which enabled it to establish a small, nonprofit landscaping business.[29]

The strategy seemed to be effective. Nevertheless, there were serious problems that, by midwinter, threatened the survival of the organization. Although it was easy to produce a large turnout for demonstrations and events, the regular membership was small and fluctuated greatly. The most faithful CIV members were, for the most part, those most in need of the services offered by the CIV (i.e., a place to eat, sleep, and drink). Even more important, funding was a serious problem. The continuation of Mike's stipend was in doubt, and in his search for alternative sources of assistance, he was repeatedly told that his organization had no programs worthy of support. Although the landscaping business would generate some overhead for the CIV, it certainly would not be enough to maintain the organization. Finally, the broader neighborhood coalitions in which the CIV was participating were also meeting strong resistance and in some cases outright defeat.[30]

It was a rather gloomy period, and for a while Mike contemplated abandoning the community organizing effort altogether. Finally he chose instead to escalate the strategy, to try to develop a more effective means of utilizing the resources and opportunities available to the Chicago Indian community.

STRATEGY: SUSTAINED DISRUPTION

Preparations for the new strategy began at the first annual CIV convention in early March 1970. Mike made an eloquent speech about the CIV's objectives and its failure, with the exception of the Tree Service, to make any progress on those objectives; then he showed several films of CIV demonstrations, including the march on Clement Stone's office to which Mike attributed the CIV's success in obtaining the loan from Stone. Mike ended by telling people that they would have to be out on the street again soon.

And they were: on March 10, after a feast of wild rice, the CIV invaded the Fourth Presbyterian Church, one of Chicago's wealthiest and most influential churches, with a vow to remain until the church promised to help them develop a housing project like the one being developed for the black community "or to resist to the last blood-stained second." The church needed its premises for a banquet that evening and worked intensely—listening to the Indians, making phone calls, arranging a meeting for the following day with representatives of the Chicago Presbytery (the governing body for all of the Presbyterian churches in Chicago)—to persuade the CIV to leave. The Indians were reluctant to appear "easy" (in their private discussions about what to do, references were made to the show of force black people would have made), but finally the group decided, on the advice of an elderly Ojibwa medicine man, to accept the offers of the church and withdraw.

The following day, in an effort to intensify the pressure, the CIV took over a deteriorating apartment building on Ainslie Street in Uptown. The building housed several Indian families and had been the source of problems throughout the winter. It was in the process of being placed in receivership to the city because of the owner's failure to make necessary repairs, but the city itself had failed to maintain the building adequately, and so the CIV moved in, demanding title to the building and assistance in its rehabilitation.

Thus began the occupation strategy that the CIV sustained over the next fifteen months. The Ainslie building served as a useful recruitment device, as Indian people heard about the takeover and came to join it, some of them becoming permanent "troops" for subsequent occupations. But the building lacked sufficient value either to the owner (who was willing to give the building to the Indians in order to be relieved of further responsibility for it) or to the city to generate significant bargaining power, and so the CIV was essentially ignored. Furthermore, although the church agreed to help the CIV acquire title to and financing for the building, the "troops" were primarily street people (some of whom had known Betty during her years on skid row), who were not really suited to a housing rehabilitation program nor to the long-term planning and perseverence necessary to obtaining such a program. They were more than willing, however, to follow Mike's lead in staging demonstrations, evidenced by the enthusiasm with which they accompanied him to a demonstration in May for the Menominee tribe up in Wisconsin).

And so, early in the morning of June 14, 1970, the CIV occupied an abandoned Nike site at Belmont Harbor along Chicago's fashionable north shore. The site was in the process of being transferred from the federal government to the city of Chicago. There was public debate about the disposition of the site, and the CIV demanded that it be given to them for a multipurpose Indian center.

The occupation generated great publicity, new participation and support, and preliminary negotiations with officials from the city, state, and federal government. But the concessions offered (e.g., another list of vacant apartments in Uptown) were meaningless, and the CIV refused to modify its demand for the land. A stalemate developed. On July 1, after a violent struggle in which Molotov cocktails were thrown and a yacht moored in the harbor was burned, the city evicted the CIV and arrested a number of Indians.

The next occupation was at a forest preserve outside the city, intended primarily as a holding action until a more strategically valuable site could be located. Then, on July 30, the CIV invaded a piece of surplus property on the grounds of the Argonne National Laboratory, an Atomic Energy Commission facility in DuPage County (west of Chicago), again demanding land and support for a comprehensive Indian center.

From a strategic point of view, the Argonne site was an excellent choice. The land was in the process of transition from federal to local hands, and considerable controversy had developed regarding its ultimate disposition. Support for the CIV was provided both by a group of Argonne scientists, who wanted the land to be used as an ecological study area and believed the Indians could play a useful role in this effort, and by a local citizens' organization that had been working for a number of years to try to obtain low-income housing for DuPage County and was happy to use the CIV presence to further that effort. In addition, the regional AEC manager was anxious to minimize trouble and avoid violence, and because of the intensity of the CIV's resistance at Belmont Harbor, he did not believe that an eviction from the Argonne site could be carried out without bloodshed. Finally, since DuPage County was a Republican stronghold while neighboring Cook County (in which Chicago was located) was a Democratic bastion, the situation offered the possibility of exploiting partisan conflicts.

The strategy paid off. The AEC and Argonne authorities opted to try for a peaceful withdrawal; the CIV was allowed to stay, and another bargaining situation was created. Further, the AEC manager sought to involve other federal agencies and finally, after repeated requests, succeeded in persuading the Federal Regional Council (an interagency coordinating body including representatives from OEO, HEW, HUD, DOL, and DOT) to address the problem. The council convened an emergency meeting on August 10 and authorized the establishment of a task force (Regional Council Task Force, RCTF) "to immediately investigate and develop solutions to the problems of urban Indians."[31] For the first time, the CIV had succeeded in generating an ongoing bargaining situation.

The first priority of the RCTF was to persuade the CIV to leave the Argonne site peacefully. The CIV, however, after an initial session in which it presented its needs and aspirations with both sophistication and apparent humility, again refused to modify its first priority, which was to obtain a piece of land. Its response to the initial offers of the RCTF—which included such things as job-training slots in Iowa, as well as promises of long-term assistance in housing—was an explosion of accusations and tears.

This time, although the CIV did not know it until later, its intransigence almost paid off. At the suggestion of the AEC manager, several members of the task force did try to persuade the White House Office of Management and Budget to allow them to request a piece of the Argonne site for the CIV. OMB commended them for their efforts to help the Indians, but said any discussion of land was out of the question. Again a stalemate developed.

For once, the stalemate did not last. The site had sufficient value to the authorities, and the desire to avoid trouble was sufficiently great that a compromise was worked out. The administrative aide to John Erlenborn, the Republican congressman from DuPage County, intervened (she was a shrewd and indominable political broker who happened to be a close friend of the assistant manager of the AEC and also had a certain sympathy for the Indians) and persuaded the Chicago Housing Authority to sign an agreement promising to build a housing project (which would include a cultural center and housing management program) in Uptown for the CIV and to locate temporary housing for them. More important to the CIV, an interim site was provided at Camp Seager, a nearby Methodist summer camp; and there were hints of continuing to help the CIV pursue its primary objective of obtaining a piece of land and developing a comprehensive Indian center.

Despite the initial excitement, this victory was essentially symbolic: The housing project hinged on a waiver of the court requirement for scattered-site integrated housing in Chicago[32] and on obtaining necessary federal funding, conditions that seriously weakened the firmness of the agreement. Moreover, the agreement required the CIV to disperse into apartments in Chicago, and the CIV members were by now totally committed to remaining together and remaining outside the city. Thus the CIV made little effort to locate housing in Uptown (which was almost nonexistent in any case).

Meantime, the Regional Council Task Force was continuing its work. It was expanded to include all the Indian organizations in the Chicago area, as well as other agencies and organizations concerned with Indian people, and its stated objectives reflected the influence of the CIV. They included not simply such conventional goals as increasing Indian employment in federal agencies but also the CIV's particular demands to provide support for existing Indian organizations and their proposals; to provide training as well as technical assistance in the development of new proposals; and to establish a comprehensive center for Indian people that would include land, housing, and other programs sought by the CIV.

Although the CIV's influence was clearly manifest in both the formation and ostensible direction of the task force, it became increasingly clear that the task force—or more specifically, its chairman, Wendell Verduin, regional director of OEO—was determined to exclude the CIV from whatever benefits were ultimately provided. Apparently, and a more thorough discussion must wait until we analyze the overall effectiveness of a strategy of disruption, Verduin was growing increasingly distrustful of this abrasive and intransigent organization, and as it became clear that the CIV had no intention of abandoning its supposedly temporary site at Camp Seager, Verduin became increasingly convinced that the CIV was not the reliable and trustworthy organization that would cooperate with the task force and bring credit to its efforts to help the Indian community. Equally important, Verduin was facing a bitter challenge from the OEO union, and when the union took up the CIV's cause, Verduin's opposition to the CIV solidified.

Verduin took a number of steps that seemed deliberately intended to isolate the CIV. First, exceptionally stringent conditions for the receipt of funds were established. Thus, in October OEO offered a $50,000 planning grant to any Indian group that could both raise $50,000 in matching funds and establish a coalition representing all of the major Indian organizations in Chicago. Given the poverty as well as the profound and well-known divisions among Indian organizations in Uptown, plus the fact that a matching funds requirement was practically unprecedented, these conditions seemed unreasonable; in fact, no group in the Indian community was able to meet them.

The CIV did manage to form a coalition. Called American Indian Organizations United (AIOU), it maintained at least six members (albeit not always the same six members) throughout the year. But Verduin raised new objections, and so the OEO union sponsored a press conference with all of the unions from the other Regional Council agencies, as well as citizen-support groups, to denounce the task force for failing to meet its promises to the CIV. Shortly thereafter, the head of the union was fired, and on December 11 the CIV was evicted from Camp Seager. Two days later, Verduin encouraged the American Indian Development and Education (AIDE) foundation, one of AIOU's principal members, to withdraw from AIOU and give testimony against the union, implying that in return AIDE would receive the planning grant. AIDE was a group of Indian people and small businesses seeking to encourage entrepreneurial and educational/cultural development among Indian people. Its director, Jim Stewart, was a long-time supporter of the CIV who, as a result of his university education and business experience, brought extremely valuable skills to the CIV. These same skills, as well as his more low-key mannerisms, made Stewart a much more attractive candidate for funding than the more abrasive and unpredictable Mike Chosa. Verduin's effort to use Stewart to isolate Chosa backfired, however, when AIDE discovered the improbability of funding and informed the press of what had happened. But the AIOU coalition was at least temporarily disrupted.

The CIV did not give up. On eviction from Camp Seager, they returned to Argonne where they were met by a massive show of force and left immediately. They spent the next month camping along the roadside, in subfreezing temperatures, until at last the governor's office found them new quarters at Camp Logan, a little-used National Guard camp in Zion, Illinois (north of Chicago).

Here a miraculous transformation occurred within the CIV: Betty Jack stopped drinking—permanently. With that, the CIV prohibited all drinking, sending those who wanted to drink back to "town" and drawing in new members who agreed not to drink. An exemplary program of communal living, leatherworking, and even a small crafts shop was developed. As further evidence of its reformation, the CIV engendered stronger outside support here than it had at any previous point; for example, the Human Relations Committee of nearby Highland Park put together a broad coalition of about 150 organizations and individuals (including church groups, women's groups, human relations councils, and Jesse Jackson's Operation PUSH) from throughout the Chicago area who supported the CIV's desire to remain at Camp Logan.

As an organization, then, the CIV was changing. In contrast to the earlier stages of the occupation strategy, when the CIV depended on a group of heavy-drinking people for the core of its support, it was now able to develop new support and move toward becoming an organization capable not simply of sustaining an occupation but also of implementing programs.

None of this, however, was sufficient to dissuade Verduin from his determination to exclude the CIV from RCTF activities. Thus, in late February, after Senator Stevenson's office had stepped in, with putative encouragement from Verduin, to help regroup AIOU, Verduin established a new body—the "Metro Committee" of the task force—to serve in place of any coalition developed by the Indian community as the official advisory group from the Indian community. Verduin did not include the CIV on the Metro Committee.

Despite its ostensible advisory role, the Metro Committee was not consulted about the one project which OEO, in conjunction with DOL and, significantly, the Fourth Presbyterian Church, finally did fund. This was a manpower training program proposed by Indians for Indians (IFI), a very small, very quiet organization headed by an elderly Chippewa whose public admission of willingness to "take the crumbs off your table" promised grateful cooperation with whatever was offered. IFI had been a member of AIOU; after it was funded, however, it withdrew.

On the other hand, AIOU's proposal for the planning grant, which was written with the help of sympathetic OEO staff and thus met the necessary standards of program planning methodology, was submitted to the Metro Committee in June. There, after several intense meetings and considerable debate between Indian and agency representatives, the proposal was rejected.

Finally, in the ultimate irony, the $50,000 committed to the planning grant was handed over to the Chicago antipoverty agency and model cities program in order to avoid having to return it to the federal coffers at the end of the fiscal year.

Shortly afterward, on July 1, 1971, the CIV was evicted from Camp Logan. Again they resisted—teargas was finally used to flush them out—and some thirty-five people were arrested. This time, after a brief regrouping in Uptown, the organization gave up. Its members dispersed, many of them going back to Wisconsin.

The influence of the CIV continued—in the lives of its members, in the issues it had raised and the programs it helped catalyze, and in the political consciousness of the Chicago Indian community. Mike and Betty and other CIV members moved on to other forms of working for Indian people. Betty completed a college program in counseling, worked with Mike on an Indian foster care program in Madison, then moved to northern Wisconsin to work as an alcoholism counselor. Mike worked as a consultant on Indian welfare programs in Wisconsin and then developed the foster care project, which employed a number of former CIV members and received CETA funding. He remained politically active: He was a member of The National Congress of American Indians (NCAI), the largest and most established of the national Indian organizations, and ironically, was sent by them in 1975 to help resolve the conflict created by the occupation of an old monastery in Gresham, Wisconsin, by a militant group of Menominees. Then, after a year of traveling across the country to visit Indian spiritual leaders, he returned to his reservation where he started a firewood business and worked with the tribal council on various reservation development efforts.

Further, the issues the CIV raised and the programs it helped to instigate remained: the Indian high school program, the IFI employment training program (which received over $300,000 in federal money in 1975), and another employment program whose initial funding resulted from CIV actions,[33] as well as a greater awareness of and attention to the needs of urban Indians, manifest not only in the continuation of the RCTF but also in such actions as the establishment of a state commission on urban Indians.[34] Within the Indian community, the traditional aversion to aggressive political action diminished somewhat as a growing number of people recognized at least the occasional need for "militant" tactics.[35]

Despite these signs of significant influence, the CIV experience does not fit the conventional model, which holds that groups that generate influence should be able to obtain concrete benefits and continue to participate in the bargaining process through which such benefits are allocated. Rather, the CIV as an organization was essentially excluded both from the established political arena and the benefits thereby distributed. What does this mean, and what does it suggest about strategic options available to the poor?

THEORETICAL IMPLICATIONS

The experience of the CIV suggests that disruption is more effective than Alinsky-type organizing as a strategy for generating collective action and bargaining power for the poor. Nevertheless, it also seems limited as a strategy for reaping benefits or developing sustained influence for those actually undertaking the disruption. Let us look more closely at these implications.

THE LIMITS OF COMMUNITY ORGANIZATION
IN MARGINAL COMMUNITIES

The Alinsky model seems to require a number of preconditions that are almost impossible for low-income, marginal groups to meet. Even Alinsky organizations require sufficient financial resources to support paid organizers and meet basic material needs, and poor people cannot generate these resources internally. Most Alinsky organizations obtain funding from some combination of indigenous community institutions—churches and local businesses—and external sources. In a marginal community, however, there are few indigenous institutions with resources to spare, and those that exist may be, as in the Chicago Indian community, too dependent on maintaining the goodwill of their patrons to risk association with an aggressive organization. Furthermore, and ironically, it is difficult for poor people's organizations to obtain external assistance—to develop proposals "worthy of funding"—because they lack the necessary education and skills (not to mention the connections and clout) and because the nature of their problems defies simple—and fundable—solutions.

This leads to the final problem. Alinsky strategy requires the use of limited issues both as a focus for collective action and as the basis for small victories that, in turn, will sustain and enhance the organization. However, as Piven and Cloward have argued, marginal groups such as the Chicago Indian community lack the ongoing institutional attachments—to homes, schools, jobs, neighborhoods—that normally provide organizing issues; and their problems—poverty, unemployment, and in the case of the Indians the demand for self-determination—cannot be defined as "specific, immediate, realizable issues." This not only hinders the organizing effort; it compounds the sense of helplessness engendered by the lack of resources and influence.

Thus, as long as it adhered to the Alinsky model, the CIV remained weak. It was able to muster occasional demonstrations and generate occasional responses, but unable to develop sustained participation or bargaining power.

THE EFFECTIVENESS OF DISRUPTION

The occupation strategy—a strategy of sustained disruption—was effective in generating ongoing collective action, raising issues, winning public support, creating bargaining power, and forcing concessions—new benefits—for the Indian community.

As a means of generating collective action, it succeeded in producing sufficient participation to sustain a fifteen-month series of occupations. It was also a costly strategy, requiring participants to abandon their homes, belongings, and jobs, and to face the possibility of violence and arrest. But this was the genius of the strategy, for the Chicago Indian community, as a marginal community and as an Indian community, contained a number of characteristics that made it uniquely suited to this strategy; indeed, the strategy actually transformed some of the obstacles to Alinsky-type organizing into resources for sustained disruption.

Thus the lack of attachments to conventional institutions made it possible to "give up everything for the cause" and join an extended occupation. The survival skills developed by marginal groups—panhandling, shoplifting, day labor—could be used as easily in the context of an occupation as on the streets of the city. And the high value in Indian culture on risk taking and courage,[36] its emphasis on sharing and communalism, lent further support to the occupation strategy. Finally, the occupation strategy solved some of the CIV's material problems: It provided housing and "office space" and also tended to generate more external assistance than had the Alinsky approach.

The occupation strategy was also highly effective in transforming the limited resources of the Indian community into new bargaining power. It took the chief resource of the Indian community—its bodies—inspired them for action, then placed them on carefully selected sites, sites sufficiently important so that the bodies would not simply be allowed to remain. And then, as long as an immediate eviction did not occur, a bargaining situation was created.

The CIV strategy was carefully calculated to reduce the prospect of immediate eviction. First, the fact that they were Indian made the authorities reluctant to use force without first trying to negotiate. Against such a clearly powerless group of people, and one capable of evoking considerable public sympathy, such action would have looked like outright brutality. Second, the strategy generated immediate and extensive publicity, which both increased support and publicized the needs of the Chicago Indian community, both of which increased the pressure. Third, the CIV tried to choose sites for which both jurisdiction and future use were unclear. Uncertainty as to jurisdiction created delay in responding to the occupation, while uncertainty as to future use made it easier for the CIV to insert its own demands; both conditions gave rise to the possibility of jujitsu—playing one side against another. Finally, by adhering to its initial demands and forcibly resisting evacuation, the CIV built credibility for both its demands and its threats, thus increasing the potential costs to its target of eviction.

As we have seen, the strategy produced steadily increasing bargaining power and generated increasingly valuable concessions, beginning with a list of vacant apartments in Uptown and culminating in a public commitment by a specially created federal interagency task force to develop the multipurpose Indian center on a land base outside the city, which was the CIV's central objective.

Nevertheless, the CIV was ultimately excluded both from the bargaining process and from the benefits thereby produced, and its exclusion reveals the limits of disruption as a strategy for generating influence.

THE LIMITS OF DISRUPTION

The strategy of sustained disruption enabled the CIV to generate sufficient pressure to necessitate a response, but not to shape that response. Rather, the response was shaped primarily by the imperatives of its targets—

the imperatives of organizational maintenance and survival—and these imperatives were in many ways incompatible with the goals of the CIV and the imperatives of its strategy.

The first imperative for the targets was to resolve the immediate crisis created by the CIV occupation, preferably by winning a peaceful termination of the occupation so as to justify the choice of bargaining rather than immediate eviction in response to the occupation. For example, at Argonne there was extensive communication between the local representatives of federal agencies and their superiors in Washington, with the latter advocating a much less conciliatory response; this put considerable pressure on those local officials to achieve a peaceful resolution of the situation so as to vindicate the decision they had made in dealing with the CIV.

Second, the targets had to contribute to the restoration of order in a broader sense, by minimizing the probability of further disruptive behavior. This meant both great concern for the kind of precedent that would be set by the response and an attempt to use the response as a means of establishing greater control over the potentially unruly community. Thus, to use the Argonne example again, the chief CIV demand was for a piece of land, but to have given the CIV a piece of land would have set a dangerous precedent for other groups. Instead, the CIV was offered apartments provided by the Chicago Housing Authority leased-housing program, which not only would not set a particularly attractive precedent for other groups but also would disperse the occupation and critically weaken the organization's influence.

Finally, the target had to "do something" for the Indians. Having admitted the presence of legitimate unmet needs in the Indian community, and having publicly formalized this admission by establishing a formal structure with the explicit purpose of dealing with those needs, it then became necessary to do something that would give proof of effectiveness in dealing with the problems for which the structure and its parent agencies had been established.

The needs of the CIV were almost diametrically opposed to its targets' imperatives. First, once the CIV adopted an occupation strategy, its organization-maintenance requirements changed. It ceased to be a storefront organization and became instead a residential group whose survival depended on the maintenance of a residential site. As long as the CIV was not given a permanent site, its refusal to evacuate those sites provided on a temporary basis inevitably developed into another crisis, thereby preventing any final resolution of that problem.

The CIV also prevented its targets from meeting their second imperative, namely, the restoration of order in a broader sense. For the CIV was committed to unprecedented goals—land, the development of comprehensive program to be run on a self-determining, communal basis—and to the struggle to develop pressure by any means possible; adopting a cooperative and essentially subordinate stance in relation to its targets, promising not to make any more trouble, would have meant relinquishing its major source of pressure. Given the irrelevance of its targets' response to the CIV objectives, abandoning the struggle for more pressure was inconceivable.

Finally, the CIV prevented its targets from "doing something" for the Indians. For the CIV was committed to goals that were difficult if not impossible for its targets to provide; it refused to adopt the grateful and cooperative behavior that was an implicit condition of receiving assistance. And it rejected those offers—such as job-training slots or leased housing—that were not only irrelevant to its goals but also threatening to its survival as an organization. Thus, as long as they were dealing with the CIV, it was impossible for its targets to "do something" for the Indians.

As a result, the targets sought increasingly to find other means of meeting their imperatives. First, as it became clear that bargaining with the CIV would not bring any benefits to its targets, the response to the inevitable crises created by the CIV's refusal to evacuate its sites shifted from attempts at conciliation to eviction; and the decision to evict rather than bargain, no matter how quickly it was implemented, essentially eliminated the value of the occupation as a source of bargaining power. Second, new relationships with the Indian community were established, relationships that both excluded the CIV and defined the role of the Indian community as purely advisory, hence purely subordinate to the decisions of the target. Third, a variety of things were done for the Indians that could be cited, as was the funding of the IFI employment program, as "a good example of effective cooperation between government and Indian people."[37] And so, although the CIV was able to force the targets into new efforts on behalf of the Indian community, the targets were able to contain, circumvent, exclude, and ultimately defeat the CIV.

The CIV's strategy was both rational and, ultimately, self-destructive. On the one hand, it seemed the best way to translate the resources available to the Indian community into political pressure, and it succeeded in generating enough pressure so that new programs and new funds were directed to the Indian community. Indeed, we can probably even say that the strategy was necessary, for all of IFI's patient waiting brought no results until the actions of the CIV made it imperative to "do something for the Indians." On the other hand, the strategy was ultimately doomed for the CIV itself, for by sustaining the strategy of disruption, the CIV only intensified the determination of its targets to minimize its participation in the benefits distributed as a result of that disruption.

STRATEGIC OPTIONS FOR THE POOR

What, then, are the options for marginal groups?

Perhaps Piven and Cloward are right: The most that the poor can do is to maximize the impact of those rare occasions when disruption is possible, for that forces some concessions, which may lead to more significant change. Or perhaps, as Alinsky would argue, groups using disruption should learn when to compromise, when to take admittedly limited gains and try to use them as the basis for further organizational development. How are we to decide?

The answer may depend in part on the objectives and priorities of a group. If the concessions offered are meaningful to a group and if it is willing to abandon its disruption and adopt instead the cooperative stance of a worthy client, then perhaps compromise is the best choice. However, if abandoning its disruption means abandoning its principal source of influence, and if the concessions offered do not provide significant progress toward its objectives, then compromise may be not only meaningless but counterproductive. It would not only *not* bring meaningful gains, it would reduce the possibility of generating further pressure in the effort to produce more meaningful gains.

The CIV did try to meet at least some of the terms of its targets and become a more worthy client (e.g., in the formation of AIOU, the preparation of the proposal for a planning grant, the internal transformation that occurred at Camp Logan). But it refused to abandon its occupation strategy, for none of the concessions actually offered were worth the cost to the organization of abandoning its occupations. Thus, had the CIV accepted any of the repeated offers of help in obtaining apartments in Uptown, it would have severely reduced its capacity to generate pressure. Not only would this have allowed the targets to claim that the CIV's needs had been met, thereby making continued disruption less legitimate, it would have ended the occupation—the immediate source of pressure—and dispersed the organization, thereby reducing its capacity to create further pressure. It is difficult to imagine a strategic justification for accepting gains that fail to contribute to the achievement of one's objectives and, worse, actually reduce the basis of one's bargaining power.

In addition, we must recall the question raised at the outset of this chapter regarding the capacity of marginal groups to sustain more conventional organizing efforts. There is no doubt that this capacity could be developed with appropriate material support and structural change (e.g., the development of institutions in which marginal groups have some stake and that can provide a basis for ongoing organizing efforts). However, it is also clear that in the case of the CIV, at least until its internal transformation at Camp Logan, many of its participants were not well suited to that kind of conventional organizing effort. Rather, their comparative advantage, so to speak, lay in maintaining a strategy of sustained disruption, and to have tried to do otherwise would, as Piven and Cloward have suggested, meant failing to do what they could do much more effectively.

Nevertheless the fact remains that sustained disruption led ultimately to the CIV's defeat. Ultimately, then, wasn't the strategy mistaken?

I think not. For not only was the alternative strategy limited, in terms of both feasibility and strategic value, the CIV strategy did have significant value both for the larger community and for its participants. Although the CIV was not itself the beneficiary, its continued disruption did continue to produce publicity for its demands and for the needs of the Indian community, did contribute to the slow acceptance of at least some of these demands, and did force the authorities to do more for the Indian community. Furthermore, a number of CIV participants experienced significant and lasting personal changes through participating in the process of disruption; and some subsequently went on to more conventional—or at least less threatening—forms of community involvement and political action.

The CIV experience suggests, then, that as long as disruption can be neither ignored nor simply repressed—a situation that itself requires careful strategic development—it will produce concessions that bring some benefits to the larger community. Furthermore, while excluded from those material benefits, the participants gain in other ways: in personal self-esteem and political consciousness. For the act of engaging in disruption, of defying rather than accepting one's lot, clearly entails a redefinition of beliefs and expectations about the status of one's community and may for some bring about both a higher sense of political efficacy and a greater familiarity with the political process.[38]

Indeed, perhaps disruption is a necessary first stage in the political evolution of an impoverished and hitherto politically subordinate group. For disruption is a highly effective means of politicizing a community and catalyzing new action, on the one hand, and of forcing new responsiveness to the community, on the other. If the bargaining process thus created can be used to obtain more meaningful gains—gains that can bring progress toward a group's objectives without undermining its capacity to continue to exercise influence—then perhaps a group can adopt less disruptive, more conventional political strategies. While it is not possible to undertake a systematic review of the evidence at this point, there is some support for this speculation in the experience of the civil rights movement (some of whose leaders went on not only to pursue conventional forms of political influence but also to create new forms, such as grass-roots community economic development),[39] as well as the experience of nationalist movements in former colonial countries.

At the same time, we must be realistic about the magnitude of the effort required if the poor are to develop the power necessary to win for themselves a better deal. Occasional disruption, bringing occasional concessions and possibly lasting influence, as well as improvement for some segments of the community, may help but is hardly likely to be sufficient. Continued pressure is necessary, and in the absence of changes making possible the development of much greater pressure through conventional forms, this is likely to require renewed disruption. The response to the recent violence in several southern black communities seems to vindicate this suggestion: After years of relative neglect, the authorities are once again at least talking about the continued presence, and in some cases the intensification, of the problems publicized by the riots of the sixties and supposedly dealt with by subsequent public policies.

To advocate disruption is not simply to condone possible harm and human suffering, it is to admit the failure of the established political process to work as it should. It is not likely to be a popular suggestion, as is indicated by the rash of critiques of the Piven and Cloward book.[40] Nevertheless, there are times when it is difficult to see a more effective means of forcing a public response to an impoverished and otherwise essentially powerless group. Given the costs of the effort, as well as the uncertainty of the outcome, there is an element of heroism in the willingness of marginal groups to undertake the struggle for political influence. Mike Chosa put it well in a speech preceding the Belmont Harbor occupation:

They say we're a bunch of drunks. Well that same bunch of drunks got a business started for Indian people.... And that same bunch of drunks are gonna stand up here in Chicago until we got housing for Indian people too. And they're gonna get jobs, you better believe it.

And after it's all over and done with, that same bunch of people, that same bunch of drunks, are still gonna be out on the street. And they know it. And yet they're willing to stand up and fight for Indian people. Every step of the way.[41]

NOTES

1. The classic expression of this point of view is probably that presented by Robert A. Dahl in *Democracy in the United States: Promise and Performance*, 3rd ed. (Chicago: Rand McNally, 1976), Chap. 28 and p. 457. For a more recent expression of this view, addressed more directly to the question of alternative strategies, see two articles by Charles V. Hamilton: "Blacks and Electoral Politics," *Social Policy*, May/June 1978, pp. 21–27; and "The Patron-Recipient Relationship and Minority Politics in New York City," *Political Science Quarterly* 94, no. 2 (Summer 1979): 211–27.

2. The best expression of this point of view can be found in Frances Fox Piven and Richard A. Cloward, *Poor People's Movements: Why They Succeed, How They Fail* (New York: Pantheon, 1977).

3. This point has been made repeatedly by both Indian spokesmen and non-Indian studies of the Indian situation. See, for example, Vine Deloria, Jr., *Behind the Trail of Broken Treaties: An Indian Declaration of Independence* (New York: Delta Books, 1974); and D'Arcy McNickle, *Native American Tribalism: Indian Survivals and Renewals* (London: Oxford University Press for the Institute of Race Relations, 1973). Indian people argue that this differentiates them sharply from other minority groups, particularly black people, whom Indians see as simply wanting what white people want. Elliot Liebow's study of marginal black men supports this argument; see *Tally's Corner: A Study of Negro Street-Corner Men* (Boston: Little, Brown, 1967).

4. The 1980 Census found 1,361,869 Indians in the United States. Department of Commerce, Bureau of the Census. *Race of the Population by States: 1980* (Washington, D.C.: U.S. Government Printing Office, July 1981). Table 1.

5. One of the best analyses of this problem is provided by Mancur Olson, Jr., *The Logic of Collective Action: Public Goods and the Theory of Groups*, rev. ed. (New York: Schocken, 1971).

6. One of the best analyses of this phenomenon is provided by Sidney Verba and Norman H. Nie, *Participation in America: Political Democracy and Social Equality* (New York: Harper & Row, 1972).

7. Alinsky's ideas are presented in several works; see, for example, his *Reveille for Radicals* (New York: Vintage, 1969) and *Rules for Radicals: A Pragmatic Primer for Realistic Radicals* (New York: Vintage, 1972). Robert Bailey, Jr., in his study of the Alinsky organization in Austin, just west of Chicago, presents a good summary of the basic Alinsky model. See *Radicals in Urban Politics: The Alinsky Approach* (Chicago: University of Chicago Press, 1974). For a survey of recent organizing experience, see the special issue of *Social Policy* on organizing neighborhoods (September/October 1979).

8. Alinsky, *Reveille for Radicals*, p. 224.

9. Alinsky, *Rules for Radicals*, p. 127.

10. Ibid, p. 126.

11. Alinsky, *Reveille for Radicals*, p. x.

12. Alinsky, *Rules for Radicals*, pp. 136–51. For example, Alinsky describes a boycott mounted by civil rights leaders against downtown Chicago department stores: Rather than attempt to boycott *all* the stores, which would have severely taxed the

organizers' resources, they focused on one store, at the height of the Christmas shopping season, and let the store's concern about loss of business to its competitors provide the principal basis of power. See *Rules for Radicals*, p. 151.

13. Ibid, p. 148.

14. Most of the successful Alinsky organizations have developed in communities that already possessed a certain level of institutional and individual resources: the church, existing neighborhood organizations, local businesses, or the socioeconomic resources generally available to working and middle-class people. See, for example, Bailey, *Radicals in Urban Politics*; John Hall Fish, *Black Power/White Control: The Struggle of the Woodlawn Organization in Chicago* (Princeton: Princeton University Press, 1973). William Ellis, in his study of the West Side Organization, also recognizes the limits of Alinsky theory in low-income communities; see *White Ethics and Black Power: The Emergence of the West Side Organization* (Chicago: Aldine, 1969).

15. The best summaries of the Piven and Cloward argument are in *Poor People's Movements*, Intro. and Chapter 1; and in a paper by Frances Piven, "Low-Income People and the Political Process," published in *The Politics of Turmoil: Poverty, Race, and the Urban Crisis*, ed. Richard Cloward and Frances Piven (New York: Vintage, 1975), pp. 73–88.

16. The concept of a "dual labor market"—the division of the labor market into a "primary labor market" containing good jobs, good wages, good benefits, good possibilities for mobility, high levels of unionization, and a "secondary labor market" containing poor jobs, low wages, no benefits, no possibilities for mobility, little unionization, and as a result of all these factors, high turnover—is now in wide use; a good summary can be found in an article by Michael Piore, "The Dual Labor Market: Theory and Implications," reprinted in *Problems in Political Economy: An Urban Perspective*, ed. David M. Gordon (Lexington, Mass: Heath, 1971), pp. 90–94.

17. Piven and Cloward, *Poor People's Movements*, p. 277.

18. Ibid, p. 353.

19. This number is considerably higher than that given by the 1970 census; however, both the BIA and the professional demographer employed by one of the service-oriented Indian organizations, as well as many others, agreed that 16,000 was a reasonable estimate.

20. For a good summary of United States policy toward Native Americans, see Harold E. Fey and D'Arcy McNickle, *Indians and Other Americans: Two Ways of Life Meet*, rev. ed. (New York: Harper & Row Perennial Library, 1970).

21. Estelle Fuchs and Robert J. Havighurst, *To Live on This Earth: American Indian Education* (Garden City, N.Y.: Doubleday Anchor, 1973), pp. 107–10; and John Kennardh White, *Patterns in American Indian Employment* (Chicago: Saint Augustine's Center for American Indians, 1971), pp. 9, 26.

22. Fuchs and Havighurst, *To Live on this Earth*, pp. 110–11.

23. Prafulla Neog, Richard Woods, and Arthur Harkins, *Chicago Indians: The Effects of Urban Migration*, Training Center for Community Programs in Coordination with the Office of Community Programs (Minneapolis: Center for Urban and Regional Affairs, University of Minnesota, 1971), p. 9.

24. Fuchs and Havighurst, *To Live on this Earth*, pp. 107–9.

25. For a brief sketch of the Indian Center, see Merwyn S. Garbarino, "The Chicago American-Indian Center: Two Decades," in *American Indian Urbanization*, ed. Jack O. Waddell and O. Michael Watson (West Lafayette, Ind.: Purdue University, Institute for the Study of Social Change, Monograph No. 1, 1973), pp. 74–89.

26. The full story of the CIV, as well as a more comprehensive analysis of its experi-

ence, can be found in my dissertation, "Heroes and Hustlers: Portrait and Analysis of the Chicago Indian Village" (University of Chicago, Department of Political Science, September 1978).

27. Planning for the experimental all-Indian high school began in the summer of 1970, after a meeting prompted by the Wrigley Field encampment between the school board and representatives of the Chicago Indian community; by the fall of 1971, the school was established in the Indian Center, funded by Title III of the Elementary and Secondary Education Act, with openings for 100 Indian students. The establishment of the school was clearly facilitated by the close relationship between the non-Indian director of the Indian Center (a trained anthropologist) and several key members of the education establishment; nevertheless, all of the Indians involved in setting up the school attributed its origins to the CIV's actions at Wrigley Field.

28. This theme can be heard in a wide variety of sources. *Akwesasne Notes*, an Indian newspaper with a national circulation of several hundred thousand, provides continuous coverage of this concern. Other sources include Deloria, *Behind the Trail of Broken Treaties*; and a reader edited by Alvin M. Joseph, Jr., *Red Power: The American Indians' Fight for Freedom* (New York: American Heritage Press, 1971).

29. National Accelerator Laboratories was located in Batavia, Illinois; their community relations and equal opportunity officer was instrumental in arranging the contract for the CIV. W. Clement Stone is an extremely wealthy insurance financier whose corporation is headquartered in Uptown; he made numerous grants to local organizations. In dealing with Indian people, he usually channeled his support through the Indian Center; however, because the Center was not responsive to Stone's desire to encourage economic development, he was willing to assist the CIV.

30. For example, one of the organizations in which the CIV was most active was the Uptown Community Health Association (UCHA), formed with the encouragement of the Chicago Board of Health to act as the citizens' advisory group for the neighborhood health center being developed under the Model Cities program. The Board of Health had backed away from UCHA when it became clear that it wanted real as opposed to symbolic participation in the governing of the new center. The coalition waged an intense struggle, including carefully staged demonstrations at Model Cities meetings; however, by winter of 1971 they recognized the hopelessness of fighting the Daley machine and abandoned their effort. (The principal health care groups within UCHA continued working, shifting their focus from the local to the federal level where they were soon successful in obtaining an NIMH grant for a community mental health consortium.)

31. Chicago Indian Village and Regional Council Task Force (Region V, Chicago), Joint Agreement, 10 August 1971. Personal copy.

32. *Gautreaux* v. *Chicago Housing Authority*, 304 F. Supp. 736 (N.D. Ill. 1969).

33. This was a program called Just Jobs, a grass-roots effort that had received nothing but discouragement from the city until suddenly, just after the formation of the Regional Council Task Force, a special Model Cities meeting was convened to explore the possibility of funding an employment program run jointly by Just Jobs and Indians for Indians. IFI, despite its initial public expression of cooperation, was reluctant to participate, but Just Jobs itself was funded.

34. An American Indians Problems Committee was established on 30 June 1971 by a unanimous resolution of the Illinois House of Representatives; Bruce Douglas, an independent representative whose district included Uptown, was elected chairman.

35. I observed countless examples of changing attitudes during my fieldwork in the

Chicago Indian community; in addition, feature articles in the *Lerner News* (Chicago's neighborhood-oriented newspaper), as well as conversations with people after I left Chicago, provided continuing information—albeit fragmentary—as to the continuing impact of the CIV. Clearly a systematic follow-up study would have helped to show the actual extent of this phenomenon.

36. An interesting study of the application of the value of risk taking to an urban situation is Jeanne Guillemin's *Urban Renegades: The Cultural Strategy of American Indians* (New York: Columbia University Press, 1975).

37. Regional Council Task Force on Urban Indians (Region V, Chicago), Minutes of Meeting of 3 May 1972.

38. This argument has been widely made, most notably perhaps by Frantz Fanon, *The Wretched of the Earth*, trans. Constance Farrington (New York: Grove Press, 1963).

39. See, for example, the article by Janice E. Perlman, "Grassrooting the System," *Social Policy*, September/October 1976, pp. 4–20.

40. See, for example, Paul Starr, "How They Fail, a Review of *Poor People's Movements*," *Working Papers for a New Society*, March/April 1978, pp. 70–73; and Robert Lekachman, "A Piece of the Action Is Not Enough; A Review of *Poor People's Movements*," *Social Policy*, November/December 1977, pp. 127–132.

41. Speech made in the People's Church, Uptown, 3 June 1971 (taped).

14

The Social Context of Strategic Success: A Land-Use Struggle in Hawaii

James A. Geschwender

This chapter analyzes the evolution of strategies and tactics utilized during the struggle of residents of Waiahole and Waikane valleys on the Hawaiian island of Oahu to prevent their homes and farms from being taken over for residential development. It is the story of a people's victory against private property rights claimed by landlords and profit sought by developers in a context where the predominance of power, legal rights, and historical precedents all appeared to be arrayed on the side of the landlords and developers.

This chapter has four sections. The first is a brief discussion of the current literature on movement strategies and tactics. The second gives a description of the background out of which the Waiahole-Waikane struggle emerged. This is followed by a description of how movement strategies and tactics evolved in interaction with opposition moves and countermoves. The chapter concludes with a consideration of theoretical concerns.

STRATEGY AND TACTICS IN SOCIAL MOVEMENT THEORY

It is an oversimplification to say, as Robert Lauer does, that "the strategies for change which movements adopt have received little attention in the literature."[1] Myriad studies of individual social movements include an analysis of movement strategies or tactics in certain specific situational contexts.[2] Some of the more general attempts to develop a theory of social movements have very little to say about the selection of strategies and tactics.[3] But it is also true that a large body of work concentrates on certain aspects of social movements. It is less oriented toward general theory but at the same time is broader than the study of specific movements. This literature includes a number of works that have focused on strategy and tactics.[4] Lauer is correct in suggesting that no existing literature spells out the particular tactics that a movement will be prone to, or will effectively use, in a given situation. Nor is such literature ever likely to exist. The spontaneous nature of social movements requires choices conditioned on situational assessments made in the light of information available. The best that theory can do is develop a compendium of factors that will affect such choices.

Turner identifies three kinds of social collectivities that must be considered in selecting social movement strategies.[5] I will add a fourth. The first is the beneficiary *constituency*, which consists of those in whose interests the movement purports to act, regardless of whether it has derived their consent to act. The second is the *target group*, which is that collectivity that must be induced to act if the movement is to have any chance of achieving its objectives. The third (not included in Turner's formulation) is the *opposition*, those attempting to influence the target group in a manner contrary to the desires of the movement. The target group and the opposition may, in different situations, be identical, overlapping, or entirely different collectivities. The fourth, the *publics*, includes at least three subtypes: *bystander publics, cooptable publics*, and *potential oppositional publics*.[6] Cooptable publics share some interests in common with the constituency and could, under favorable conditions, be activated as movement supporters. The potential oppositional publics share some interests with the opposition and could, under unfavorable conditions, become movement opponents. Bystander publics, for the most part, share few interests with either the constituency or the opposition and will not usually become either movement supporters or opponents unless their normal life styles are in some way disrupted. If activated, they become either supporters or opponents depending on the manner in which they define the situation.

There are three basic types of strategies: persuasion, bargaining, and coercion.[7] *Persuasion*, the attempt to elicit the desired response from the target group through symbolic manipulation, is the most desired from the movement's perspective because its use does not cost anything. It is also the least effective strategy as the only incentive for the target group to act in the desired manner is the possibility of a sense of moral well-being. Consequently, persuasion tends to be used only when a movement lacks access to resources needed for either bargaining or coercion. *Bargaining* is the attempt to exchange some resource in the possession of the movement, but desired by the target group, for the desired action on the part of the target group. For this to be a viable strategy, the movement has to have, and be willing to give, something the target group wants. *Coercion* is the threat to inflict costs on the target group if it fails to act in the desired manner. This requires that the movement have the capability of, and willingness to, inflict such costs. Social movements often develop among segments of the population excluded from existing decision-making apparatus and for whom the existing balance of power is arrayed to their detriment. The selection of a coercive strategy lays a movement open to severe retribution and will normally be chosen only in the absence of viable alternatives.

Lauer notes that strategies simultaneously bear a relation to the achievement or failure of movement objectives; have an impact on the recruitment, retention, and commitment of members; and present the movement's face to the public.[8] Turner and Killian say the same thing using different language.[9] Each acknowledges an element of rationality in the selection of strategies that have some reasonable potential of achieving movement objectives and an expressive element oriented toward the values and attitudes of movement adherents. One must also consider the potential impact of strategies in gaining or losing support among the various publics. The ideal strategy would be consistent with the values possessed by movement adherents, would be rationally effective in influencing target-group actions, would not activate any potential oppositional groups, would attract the support of cooptable publics, and, at worst, would not involve bystander publics.

This ideal strategy is virtually impossible to achieve. Social movements are not simple, unidimensional phenomena. They tend to have a varied membership and multiple objectives.[10] Gerlach and Hine suggest that movements normally have two levels of objectives.[11] There may be a relative consensus among participants about general goals and a great deal of dissensus on specific ones. Thus it is difficult to find strategies that will achieve heterogeneous and often contradictory objectives and that also satisfy heterogeneous and often contradictory participant values. This selection is complicated by the fact that the degree to which the movement constituency and the various publics will accept a given strategy as plausible (i.e., both potentially effective and morally acceptable) is a function of a changing social context.[12] These problems are analyzed after we consider the background of the Waiahole-Waikane movement.

THE CONTEXT

Hawaii shares with all island chains the problems of a finite land base.[13] Limited amounts of land normally are accompanied by disagreements over appropriate usage and almost invariably lead to conflict over ownership and control. In traditional Hawaiian society all land was owned and controlled by the monarch. Others could use it at his pleasure for purposes and durations that won his approval. Missionaries who came to Hawaii maneuvered to acquire a great deal of influence over the Hawaiian monarchy. Other *haoles* (Caucasians), often members of the missionary families, moved into trade and commerce and began the development of large-scale agriculture. They did not believe that commercial agriculture had much future in Hawaii unless the system of land ownership was changed, and pressure was exerted on the Hawaiian king to transform the land system.

Individual ownership of land was established and the land was distributed. Roughly 1 million acres (24 percent of the total) became crown lands;

1.6 million acres (39 percent) were given to the *alii* (Hawaiian chiefs); and the remaining 1.5 million acres (37 percent) came under government control. About 30,000 acres were taken from the government portion and given to commoners who could prove long-term continued agricultural use. It was not long before the land moved into the hands of a small number of *haoles*. The degree of land concentration continued to increase as Hawaii first experienced a planters' revolution overthrowing the monarchy, then annexation to the United States, and finally admission to statehood.

By 1965 the state government owned approximately 39 percent of all land, with the federal government owning another 10 percent. The remainder of the land was highly concentrated in relatively few hands, with 72 private owners possessing 47 percent of all the land in the state (18 possessed 40 percent, and as few as 7 possessed 30 percent). This left the vast bulk of Hawaii's population with less than 5 percent of the state's land. Even these figures understate the extent of land concentration because they omit the fact that 18 of the private landowners leased almost 25 percent of all land owned by state and federal governments.

Immigration and reproduction increased the population of Hawaii to 786,561 by 1970. Almost 80 percent of the state's population was concentrated on Oahu. The development of bigger and faster aircraft sparked a fantastic growth of tourism with Oahu remaining the primary destination. Land was at a premium. Increasing amounts of land needed to be diverted into residential developments, while additional amounts had to be taken over for tourist facilities. Yet there was also concern that nothing should be done to interfere with two major commercial crops: sugar and pineapple. Some of the less profitable sugar and pineapple lands were converted into residential and tourist developments, but most of the burden of changed life style was borne by the small farmer and rural dweller.

Waiahole and Waikane[14] are two valleys located on the windward side of Oahu. Mountains separate them at the head of the valleys, but they merge to form a broad plain at their ocean ends. A high mountain range separates the valleys from urban Honolulu, but two cross-island highways bring them within a 45-minute drive. The combination of their rural location and relative proximity to urban Honolulu rendered them desirable as potential development sites. In 1890 Lincoln McCandless began acquiring land in the valleys through techniques neither more nor less moral and legal than those used by other *haoles* to acquire Hawaiian lands. His activities differed from some of the others only in that, as a member of the territorial legislature, he helped write the laws he used to his own end. He soon owned most of the more desirable land in the valleys, but a number of scattered small plots were owned by others. When McCandless died in 1940, his heirs continued to lease land to small farmers and others but they foresaw the potential for development and made preparations. Between 1956 and 1958, tenants were informed that potential development prevented issuance of any more long-term leases. Tenants could remain only if they would accept month-to-month leases and vacate on receiving a 28-day notice. This situation continued until December 1, 1973, when the McCandless heirs submitted to the state a letter of intent to reclassify 1,337 acres of agricultural land in Waiahole and Waikane (752 acres to urban and 585 acres to rural or large-lot residential classifications).

The residents of the two valleys were not informed of the filing, but their suspicions were aroused by the presence of outsiders driving expensive cars down their country roads. Suspicions were intensified during February and March 1974 when Robert Anderson, a faculty member in the College of Business Administration at the University of Hawaii, surveyed valley residents for the development planners under the pretense of conducting scholarly research. Rumors circulated that Joe Pao, a man with a controversial and questionable reputation, would be developing the valleys. Bob Nakata, lay organizer of a religiously supported youth project in Kahaluu (a neighboring valley) and nephew of one of the farmers in Waiahole, was conducting a farming survey in Waiahole-Waikane at the time. He had a background in community organizing and discovered the existence of the letter of intent. This gave residents of the two valleys time to organize and prepare prior to an immediately threatening situation.

A meeting of Waiahole and Waikane residents was held on April 8, 1974, and the Waiahole-Waikane Community Association (WWCA) was formed, a steering committee organized, and monthly meetings scheduled. Bobby Fernandez was elected president of the association. The full implications of the development plans became more apparent with the submission of a revised rezoning request on June 30, 1974. It, and subsequent elaborations, described the development program as involving three five-year stages with the completed development to include some 6,700 housing units for a residential population of approximately 20,000 persons. The WWCA was determined to prevent development if at all possible.

THE ACTORS

We may readily identify several relevant social collectivities: the constituency, the opposition, target groups, and various publics. It is a bit more difficult to precisely designate those early activists who gathered information, called meetings, and generally provided the initial impetus to the defense movement. Perhaps this is the reason why that particular category is so frequently missing from lists of relevant social collectivities analyzed in general works on social movements. In the case of Waiahole-Waikane, and probably in most social movements, this group of early activists included a combination of some members of the movement constituency and persons currently or previously active in related social movements, particularly those aimed at the retention of an agricultural life style on windward Oahu and the prevention of further urban sprawl.

THE CONSTITUENCY

The constituency of the defense movement was that population of people who either lived or farmed in the Waiahole and Waikane valleys. For the most part the constituency was made up of long-term residents of the valleys who had a high school education or less, incomes generally under $10,000, and were either farmers or blue-collar workers who also farmed small plots.[15] They were ethnically mixed. Almost half (46 percent) were pure or part-Hawaiian; 20 percent were Japanese American; 17 percent, Filipino American; 12 percent, *haole*; and 5 percent, other. Many of the Hawaiians and part-Hawaiians were descendents of the original settlers and had heard family tales of the manner in which they had been "cheated" out of their land by Lincoln McCandless.

THE OPPOSITION

The two major figures among the opposition were Joe Pao and Loy McCandless Marks. Pao, a developer with a long history of residential development, formed and became the head of Windward Partners solely in order to develop the Waiahole and Waikane valleys. Marks was the McCandless heir who, during the course of the struggle, acquired full title to the two valleys through a land swap with the remaining heirs. Both individuals believed in the rights of owners of private property to do pretty much as they pleased with their property. Marks was faced with rising costs of living, escalating land values, and relatively declining rental incomes. She saw her opportunity to sell the land to Pao as a solution to her problems and did not perceive any moral or legal barriers to such a step. Pao saw the opportunity for great profit in developing this land area in the same manner that he had developed so many others.

TARGET GROUPS

Ultimately the final resolution of the struggle would require actions by various governmental representatives including the governor of Hawaii, the mayor of the city and county of Honolulu, the members of various state and city land-use and zoning boards, and state and city legislators. A complex and time-consuming process is required to take land currently classified agricultural, have it reclassified urban, and actually construct dwelling units on it. The entire island of Oahu is part of the city and county of Honolulu, which has responsibility for zoning and the issuance of building permits. However, the state of Hawaii, through its Land Use Commission, retains jurisdiction over land classification. Thus any potential developer must first petition the state for a change in land classification from agricultural to urban. If this is granted, the developer would then petition the city for necessary zoning changes and building permits. Past precedent suggested that this process rarely proved to be much of a barrier to developers. But it is not necessarily the case that all development would be blocked even if the state were persuaded to deny land reclassification. Hawaii's land classification laws require that land classified agricultural be retained in two-acre or larger lots but do not require that it actually be used for agricultural purposes. Thus it would be possible to use agricultural land, assuming receipt of the necessary building permits, to develop a luxury residential area with each dwelling unit erected on a two-acre lot.

The public officials who decide upon reclassification, rezoning, or the issuance of building permits are required to act within the context of existing law (or to reformulate the law), but they are responsive to pressure. The entire framework of laws is aligned on the side of the landlord and is designed to protect private property rights. Politicians need campaign contributions in order to be reelected, and the poor do not contribute much. Past precedent favored the approval of necessary zoning alterations and the issuance of the needed land-use permits as had been done for countless other areas slated for development. Thus the most probable outcome was that the residents of Waiahole and Waikane would be evicted and their valleys developed. The one hope lay in the fact that the various public officials were also bound to consider the greater good of the community and that sufficient public pressure might convince them that the interests of the community could be best served by preventing development of the valleys.

THE PUBLICS

Persons in finance, commerce, development, or construction would logically be members of potential oppositional publics, as would any who were ideologically committed to private property and free enterprise without governmental interference. The bystander public included those who were not members of either the oppositional public or the cooptable publics (discussed below). They would be unlikely to become activated unless the struggle offended their sense of property or their commitment to law and order. A wide variety of cooptable publics had been created by recent developments or related political movements. Issues that might motivate members of the public to support the WWCA would include land, environment, agriculture, racial/ethnic nationalism, class solidarity, and radical politics.

Land. Land ownership and land laws became an issue in Hawaii in recent years as more people became concerned over tenants' rights. This was equally true of urban residential tenants and agricultural tenants. As of 1974 the overwhelming majority of homeowners in Hawaii owned their houses but leased the land on which they sat. When leases expired, the landlord held all the high cards. If agreement on rent proved impossible, the tenant had to move the house to another lot, leaving behind landscaping and other improvements. Land rentals in several middle- to upper-middle-class neighborhoods were being renegotiated at this time, and tenants faced dramatic increases. These homeowners potentially could be induced to empathize with the plight of Waiahole-Waikane residents.

Environment. The tremendous growth of Oahu's population combined with increased tourism caused drastic changes in the environment in a relatively short space of time. As urban concentration spread rapidly outward from Honolulu, rural valley after rural valley was taken over for residential or tourist use. Water quality rapidly deteriorated. Kaneohe Bay (on the windward side) was clean and pure a decade ago and now seems to be polluted and rapidly dying. Little of its once famous coral beds remain alive. Waikiki Beach was once closed for a day because of its polluted condition. There are claims of sightings of pockets of smog. Highway congestion has long since gone beyond the tolerable stage, and there is no place to build highways without massive destruction of environmentally and/or historically important sites. The environmental movement of the sixties remains strong in Hawaii. Perhaps here, more than elsewhere, people are aware of their surroundings because so much time is spent outdoors. There was much concern that the Waiahole-Waikane development would remove one of the few remaining rural areas and contribute to increased pollution and highway congestion.

Agriculture. Hawaii has almost a single-crop economy. Its major sources of income are tourism, sugar production, and governmental (military) expenditures. Pineapple is a distant fourth. Thus there is total concentration of the best agricultural land in sugar and pineapple. Hawaii has to import most of its food and manufactured products. It is highly vulnerable to dock or shipping strikes. Legislative attempts to control the strike threat have been less than successful. Consequently, lip service has been paid to the idea of making Hawaii agriculturally self-sufficient. Thus, resistance would be expected to any attempt to remove from agriculture two valleys that produced over half of the sweet potatoes grown in Hawaii as well as the majority of Oahu's bananas and papayas.

Racial/Ethnic Nationalism. In recent years there has been a resurgence of Hawaiian nationalism. Hawaiians have seen *haoles* introduce diseases that decimated their people, disrupted their social system, destroyed their religion, alienated their land, overthrew their monarchy, and established a new society in which they occupy a very low position in the racial stratification order. Most of the immigrant groups imported to work on sugar plantations under penal labor contracts have had greater success in modern Hawaii. Ethnic tension has been heightened by the military's continual use of Kahoolawe as a target island despite its historical and religious importance to Hawaiians. Evictions of people from Waiahole-Waikane to make room for development could be viewed as another example of the exploitation of native Hawaiians.

Class Solidarity. Members of the working class and the unemployed were potential supporters in any battle against the economic elite. Hawaii has been a tightly controlled and rigidly stratified society, totally manipulated by a small group of *haoles*. The school system (the traditional instrument of democratization and individual advancement) was segregated first through the mechanism of standard English schools and later by the extensive use of private schools. Private schools enroll almost as many students as public schools even today.

Labor unions did not threaten the economic elite until after World War II. As was occasionally true on the mainland, unions were built by ideologically committed people with radical political orientations. They talked and thought the language of class conflict. While unions did become conservative and establishment-oriented once they became powerful enough for the economic elites to accept them, they nevertheless left a heritage of radical thought and action that could be built upon in developing another movement.

Radical Politics. The most important potential supporters were those who could be attracted for ideological reasons. A committed group of political activists had been in Hawaii since the 1960s. They had a sophisticated political orientation, a commitment to building a just society, a dedication reflected in almost total involvement in any struggle once undertaken, and a willingness to risk their personal well-being for a cause in which they believed. This group resembled in many ways the people who built the International Longshoremen's and Warehousemen's Union (ILWU) in Hawaii, the CIO on the mainland, and those who had been at the forefront of so many struggles for human rights. Perhaps the most visible radicals were those affiliated with the Revolutionary Communist Party (a "new" Communist Party oriented toward Maoist thought), but several other groupings would be prone to support the Waiahole-Waikane movement for ideological reasons.

THE SELECTION OF TACTICS: PHASE I

The movement to defend Waiahole-Waikane had two historical phases characterized by differences in the composition and outlook of the leadership, differences in the strategies and tactics selected, and differences in which of the various cooptable publics were activated to support the movement. The first elections of the WWCA (April 1974) found the executive board dominated by larger farmers and landowners who believed that retention of their life style depended on keeping the valleys in agriculture. The executive board decided to resist eviction and development but at the same time to confine their activities to those that were legal and more or less respectable. They attempted to inform the public that development of the valleys would mean loss of land from agriculture, increased urban sprawl, increased highway congestion, further loss of open space, and continued environmental damage. This strategy attracted some sympathy and support from segments of the cooptable publics.

No attempt was made to link the Waiahole-Waikane situation to the larger issue of tenants' rights as it affected middle-class homeowners, but a newspaper article on this connection attracted some support along those lines. No overt appeal to Hawaiian nationalism was made, but some Hawaiian organizations, primarily composed of middle-class members, saw the connection and offered their support. There was little attempt to elicit aid on the basis of class consciousness or from those involved in radical politics. In fact, when a few radicals came to offer their aid, they created a certain amount of fear and discomfort but were allowed to stay primarily because they moved slowly and generally kept a low profile.

The first round of the battle took place at the State Land Use Commission hearing (originally scheduled for October 10, 1974) to consider Windward Partners' request to reclassify the valleys as urban as a first step toward residential development. The parties gathered at the appointed time, but the meeting was postponed until October 21. A large crowd of WWCA supporters had shown up for the first meeting, and there was some suspicion that the postponement may have been manipulated to keep people away, but more than 800 WWCA supporters came to the rescheduled hearing. They carried signs, sang, and chanted. The tenants presented the commission with an anti-development petition signed by 20,000 people, including U.S. Senator Daniel Inouye and Randolph Crossley, the Republican gubernatorial candidate.

The general consensus was that the tenants' case was well received. Frank Fasi, mayor of Honolulu, had already indicated his desire to see the area retain its low population density, and George Ariyoshi, the Democratic candidate for governor, had indicated his desire to see the area remain in diversified agriculture. The developers may have anticipated a defeat because between the hearings and the announcement of a decision, they made a compromise offer to the WWCA, which was rejected. Jockeying back and forth, mainly intended for public consumption, continued until December 20, 1974, when the State Land Use Commission voted 7 to 0 (with two abstentions) to reject the rezoning request. In little over a year since the initial letter of intent to rezone the land the tenants had won—or so it seemed.

The WWCA soon found that it was not possible to discourage monied interests simply by beating them in the first round. Plans can be reworded and new applications submitted. It is not necessary to apply for approval of a three-step project that will take 15 years to complete. One can always apply for approval of a single stage at a time. This, in effect, is what the developers did after laying a bit of groundwork.

During the second year of contention Loy McCandless Marks acquired full title to the two valleys through an exchange with the other heirs, and all tenants were informed that leases would have to be renegotiated at higher rentals. The WWCA formed a negotiating committee with power to negotiate all leases and hired Michael Hare to act as their attorney. On May 22, 1975, Joe Pao purchased part of Waikane (the site scheduled for earliest development) outright, arranged to purchase the remainder of Waikane after reclassification was approved, and acquired an option to purchase Waiahole that had to be exercised by November 1, 1977, or the deposit would be lost. On June 3 the Waiahole tenants received letters notifying them of new rental rates, effective July 1, which ranged between one and one-half and eight times the old rate. The tenants objected to the magnitude of the increases and agreed not to pay. On July 1, 92 of 120 leasees presented a common check to Marks's rent collector for rents at the old rate. The check was refused. The tenants set up a trust fund controlled by their attorney, Michael Hare, into which they continued paying rent at the old rate.

On June 26 a newspaper article reported that Joe Pao had submitted a request to the City Department of Land Utilization for approval of subdivision lines in order to make possible the construction of a two-acre lot subdivision in Waikane. It was not entirely clear whether he did this as a backstop in case he lost on his rezoning request or as a psychological tactic to undermine the confidence of his opposition. His public statements stressed his primary goal of having the area reclassified urban and developing it for small lot residential use.

It was about this time that Windward Partners was formed. It instigated a three-pronged propaganda campaign. The first stressed that the development would help solve the island's need for low-cost housing as the houses would range between $40,000 and $300,000 in cost. The second prong was to argue that the delay in construction was costing many people jobs at a time of high unemployment. The third involved a refusal to meet with the WWCA on the grounds that it was manipulated by "outside rabble rousers." This later blossomed into a full-scale red-baiting campaign.

The WWCA responded with a propaganda/educational campaign that questioned Pao's reputation and integrity as a developer, attacked his high-handed mode of operation, and questioned the legal basis of the McCandless land titles. Marks moved on July 17 to split the unity of the WWCA. She offered Waiahole tenants new one-year leases (but cancellable with a 60-day notice) at rental rates below those stated in the original letter. This move was made tactically feasible because Waiahole was not included in the first five-year development plan. Some tenants accepted the offer, but most refused. This weakened but did not destroy the WWCA. The WWCA propaganda campaign was aided when the *Honolulu Advertiser* published an article on July 22, 1975, detailing Pao's controversial past as a developer and quoting him to the effect that all of Oahu should become residential with agriculture relegated to the outer islands. In August 1975 Windward Partners accepted a WWCA rental check for those tenants living in Waikane on Windward Partners' land but indicated that this check covered overdue rent and its acceptance did not imply any future commitments on the part of Windward Partners.

This series of events initiated a distinction between the legal and political status of the leasees in the Waiahole and Waikane valleys. Nine families lived in that portion of Waikane Valley already purchased by Pao and slated for development during the first five years. They faced imminent eviction as part of the program of land clearance to enable the land to be prepared for construction. Neither Pao nor Marks exhibited any immediate concern over the status of those tenants residing in the remainder of Waikane, but Marks did appear to be worried by the militance of the Waiahole tenants. She may have been afraid that they would cause so much trouble that Pao might choose not to exercise his option to buy, the sale of Waiahole would be canceled, and she would be stuck with her funds tied up in land that was not returning the desired yield. Thus she committed herself to evicting the Waiahole tenants.

The fact that the Waiahole tenants had withheld rental payments at the new rates provided Marks with the justification for serving eviction notices. The Waiahole tenants were ordered to appear in court August 14, 1975, the same day that Pao filed an official request with the City Department of Land Utilization to develop 130 large houselots in Waikane. Governor Ariyoshi announced his desire for the state to prevent evictions and keep the valleys agricultural, but he did not specify how. The nine Waikane tenants also received notices to vacate when their leases terminated on September 30, A complex series of legal moves and countermoves ensued that are too detailed to be of much relevance to our central concern. These eventuated on April 22, 1976, in an order granted by Judge Fong to repossess the lands of the nine Waikane tenants and on May 5 in an eviction order of the 79 Waiahole tenants who had rejected the offer of one-year leases. The Waikane evictions were delayed pending appeal, and the Waiahole evictions were postponed several times prior to the final confrontation (described below).

Meanwhile, the WWCA announced its intention to resist all evictions. On September 8, 1975, it held a rally near the Waiahole elementary school with potluck lunch, speeches, entertainment, and hiking and jeep tours of the valley. Between 500 and 600 people attended. The jeep tours were continued on subsequent dates to help acquaint the public with the environment that would be destroyed by development and to try to generate enough public support to influence the decision of the City Department of Land Utilization. On January 24, 1976, the department rejected Pao's request for approval of large-lot construction in Waikane, and on March 11, 1976, they rejected a revised version of the same request. In between these two rejections Pao submitted a new proposal to the WWCA asking them to withdraw their opposition to development in exchange for certain compromises on the amount of land to be retained for agricultural use. This was rejected by the WWCA as a very minor revision of earlier unacceptable proposals. It was at this point that Judge Fong's eviction orders (cited above) were issued and that Pao submitted a request to the State Land Use Commission to have 491 acres of Waiahole reclassified urban.

Movement activists were beginning to feel the fight was endless. They kept winning victories that dissolved into thin air when a new proposal was submitted. They constantly had to fight three different battles: against reclassification, against large-lot development, and against eviction. Even if reclassification was eventually and finally defeated, large-lot development might still take place. And if that could also be prevented, the tenants might still be evicted. Consequently, the WWCA becme louder and more vocal, although it did not alter its basic strategy. Each court appearance was accompanied by a rally. Each negative court decision was met with the chanting of phrases, in and out of the courtroom, such as "Hell No! We Ain't Moving!" Other marches and rallies took place. A benefit concert was held in the bandshell at Waikiki featuring many of the biggest names in Hawaiian folk and popular music and a display of the sights, sounds, and feel of country living. But it became increasingly apparent that these tactics were not working. Time seemed to have run out when a court order set October 1, 1976, as the eviction date for Waiahole. No further delays seemed likely.

STRATEGY AND TACTICS: PHASE II

The WWCA had long experienced internal tensions. One group of primarily urban workers formed a caucus called Up In Arms. They argued that the tactics used had attracted support mostly from middle-class persons who marched, signed petitions, and gave money. Victories were achieved, but none were final—yet a single defeat would mean the end of the struggle. They argued that there was no hope for the WWCA unless it developed a more militant, class-oriented line. Elections in early 1976 gave Up In Arms a majority of the steering committee, moving the WWCA toward more militant confrontation tactics. They welcomed support from some of the more radical elements in Hawaii, including the Revolutionary Communist Party. They did not deliberately drive away supporters of any particular class or political persuasion, but they did choose to reorient themselves toward a different sector of the cooptable public. The WWCA developed a program of unifying the defense of Waiahole-Waikane with other working-class and community struggles. Members of the WWCA participated in all demonstrations and confrontations affecting their allies, and members of those groups came to the aid of the WWCA. These changes in style and content of the defense movement alienated many middle-class supporters who had been initially attracted because of their involvement in environmental and life-style issues. They, along with some of the larger landowners and farmers in the valleys, drifted away from the WWCA.

A mass rally was held on September 25, 1976, in preparation for the October 1 eviction date. Again there was a potluck lunch, speeches, and songs, but the highlight was an eviction drill. A siren signaled the section of land under impending police threat. From 600 to 1,000 people rushed to the house in question and circled it with linked arms several rows deep. People playing the role of police attempted to break through and were repulsed time and time again. The drill received good coverage in the media and served the dual purpose of dress rehearsal and demonstration to the authorities of the intention to resist evictions.

The eviction date was again postponed until all appeals could be heard. The court indicated its willingness to grant a stay if the rent trust fund were turned over to it, but the WWCA refused and concealed the location of the fund, out of concern it would lose all leverage once it lost control of the Trust Fund. Windward Partners made one final compromise offer to the WWCA, which was refused, as was the WWCA counteroffer. January 3, 1977, was set as the new Waiahole eviction date.

On January 2 (the end of the third year of struggle) a tent city was set up in Waiahole. Tents were erected by student groups (the Revolutionary Student Brigade and Students United for Land and Housing), worker groups (pineapple workers, sugar workers, the unemployed, and civil service workers), youth groups, GI's, and others without affiliation. On January 3 the sheriff served writs of possession, effective immediately. The writs were accepted and burned while the road leading into the valley was blocked by an arm-linked force of several hundred people. The sheriff departed. By Tuesday, January 4, people were drifting away and the tent city dwindled to token size. Teams were sent out to leaflet and picket at numerous sites throughout the city asking the public to phone officials demanding their intervention to stop the evictions.

Around 11 p.m. on January 4 word came that the police were on their way to carry out the evictions. The tenants, the tent city residents, and an "on-call reserve force" mobilized and blocked a half-mile stretch of the Kamehameha Highway, preventing all access to the valley. This blockade stopped all traffic on the windward side as the highway is the only connection with the rest of the island. It lasted over an hour until trusted police sources promised that no police eviction team would come that night. Governor Ariyoshi was convinced by these events that no evictions could take place without a major confrontation that would most likely escalate into violence. Consequently, he convinced Marks to postpone the evictions until March 1 while attempts were made to develop a nonviolent solution.

Much happened in the next fifty days. The State Land Use Commission held hearings February 9 and 10 on Pao's request to have Waikane reclassified urban. The WWCA was successful in having the hearings held in Waiahole, and large numbers of supporters came. At one point an 83-year-old woman testified in Hawaiian (one of the two legal languages in Hawaii) and then requested a song as part of her testimony. The request was granted, and a large choral group of residents gave a moving rendition of a song written for the struggle. The City Department of General Planning submitted testimony that reclassifying either valley urban was contrary to the Oahu General Plan adopted by City Council just that January. The State Department of Planning and Economic Development submitted testimony that such reclassification was contrary to the state's Windward Regional Plan and that the amount of new housing resulting would have no significant impact on the state's housing problem.

This period was also marked by continued public pressure. A second benefit concert was held at the tent city and again attracted many locally popular musicians. An overflow crowd of about 6,000 people caused a massive traffic jam, tying up windward traffic for hours. As March 1 approached, additional pressure was placed on Governor Ariyoshi to act. Then, on February 26, 1977, he announced that, contingent on Windward Partners allowing their option to lapse, the state would buy 600 acres of Waiahole for $6 million and that arrangements would be made for current residents to live in and farm the valley with long-term leases at fair rentals.

This was a tremendous victory for the WWCA and its supporters, although the victory was not total. The settlement did not include Waikane and left the nine families still threatened with eviction, and it did not include the portion of Waiahole Valley located on the ocean side of the Kamehameha Highway, on which twelve families lived. The governor promised to give these people priority if room remained in Waiahole. This was also a good deal for Marks. Although the price was probably less than that offered by Pao, it was a guaranteed sale. Marks could continue to try to sell to Pao and then, if Windward Partners chose not to exercise its option, could still sell to the state.

Joe Pao died on April 18, 1977. In August the State Land Use Commission rejected the request to reclassify Waikane. In the light of unfavorable public actions, Windward Partners chose not to exercise its option, and the state purchased Waiahole. As of July, 1981, the state has still not announced its plans for the valley. It remains much as it was before the struggle began. Some limited development has taken place in Waikane. Of the nine families stated for eviction, one worked out a private deal, the details of which are unavailable, and the remaining eight negotiated an exchange. Windward Partners gave them free homelots in exchange for their agreement to cease and desist all opposition to attempts to develop Waikane. The agreement required the WWCA to also agree not to oppose limited development of that one portion of Waikane but left them free to act otherwise. Approval has been granted for the construction of 26 dwelling units on two-acre lots and 5 units on smaller lots. It is unlikely that additional construction will be approved in the near future.

THEORETICAL IMPLICATIONS

The key to the people's victory in the Waiahole-Waikane struggle was the transformation of leadership. This led to a change in strategies and tactics accompanied by a change in the cooptable publics that were a source of additional supporters. Without this transition, the movement was doomed to failure. This is not to say that the WWCA was mistaken in its initial choice of strategies, tactics, and cooptable publics. On the contrary, I would argue that the first phase was a necessary precondition for the second phase of the movement.

The WWCA was composed of persons with relatively little power and/or influence in the Hawaiian social structure. They were engaged in an endeavor for which there was no precedent. All previously successful struggles over land use in Hawaii had involved state land. Never before had private property rights been successfully challenged. Consequently, the WWCA could not simply select tactics that had worked elsewhere. They had to design and use tactics consistent with the values held by them and the majority of the cooptable publics.[16] Their activities had to be viewed as plausible given the social context existing at a particular time.[17] But both values and the definition of the social context changed as a consequence of experience.

The WWCA initially defined their struggle as one to retain land in agriculture and rural space while preventing urban sprawl, increased highway congestion, and further environmental deterioration. These issues attracted a broad range of support from middle-class individuals who would also be receptive to the polite tactical forms of signing petitions, donating money, and token picketing. They would not be receptive to strident confrontation-oriented tactics that held the potential of causing violence. Ultimately, they appeared to believe in the rights of owners of private property to do as they wished consistent with the public interest, and they hoped to convince either Marks or public officials that it was in the public interest not to allow Waiahole and Waikane to be developed. Some voiced a distinction between this cause and that of the tenants facing evictions. They were willing to concede the right of landowners to evict tenants, but still wished to prevent development if it could be done without undue violation of public order. They were quite different from the middle-class civil rights activists in the early sixties who were willing to use confrontation tactics on behalf of a cause they believed to be morally right and thought to be supported by the Constitution of the United States. That level of ideological commitment was lacking among most middle-class supporters of the WWCA; political radicals were the notable exception.

Initially the WWCA followed a moderate line of struggle and won decisions on zoning and land use. But developers and landlord kept coming back with new proposals and new plans. This increased the political sophistication of the WWCA, for they realized they were in for a long, hard struggle with no holds barred. This also changed the social context as the public increasingly perceived the developers as unconcerned about the opinions and welfare of state and city agencies or of the general public. When the developers were defined as selfish and greedy, an increasing tolerance for more strident tactics emerged. The WWCA had succeeded in getting the public to define as unjust that which it had always defined as just: the unrestricted use of private property for the benefit of its owners.

The shift toward more confrontational tactics was made possible by a shift in leadership within the WWCA. All social movements are heterogeneous in composition. The values and ideology that the movement as a whole expresses will be a function of which segment occupies leadership positions. It is probable that the urban workers of Up In Arms developed their class consciousness during the struggle as a consequence of the educational efforts of some of WWCA's more radical supporters. It is also possible that some came from the radical tradition of organized labor in Hawaii. Whatever the source, their class consciousness led them to redefine the struggle and seek to activate a different cooptable public. Working-class and middle-class persons have different values and will be receptive to the use of different tactics. The activation of the working class and radical segments of the public brought into the movement people who were more willing to use confrontation tactics and who were not, as a matter of principle, overly afraid that these might escalate into violence. It is doubtful if the occupation of the valley and the blockade of the highway would ever have taken place if the movement had not been transformed from one relying on middle-class support to one that relied primarily on radical and working-class support. It is clear that the movement would have lost all if it had obeyed the law and vacated when the sheriff tried to evict. It is also clear from Governor Ariyoshi's public statements that the state would not have purchased Waiahole if it were not for the clear and present danger that a violent confrontation would result from any attempt to evict the tenants.

Social movements are ever-changing phenomena. The selection of appropriate strategies and tactics must take into account many things including the nature of the target group, the nature of the opposition, the social composition and values of the constituency, the social composition and values of each of the various publics, along with the social context existing at any given historical moment. There is no simple a priori rule that allows one to select the most effective tactics. Nor are there any tactics that may automatically be ruled out. Strategic success requires the selection of tactics and the activation of cooptable publics that will yield the unique combination that can exert maximal pressure upon target groups and/or the opposition. In many cases, as in Waiahole-Waikane, this will involve the use of confrontational tactics. In other cases it will not. This will be a function of the unique sociohistorical context within which the struggle is located.

NOTES

1. Robert H. Lauer, *Social Movements and Social Change* (Carbondale: Southern Illinois University Press, 1976), p. 81.

2. E.g., Stokely Carmichael and Charles V. Hamilton, *Black Power: The Politics of Liberation in America* (New York: Random House, 1967); Francis Fox Piven and Richard A. Cloward, *Poor People's Movements: Why They Succeed, How They Fail* (New York: Pantheon, 1977); James A. Geschwender, *The Black Revolt: The Civil Rights Movement, Ghetto Uprisings, and Separatism* (Englewood Cliffs, N. J.: Prentice-Hall, 1971); and idem, *Class, Race, and Worker Insurgency: The League of Revolutionary Black Workers* (New York: Cambridge University Press, 1977).

3. E.g., Neil J. Smelser, *Theory of Collective Behavior* (New York: Glencoe, Free Press, 1963); John D. McCarthy and Mayer N. Lald, "Resource Mobilization and Social Movements: A Partial Theory," *American Journal of Sociology* 82 (May 1977); 1212–41.

4. E.g., Lewis M. Killian, "Social Movements," in *Handbook of Modern Sociology*, ed. Robert E. L. Faris (Chicago: Rand McNally, 1964), pp. 426–55; idem, "The Significance of Extremism in the Black Revolution," *Social Problems* 20 (Summer 1972): 41–49; Ralph H. Turner, "Determinants of Social Movement Strategies," in *Human Nature and Collective Behavior: Papers in Honor of Herbert Blumer*, ed. Tamotsu Shibutani (Englewood Cliffs, N. J.: Prentice-Hall, 1970), pp. 145–64; Ralph H. Turner and Lewis M. Killian, *Collective Behavior, 2nd ed.* (Englewood Cliffs, N. J.: Prentice-Hall, 1972); Anthony Oberschall, *Social Conflict and Social Movements* (Englewood Cliffs, N. J.: Prentice-Hall, 1973); Harvey A. Hornstein et al., *Social Intervention: A Behavioral Science Approach* (New York: Free Press, 1971); William A. Gamson, *The Strategy of Social Protest* (Homewood, Ill.: Dorsey Press, 1975); William R. Anderson and Russell R. Dynes, *Social Movements: Violence and Change* (Columbus: Ohio State University, 1975); Robin M. Williams, Jr., *Mutual Accommodation: Ethnic Conflict and Cooperation* (Minneapolis: University of Minnesota, 1977); Lauer, *Social Movements*; and idem, *Perspectives on Social Change* (Boston: Allyn and Bacon, 1973).

5. Turner, "Determinants of Social Movement Strategies," pp. 149–52.

6. Potential oppositional publics were not included in the original Turner formulation but were added in Turner and Killian, *Collective Behavior*, pp. 292–93.

7. Turner, "Determinants of Social Movement Strategies," pp. 147–49.

8. Lauer, *Social Movements*, pp. xix-xxii.

9. Turner and Killian, *Collective Behavior*, pp. 291–97.

10. Lauer, *Social Movements*, pp. xx-xxi; Killian, *Social Movements*, pp. 451–52.

11. Luther P. Gerlach and Virginia H. Hine, *People, Power and Change: Movements of Social Transformation* (Indianapolis: Bobbs-Merrill, 1970), p. 165.

12. J. Kenneth Benson, "Militant Ideologies and Organizational Contexts: The War on Poverty and the Ideology of Black Power," reprinted in Lauer, *Social Movements*, pp. 107–25.

13. For a description of Hawaiian history, see Gavan Daws, *Shoal of Time: A History of the Hawaiian Islands* (New York: Macmillan, 1968); Lawrence Fuchs, *Hawaii Pono: A Social History* (New York: Harcourt, Brace and World, 1961).

14. Much of this portion of the paper is derived from a combination of participant observation on the part of the author, interviews with other participants, and newspaper accounts. News stories in the *Honolulu Advertiser* and the *Honolulu Star Bulletin* on or near the dates cited in the text provide news accounts of the events described.

15. Robert Anderson, "Report on Waiahole-Waikane" (unpublished ms., 1974).

16. Turner and Killian, *Collective Behavior*, pp. 293–95.

17. Benson, "Militant Ideologies."

15

The Use of Terrorism by
American Social Movements

Ernest Evans

Terrorism has generated a great deal of intellectual controversy
in the past decade. There have been frequent debates among scholars, government officials, and the public on the morality and efficacy of terrorism. This
chapter addresses the use of terrorism by American social movements with the
intention of answering the following question: In what circumstances has the
use of terrorism furthered (or not furthered) the aims of American social
movements?

The topic of terrorism is so surrounded by controversy that getting agreement on a definition of the term is difficult. Besides, terrorism does not lend
itself to simple definitions. Rather, terrorism must be seen as a political phenomenon having a number of characteristics:

1. Terrorism is violence intended to produce an effect on a group larger
   than the immediate victims of the violence. Perpetrators of such violence
   hope that the effect it produces will enable them to attain their political
   goal. This intended effect on others distinguishes terrorism from ordinary criminal violence. Any act of criminal violence may terrify people besides the victims of the act, but terrorizing others is not the purpose of
   most ordinary crimes.[1]

2. One effect of terrorism is fear on the part of those who witness the act, whether directly or through the mass media. Hence the word "terrorism" to describe such acts. Those resorting to terrorism hope that the fear and terror their acts generate will enable them to coerce those who would otherwise oppose their policies.

3. Terror is not the only effect the practitioners of terrorism hope to produce. A terrorist group may believe that spectacular acts of violence will publicize its cause. Various Palestinian terrorist organizations hope that acts of terrorism will aggravate relations between states sufficiently to prevent an international outcome that harms their interests.[2] Acts of terrorism have been motivated by a desire to attain material rewards for terrorist movements. The perpetrators of political kidnappings have usually included among their demands the payment of ransom money and the release of captured terrorists. And, very often, terrorist movements hope to provoke a government into adopting repressive measures in response to their acts of violence.[3]

4. Terrorism can be resorted to by groups that want to initiate changes in the social and political order and by groups that want to prevent such changes. In other words, terrorism can be used by counterrevolutionaries seeking to prevent societal charge and by revolutionaries seeking radical changes in society.

5. Terrorism can be used by both state and by nonstate groups. Currently terrorist activities are usually engaged in by groups that are out of power. It is often forgotten that the origin of "terrorism" was the Reign of Terror, which took place in 1793–94 during the French Revolution, and witnessed the execution of thousands of the enemies of the revolution by Robespierre and the Committee on Public Safety. The word "terror" has been applied to government activities in later eras, perhaps most notably during Stalin's Great Terror in 1936–38 when Stalin executed millions of Soviet citizens in a successful effort to destroy opposition to his rule.

The foregoing attributes of terrorism can be summarized in the following definition: Terrorism is the use of violence to produce certain effects, including fear or terror, on a group of people so as to advance a political cause; such terroristic violence can be employed by movements seeking changes in the status quo and movements opposing changes in the status quo, and by both nonstate groups and states.

One final point should be noted about the problem of defining terrorism. There has been an unfortunate tendency by participants in debates over terrorism to try to define the subject in such a way that one's own nation, cause, or movement is not guilty of participating in terrorism, while one's opponents are guilty of being terrorists. To this end a vast array of political phenomena are characterized as terrorism. In other words, the only general agreement on the definition of terrorism seems to be that whatever it is, it is a deplorable practice that only the other side engages in. These attempts to absolve one's own side from the charge of being terrorists results in a twisting of reason and logic that in turn leads to convoluted and confused definitions of terrorism.[4]

This manipulation of definitions of terrorism is unnecessary because it rests on a false premise: that terrorism is never morally justified and that hence the case for one's position in a given dispute is weakened if one is guilty of terrorism. While this chapter does not address moral issues of political violence, neither does it accept the premise that all terrorism is morally wrong. On the contrary, in certain circumstances a resort to terroristic violence can be as morally justifiable as any other use of force, such as the protection of public order within domestic society and the defense of one's country in international society, widely accepted as morally legitimate.

While terrorism has frequently been resorted to by states and social movements, the efficacy of its use has often been disputed. Leaders of a number of movements and causes have argued that the use of terrorism is not an effective means of achieving goals. For example, around the turn of the century, Bolshevik leaders V. I. Lenin and Leon Trotsky attacked the rival Social Revolutionaries for engaging in terrorism. Lenin and Trotsky had no moral objections to terroristic violence, but both felt that what was needed to bring down the czarist government was a disciplined mass movement rather than small cells of terrorists.[5]

Debates over the efficacy of terrorism have also taken place within the context of American politics. The escalation of the Vietnam war that began in 1965 and the acceleration of the struggle for civil rights that began in 1963 led to major debates within the antiwar and black movements on the use of violence, including terroristic violence, as a means of achieving their aims. Each of these debates is sufficiently important to warrant some discussion.

The antiwar movement was a diverse collection of people. It included pacifists like the Quakers and the Catholic Worker movement, believers in the politics of realism like Hans Morgenthau and George Kennan who felt that American national interests were not being served by the Indochina war, members of the liberal wing of the Democratic party like Senators Robert Kennedy and Eugene McCarthy, individuals with a long history of involvement in radical causes like Norman Thomas and Howard Zinn, and members of New Left groups like the Students for a Democratic Society. Thus, when one generalizes about the attitudes of the antiwar movement toward terrorism, it must be recognized that such generalizations are oversimplifications of the views of a diverse movement. Keeping this caveat in mind, let us look at the debate in the late sixties and early seventies within the antiwar movement over the use of terrorism.

The first major action of the antiwar movement was a demonstration in Washington, D.C., in April 1965 to protest the Johnson administration's escalation of the Indochina war.[6] For the next few years the antiwar movement, including its most militant New Left elements such as the SDS, pursued a policy of nonviolent opposition to American involvement in Indochina.[7] However, under the pressures of the traumatic events of 1968 (the assassinations of Martin Luther King and Robert Kennedy, the Democratic National

Convention in Chicago, and the election of Richard Nixon), certain elements within the New Left wing of the antiwar movement began to advocate using violence. During the Christmas holiday season in 1969 the Weatherman faction of the SDS (SDS had broken up into several factions during the summer of 1969) announced that it was going underground to wage a campaign of terrorist violence against the American government.[8]

The Weatherman faction, which later changed its name to the Weather Underground so as to eliminate the sexism inherent in the use of the term "Weatherman," justified its decision to resort to terrorism with the argument that nonviolent efforts at social and political change were ineffective. A member of the Weather Underground made the following statement to a Chicago audience:

> Non-violent marches have their place, but they won't bring about the changes necessary for freedom. Capitalism won't crumble because of moral protest. It didn't in India, where only the color of the agents of the oppressors changed. Once again: revolution, liberation and freedom must be fought for.[9]

The first public communique of the Weather Underground argued:

> Ever since SDS became revolutionary, we've been trying to show how it is possible to overcome the frustration and impotence that comes from trying to reform this system. Kids know that the lines are drawn; revolution is touching all of our lives. Tens of thousands have learned that protest and marches don't do it. Revolutionary violence is the only way.[10]

The decision of the Weather Underground to resort to terrorism was sharply criticized by other leftist and antiwar groups. The Trotskyist Socialist Workers party, which played a key role in organizing mass demonstrations against the Indochina war, argued that the resort to terror by groups like the Weather Underground would be ineffective. The introduction to a collection of Trotsky's writings on terrorism that was put out in 1974 by the SWP argued that the terrorism practiced by the Weather Underground would not be effective in promoting revolutionary change:

> Trotsky's opposition to individual terrorism did not flow from any pacifistic, moralistic, or ethical aversion to violence under any circumstances, or from reformist illusions about the possibility of peaceful social revolution. Rather it flowed from an understanding of the basic ineffectiveness of individual terrorism as a strategy for social change.[11]

A debate on the use of violence similar to that which took place within the antiwar movement began within the black movement in the 1960s and has continued to the present. Just as the failure of peaceful marches to bring a quick end to the Indochina war pushed a number of people in the antiwar movement toward violence, so too the failure of the peaceful civil rights movement to achieve immediate racial equality, coupled with the emergence of a white backlash against black demands, led a number of blacks to advocate violence, including terrorism, as a means of ending the inferior position of blacks in American society.[12] In the years since the mid-1960s there have been several shootouts between police and the Black Panthers (established in 1966) and the Black Liberation Army (established in 1971); a number of police officers and black militants have been killed.[13]

Debates among members of the radical left and the black movement on the use of violence to attain their ends have continued into the 1980s, although with the ending of the domestic turmoil of the late sixties and early seventies the saliency of such debates to American public life is less. These debates on the efficacy of the use of violence were necessarily inconclusive because there is no simple answer to the question whether violence, including terroristic violence, is effective in promoting social change in America. The answer is at best conditional: Terroristic violence has been successful in certain circumstances in American history and unsuccessful in others. Specifically, a review of American history shows that revolutionary movements that resort to terrorism do not thereby succeed in furthering their causes, while status quo movements have in certain circumstances successfully used terrorism to further their aims.

Recent American history offers numerous examples of the futility of the resort to terrorism by movements seeking radical changes in American society. The Weather Underground has no significant achievements to show for its decade of clandestine existence; a number of its members have either surrendered to the authorities or dropped out of the organization. The Symbionese Liberation Army's members are either dead or in jail. The emergence in the late sixties and early seventies of militant black groups such as the Black Panthers and the Black Liberation Army has done little to advance the cause of racial justice in America; on the contrary, these groups merely gave rightist demagogues an issue on which to arouse a white backlash against the civil rights movement. And the FALN (Fuerzas Armada de Liberación Nacional Puertorriquena, or Armed Forces for the National Liberation of Puerto Rico) has had little success in mobilizing Puerto Rican opinion in favor of independence; the overwhelming majority of Puerto Ricans continue to be in favor of either statehood or a continuation of Puerto Rico's commonwealth status.

The failure of revolutionary violence in America stems from a key fact about American society: There have never been any mass-based movements of the extreme left in the United States. In America movements of the extreme left, whether Moscow-line parties such as the Communist party, USA, or Trotskyists such as the Socialist Workers party, or Maoists such as the Progressive Labor party, have remained very small organizations.

Mass-based extreme left movements in America would bring two vitally needed sources of support to revolutionary terrorism. First, such movements would provide a pool of potential recruits for groups engaging in terrorism. Terrorist groups need a constant stream of recruits because of the high turnover rate resulting from arrests, deaths, and desertions. It is of course true that not all members of extreme left groups believe in terrorism (*vide* the quotation cited from Trotsky's writings and put out by the Socialist Workers party). The point is that in countries with large extreme left movements there is a ready-made organizational structure that terrorists can tap for recruits; witness, for example, the success of the Red Brigades in Italy in recruiting disaffected members of the Italian Communist party.[14] Similarly, the Provisional Irish Republican Army has had little difficulty in recruiting members from large segments of the Catholic population of Ulster radicalized by sectarian violence. Second, the lack of mass-based extreme left movements in America means that few are willing to rationalize and apologize for revolutionary violence; thus, in the United States there is little legitimacy accorded to such violence.

A key to understanding the use of violence in America is the fact that, as Richard Hofstadter argued, most American violence has been in defense of the established social order:

> ... one is impressed that most American violence—and this also illuminates its relationship to state power—has been initiated with a "conservative" bias. It has been unleashed against abolitionists, Catholics, radicals, workers and labor organizers, Negroes, Orientals, and other ethnic or racial or ideological minorities, and has been used ostensibly to protect the American, the Southern, the white Protestant, or simply the established middle-class way of life and morals. A high proportion of our violent actions has thus come from the top dogs or the middle dogs.[15]

There has clearly been a lot of pro-status-quo violence in America, including a great deal of terroristic violence. And much of this violence has been successful in achieving the goals of those who initiated it. The key reason why violence by movements in favor of the status quo has been more successful than violence by revolutionary groups is that there have been a number of American mass-based movements of the extreme right.[16] The 1850s saw the antiimmigrant American party (also known as the Know-Nothings) emerge as a major electoral force.[17] In the 1920s the Ku Klux Klan experienced a nationwide revival; its membership reached a peak of 5 million in 1925.[18] And in the 1968 presidential election George Wallace received almost 10 million votes, some 13 percent of the total vote cast.[19]

Not all extreme right organizations have endorsed terrorism, but the existence of such mass movements helped rightist terrorists in two ways. First, these movements gave rightist terrorist groups a clearly identifiable pool of potential recruits; and second, the existence throughout much of American history of mass-based movements of the extreme right has meant that members of the extreme right who engaged in violence, including terroristic violence, have had people willing to rationalize and apologize for their actions. Hence the legitimacy in American society of pro-status-quo violence is higher than that of revolutionary violence.

In the Reconstruction period after the Civil War, federal government efforts to establish racial equality in the South were thwarted by the Ku Klux Klan.[20] The revived Klan of the 1920s was so powerful that it was the dominant force in the politics of a number of states.[21] American radical movements such as the Industrial Workers of the World (IWW) and the Socialist party were dealt crippling blows after World War I when these movements were subjected to frequent incidents of violence orchestrated by right-wing groups.[22] And the wave of bombings of abortion clinics in the years since the 1973 Supreme Court decision legalizing abortion has hindered efforts to make abortions available.

Rightist terrorism is not always successful. Specifically, for a campaign of status quo terrorism to be successful, the following condition has to be met: Local authorities and the federal government have to be either unwilling or unable to take repressive measures against the movement engaging in terrorism in defense of the established social order. To illustrate the importance of governmental complicity and/or indifference to the success of a campaign of rightist terrorism, consider two cases of such terrorism, one of which was successful one of which was not. Both cases involve the Ku Klux Klan. The first concerns the successful efforts of the Klan to thwart the aims of the federal government during Reconstruction and the second concerns the unsuccessful attempt by the Klan in the 1960s to prevent the achievement of civil rights movement goals in the South.

In the aftermath of the South's defeat in the Civil War, the federal government sought to force the southern states to guarantee the political rights of newly freed slaves. The majority of white southerners was in no mood to accept blacks as their political equals. Almost immediately, white southerners began to use violence to intimidate blacks. In Texas, a U.S. attorney estimated that a thousand blacks a year were killed from 1868 to 1870. In Louisiana, Union General Philip Sheridan estimated that from 1866 to 1875 thirty-five hundred people, almost all of them black, were killed or wounded.[23]

The most important organization behind this violence was the Ku Klux Klan. The Klan was founded in Pulaski, Tennessee, in 1865 by a group of Confederate veterans. Initially intended as a secret society of war comrades, it soon evolved into a political organization dedicated to white supremacy. By the middle of 1868 the Klan was organized in all of the former states of the Confederacy.[24]

The two Presidents during Reconstruction, Andrew Johnson and Ulysses Grant, were reluctant to take action against the Klan. Johnson was basically out of sympathy with the aims of Reconstruction, and Grant preferred that southern officials "exhaust their own military resources first" before asking for assistance from the federal government.[25] Even had the federal government been determined to use force to implement the goals of Reconstruction, its ability to do so would have been limited by the small size of the U.S. Army: By 1867 this force numbered only 20,117 men.[26]

State and local governments in the South were also unable or unwilling to take action against the Klan. Authorities who tried to implement Reconstruction had only weak and poorly trained militias at their disposal. And as Reconstruction progressed an increasing number of state and local governments in the South came under the control of white southerners determined to maintain white supremacy. White supremacist authorities turned a blind eye toward Klan violence.[27]

In the end the Klan succeeded in defeating the attempt by Republicans to achieve political equality for blacks in the South. Northerners grew weary of trying to coerce the South and finally agreed to end Reconstruction as part of the settlement of the disputed presidential election of 1876.[28]

In the 1960s the Klan's various branches used violence in an attempt to prevent the civil rights movement from achieving its goals in the South. In the summer of 1964 three civil rights workers were murdered in Mississippi by the White Knights of the Ku Klux Klan. Several members of this Klan faction were later convicted of violating the constitutional rights of the three civil rights workers and were sent to prison. In early 1965 a civil rights worker named Viola Gregg Liuzzo was murdered by the Klan while driving on the Selma to Montgomery highway; three Klansmen were convicted of violating Liuzzo's constitutional rights.[29] This campaign of violence failed to prevent the ending of white supremacy in the South because neither the federal government nor state and local authorities were prepared to tolerate Klan violence.

The history of the use of terrorism by social movements in America clearly shows that terrorism does not necessarily help such movements to achieve their aims. Two preconditions must be fulfilled for a terrorist campaign to achieve the goals of the social movement sponsoring the campaign: (1) the social movement must have a significant degree of mass support; and (2) federal, state and local authorities must be unwilling or unable to take repressive measures in response to the campaign of terroristic violence. When these preconditions have not been present, terrorism has not succeeded in furthering the aims of American social movements.

NOTES

1. Brian Jenkins, *International Terrorism: A New Mode of Conflict* (Los Angeles, Calif.: Crescent Publications, 1975), p. 1.
2. For example, in December 1973 a group of Palestinian *fedayeen* machine-gunned passengers and firebombed a parked airliner at the Rome airport, killing thirty-two people. The terrorists then hijacked another airliner and flew to Kuwait. The *fedayeen* were apparently trying to raise tensions in the Middle East in the hope of sabotaging the Geneva Peace Conference. See *New York Times*, 18 December 1973.
3. For a discussion of the various objectives of a campaign of terrorism, see Ernest Evans, *Calling a Truce to Terror: The American Response to International Terrorism* (Westport, Conn.: Greenwood Press, 1979), Chap. 3.
4. See, for example, the wide variety of definitions of terrorism offered in the speeches by various countries during the 1972 United Nations debates on international terrorism. *Official Records of the General Assembly*, 6th Committee, 27th sess., passim. Brian Jenkins has noted that there are severe difficulties in defining terrorism because of the tendency to use the word to describe a large and varied range of political phenomena. See *International Terrorism*, pp. 1–2. For a good discussion of the various characteristics of terrorism, see Chap. 1 of Paul Wilkinson's *Political Terrorism* (New York: Wiley, 1974). In Chap. 2 of this book Wilkinson uses the definition offered in Chap. 1 to develop a typology of terrorism.
5. V. I. Lenin, "Why the Social Democrats Must Declare Determined and Relentless War on the Socialist Revolutionaries" (1902) and "Where to Begin" (1901), cited in *Lenin Reader*, ed. Stefan Possony (Chicago: Henry Regnery, 1966), pp. 470–72; Leon Trotsky, "The Marxist Position on Individual Terrorism," in *Leon Trotsky: Against Individual Terrorism*, ed. Will Reissner (New York: Pathfinder, 1974), pp. 5–9.
6. See Kirkpatrick Sale, *SDS* (New York: Vintage, 1974), pp. 173–91, for a description of the events leading up to this demonstration and the demonstration itself.

7. For an analysis of the antiwar movement and the question of violence, see Jerome Skolnick, *The Politics of Protest*, A Staff Report to the National Commission on the Causes and Prevention of Violence, 1969, pp. 21–61; for a discussion of the SDS's role in the antiwar movement in 1965–68, see *SDS*, Chaps. 12–20.

8. See Chaps. 21–25 of *SDS* for a discussion of how many members of the SDS became increasingly supportive of violence in the years 1968–70.

9. Ibid., p. 631.

10. Ibid., pp. 631–632.

11. *Leon Trotsky*, p. 3.

12. For a discussion of black militancy in the 1960s, see *The Politics of Protest*, pp. 97–135.

13. Samuel T. Francis and William T. Poole, *Terrorism in America: The Developing Internal Security Crisis* (Washington, D.C.: Heritage Foundation, 1978), pp. 6–8.

14. Vittorfranco S. Pisano, *Contemporary Italian Terrorism: Analysis and Countermeasures* (Washington, D.C.: Library of Congress Law Library, 1979), pp. 46–47. Claire Sterling's *The Terror Network* (New York: Holt, Rinehart and Winston, 1981) argues in its discussion of terrorism in Italy (see Chap. 11) that the Red Brigades have benefited enormously from the existence in Italy of a sizable segment of public opinion that is sympathetic to their aims.

15. Richard Hofstadter and Michael Wallace, eds., *American Violence: A Documentary History* (New York: Vintage, 1971), p. 11.

16. For an analysis of these various extreme right movements, see Seymour Martin Lipset and Earl Raab, *The Politics of Unreason: Right-Wing Extremism in America, 1790–1970* (New York: Harper & Row, 1970).

17. Ibid., pp. 47–59.

18. George Thayer, *The Farther Shores of Politics: The American Political Fringe Today* (New York: Simon and Schuster, 1968), p. 83.

19. Lipset and Raab, *Politics of Unreason*, p. 379.

20. Marvin Maurer, "The Ku Klux Klan and the National Liberation Front: Terrorism Applied to Achieve Diverse Goals," in *International Terrorism in the Contemporary World*, ed. M. H. Livingston, L. B. Kress, and M. Warek (Westport, Conn.: Greenwood Press, 1978), pp. 148–49.

21. Thayer, *Farther Shores of Politics*, pp. 82–85.

22. Hofstadter and Wallace, *American Violence*, pp. 351–56.

23. Ibid., p. 223. See pp. 101–5 and 218–29 of the Hofstadter and Wallace volume for contemporary descriptions of some of the violent incidents during the Reconstruction era.

24. Maurer, "Ku Klux Klan and National Liberation Front," pp. 147–48.

25. Ibid., p. 140.

26. Ibid., p. 138.

27. Ibid., pp. 139, 147.

28. Ibid., pp. 147–49. In the 1876 presidential election between Democrat Samuel Tilden and Republican Rutherford Hayes there was a dispute over who was the legitimate winner; there were charges of electoral fraud in several states. The dispute was resolved by the following compromise: Hayes, the Republican candidate, was allowed to take office; in return, the Republicans agreed to bring the Republican-initiated and -supported Reconstruction period to an end.

29. Thayer, *The Farther Shores of Politics*, pp. 96–99. There have been charges that the shot that killed Mrs. Liuzzo was fired by Gary Thomas Rowe, an FBI informant who was in the car with the Klansmen who killed Mrs. Liuzzo. Two Birmingham policemen claimed that Rowe had confessed to them that he had killed Mrs. Liuz-

zo. Rowe denied that he had made any such confession. (*New York Times*, July 18, 1980). In December 1980 Attorney General Benjamin Civiletti stated that a two-year internal inquiry in the Justice Department had produced no "credible evidence" that Rowe had fired the shot that killed Mrs. Liuzzo. (*New York Times*, December 16, 1980). The Liuzzo family, not believing Rowe's denials and the Justice Department's claims, has filed a $2 million suit against the FBI. The suit is now slowly working its way throught the court system; in February 1981 a Federal District Court refused a Government request to dismiss the suit. (*New York Times*, February 26, 1981).

16

Conservative Tactics in Social Movement Organizations

David P. Gillespie

Accounts of social movement organizations often interpret the moderation of tactics and the institutionalization of conflict as signs of growing organizational conservatism. According to this view, the adoption of more conservative tactics by a social movement organization (SMO) shows that its leaders have sought accommodation with the organization's opponents. Leaders' motives for accommodation are the protection of their own positions and their access to material incentives offered by opponents, as well as the prestige of associating with the powerful. Such accommodation requires that uncontrolled attacks on opponents be replaced by modes of conflict that are regularized and predictable. The new conservative tactics render the SMO less effective and signify the substitution of survival for the original instrumental goal.

That increasingly conservative tactics should be interpreted as indications of SMO weakening and goal displacement is not surprising; there is a longstanding, respected theoretical explanation for such a view. The Weber-Michels model (Zald and Ash 1966) predicts that goal transformation in SMOs always results in greater conservatism (the accommodation of goals to the demands of dominant societal actors). The transformation is not limited to

The author wishes to acknowledge the support of a National Institute of Mental Health traineeship and a Department of Housing and Urban Development Research Grant H-2617RG during the period of data collection.

SMOs; any emergent organization that attempts to ensure its existence risks displacing its original goals with that of survival. The displacement occurs through an exaggerated attention to organizational maintenance or through subordinates' perception of standard procedures as ends in themselves (Gerth and Mills 1946; Sills 1957, p. 62).

But SMOs encounter an enhanced risk of goal displacement in two respects. On the one hand, like other organizations, SMO survival may require accommodation to the demands of powerful external actors. But SMOs are commonly "challenging" organizations (Gamson 1975) that attempt to change the behavior of these actors. Since they resist change, the accommodation these actors require may simply preclude attainment of the SMOs' original goals; the SMO faces the choice between secure existence—perhaps through public funding—or goal attainment. Unlike other organizations (e.g., voluntary service organizations), it cannot have both. On the other hand, the tendency to oligarchy presents a particular problem for SMOs (Michels 1962). Unlike most utilitarian organizations, many SMOs emerge with a commitment to democratic control, and *this* goal is automatically displaced by increased oligarchization. But beyond this, the mobility of SMO staff may be lower than that of other executives. If other organizations have not legitimized the SMO, a displaced leader cannot look forward to such a position elsewhere. To protect their interests, then, SMO leaders can be expected to take extraordinary steps, among them maintaining peace with the environment at any cost. Particularly for SMOs, oligarchy reinforces the already strong goal of survival.

This theoretical orthodoxy is enhanced by extensive empirical confirmation. Organized labor, for instance, is often identified as a movement that has prospered through the sacrifice of its initial radical goals. One popular view holds that the collaboration between unions and corporations has been so thorough that not only can industrial conflict be carefully regulated by the state but union leaders become the very agents of their supposed adversaries (Dahrendorf 1959, p. 263; Miliband 1969; Aronowitz 1973). Piven and Cloward's (1979) analysis of the National Welfare Rights Organization is a recent instance of case studies that support the theory. This SMO rapidly replaced confrontation tactics with lobbying and negotiation, and produced leaders who fiercely protected their positions at the expense of building an enlarged and broad-based membership. This accommodation and oligarchy left a drastically weakened organization.

Despite the scarcity of empirical exceptions, students have occasionally questioned the inevitability of conservatism for SMOs. Gusfield (1968) concluded that there appears to be no inherent or necessary relationship between increasing bureaucratization and conservatism in SMOs. Zald and Ash (1966) argued that the transformation of SMOs—to greater radicalism as well as conservatism—is conditioned on internal and external developments. Beach (1977) and Jenkins (1977) specified the conditions under which SMOs become more radical, while Rothschild-Whitt (1976) and Gillespie (1980) examined characteristics of SMOs and their environments that enable them to maintain democratic control.

This chapter reports some of the findings of a comparative analysis of twenty tenant organizations and the parent organization that helped establish them. The study extends the specification of the Weber-Michels model (1) by examining an instance in which the selection of more conservative tactics by SMO leaders was not accompanied by the displacement of original goals, and (2) by evaluating the effectiveness of the conservative tactics for the attainment of four organizational goals.

DATA

The data reported here are part of a study of all organized tenant activity in Madison, Wisconsin, over a seven-year period. This activity occurred at two levels of organization. The Madison Tenant Union (MTU) was (and remains) concerned with tenant welfare throughout the city. Individual tenants joined the MTU to support tenant advocacy and receive selective benefits of information and protection. But the MTU also served as a center for training and deploying organizers. The primary activity of organizers was to establish and sustain organizations of tenants who rented from a common landlord. Organizers helped build these smaller organizations, termed "locals," throughout the city and its suburbs.

Detailed organizational histories were assembled for both the MTU and each of the twenty locals* it helped establish during the period June 1969 to December 1976. The primary data source was a combination structured and unstructured† interview schedule; it requested information on the emergence, tactics, and effectiveness of each organization. Ninety personal interviews were completed with landlords, tenant leaders‡ of each local, and MTU organizers. Interviews were supplemented by documentary analysis of MTU and leaders' files on each organization, § and by participant observation of MTU meetings, training sessions, and day-to-day business. Data gathering began in September 1975 and continued for fifteen months.

ADOPTION OF CONSERVATIVE TACTICS

U.S. tenant organizations did not appear in the 1960s for the first time. During the 1890's, after World War I (in response to a housing shortage), and

---

* "Local" was operationalized as an association of tenants (1) who rented from a single landlord, (2) in which tenant members conceived of themselves as an ongoing organization (3) with improved housing as the primary objective, and (4) who reached the stage of organization in which formal demands or proposals were presented to the landlord. Six "prelocals," associations that satisfied at least one but not all four criteria, were included in the study, but are not included in data on the twenty locals.

† The unstructured portion of each interview conformed to what Dexter (1970, p. 5) termed the "elite" interview, in which "the investigator is willing, and often eager to let the interviewee teach him what the problem, the question, the situation, is. . . ."

‡ "Tenant leader" refers not to an MTU organizer but to a member of a local who assumed leadership responsibilities in that organization.

§ The files consisted of minutes of meetings; letters exchanged by the MTU, locals, landlords, and management companies; written agreements with landlords; tenant newsletters; and city and MTU press reports.

during the Great Depression (in reaction to mass evictions), tenants formed radical though short-lived organizations. But during the sixties the convergence of social forces and political movements* spawned the most extensive tenant organizing in U.S. history. This contemporary tenant movement began in New York City in 1963 when several CORE chapters and Jesse Gray, a local black organizer, launched a series of rent strikes in Harlem (Naison 1972). In Chicago, intensive organizing by civil rights and community organizations, with trade union support, produced forty-five separate tenant associations in 1966 (Davis and Schwartz 1966).

Marcuse (1973, pp. 50–51) reported the tenant union movement's rapid growth:

> The movement spread to other cities in 1967 and 1968. Cleveland, under SCLC's leadership again; San Francisco . . . ; Detroit, where UAW support and the organizing tradition were powerful; Boston, Philadelphia, Milwaukee, St. Louis, and Muskegon Heights, and probably 25 other major cities, all saw active organizing, rent strikes. . . .

Early in 1969 the New York and Chicago tenant organizations, with the American Friends Service Committee, sponsored a meeting that began the National Tenants Organization. By the end of the year the organization had over sixty affiliates, predominantly in public housing. These organizations shared common objectives: Tenant members sought building repairs and maintenance, freedom from rent increases, and greater control over decisions affecting their tenancy.

Since the Madison Tenant Union was not founded until the summer of 1969, this development of the tenant movement in other cities provided the new organization with a model of established tactics. Indeed, during their period of planning, MTU founders undertook careful study of the tenant movement in two other cities: New York City and Ann Arbor, Michigan. The organizations in these cities had different constituencies—poor blacks in New York and middle-class university students in Ann Arbor; they also addressed different problems—deteriorated dwellings and rent increases. Yet they had adopted the same tactics—mass organizing and the rent strike.

First, the organizations attempted to mobilize *all* tenants in particular sections of the city. This meant attempting to influence all landlords with property in those areas. Second, if tenants' initial demands for repairs or rent reductions were denied, the organizations' standard response was to organize a rent withholding action, the "rent strike." Since neither the mass organizing of tenants to oppose their landlords nor the breaking of a legal covenant had been legitimated by powerful actors in either city, these constituted radical tactics.

---

* These included (1) the posturban renewal housing shortage encountered by the poor, particularly the black poor who had migrated to urban areas; (2) the civil rights movement, with its emphasis on community organization; (3) the Great Society Program's funding of community organizers and poverty lawyers; and (4) the mobilization of college students around civil rights and Vietnam war issues.

By the time their 1969 deliberations were completed, MTU founders had decided to *avoid* both tactics. Rather than organize tenants* by geographic area, they would organize only tenant locals, organizations composed of tenants of particular landlords. Rather than use the rent strike as the standard weapon of influence, the MTU would adopt a collective bargaining model for its relationship with landlords. Together with the tenant local, it would seek the landlord's recognition of its right, based on members' signed authorizations, to represent tenants. Through formal bargaining, it would attempt to secure the landlord's written agreement to building improvements, a grievance procedure, and a model lease. The rent strike would be used as a threat, but would be held as a last resort. Locals would strike only if a series of less extreme tactics, such as mass meetings, picketing, and publicity, failed to force landlords to bargain "in good faith."

Why this accommodation? What could have led these organizers to reject tactics of massive, disruptive protest—the very tactics that Piven and Cloward (1979) have argued are most effective? Were MTU founders coopted by their opposition? Did they anticipate public funding that precluded their breaking the rules of the game? Or were they simply attempting to protect their positions of leadership by developing a long-lived, stable organization?

Examination of this period suggests that none of the processes predicted by the Weber-Michels model account for the MTU's rejection of the movement's radical tactics. Instead, reasons for the rejection include the experience of previous tenant organizations, the experience of organizers in the antiwar movement, and the attractiveness of tactics developed by the trade union movement.

PAST EFFECTIVENESS OF RADICAL TACTICS

MTU founders gathered extensive intelligence on the effectiveness of tenant action in New York and Ann Arbor. Through discussions with tenant organizers from both cities, written accounts of the New York strike, and visits to Ann Arbor while the rent strike there was in progress, the MTU staff reached several conclusions about the effects of mass organizing and the rent strike.

First, at least in Ann Arbor, organizing by geographic area resulted in no one landlord being "hit hard enough that he had to bargain" (Groban 1970). The founders decided that to force Madison landlords to comply with tenants' demands, it would be necessary to organize all or most of a particular landlord's tenants, regardless of whether they lived in contiguous locations or not.[†] Founders also argued that organizing by geographical area made effective

---

* Organizers did invite all tenants of the city to join the MTU. Incentives for membership included help with the check-in and check-out procedures, use of a model lease that individuals could urge their landlords to adopt, subscription to the *MTU News*, and the attraction of supporting an organization that worked for the welfare of all tenants. But unlike the locals it established, the MTU did not attempt to influence landlords through the collective action of its at-large members.

† Of course, the mobilization of all tenants in the city would influence landlords, but was beyond the organizing capabilities of the emergent MTU.

targeting impossible. They suggested that landlords could be divided into three kinds, each of which would influence the outcome of tenant organizing. In "ma and pa" operations of few units, landlords usually lived on the premises. Since their properties were expected to be in relatively good condition and their supply of capital limited, these landlords were judged not suitable for organizing against. In contrast to these were very large landlords, both individuals and corporations, who owned hundreds or thousands of units (often) in several cities. Organizing all the tenants of such owners would probably be impossible, and the fraction of tenants that did organize would exert little influence. But there were also "middle-level" landlords who owned between ten and two hundreds units. A subset of these landlords was considered particularly vulnerable: those landlords purchasing property on land contract who depended on tenants' rent payments for their own property payments.* These landlords understood that if tenants withheld rent, landlords might be forced to refinance their debts or even foreclose. If middle-level landlords could be carefully selected, the probability of successful tenant action would be enhanced. Organizing by geographic area precluded such selection.

Second, Ann Arbor and New York tenant organizations were forced into court when landlords attempted to evict striking tenants or sue for back rent. Immediately, the tenant organizations became dependent on other actors, over whom they had little control. They were forced to find defense attorneys committed to the strike, whatever its duration, and willing to include tenant leaders in decision making. They were forced to persuade building inspectors to examine buildings, record violations, and produce records in court. They were forced to rely on judges to withhold rent held in escrow from landlords until they had completed building repairs. Without the cooperation of each of these actors, tenant actions could not be effective. Moreover, attorneys' fees and court costs placed enormous financial burdens† on tenant organizations. Since poor tenants were unable to pay their own legal expenses, successful fund raising became an additional requirement for success, and made the organizations dependent on still other third parties for contributions.

Third, customary court practices lent certain advantages to landlords. Court summonses never delivered to tenants ("sewer service") could result in default judgments against them. Some tenants who did receive summonses were so threatened by the prospect of having to appear in court that they paid their rent or vacated their apartments (Lipsky 1970). Landlords could request repeated delays in court to reduce support for the strike; because of tenants' fears of suits and evictions, tenant organizers could not sustain support for a strike indefinitely (Jennings 1972). To each of these disadvantages of court action, MTU founders were forced to add the failure of Wisconsin law—unlike that of New York or Michigan—to provide for legal rent withholding. They predicted that rent strikes in Wisconsin would be overturned in state courts.

* The easing of on-campus residence rules by the university produced sharply increased demand for rentals in Madison during this period. Investors immediately purchased single-family dwellings and transformed them to student rentals.
† For instance, the first attorney retained by the Ann Arbor Tenant Union accepted payment of $5,000, and then withdrew his services before the termination of the strike (Katz 1970).

Finally, founders of the MTU concluded that use of the rent strike had produced goal displacement. In New York and Ann Arbor, the long-range goals of protecting and mobilizing tenants had been replaced by the determination to mount a successful strike. The appeal to third parties, the need to convince threatened tenants to maintain the strike, and the continual search for funds left organizers no time or energy for other pursuits.

EFFECTIVENESS OF ANTIWAR PROTEST

Antiwar demonstrations in Madison had begun in 1964, and many founders of the MTU were veterans of this movement. They were disillusioned. It seemed obvious that the years of protest in Madison and other cities had failed to force an end to the war. But they identified another failure. Many participants had approached the war protest as a means of calling attention to other class-related issues. In particular, they had hoped it would serve as a vehicle for increasing the class consciousness of working- and middle-class individuals. Yet the form that their protest had taken, often violent encounters with the police and military, had alienated the very objects of these efforts to increase consciousness. The backlash against student protesters had been severe.

These veterans of past protest reasoned that by avoiding disruptive protest they might increase the effectiveness of their organization, and they would certainly make it more acceptable to potential members and sympathizers. A key requirement for the new organization would be the selection of tactics that were legitimate in the eyes of nonstudents; the massive rent strike would not meet this criterion.

AVAILABILITY OF AN ALTERNATIVE MODEL

MTU founders concluded that the trade union movement had more to recommend it than either the tenant or antiwar movements. After its early years, it had successfully influenced employers through collective bargaining while maintaining legitimacy in the eyes of much of the public. MTU founders resolved to adopt organized labor's tactics. Landlords would be presented with proof of majority tenant support for MTU affiliation. If the landlord refused to bargain, public announcement (or threatened announcement) of the refusal, mass meetings, and picketing might suffice to bring the landlord to the bargaining table. If the landlord persisted in refusing to bargain despite increasingly aggressive tenant tactics, a rent strike would be necessary, but it would be legitimate in the opinion of much of the public. After all, tenants had attempted an orderly settlement. Use of tactics so familiar to working-class residents was expected to win not only widespread sympathy for the organization but also actual members.

MTU founders were also attracted by the trade union organizing model and structured the MTU to be a parent union that established discrete locals. These locals would receive organizing assistance and instruction from the MTU; once organized, the locals' representatives would help determine MTU policy. Since MTU and local representatives would attempt to negotiate all conditions affecting tenancy on behalf of members, there would be no dependence on such third parties as attorneys, courts, or city employees.

In short, MTU founders selected tactics on the basis of other tenant organizations' experiences, the failure of antiwar protests, and the effectiveness and legitimacy of trade union tactics. My investigation suggested that these three considerations were accompanied by none of the reasons predicted by the Weber-Michels model for an SMO's selection of conservative tactics. First, there is no evidence of any agreement, implicit or explicit, between the MTU and landlords. Careful observers of Ann Arbor themselves, Madison landlords expected a similar mass rent strike from the new organization and prepared to forcefully resist,* not to coopt, the MTU. Second, given local citizens' reaction against antiwar protests and a conservative city administration, there was not a hint of public funding for the organization in return for the avoidance of disruptive tactics. Third, since most of the student founders expected to live in Madison only temporarily, there is no reason to suspect that they chose safe tactics in order to protect their future leadership positions.

SUCCESS OF CONSERVATIVE TACTICS

The case of the MTU challenges the conventional wisdom that the choice of more conservative tactics by SMOs signals their having "sold out." But the notion remains that in comparison to radical tactics, conservative tactics are necessarily weak and ineffective—why else would SMO opponents prefer them? Evaluation of MTU outcomes during the organization's first seven years addresses this question of the effectiveness of conservative tactics. Since the MTU had no single purpose, evaluation requires the separate examination of each of its goals.[†]

ESTABLISHING "SUCCESSFUL" TENANT LOCALS

From the perspective of MTU organizers, a major requirement for local success was that landlords agree to collective bargaining. Five levels[‡] of legitimation of collective bargaining were adapted from Gamson's (1975) analysis. Among these, the presence of negotiations[§] between landlord and tenant representatives was selected as indicating a level of intermediate success in the acceptance of collective bargaining. Thirteen of the twenty locals achieved negotiations.

---

* Several landlords added clauses to their 1969–70 leases forbidding tenant union affiliation or rent withholding.

† This evaluation addresses only those goals attainable through the organization of locals and collective bargaining. Thus it does not consider (1) the MTU's attainment of its goals of tenant education, tenant counseling, and lobbying for pro-tenant legislation at the state and city levels; or (2) locals' attainment of increased interaction among tenants and increased ability to control deviant tenants.

‡ The five levels were (1) informal acceptance of tenant representatives as valid spokespersons for tenants, (2) negotiations, (3) consultation with tenant representatives, (4) the signing of formal agreements with the organization, and (5) the signing of an agreement formally recognizing the organization as sole collective bargaining agent for tenants.

§ "Negotiations" is defined as one or more prearranged meetings between the landlord (or the landlord's agent) and tenant representatives in which the landlord does not rule out the possibility that he or she will discuss and comply with at least one tenant demand.

TABLE 16.1/Benefits at Landlord Expense, by Legitimation
by Landlord

| | Legitimation | |
Benefits	Negotiations or Stronger	None
One or more	11	4
None	2	3

In contrast to organizers, many tenant members of the locals had only a limited interest in the success of collective bargaining. Instead, these tenants had organized to get something from the landlords: improved services and protection from increased housing costs. An indication of success from the tenants' perspective, then, was that the local gain at least one benefit "at landlord expense."* Fifteen of the twenty locals reported a total of forty-one such benefits.† These measures of legitimation and benefits are combined in Table 16.1.

Eleven of the twenty locals met the criteria for success for both measures. Two locals achieved legitimation by the landlords but were denied benefits, and four achieved benefits without legitimation. Three locals achieved success in neither respect.

Examination of all twenty locals is not a satisfactory test of the utility of collective bargaining tactics. Several events during the period from 1969 to 1971 made landlords particularly resistent to the demands of organized tenants. First, having heard rumors (preceding the MTU) of a mass strike among students scheduled for the 1969 school year, many landlords were determined to resist *any* demands by organized tenants. Second, the late 1960s and early 1970s saw a nationwide reaction against student political activism fueled by a progression of campus demonstrations, riots, and building takeovers. Since the first MTU locals consisted mostly of students, landlords perceived them as organizations closely related to those responsible for the earlier violent and destructive episodes in the city. Third, during this same period, the destruction ("trashing") of apartments by departing students, as well as attacks on the persons and personal property of unpopular landlords, was not uncommon in Madison. Respondents suggested that students responsible for these actions perceived themselves to be exploited; they were forced to pay what they considered high rents for deteriorated housing by landlords taking advantage of an excess demand for housing in the vicinity of the university. Despite the MTU's public position against destruction of property and violence against persons, it did not at first escape association with these acts.

---

* The local attained such a benefit (1) if tenant respondents reported at least one new advantage received as a result of their collective action, (2) if the new advantage involved a cost for the landlord, and (3) if the new advantage was not a one-time-only or "trivial" (in tenants' estimation) maintenance procedure.

† For instance, ten locals reported improved general maintenance; seven reported a rent decrease or postponement of a rent increase; five reported that a resident or property manager was replaced at their request; and so on.

TABLE 16.2/Benefits at Landlord Expense, by Legitimation by Landlord Late Locals Only

Benefits	Legitimation	
	Negotiations or Stronger	None
One or more	8	1
None	1	0

During the 1971–73 period, student-community relations thawed. Landlords found that a mass rent strike was never initiated. Antiwar protest subsided. When a new mass transit system and apartment construction on the city's fringe relieved the overcrowded rental market, destructive acts by student tenants ceased. As a result, the ten locals established after 1971 did not experience the extreme landlord opposition of earlier years. They therefore provide a test of the effectiveness of landlord-tenant collective bargaining under typical conditions. Table 16.2 shows that among these ten "late" locals, eight achieved both negotiations and one or more benefits; one gained only negotiations, while another gained only benefits; and no local failed to achieve either measure of success.

Examination of higher levels of legitimation and benefits reinforces the conclusion that MTU locals were more successful during the later, politically relaxed, period. Six of the ten late locals achieved the higher legitimation of a written agreement,* while only one of the ten early locals won such an agreement. Similarly, the late locals reported twenty-seven benefits, a disproportionate share of the forty-one benefits gained at landlord expense by all twenty locals.

ORGANIZING NONSTUDENTS

Several founders of the MTU selected housing as an organizing issue because it promised the opportunity for developing class consciousness among nonstudents that antiwar protest had not. One explained that at a level beyond the concern with housing, "We wanted to give people more control over their lives, but we also wanted to create activists. We wanted to create people who were sensitive to power relations† in a lot of different areas of their lives." One measure of whether such messages reached nonstudents is the portion of locals with nonstudent majorities.‡

* Any agreement signed by both the landlord or the landlord's agent and tenant representatives.
† For instance, during door-knocking campaigns to build support for a local, MTU staff regularly called tenants' attention to the question of equity: Why should the landlord, not the tenants, eventually gain ownership of a property paid for by tenants?
‡ MTU organizers also made contact with nonstudents when they attempted to establish locals that never became organizations, and when they communicated with tenants who did not belong to locals via the *MTU News* and the telephone advising service (some 3,700 calls received during 1975). Yet relative to these contacts, interaction between organizers and tenant members of the locals was intensive and of long duration. The frequency of nonstudents locals is therefore a measure of the strongest opportunity of staff to politicize nonstudents.

The record is mixed. Eleven of the twenty locals were predominantly nonstudent. But not surprisingly, as antistudent backlash waned during the early 1970s, the MTU increased its ability to attract nonstudents. Seven of the ten late locals were nonstudent. Particularly during this later period, then, the MTU provided a vehicle for leftist university students to approach other groups: young white and blue-collar workers, the poor living in public housing, and the aged. The organization's tactics partly account for its acceptability to these tenants.

ORGANIZATIONAL SURVIVAL

MTU founders envisioned a city level organization and locals that would provide enduring protection for tenants. Since the problems and needs of tenants were not likely to be resolved in the near future, there would be a continuing need for the organizations. Did they survive?

The MTU was clearly successful in this respect. At this writing, it has been in continuous operation for twelve years. This longevity is at least partly explained by the MTU's use of conservative tactics. As part-time student volunteers declined in the 1970s, city appropriations and VISTA placements became crucial in supporting a smaller number of full time organizers. Had the MTU developed a more radical reputation, these external sources of support would not have been available.

In contrast, MTU locals were comparatively short-lived. Their period of activity ranged from two to forty-eight months, with a mean and median span of eleven and seven months respectively. But the short life of locals can be attributed to the MTU's choice of conservative tactics in only two cases. In those two locals, members disbanded in response to complete opposition by landlords to collective bargaining demands. The reasons for the dissolution of other locals were goal attainment, unsuccessful rent strikes, and, by far most frequently, the rapid turnover of members.* Each appeared to be unrelated to the MTU's selection of tactics.

AVOIDING LITIGATION

Founders of the MTU knew that the records of other tenant organizations in court were not enviable. To the detriment of their organizations, the best known tenant unions had used the rent strike as the main tactic of influence, and had been forced to turn all their energies to court defenses against eviction. The founders resolved to replace court-centered dispute processing with the collective bargaining system.†

They were largely successful: Tenants organized by the MTU were forced

---

* The high mobility of tenants is explained by the temporary residence of university students in the city and the age of tenants in the nonstudent locals: 60 percent of tenants were 18 to 30 years of age. Departing members of a local were hard to replace. New tenants often no longer experienced the problems responsible for the formation of the local, and they often arrived after most leaders of the local had departed.

† Moreover, individual tenants had not been making use of small claims court to resolve their grievances with landlords (Gillespie 1977), so the grievance procedure was designed to work for individuals where the court had failed.

into court only three times. In each instance litigation followed rent strikes* called to compel landlords to sign or honor written agreements.

MTU experience with rent strikes in court confirmed the founders' decision to avoid litigation. In addition to the time and money required by court action, tenants required an immense amount of encouragement by organizers to maintain the strike. Of four strikes that began simultaneously in December 1970, three failed because tenants were not adequately prepared, organizers did not have enough time to spend conferring with strikers, and money was not available to pay court costs and legal fees. In an important respect the strike was a weak as well as a costly tactic. Because of their fear of the court and of eviction, tenants' participation in the rent strike was low relative to other tenant local activities. Local records showed a mean of only 40 percent and a median of 36 percent *initial* participation in the strikes. Over time, many of these participants defected from the strikes.

CONCLUSIONS

The first conclusion of this analysis is that an SMO's selection of conservative tactics can be motivated wholly by a concern for effectiveness; it need not indicate any compromise of movement goals. The second conclusion is that conservative tactics can produce moderate to high realization of organizational goals. In this instance, conservative tactics were considerably more effective in the pursuit of four goals during a period of political calm than during an earlier period of tension.

These findings have practical significance beyond their theoretical implications. Unqualified acceptance of the Weber-Michels model of SMO transformation permits the extreme conclusion that social movements should *avoid* organization (Piven and Cloward 1979). But this study, like previous specifications of the conditions under which the model makes inaccurate predictions, can serve social movement leaders by indicating when increased organization will not be counterproductive.

Because they attempt to change society or its members, SMOs are everywhere subject to repression and cooptation. When SMOs can substitute conservative for radical tactics, dominant societal actors will perceive SMOs as less threatening and will be less likely to attempt to undermine them. This forbearance may be critical. The Weber-Michels model suggests that external threats and incentives are responsible for goal displacement and oligarchization within SMOs. By avoiding unnecessary conflict with their environments, SMOs make themselves less subject to both external attacks and internal transformations.

REFERENCES

Aronowitz, Stanley
   1973   *False Promises: The Shaping of American Worker Class Consciousness.* Hightstown, N.J.: McGraw-Hill.

* In five cases of strikes called for this reason, tenants were not forced into court.

Beach, Stephen W.
  1977 "Social Movement Radicalization: The Case of the People's Democracy in Northern Ireland." *Sociological Quarterly* 18: 305.

Dahrendorf, Ralf
  1959 *Class and Class Conflict in Industrial Society.* Stanford: Stanford University Press.

Davis, Gordon J., and Michael W. Schwartz
  1966 "Tenant Unions: An Experiment in Private Law-making." *Harvard Rights-Civil Liberties Review* 2: 237.

Dexter, Lewis Anthony
  1970 *Elite and Specialized Interviewing.* Evanston: Northwestern University Press.

Gamson, William A.
  1975 *The Strategy of Social Protest.* Homewood, Ill.: Dorsey Press.

Gerth, Hans J., and C. Wright Mills, eds.
  1946 *Max Weber: Essays in Sociology.* New York: Oxford University Press.

Gillespie, David P.
  1977 "Tenant Unions and Collective Bargaining." Ph.D. dissertation, University of Wisconsin–Madison.
  1980 "Strength in Weakness? Barriers to Oligarchy in Social Movement Organizations." Paper presented at the annual meeting of North Central Sociological Association, Dayton.

Groban, Debbie
  1970 "City-wide Rent Strike." *Madison Tenant Union News,* 14 October, p. 1.

Gusfield, Joseph R.
  1968 "Social Movements: The Study." Pp. 445–52 in David Sills, ed., *International Encyclopedia of the Social Sciences,* vo. 14. New York: Macmillan.

Jenkins, J. Craig
  1977 "Radical Transformation of Organization Goals." *Administrative Quarterly* 22: 4.

Jennings, Thomas
  1972 "A Case Study of Tenant Union Legalism." Pp. 47–62 in Stephen Burghardt, ed., *Tenants and the Urban Housing Crisis.* Dexter, Mich.: New Press.

Katz, Stuart
  1970 "Rent Strikes and the Law: The Ann Arbor Experience." *Yale Review of Law and Social Action* 1: 14.

Lipsky, Michael
  1970 *Protest in City Politics: Rent Strikes, Housing and the Power of the Poor.* Chicago: Rand McNally.

Marcuse, Peter
  1973 "The Rise of Tenant Organizations." Pp. 49–54 in Jon Pynoos et al., eds., *Housing Urban America.* Chicago: Aldine.

Michels, Roberto
  1949 *Political Parties.* Glencoe, Ill.: Free Press.

Miliband, Ralph
  1969 *The State in Capitalist Society.* New York: Basic Books.

Naison, Mark D.
  1972 "Rent Strikes in New York." Pp. 19–34 in Stephen Burghardt, ed., *Tenants and the Urban Housing Crisis.* Dexter, Mich.: New Press.

Piven, Frances Fox, and Richard A. Cloward
  1979 *Poor People's Movements: Why They Succeed, How They Fail.* New York: Vintage.

Rothschild-Whitt, Joyce
  1976 "Conditions Facilitating Participatory-Democratic Organizations." *Sociological Inquiry* 46: 75.

Sills, David
   1957   *The Volunteers*. Glencoe, I11.: Free Press.
Zald, Mayer N., and Roberta Ash
   1966   "Social Movement Organizations: Growth, Decay and Change." *Social Forces*
          44: 327.

Anti-Vietnam War March, Chicago, 1967.

Part 5
Decline

Movements are inherently unstable. Because they are an unpredictable combination of conflicting tendencies in an ever-changing environment, they inevitably decline. But the causes and consequences of decline vary. Some movements decline because the grievances that stimulated them are resolved. Some movements are repressed successfully. Some fall apart because their resources disappear, the cost of participation becomes too high, or internal bickering splits them into competing factions. A movement may have a major transformative effect on society or it may pass as a ripple, leaving no lasting effects. It may leave new organizations or institutions in its wake to try a different approach to the problems it tackled, or it may withdraw and speak only to the converted. It may change its goals to maintain its existence or may change its existence in response to new goals. It may decline as a social movement while continuing to develop as a social club, an interest group, or something else. Decline may be inevitable, but the type of decline is not.

Miller identifies four patterns of decline: success, cooptation, repression, and failure. Success is a primary cause of movement decline and is sometimes consciously avoided by movement leaders, who deliberately alter their goals to avoid achieving them. This happened to SDS. The more successful it was, the more it attracted attention from the authorities and participants who wished to change it and the goals of the student movement at large. It was finally split by two factions whose goals were so unrealistic that both sides could safely assume that only the most committed would join them.

The two chapters on the civil rights movement illustrate a similar decline pattern, but for somewhat different reasons from that of SDS. The civil rights movement was successful not only in attracting attention but in achieving its initial goals of removing legal segregation and barriers to black voting in the South. This success stimulated it to go further, demanding a share of societal power in the North as well as the South. This, coupled with urban riots, brought factionalism, a loss of financial resources, and government repression. McAdam gives an overview of this process for the entire movement; Stoper analyzes how it affected a single organization. Her focus on SNCC shows how a movement organization created for one set of circumstances unsuccessfully tried to adapt itself to another. It illustrates one reason movement organizations are so unstable.

Bromley and Shupe's study of the Unification Church illustrates a different kind of repression—one engaged in by private individuals more than government authorities. People who felt their basic values and families threatened fought back. Since the inherent bias of social institutions and values was already on their side, they were able to force the Unification Church into withdrawing from active proselytization into more of a holding pattern.

Burghardt's chapter is not on a movement or movement organization so much as on how the consequences of success can create the means of future failure. The labor movement was *the* Social Movement of the nineteenth century. Although it still calls itself a movement, it long since "institutionalized" into a powerful part of the established order. A consequence of this is not only the forswearing of militant movement tactics in exchange for organizational stability, but active "social control" efforts to prevent new movements within its ranks. Several unions have developed rank-and-file caucuses in the last few years who are trying to push union leaders into more confrontational postures in hopes of greater gains for members. The Coalition for a Better Contract within the New York City Transit Union was one of these (actually a coalition of three such caucuses). Although it forced a strike contrary to the leadership's inclination, it failed to achieve with this action real gains or even power for itself within the union. Burghardt analyzes why this movement within an institutionalized movement had such a short life.

Although the term "decline" implies failure, a conclusion that movements inevitably fail would be inaccurate. Many movements described in this book were highly successful. The fact that they inevitably declined *as movements* illustrates movement instability, not movement failure. The fact that instability is inherent and decline inevitable should not discourage movement participation so much as it should encourage movement participants, in so far as possible, to delay decline and structure its direction. The realization that social movements are not only an intrinsic part of American society but usually temporary should make it possible to maximize their impact while they are at their most powerful.

17

The End of SDS and the Emergence of Weatherman: Demise Through Success

Frederick D. Miller

In recent years, scholars of social movements have turned from studying the psychological underpinnings of individual social movement participation (Hoffer 1950, Feuer, 1969, Gurr 1970) to studying the structure of social movement organizations (Gerlach and Hine 1970), their place in the political system (Tilly, Tilly, and Tilly 1975) and factors that influence their success or failure (Zald and Ash 1966, McCarthy and Zald 1973, Gamson 1975). This has entailed a shift from the perspective of agents of social control whose interest is in controlling individual actors to that of social movement leaders whose interest is in why movements succeed or fail, with an emphasis on how to make them succeed (cf. Gamson 1968). Movement participation has generally been studied in terms of personality psychology, but what happens to movements is the study of organizations; hence it draws on organizational, political, and economic models. These newer organizational theories of social movements have been loosely gathered under the title "resource mobilization theory" because of the emphasis they place on the role of resources—money, expertise, access to publicity, paucity of social control—in determining the course of social movements.

This chapter examines factors that contribute to the decline of social movements and the organizations that comprise them. Starting from the perspective that movements are developed by mobilizing resources, it is possible to define influences that make resources less available to organizations or make organizations lose interest in resources they might otherwise seek. The operation of such factors is illustrated with two examples of organizational decline and failure: the splitting and collapse of Students for a Democratic Society (SDS) in 1969, and the foundering of Weatherman, the most notorious group to emerge from that split.

A MODEL OF MOVEMENT DECLINE

Most social movements consist of a variety of social movement organizations that, with varying degrees of cooperation or competition, seek to mobilize people and press demands. The history of a movement and its organizations is broadly determined by three factors: events in the world that influence the availability of resources and the success of tactics; movement ideologies that influence tactical and structural choices; and movement organizational structure, which also influences tactics and ways of accessing and mobilizing resources. Since all three of these factors are related to one another, they cannot be studied independently. Both movement ideology and structure, which shape each other, are created by the members' adaptive responses to external forces. Once created, neither ideology nor structure is static; both influence strategic choices that organizations make and remain somewhat responsive to external events. Strategic choices made at any time influence the range of choices that an organization will have available later. The history of any movement organization is determined by an interaction between factors internal to the organization and factors in the outside world.

The decline of specific social movement organizations does not always herald the decline of an entire social movement. Individual organizations may come and go within a movement, the replacement of one by another signifying vital growth and change. The movement as a whole declines only when all social movement organizations decline, leaving no group to effectively embody the goals of the movement, or when there no longer is a potential constituency for organizations to mobilize. In either situation, the movement may cease to exist. Four separate broad features—repression, cooptation, success, and failure—can bring about such decline in movements or individual organizations.

REPRESSION

Repression occurs when agents of social control use force to prevent movement organizations from functioning or prevent people from joining movement organizations. The variety of repressive tactics includes indicting activists on criminal charges, using infiltrators to spy on or disrupt groups, physically attacking members and offices, harassing members and potential recruits by threatening their access to jobs and schools, spreading false information about groups and people, and anything else that makes it more difficult for the movement to put its views before relevant audiences. Repressive actions may be defined as legitimate by the state for example, when it passes laws banning political parties or suspending civil liberties in emergencies, but they are never legitimate from the perspective of the movement. For both the agent of social control and the movement, the most relevant judge of legitimacy is the population at large. In the late sixties, public opinion polls found that large majorities of Americans, who saw crime as the country's most serious problem, took lenient views of violent police tactics used to stop political groups and demonstrations. In such a climate the repression of dissidents can be carried out rather easily.

As Gerlach and Hine (1970) point out, a weak attempt at repression may actually help a social movement organization by increasing solidarity among members who share the burden of repression. Above a certain point, however, repression disrupts an organization: if leaders and members are killed or jailed, if its activities are disrupted, or if the resources required to keep it going are inadequate to meet the increased costs of maintaining the group. Repression can destroy an entire social movement in a similar fashion by raising the costs for potential recruits and supporters beyond what they are willing or able to pay. The issues and grievances the movement addresses may still exist, but movement activity may start again only when the repressive cost comes down.

COOPTATION

Cooptation strategies are brought into play when individual movement leaders are offered rewards that advance them as individuals while ignoring the collective goals of the movement. Such rewards serve to identify the interests of those coopted with those of the dominant society. People who are coopted often argue that by joining the opposition they are doing what can best further the movement, but generally it is easier to control people once they are dependent on an organization than when they are leading independent opposition organizations. This form of cooptation only hurts movement organizations when it removes irreplaceable members. It is most likely to be effective with movements of powerless constituencies who have few skilled activists.

A different means by which movement organizations are coopted was described by Robert Michels (1962) in his classic work on European socialist parties. He propounded an "iron law of oligarchy" according to which movement organizations have inherent tendencies to bureaucratize, centralize authority, and withdraw from political activity, regardless of their prior success. Michels argues that leaders who hold office for long periods cannot avoid becoming more concerned with retaining their positions and perquisites than with pressing movement demands. Since being an organizational leader offers them more rewards—and often more money—than they could get from any other available occupation, they curtail radical activity in the interest of maintaining the organization and their position within it.

SUCCESS

While every movement should seek and be able to enjoy success or victory, success is actually a bit more complicated. Growing by attracting new constituents and winning on particular issues both pose problems for social movements. It is conceivable that a movement could set goals, accomplish them, and subside, with success obviating the need for the movement. This is rare, however, probably limited to instances where people organize solely to achieve one goal. For example, if residents of an area mobilize to prevent construction of a new airport, and win their demand, the movement may demobilize without regret. The woman's suffrage movement was one of the rare movements to do this. But few movements that comprise many organizations raise single demands that can be satisfied. They present multifaceted programs, and the accomplishment of some demands leads to the raising of others. Few movements see the satisfaction of all their demands. Instead, they make or are forced into compromises that only sometimes are advantageous to the movement.

In obtaining concessions from the dominant system, movement organizations often have to relinquish some portion of their claim to represent an independent radical opposition. This process of *absorption* brings social movement organizations into the structure of interests in the polity, converting them into interest groups. The successful group, taking on increased responsibility and resources, tends to be more rigid and bureaucratic than a social movement organization. Funds make it possible to replace volunteers with professional staff, and responsibility discourages the spontaneous and freewheeling qualities often associated with movement organizations. When the absorption of social movement organizations causes a large number of constituents to identify their interests with those of the dominant society, the movement ceases to exist as a movement. It no longer has a role as an opposition to the polity.

Problems identified with success can affect movement organizations well before demands are realized. An organization that attracts attention and members is undergoing a form of success. Certainly, voluntary political organizations want to grow. Yet growth can change or even harm an organization. Recruits may be less committed to the organization than older members, or may differ in their beliefs in ways that encourage factional splits. A small organization may find it difficult to find roles for new members and thus may not be able to hold recruits, alienating potential constituents in the process. Finally, rapid growth may swamp available resources, limiting the amount that organizations can accomplish while they struggle to integrate members.

Besides drawing members, growth can attract organizations that seek to attach themselves to the movement. New movement organizations often start by seeking to share resources developed by older groups. For example, many ethnic minorities have organized themselves in emulation of black Americans, and such groups as the handicapped seek to be identified as a form of minority in the hope of reaping collective benefits. The danger this poses for the initial movement is that new arrivals can become competitors for resources and members, draining the resources of the originally successful group.

FAILURE

Success is a desirable end that brings problems. Failure is simply undesirable. With hindsight, organizational failure can often be identified as due to strategic or structural errors. A combination of skill and luck is required for an organization to press its demands successfully. Organizations often adopt ineffective strategies or experience organizational problems. Failure at the organizational level takes two major forms: factionalism and encapsulation.

Factionalism arises from the inability of the organization's members to agree over the best direction to take. While a movement may contain many factions, and even gain intellectually from the tensions of debate, a single organization can be halted by disunity. Factional dispute can prevent policies from being set, or can cause resources needed to raise demands to be squandered in fights within or between organizations. To the extent that the movement and its members are struggling with each other, they cannot attend to external political matters.

Encapsulation occurs when a movement organization develops an ideology or structure that interferes with efforts to recruit members or raise demands. This can come about in several ways. Under the pressure of repression, a group may prevent infiltration by cutting off the access by which potential members may join. Alternately, members may develop such strong cohesion among themselves that outsiders become unwelcome. In prolonged interaction, a group may develop an ideology that is internally coherent but virtually unintelligible to recruits and outsiders who do not share all of the members' assumptions. Such groups are not uncommon in movements; they constitute the fringe of organizations that appears strange to outsiders. An encapsulated organization may find it easy to maintain its dedicated core of members, whose identities are linked to the group and who may have few outside contacts, but such groups have little chance of growing or increasing their influence. Most strikingly, they may lose interest in such things, contenting themselves with maintaining their encapsulated existence.

Failures at the level of individual social movement organizations need not harm the social movement as a whole. Factionalism and encapsulation may clear away some social movement organizations and leave the field open for more creative and successful ones. But beyond a point, the failure of individual organizations can leave the movement without effective groups or can identify the movement as one that cannot realize constituents' goals. When this happens, the movement itself will decline. Persistent factionalism will squander resources and divert attention from recruitment and raising demands. Encapsulation will prevent a movement from speaking for any sizable constituency. There are particular moments at which recruits and resources are available to movements and the distribution of power is such that a movement can mobilize effectively. When movement organizations lose such chances through tactical blunders, they can seldom be recovered. With hindsight, one can often spot errors that led movements to decline, but for those engaged in politics these are often matters of trial and error.

In summary, four broad sources of movement decline—repression; cooptation; success; and failure—have been briefly identified. The decline of specific movement organizations and movements is usually caused by combinations of these factors. In the next section, we consider two linked case histories of organizational decline in order to illustrate some of these processes in action.

THE END OF SDS

HISTORICAL OVERVIEW

Students for a Democratic Society (SDS) was the largest and most influential organization in the 1960's American New Left. Its history encompasses most aspects of New Left organization, ideology, and tactics. SDS grew out of white students' involvement in the southern integration and voting registration struggles of the early sixties. It played a central role in the movement for student power and freedom, as well as in the first years of the opposition to the Vietnam war and the military draft. In addition, SDS sponsored community organizing projects in the mid-sixties and served as a major base from which the women's movement sprang. When SDS collapsed in a factional struggle in 1969, the contending factions defined it as a revolutionary group dedicated to overthrowing the American government, certainly no longer interested in student issues. By then, SDS was regarded by government and law enforcement officials as a dangerous subversive group. This was hardly how it organized itself.

SDS was founded in 1960 to replace the Student League for Industrial Democracy, the youth branch of the League for Industrial Democracy (LID, a small, moderate left group that survived the McCarthy era by espousing anticommunism and moderate support for liberal reforms). LID and its student affiliate stressed education rather than political action. The tiny original SDS sponsored conferences on northern campuses to publicize the civil rights movement. In June 1962, SDS issued the Port Huron Statement, a position paper that accurately expressed many students' discontent with the conformity and conservatism of American life in the fifties. As an alternative, SDS proposed a more participatory and communal society, and called for an alliance of civil rights groups, pacifist and antinuclear weapons groups, students, liberal organizations, and liberal publications to push the Democratic party in a progressive direction.

The Port Huron Statement was widely praised on campuses, but the organization grew slowly over the next several years. During that period, members started to question the liberal reformist approach of the Port Huron Statement because of the failure of the Kennedy and Johnson administrations to support civil rights and antipoverty efforts adequately and because of the escalation of the Vietnam war. At the same time, SDS was unsure of what sort of political action to emphasize. While its resources and strength lay in college campus chapters, from 1963 through 1965 the major national effort of SDS went into the Education Research Action Project, a series of marginally successful community organizing projects in poverty areas.

In April 1965, SDS organized the first Washington march against the war in Vietnam. The march was a surprising success, drawing over 15,000 demonstrators, most of them students. This led to a surge in membership to over one hundred chapters. During the next two years, SDS made starts at leading antiwar and draft-resistance struggles, but declined regular involvement in the succession of umbrella mobilization committees that led most national antiwar protest. SDS leaders feared that opposition to the war was too narrow a focus from which to build a movement for general societal reform.

Nevertheless, the number of campus chapters continued to grow as local chapters led student power struggles, movements against university complicity with the war and draft, and other fights. Each major struggle brought more members to the organization; it is estimated that as many as 100,000 joined in 1969 alone. Yet, at the height of success, measured in terms of membership and publicity, both the national organization and many of the chapters appeared to tear themselves apart. In 1969, SDS collapsed into a variety of small factions, none of which proved capable of maintaining SDS as a potent force in national politics.

Our task here is to interpret this collapse. A detailed history of SDS cannot be offered in these few pages. Interested readers should consult Kirkpatrick Sale's (1973) thorough volume and the excellent analysis of the development of New Left ideology by George Vickers (1975).

SDS STRUCTURE AND SUCCESS

SDS claimed to have no ideology in its early days, but this claim of nonideology was itself an ideological position. It stood for rejecting other current ideologies—both Communist party Marxism, with its overtones of authoritarian Stalinism, and cold war liberal red baiting, with its overtones of repressive McCarthyism—but not for rejecting having any beliefs at all. SDS favored racial equality, integration, disarmament, and an end to poverty. More importantly, the New Leftists saw the exercise of centralized authority in any system as undemocratic. They wished to create "participatory democracy" by decentralizing authority and inviting all people to participate in collective decision making.

The openness of this system allowed SDS to encompass a broad diversity of views and led to an organization that was always loosely structured. There was a National Office, which maintained membership lists, put out a newspaper, and tried to provide publications to chapters. National officers kept communications open between chapters, encouraged new chapters, and provided whatever advice and help they could. The National Office was always short of money, behind schedule on mailings and recordkeeping, and generally chaotic. This left the chapters free to pursue issues they chose with more or less militance. Annual national and regional meetings passed resolutions on broad strategy issues, but the local chapters retained control over implementation. Most chapters were on college campuses, though some existed in other organizations or high schools.

This loose participatory structure, which worked well to incorporate members when the organization was small, was a source of problems as the organization grew larger. Since decisions were made in open meetings where all people had voice and vote, people with staying power and vocal volume could exercise power, regardless of whether they had good ideas. People who could last through the inevitably lengthy group meetings were often the most influential. Furthermore, it allowed organized factions to dominate decision making. Since only a portion of the total members generally involved themselves in decision making, a block of disciplined people representing one view could carry disproportionate weight in the organization.

For a time these matters seemed unimportant. In the summer of 1968, SDS was at the height of its success. Campus activism had increased steadily, climaxing in the dramatic SDS strike that closed Columbia University over war-related research at the university and university plans to expand into the neighboring Harlem community. Yet this success contained all the seeds of the SDS downfall, for while it brought members, public interest, and even some victories, it put strains on SDS's structure and ideology that the organization could not bear.

By 1968, SDS's successes had evoked a two-pronged response from campus authorities and government officials. On the one hand, officials harassed members and potential recruits, making political activity more difficult. At the same time, some liberal politicians sought to incorporate moderate leftist positions into liberal Democratic party politics. The simultaneous presence of both responses illustrate the diversity of authority in the United States. Both tactics had the same impact: to lessen the impact of SDS.

Government and police harassment of SDS and other New Left groups in the late sixties and early seventies was very wide ranging. The CIA, the FBI, the Defense Department, and many local police departments, kept files on left-wing activists. State laws were passed to cut off scholarships and loans to student activists. In some instances, draft boards took away draft deferments from students who participated in antiwar activities. Students were recruited to spy on campus radical activities. SDS activists were expelled from many schools, and on some campuses SDS was banned. Rumors abounded that university admissions officers were checking applicants' political views to screen out activists. Police agents joined SDS chapters, where they spied, disrupted activity, and at times tried to provoke groups to violent or foolish action. At the University of Texas, a state police undercover agent was elected president of the campus SDS chapter. University officials freely called police to quell demonstrations on campuses. Government officials and presidential candidates excoriated campus protest as the worst social problem in America and the major obstacle to peace in Vietnam.

The full extent of this repressive and disruptive activity has not yet been documented. It is clear that it raised the cost and danger of being active in SDS, driving out some members and scaring off potential recruits, as well as wreaking havoc with the open, communal tone that had once been the hallmark of SDS chapters. The participatory democratic style was particularly vulnerable to infiltration because any recruit could assume an active role. Given infiltration and spying, members no longer knew if recruits or even old friends could be trusted. As that happened, chapters were forced to operate less democratically, which made them less attractive to potential recruits drawn to the New Left's participatory style. Chapters and their leaders had to devote time to defending themselves from legal and illegal attacks; this diverted time from political organizing.

Many movement members have argued that government repression destroyed SDS (cf. Oglesby 1974). However, repression can only be held to be the sole cause of SDS's demise if one ignores the other problems that success created and that SDS failed to solve. There can be no doubt that repression made it harder to solve those problems, but repression was not the only problem SDS faced.

Some of the group's more appealing moderate positions began to enter the realm of accepted political debate. By the spring of 1967, liberal politicians were giving friendly speeches at antiwar rallies, defining moderate opposition as an acceptable part of the political spectrum. Student demands for curriculum changes and relaxed parietal rules, as well as for a voice in university governance, were accepted at many institutions. These successes posed the threat of absorbing a portion of SDS's position into the political mainstream. Many national and chapter leaders who feared that such success would lead to compromises on crucial issues avoided absorption by adopting more extreme left-wing positions. This process of moving leftward to avoid being caught in the mainstream involved the danger that leaders would become too extreme to successfully recruit potential supporters. Alienating one's base in that fashion can make it impossible to mobilize a social movement.

Liberals were not the only politicians attracted by SDS's success. Other left-wing organizations grew interested in SDS because they saw it as a place to recruit for their own groups. One such group that had a major impact on SDS was the Progressive Labor party (PL) and its youth group, the Worker-Student Alliance (WSA). PL was an old left organization, rigidly disciplined, autocratic, disdainful of the youth-oriented counterculture, and ideologically dedicated to organizing the working class. Where SDS had a chaotic structure and a loose ideology, PL offered tight discipline and absolutist ideology. PL members started joining SDS in 1966; by 1968, PL factions were battling the national SDS leadership for control of the organization. SDS's participatory democratic structure favored PL in this struggle. SDS felt bound not to exclude people of any political persuasion, and PL found it could control open meetings by sending organized groups willing to stay until they had a majority. PL-SDS wrangling split many chapters and turned several national and regional meetings into unproductive squabbles. While SDS leaders were struggling with the various organized interests their success had attracted, they were also attracting recruits. Every time SDS led a major struggle, membership rolls and the number of chapters swelled. The loose structure of many SDS chapters made it difficult to find roles for recruits. While they were free to have a voice, many were unsure of what to say or how things were to be done. Nor was it easy to figure out SDS chaos. Chapters often were based on the friendship of people who got around to doing chapter work in sporadic bursts. This difficulty of integrating recruits worked to PL's advantage. PL could offer recruits a place in a well-defined structure, increasing PL's strength within SDS chapters. As Andrew Kopkind, a leftist commentator, put it:

> P.L. overwhelms newly politicized students with its sophisticated Marxism-Leninism on the one hand, and its simple promises of workable work-in programs on the other.... With its simple strategy of instant revolution by the working class and its logical and disciplined structure, P.L. appeals to young people who are tired of the tentative experimentalism and undiscipline of SDS organizing." (Cited in Jacobs 1970, pp. 17–18)

OTHER CURRENTS IN 1968–69

While PL fought SDS for leadership, the SDS leadership at both chapter and national levels was further split by the growing demands of women to assume leadership positions. Though never officially barred from power, women had for the most part been shunted into secondary roles in SDS. Women often performed essential but boring office work or leafletting, while men made decisions and assumed the more glamorous public roles. As women demanded a greater share of authority, men were more often incredulous than sympathetic—perhaps because they were unwilling to see themselves as oppressors. This conflict further split SDS. Male leaders' occasional requests that women hold off their demands until PL had been confronted only exacerbated the issue.

The battle with PL also influenced SDS's ideology. In seeking to avoid absorption, SDS had turned to Marxist ideas. This led to battles with the PL version of Marxism. For many of the newer recruits these struggles seemed odd at best. Many recruits were drawn to SDS not by left-wing ideology but by their opposition to the war and the draft, which was based on a mixture of humanitarian beliefs, a desire to avoid going to Vietnam, and their attraction to the counterculture. The struggle over the correct line for revolutionary anti-imperialism created a gulf between movement leaders and people who were potentially mobilizable for an antiwar movement.

In two major instances, the Columbia strike and the spring 1969 Harvard strike, it appeared to SDS leaders that this gap was closed. The appearance was illusory. In both instances, police violence galvanized large portions of the student body to strike under the leadership of SDS chapters whose actions had provoked the police presence. But in both cases the new recruits were more committed to opposing police brutality than to supporting demands raised by SDS leaders. As a result, both strikes eventually hurt campus SDS chapters. Liberal reforms wooed away the bulk of this new support and left the SDS leaders angered with their constituents over the desertion. Since the issue that mobilized students was police brutality, campus administrators learned to avoid problems by getting court injunctions to stop demonstrations, rather than send in the police. SDS could not repeat the Columbia/Harvard tactics.

WHERE WEATHERMAN CAME FROM

The Weatherman faction emerged in SDS in 1968 as an answer to PL's growing aggressiveness and the widening gap between SDS and most leftist students. Regardless of its actual impact, Weatherman attracted enormous attention by calling for immediate revolution. The idea of an armed revolution in the United States may seem farfetched today, but in the late sixties it seemed close at hand. As the Weather Underground stated in *Prairie Fire*, a 1974 position paper:

> The year 1968 was a high point and a turning point. It is not surprising that the maturing of the movement took place at a time when the world was in flames. 500,000 U.S. troops were dealt a staggering blow by the Vietnamese popular forces during Tet. Armed struggle raged throughout Latin America and the

Palestinian liberation forces emerged in the Mideast. Student movements in France, and throughout the industrialized world were in full revolt, challenging their own governments and demonstrating open solidarity with the people of the world. The Chinese Cultural Revolution was unleashing a new dimension to class struggle. (p. 8)

The success of the Vietnamese in stalemating American military power was seen as a demonstration that America was not invincible. Though Che Guevara had died in 1967 trying to foment revolution in Bolivia, his slogan that there should be "two, three, many Vietnams" seemed to be embodied in the emergence of such revolutionary groups as the Tupomaros in Uruguay, Frelimo in Mozambique, and Fatah in the Middle East. Student movements were also becoming increasingly militant. In France in May 1968 a coalition of students and workers brought the country to the brink of revolution. Strong left-wing student movements appeared in Germany and Japan, and substantial opposition to the Vietnam war was demonstrated in many other countries. In the United States, armed black militant groups, most notably the Black Panthers, were proclaiming revolution and affirming their ties to liberation movements in the Third World. The murders of Martin Luther King and Robert Kennedy in 1968 seemed to symbolize America's unwillingness to heed those who urged moderate reforms. The brutal handling of antiwar demonstrators at the Democratic National Convention in Chicago, which a majority of Americans applauded in public opinion polls, and the subsequent election of Richard Nixon further demonstrated conservative intransigence in American politics. In September 1968 an International Conference of Revolutionary Youth was held at Columbia University. While its open sessions were often chaotic and divisive, the meeting did bring Americans into contact with radicals from many countries. As one looked across this international scene, it was not hard to believe that a worldwide revolutionary struggle against an increasingly reactionary America was in progress.

The SDS regional conferences during the 1968–1969 academic year saw increasingly angry struggles between PL followers and supporters of the SDS National Office. The two sides argued over which social class would make the revolution and what tactics should be followed. PL hewed to the traditional Marxist view that the working class must make the revolution and that students should subordinate their struggles over the draft and campus rights to the task of building worker-student alliances. Furthermore, PL took two stands that infuriated many SDS members. PL attacked North Vietnam because it took aid from the (anti-Chinese) Soviet Union. PL also opposed the Black Panthers and other black nationalist groups because they organized on national rather than class lines, a contradiction of Marx's insistence that class struggle cuts across all national and ethnic interests.

A group of Columbia veterans and National Office workers prepared an anti-PL paper for the 1969 SDS National Convention, taking the paper's title "You Don't Need a Weatherman to Know Which Way the Wind Blows" from a Bob Dylan song. The "Weatherman" paper argued that Third World opposition to American imperialism was the most important movement in the world and that the black liberation movement in America was the crux of the struggle because it represented the Third World in America. The role of white radicals was to support this process, not lead it; since the black movement would triumph by itself if necessary. The white youth movement was to be built around the issues of black liberation and the worldwide struggle against imperialism, not around the counterculture. It should abandon organizing college students and instead should recruit working-class and dropout youths into small disciplined collectives that would form the basis of a revolutionary party.

While the ideology has obvious flaws, it did place SDS in a framework of world revolution. It avoided absorption into established politics by calling for the complete overthrow of established politics. It countered PL's tactic of organizing workers and students by emphasizing recruitment of disaffected blue-collar youths. It called for abandoning the problem-riddled participatory democratic system. While the problems with the Weatherman position will become clear enough, it did try to answer each of SDS's problems.

SCHISM

The struggle between PL and SDS reached its climax at the June 1969 National Convention in Chicago. The details of this meeting are adequately reported by Sale (1973). PL had brought enough supporters to hold a small majority at the convention, even though they were still a minority in SDS. Also in Chicago were the Weatherman paper faction and its supporters—who called themselves the Revolutionary Youth Movement (RYM)—and a smaller number of unaffiliated delegates. The rancorous and disorderly convention ended with RYM expelling PL from SDS, and PL claiming to be the true SDS. SDS was finished as a New Left organization.

From the shambles, PL pursued its worker-student efforts in SDS's name to little avail on most campuses. After some years, PL discarded the SDS name as useless. The RYM group set about maintaining it's own SDS, organizing youth along the Weatherman paper's lines and planning an action for the fall in Chicago against the war and the trial of the Chicago Eight, prominent activists accused of fomenting riots at the 1968 Democratic convention. RYM soon split again, the Weatherman paper authors arguing for more militant action, while a separate faction calling itself RYM 2 called for more recruiting and organizing before taking militant action. RYM 2 soon petered out, while Weatherman continued in operation. We will follow the Weathermen because they were more successful than PL or RYM 2 at remaining in the public eye.

WEATHERMAN: STRUCTURE AND TACTICS

Weatherman ideology emerged as a response to both PL and several problems and events in 1968. This ideology, and the need for security from repression, determined Weatherman's structure. Weatherman faced severe repression of its revolutionary activism and some continued PL harassment. In response, Weatherman organized small collectives of acquaintances who maintained extremely strict criteria for screening new members. Weatherman ideology demanded that each member break all ties with American culture and be ready to die for the revolution. Members were expected to relinquish all possessions, abandon all monogamous relationships, and limit contact with people outside Weatherman.

The Weather Machine (Weatherman fell out of favour as a name because of its gender connotation) had a three-part structure. At the top was the Weather Bureau, perhaps twenty-five people. They were a tightly knit group of old friends and movement veterans. There was little turnover in this group. It dictated national policies to the local level and sporadically published a national newspaper. As in SDS, local collectives had a good deal of autonomy in day-to-day matters, although Bureau members would occasionally reorganize local collectives. The disruptive impact of such arbitrary leadership is described in Susan Stern's (1975) memoir of Weatherman in Seattle.

The collectives were scattered around American cities. They had five to twenty-five members, with perhaps a total of five hundred people involved at any time. Most collectives saw moderate turnover, often spurred by groups expelling disruptive members. Each collective had three internal aims: deepening members' knowledge of and trust in each other; learning medical, legal, defense and propaganda skills; and engaging in internal political education. In addition, each collective had the external goal of recruiting participants for the fall Chicago National Action. Weather ideology dictated that working-class white youth were so alienated (by the war and the lack of meaningful jobs) that the demonstration of the existence of a fighting movement that would act rather than talk would rally them to its side. Thus Weatherman leafletted and recruited at high schools and hamburger joints and staged violent actions to show their fighting preparedness, such as briefly seizing high school or college classrooms. The actions were provocative but not successful as organizing devices.

Every collective did attract some hangers-on, people who never became members but who did some work and would attend rallies. There was a lot of turnover among the hangers-on. Weather persons were intolerant of people not totally committed to their extremist politics. Weatherman's insistence on ideological purity greatly widened the gap between leaders and potential followers that had started in SDS.

This rigidity was symptomatic of a major problem in Weatherman structure: It made little provision for vertical mobility, either into or within the organization. Weatherman officially denied the need for any white movement within the revolution, yet most of its efforts during the summer of 1969 were directed toward recruiting members. Still its uncertainties about recruitment were obvious in the difficulties facing those who wished to join collectives. To join, one had to demonstrate sincerity and trustworthiness. That could be done only through participation in collective actions. Yet, since most actions required secrecy, only collective members could be included in them. Thus it was easier for recruits to form a new collective than to join an existing one, although that involved the very difficult task of recruiting a group of people. In practice, Weatherman was so tightly organized that it had no mechanism for growth.

It similarly was difficult for people to move from a collective to the

Weather Bureau, as the Bureau was a cohesive group with little interest in training new leaders. Leadership at the collective level seemed to be awarded on the basis of familiar New Left criteria of volume and longevity at meetings, but these were augmented by new criteria of merit—bravery in action, radical attitudes, toughness. Other left-wing groups criticized the Weatherman for espousing "macho" virtues.

WEATHERMAN IN ACTION

Weatherman's history was brief. They attracted attention because they carried part of the SDS mantle and because of their promotion of violence; but their accomplishments were small. Though Weatherman declared many of its militant actions to be successes because they demonstrated members' willingness to fight and because they increased collective cohesion, these actions drew few recruits and little praise. The Chicago National Action, renamed the Days of Rage, drew between 500 and 800 participants, instead of the 5,000 predicted by the Weather Bureau. Those hundreds proceed to "trash" Chicago's Gold Coast and battle the Chicago police. Their courage attracted much attention among leftists but few recruits, and it resulted in 300 arrests, the posting of $750,000 in bail, and a conspiracy indictment against twelve Weatherman leaders. After Chicago, the Bureau grew disenchanted with attempts to recruit members and recognized it could no longer afford aboveground action. At a desultory War Council in Flint, Michigan, at the end of December, most remembered because Bernardine Dohrn of the Weather Bureau made a speech praising convicted murderer Charles Manson, the Bureau announced that the core of the organization was to go underground. There it carried out bombings of symbolic targets—including the national capital—when no people were present and printed occasional papers. Three Weatherpersons died in an accidental explosion while making bombs in Greenwich Village in March 1970. In 1975, Senate investigators estimated that forty Weathermen were still underground.

The lack of vertical mobility in Weatherman prevented organizational growth. This meant that at best the group could only maintain itself as a stable organization. Yet even that proved impossible, as the collective's membership dwindled under the dual pressures of external harassment and the rigors of collective life. While these rigors—much work, self-sacrifice, organizationally ordered sex with all of one's brothers and sisters, group LSD trips, lengthy and often brutal criticism sessions—served one useful function by making Weatherman very difficult for informers to infiltrate, they also made life in the organization difficult to sustain. Some sense of what this was like is conveyed in this description from Weatherman Shin'ya Ono.

> New people began to learn what discipline means when no one was allowed to stay out of these collective discussions and collective tasks. People who preferred to read were compelled to join. People who fell asleep were woken up. Smoking was prohibited. Seating was "arbitrarily" changed according to the demands set by political criteria. Politics in command. Everything for the revolution. People began to get some sense of what these well-known Maoist slogans meant.

We slept six hours and resumed our struggle in the morning. . . . (Jacobs 1970, p. 253).

The emphasis on toughness, on treating people as political objects whose incorrect lines were to be smashed, took its toll of members. At the same time, indictments and court costs for Weatherman's illegal actions were building up. A major reason for going underground was to escape these indictments, a task at which the underground organization proved very successful.

By the fall of 1969, major rifts were developing between Weatherman and the rest of the left. The worse things got for Weatherman, the more intransigent the group became in insisting that leftists who did not commit themselves to Weatherman were enemies of the movement. While many on the left had admired Weatherman courage, there was less sympathy for the extremity of Weatherman's fascination with violence and the ineffectiveness of its tactics.

Weatherman's position rested on a prediction that the war in Vietnam would not stop with a Hanoi victory but would be only the first step in a rising crescendo of Third World assaults that would lead to America's downfall—an ironic echo of the "domino theory" that justified America's presence in Vietnam on the grounds that Vietnam was the first step in a chain that would end with the invasion of America. Weatherman's self-justification further rested on its ability to rally disaffected white youths to support a black revolution. However, the Black Panthers, Weatherman's proclaimed revolutionary vanguard, were increasingly placed on the defensive by government repression that climaxed in the murder of two Illinois Panther leaders by Chicago police in December 1969. Instead of leading the revolution, the Panthers were fighting for their lives, heading toward their own schism, and leaning on white radicals for help.

This package of ideology and strategy had been developed to counter the position of PL, as well as to describe the world. When it was disconfirmed, and Weatherman faced an increasing lack of sympathy from the rest of the left and even the Panthers, plus a growing list of indictments and trials, Weatherman folded its aboveground operations. It never truly had established a constituency.

EXPLAINING ORGANIZATIONAL DECLINE

Somewhat different explanations have to be offered for the decline of SDS and Weatherman. Nevertheless, both instances illustrate how a variety of causes may converge in the downfall of any organization.

SDS suffered from each of the causes of movement organization decline outlined earlier in this chapter except cooptation, and cooptation was not used only because the demands of the student movement made few incentives for cooptation desirable to its leaders. Primarily, SDS's decline was set in motion by the organization's rapid and surprising success. Success brought the weight of new members, the assault by PL, the mixture of repression and absorption, and the resulting factionalism and tactical blunders. The irony is that success is precisely what a movement should seek, even though the price of immediate success sometimes is long-term failure. For SDS, the biggest problems brought by success were the threats of absorption and factionalism.

A number of SDS positions were absorbed by the political system. The McCarthy and Kennedy campaigns in 1968 showed the enthusiasm with which civil rights and antiwar stands could be channeled into mainstream politics, and though SDS was gone, most of the Port Huron Statement was incorporated by the liberal wing of the Democratic party by 1972. Why, then, did SDS continue to radicalize rather than become an interest group? The answer may lie in the unique position of students as people whose lives are in transition. Most political groups have permanent interests to protect. For workers, the permanent recognition of their rights as workers, though restraining union militance, may be worth trading some immediate demands for. But students have only their demands; they have no permanent position to protect. Thus the compromises involved in absorption have little attraction for student leaders. The student movement sacrifices nothing by pressing demands with renewed vigor, even after winning some victories.

The position of students has two important corollaries. First, because students often demanded things for others—the Vietnamese, the poor, the minorities—rather than for themselves, there were few incentives with which to coopt SDS leaders. They often were people who had chosen not to seek available positions of wealth and power. Second, the constituency of student organizations had to be renewed annually. While a few university towns became centers for superannuated student hangers-on, the annual turnover in students meant that veterans were lost to graduation, and new ranks had to be recruited from entering students. The problem that recruiting new members posed for the New Left as a whole will be considered below.

The factionalism to which SDS succumbed was the cost of a success encouraged by the participatory democratic structure. This structure works well in organizations that are small or in which consensus is high about everything except details. But when powerfully divisive issues arise, the participatory approach lacks means to limit the length or acrimony of debate or protect the organization from irrelevant or deliberately destructive intrusions. Since it assumes that a consensus can be achieved on every issue, it is ill equipped to hold an organization together when factions absolutely fail to agree. It is tempting for the losing faction to form its own group, where it can have its own consensus. In order to survive, SDS would have had to adjust its structure to its changing size. Given that one of SDS's founding principles was to decentralize and democratize authority, this may have been impossible. The new groups like Weatherman rejected democracy completely, and a traditional centralized democracy had no defenders.

The repression directed at SDS did not physically destroy chapters, but it did create a climate of fear and divisiveness. The open participatory structure was particularly ill suited to prevent or counter repressive responses. The structure made SDS easy to infiltrate or disrupt. Repression was a background against which the factionalism and inability of SDS to mobilize newer students played out the organization's collapse.

The problems that led to Weatherman's decline were more straightforward. Weatherman's narrow ideology, more a response to PL than a tested or pragmatic plan, greatly limited Weatherman's tactical choices. At a time when antiwar and student movement resources appeared to be cresting, Weatherman turned to organizing a new constituency—blue-collar youth—with whom they had little contact or experience. Yet even this organizing attempt was extremely tentative. Weatherman's structure made it difficult for anyone to join the organization. Weatherman had set itself up as an encapsulated group. The multifaceted nature of this encapsulation should be noted. Weatherman's positions made most people and New Left groups turn away from it at the same time that Weatherman was losing interest in organizing people, substituting an apocalyptic vision of an uncontrollable violent world revolution.

An encapsulated group can maintain itself. As its members cut their ties to other groups, their cohesion with one another may assume greater importance and keep the group together. Two factors worked against this in Weatherman. One was the intense pressure that the constantly politicized life placed on members, encouraging some people to quit. The other was the mounting weight of trials, fines, and indictments. This legal repression went largely unchallenged by outsiders because the government easily convinced most people that the threat posed by Weatherman—a group advocating violence and lawlessness—justified a strong response. This did not require a deliberate campaign of persuasion. Weatherman, in spite of its large pool of initially available resources, lasted less than one year.

EXPLAINING MOVEMENT DECLINE

The decline of any particular movement organization need not signal the decline of the movement. Nevertheless, the decline of SDS in the late sixties was coterminous with the decline of the New Left and the student antiwar movement in general. What makes this surprising is that there still appeared to be a large constituency for the student movement in the late sixties; indeed, the protests following the Cambodia invasion and the Kent State killings in May 1970 were the largest campus demonstrations ever. There also were several organizations, such as the Socialist Workers party, that tried to mobilize such people. Decline in activism is all the more striking given the absence of an immediate parallel decline in radical beliefs. Gold, Christie, and Friedman (1976), studying the Columbia class of 1972, found little evidence that students' acceptance of New Left ideology had declined from 1968 to 1972, although activism had clearly dwindled.

Still, the movement declined. The reason was not that New Left organizations no longer existed, nor that they lacked constituents and resources, but that their collective ability to speak for their constituency had faded because of factionalism, absorption, and repression. The opportunities presented in the sixties had passed and could not be recovered.

The external climate became less hospitable for movements when Richard Nixon became President in 1969 and the climate and pace of repression began to pick up. Nixon claimed to be ending the war. While overtly and covertly widening the war on some fronts, he did withdraw American troops and first limited and then ended the draft. This served to lessen the war's impact as an organizing issue.

The internal climate was less hospitable as well. By 1969, any large demonstration or organization would draw factions whose attitudes were radicalized far beyond those of the mass of constituents. The radicals no longer wanted to build an antiwar movement but were pushing toward revolution. Weatherman was only one example of this. Such groups had a dampening effect on all efforts to mobilize a mass movement among more moderate students, both by attracting more intense repression and by bidding the cost of movement membership higher.

At the same time, the mass of potential constituents was being wooed by a series of concessions: the draft lottery, extension of the franchise to eighteen-year-olds, school breaks for electoral politics, promises of withdrawal from the war, loosening of marijuana laws—that the older leaders could write off as inadequate but that could satisfy less ideologically integrated constituents. As the cost of participation rose, especially after the killings at Kent State, it became harder to mobilize people to push for additional concessions. To the extent that such people sought personal satisfaction through social movement participation, newer movements for women's rights and environmental protection offered activism with less risk. All these trends were accompanied by a chorus of "the sixties accomplished nothing," led by politicians and academics who were glad to see the old activism fade, supported by radical activists who wrote off the gains of the sixties as woefully short of their goals, and joined by younger students who were unaware of what changes the sixties had wrought.

CONCLUSIONS

The history of SDS shows that social movements are difficult to maintain. If a movement fails, it fails; but even if it succeeds, it may fail. A few points can be emphasized from the SDS and Weatherman experiences.

1. Structures must be flexible. The organization that works well at one size or on one issue may not work well at others. The participatory structure of SDS was fine for a small, cohesive group, but it allowed factionalism to flourish as the group grew. Since the organization was dedicated to its decentralized, participatory structure, it was unable to make adjustments when necessary.

2. Organizations must plan for new members. If members are sought, a group should have routes for joining (which Weatherman did.not) and roles and positions for people who join (which SDS often did not).

3. Gaps between the tactics and goals endorsed by leaders and those sought by members must be addressed. This is a long-standing issue in revolutionary theory—should the leaders articulate the members' views, or should the leaders take a vanguard position and pull the members forward? There is no simple answer to this, but when the leadership reaches so far into the vanguard that it can no longer communicate with

its constituency, something is wrong. This was a problem for Weatherman.

4. Movement organizations must identify and focus their energies on their primary enemies. When they put more resources into fighting each other than seeking collective goals, the movement has a serious problem. Structures that allow or encourage resources to be channeled into factionalism are flawed and should be replaced.

REFERENCES

Feuer, L. S.
  1969   *The Conflict of Generations.* New York: Basic Books.
Gamson, W. A.
  1968   *Power and Discontent.* Homewood, Ill.: Dorsey Press.
  1975   *The Strategy of Social Protest.* Homewood, Ill.: Dorsey Press.
Gerlach, L. P., and V. H. Hine
  1970   *People, Power, Change: Movements of Social Transformation.* Indianapolis: Bobbs-Merrill.
Gold, A. R.; R. Christie; and L. N. Friedman
  1976   *Fists and Flowers: A Social Psychological Interpretation of Student Protest.* New York: Academic Press.
Gurr, T. R.
  1970   *Why Men Rebel.* Princeton: Princeton University Press.
Hoffer, E.
  1951   *The True Believer.* New York: Harper & Row.
Jacobs, H.
  1970   *Weatherman.* San Francisco: Ramparts.
McCarthy, J. D., and M. N. Zald
  1973   *The Trend of Social Movements in America: Professionalization and Resource Mobilization.* Morristown, N. J.: General Learning Press.
  1977   "Resource Mobilization and Social Movements: A Partial Theory." *American Journal of Sociology* 82: 1212–41.
Michels, R.
  1962   *Political Parties.* New York: Free Press.
Oglesby, C.
  1974   "SDS Death: Panthers, PL, Weatherpeople." *Boston Phoenix,* 4 June.
Sale, K.
  1973   *SDS.* New York: Random House.
Stern, S.
  1975   *With the Weathermen.* Garden City, N.Y.: Doubleday.
Tilly, C.; L. Tilly and R. Tilly
  1975   *The Rebellious Century, 1830–1930.* Cambridge, Mass.: Harvard University Press.
Vickers, G. R.
  1975   *The Formation of the New Left.* Lexington, Mass.: Lexington Books.
Zald, M. N., and R. Ash
  1966   "Social Movement Organizations: Growth, Decay and Change." *Social Forces* 44: 327–41.

18

The Decline of the Civil Rights Movement

Doug McAdam

The most significant insurgent challenge to arise in this country during the last quarter of a century was the black protest movement of the 1950s and 1960s. Its significance derives from two sets of consequences: It stimulated other movements of the period, such as women's liberation and the student movement, and it resulted in important changes affecting many blacks. Although it never effected the fundamental restructuring of American society sought by many insurgents, the civil rights movement nonetheless created new opportunities, overturned an anachronistic regional caste system, and sparked something of a politico-cultural renaissance within the black community. Like all insurgent challenges, the black movement nonetheless waned as the 1960s drew to a close. Why? What can existing perspectives on movement decline tell us about the fate of the black movement?

EXISTING THEORIES

There are three theoretical perspectives on movement decline: the classical model, resource mobilization, and the political process model. The classical model associates movement decline with three processes: oligarchization, conservatization, and institutionalization (Weber in Gerth and Mills 1946, pp. 297–301; Messinger 1955, pp. 3–10; Michels 1959). Oligarchization involves the emergence of an elite that comes to exercise disproportionate control over the movement organization. These "leaders" share an interest in the organization's survival as a prerequisite of maintaining their privileged position within the organization, *even* when this survival requires the subordination of the movement's original goals. Consequently, oligarchization leads to the displacement of original goals with more conservative ones. When the personal interests of the movement's elite are inextricably linked to the survival of the organization, they avoid mobilizing an opposition capable of damaging the organization. The result is a diminution in radicalism as the leaders seek to accommodate to the viewpoints of dominant groups in society.

Institutionalization involves the development of a hierarchical organization, an explicit division of labor, and established administrative procedures. While created to facilitate organizational functioning, these inevitably dampen member enthusiasm and creativity in favor of predictability and organizational stability. Thus institutionalization encourages movement organizations to shift resources from achieving their original goals to maintaining their current structure.

Resource mobilization proponents have not explicitly advanced a theory of movement decline; theirs is a more general model of movement dynamics from which some implicit assumptions regarding the decline of insurgency can be drawn.* This model postulates that the emergence and development of a social movement is primarily a function of the resources available to support insurgency (McCarthy and Zald 1973). Unfortunately, many groups in society simply lack the resources to generate a movement on their own (Oberschall 1973). In such cases, movements must depend on external "sponsors." If external resources trigger a movement in the first place, this model implies that a significant withdrawal of such support would precipitate its decline.

The emphasis of the classical and resource mobilization models is strikingly different. The former focuses on processes *internal* to the movement, while the latter suggests that the dissolution of insurgency is primarily due to the withdrawal of *external* support. I propose that undue emphasis on either internal or external processes misses the dynamic interplay between the two that shapes a movement throughout its history. This fundamental premise lies at the heart of a third model of social insurgency.

The political process model emphasizes three factors that are crucial to the ongoing development of a movement: the organizational strength of movement forces; the "structure of political opportunities" (Eisenger 1973) available to insurgents to any point in time; and the response of other groups to the challenge posed by the movement. A significant negative change in any one of these factors is expected to diminish the ability of insurgents to sustain collective protest.

---

* Resource mobilization is little more than a label applied indiscriminately to a disparate group of theorists. So divergent are some perspectives to which the label has been applied that continued adherence to our present use of the term threatens to obscure important differences between distinct schools of thought. To remedy the confusion, Perrow (1979) has suggested a distinction between what he calls RM (resource mobilization) I and RM II. RM I refers to the works of Oberschall, Gamson, and Tilly, among others; RM II is represented by the work of McCarthy and Zald. I am solely concerned with the McCarthy/Zald version of resource mobilization here.

THE DECLINE OF BLACK INSURGENCY

This chapter assesses the analytic utility of each model as an explanation for the decline in black insurgency in the late 1960s through content coding of relevant story synopses contained in the *Annual Index* of the *New York Times*. This provides a rough measure of the pace of black insurgency between 1948 and 1970.* The results show a general rise in movement activity between 1955 and 1965 followed by a steady decline thereafter. The causes of that decline occupy the remainder of this chapter.†

The conservatization predicted by the classical model clearly did not occur. Instead, the movement grew progressively more radical as the decade wore on. It shifted its demands from the integration of blacks into various areas of life to a more fundamental restructuring of this country's dominant political and economic institutions. As Stokely Carmichael asserted, "Integration is irrelevant. Political and economic power is what black people have to have" (quoted in Killian 1975, p. 106). This shift was also accompanied by a fundamental change in tactics. From strict adherence to nonviolence during the civil rights phase of the movement, many insurgents had, by decade's end, come to openly espouse violent insurrection. Nor did *oligarchization* or *institutionalization* take place to any great extent. Faced with a growing dissensus over the substantive and tactical thrust insurgency should take, direction over the movement became increasingly fragmented and decentralized as the sixties wore on.

The implicit linkage stressed by some resource mobilization theorists between external resource support and the pace of insurgency is also found wanting in the case of the black movement. As can be seen in Figure 17.1, the decline in black insurgency in the latter half of the 1960s occurred in the face of continued high levels of external funding. In general, throughout the study period, outside support increases sharply *following*, rather than preceding, peaks in insurgent activity.

Instead, the decline of the black movement is best understood as a complex by-product of the three sets of factors noted earlier. Specifically, it was changes in (1) the internal strength of movement forces, (2) the external "structure of political opportunities," and (3) the response of other groups to the movement that helped trigger the decline in black insurgency between 1966 and 1970.

---

* In the indexes for 1948–70 all story synopses under "Negroes-U.S.-General" and "Education-U.S.-Racial Integration" were coded according to criteria drawn up prior to the start of research. The decision to code only these headings was based on a careful examination of the classification system and cross listings for several years in the *Index*, which convinced me that the overwhelming majority of events relevant to the movement was contained under these headings. That any number of other potentially relevant headings are in the *Index* is readily conceded, but the sheer volume of listings made it absolutely necessary to restrict coding in some fashion. For instance, in 1969 no less than 718 other *Index* headings were listed as relevant listings under the general category "Negroes-U.S.-General."

† For the purposes of this analysis, movement-initiated activity is defined as any action, speech, or statement initiated by a black (or racially mixed) group or individual actively working to further racial equality in the United States.

Figure 17.1 Number of Movement-Initiated Events and Level of External Financial Support, 1948–70.

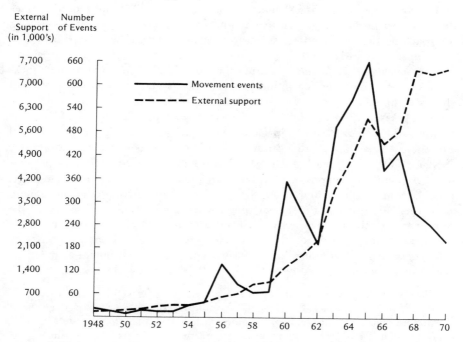

Source: For NAACP, Annual Reports for the National Association for the Advancement of Colored People, 1961–70; for CORE, Melier and Rudwick, 1973: 97, 149, 225, 335, 411, 420–30; for SCLC, Brink and Harris, 1963: 115; Clayton, 1964: 14; Lomax, 962: 94, Muse, 1968: 276; for SNCC, Melier, 1971: 25; Oberschall, 1977: 3; Zinn, 1965: 10. Data on Urban League was unavailable for inclusion in the chart. Where absolute dollar amounts were unavailable, knowledgeable estimates were substituted.

SHIFTING ORGANIZATIONAL STRENGTH, 1961–70

In any conflict situation the strength of a particular group is determined as much by the deployment of its forces as by its absolute numbers. However, theorists have disagreed as to the optimum distribution of a movement's personnel. Following Gerlach and Hine (1970), some have emphasized the advantages of a decentralized structure of local protest units. Other theorists have stressed the need for a more centralized structure, arguing that insurgents must be able to concentrate movement personnel and resources if they are ever to become an effective political force. Gamson's finding that movements with centralized organizational structures tend to be more successful than ones with decentralized structures has often been cited as evidence supporting this latter position (Gamson 1975).

My contention is that an optimum deployment of movement forces combines elements of both these structures. Strong organizations linked together by means of a reticulate structure would seem to preserve the functional benefits of the decentralized structure—resistance to repression, encouragement of innovation—without sacrificing the minimal concentrations of resources needed to sustain effective political action. In the black movement, something approaching this intermediate structure was achieved in the early sixties only to collapse by decade's end.

Organizational Proliferation. During the early 1960s four organizations jockeyed with one another for influence over the movement and the increased shares of publicity and money generated by protest activity. They were the National Association for the Advancement of Colored People (NAACP), the Southern Christian Leadership Conference (SCLC), the Congress of Racial Equality (CORE), and the Student Non-Violent Coordinating Committee (SNCC).* On the strength of Dr. Martin Luther King's extraordinary popular following and media appeal, SCLC was frequently able to preempt the stage, though none of these four groups succeeded in dominating the movement. Still, their attempts to do so lent much needed vitality and diversity to the movement. Each organization carved out a unique program, style, and mode of operation that broadened the movement's recruiting and financial bases by offering a range of organizational alternatives from which potential members and benefactors could choose. As Clark (1970, p. 295) described it:

> The civil right groups vary in organizational efficiency as well as in philosophy, approach, and methods. The rank and file of liberal or religious whites might be more responsive to the seemingly nonthreatening, Christian approach to Martin Luther King, Jr. More tough-minded and pragmatic business and governmental leaders might find a greater point of control with the appeals and approaches of the NAACP and the Urban League. The more passionate Negroes and whites who seek immediate and concrete forms of justice will probably gravitate toward CORE and SNCC.... The variety of organizations and "leaders" among Negroes may be viewed as ... the present strength of the movement rather than a symptom of weakness. Each organization influences the momentum and pace of the others. The inevitable interaction among them demands from each a level of effectiveness and relevance above the minimum possible for any single organization.

In addition to the positive effect that these organizations had on one another, their collective presence also confronted movement opponents with four sources of pressure. This considerably increased the difficulties and cost of defeating or containing the movement by not allowing opponents to concentrate resources for a concerted campaign of social control directed at any one group. After 1965, however, the dominance of the "Big Four" within the movement waned considerably. Table 17.1 captures this trend.

---

* Some have argued that the National Urban League should be included but its influence was greater in social welfare and business circles than within the movement. Indeed, the organization's visibility within the "liberal establishment" of foundations, academia, and social welfare groups may help account for the prominent role ascribed to it by writers largely drawn from that same "establishment" (cf. Clark 1970). Few protest activities or movement campaigns involved the Urban League. The *Times* data attribute the following yearly event totals to the Urban League: 1955–1960, 26 (12%); 1961, 7 (6%); 1962, 13 (12%); 1963, 21 (8%); 1964, 25 (8%); 1965, 7 (2%); 1961–65, 73 (7%).

TABLE 17.1/Distribution of All Events Initiated by Formal Movement Organizations, 1961–70

Organization	1961–65 %	1961–65 N	1966 %	1966 N	1967 %	1967 N	1968 %	1968 N	1969 %	1969 N	1970 %	1970 N	1966–70 %	1966–70 N
NAACP	24	(265)	21	(50)	27	(53)	16	(25)	16	(21)	21	(20)	21	(169)
CORE	22	(244)	4	(10)	18	(36)	7	(10)	6	(8)	2	(2)	8	(66)
SCLC (including M. L. King)	23	(257)	23	(56)	25	(49)	36	(55)	18	(24)	8	(8)	23	(192)
SNCC	6	(62)	9	(22)	4	(8)	1	(2)	0	(0)	1	(1)	4	(33)
Other movement organizations	15	(168)	23	(55)	17	(34)	33	(49)	56	(76)	59	(56)	33	(270)
Multiple movement organizations	10	(110)	20	(49)	8	(15)	7	(11)	4	(6)	8	(8)	11	(89)
Total	100	(1,107)	100	(242)	99	(195)	100	(152)	100	(135)	99	(95)	100	(819)

Source: Annual Index of the New York Times, 1961–70.

In 1967 the four organizations initiated 74 percent of all events credited to formal movement organizations. By 1970 the proportion dropped to barely 32 percent. While only 15 percent of all events initiated by formal movement organizations in the 1961–65 period were attributed to groups other than the Big Four, the comparable proportion for the succeeding five years was 33 percent. Indeed, between 1968 and 1970 "other movement organizations" accounted for nearly half (47 percent) of all events initiated by formal movement groups. By the end of the sixties then, the structure of centralized national groups that had dominated the movement in the early 1960s had been replaced by a highly fluid, segmented structure of small, loosely connected local organizations.

At the root of this disintegration was the devaluation of integration as *the* fundamental goal of the movement. From 1955 through the mid-1960s black insurgency had focused almost exclusively on the issues of voter registration and desegregation of public facilities. During the late sixties this was replaced by a concern for many issues. Police brutality, institutional racism, international colonialism, the development of black pride, the establishment of black studies programs on college campuses, and many other issues came to be embraced by insurgents. Ironically, this substantive shift owed much to the early successes enjoyed by insurgents, who, in eradicating legal segregation, had come to realize the limited value of their victories. As Bayard Rustin expressed it, "What is the value of winning access to public accommodations for those who lack money to use them?" (Rustin 1965, p. 28). However warranted this shift was, it nonetheless deprived the movement of the single dominant issue around which the diverse insurgent factions could be organized.

By the late sixties the substantive focus of the movement had clearly shifted from questions of caste to class. This change required a redefinition of the movement's opponents. Such traditional enemies as the southern sheriff, the hooded night rider, and the ax-wielding restaurant owner were replaced by the principal political and economic elites of the country as those ultimately responsible for the perpetuation of racism. This shift in targets also reflected the movement's growing hostility toward a federal establishment it felt had shown itself in the tough southern campaigns of the early 1960s to be a less than aggressive advocate of black rights.

This growing disaffection and its effect on the goals pursued by insurgents provides an excellent illustration of how the interaction between processes internal and external to a movement shape the development of insurgency over time. The shift in goals discussed here owed as much to the actions (or lack thereof) of federal officials as it did to the organizational dynamics of insurgent groups. In turn, this substantive shift posed a far greater threat to existing political and economic interests in this country than had the earlier civil rights phase of the struggle. Thus, in response to this shift, both the federal government and other parties to the conflict modified their responses toward the movement in ways that were to contribute greatly to the decline of black insurgency.

The Rise of Intramovement Conflict. Even at the peak of black insurgency in the early 1960s, there existed considerable competition among the Big Four for the money and publicity needed to sustain their operations and position within the movement. At the same time the strong substantive and tactical consensus that prevailed during the early sixties prompted movement groups to set aside their rivalries to work together in numerous joint campaigns. However, after 1965 any semblance of cooperation was to crumble in the face of the growing ideological and tactical differences that increasingly split the movement (and often at times the organizations themselves) into two antagonistic factions.

Poised on the one hand, were traditional integrationists including SCLC and NAACP who continued to eschew violence as unacceptable and/or ineffective. Aligned in increasing opposition to the integrationists was the so-called Black Power wing of the movement, with its rejection of integration as *the* fundamental goal of black insurgency and its approval of violence as an acceptable addition to the movement's tactical arsenal. The remaining two members of the Big Four—CORE and SNCC—were in varying degrees associated with this wing of the movement.

Relations between these two wings declined steadily after 1965 with charges of extremism, reverse racism, and "Uncle Tomism" regularly exchanged. Even within the factions there was considerable conflict. Relations between SCLC and the NAACP cooled noticeably following Martin Luther King's 1965 criticism of the Vietnam war. Two years later, two rival black power groups, US and the Black Panthers, staged a shootout in Los Angeles that stemmed, in part, from ideological differences over the direction the movement should take.

This basic division could also be found *within* specific movement organizations. Meier and Rudwick, for example, have documented the role such disputes played in the decline of CORE affiliate strength in the mid to late sixties. Representative of these disputes was one that split the Seattle chapter of CORE into a "conservative" faction and a dissident group called the Ad Hoc Committee. To quote at length from the author's account of the dispute:

> ...Ad Hoc members were charged with circulating "divisive and derogatory allegations" that the chapter leaders had conspired to thwart direct action projects and had 'foisted a compromising agreement on the membership.' Ad Hoc people attacked the chapter's black chairman and vice-chairman as "too respectable" and too fearful of losing their jobs and homes by participating in militant tactics.... Defeated in its attempt to oust the chapter's established leadership in the next election and hoping to function independently as a ghetto-oriented organization, the Ad Hoc Committee withdrew, and soon after disintegrated. Meanwhile, amid the accusations and counteraccusations, a number of others left the Seattle Chapter, disgusted by the "lack of faith and trust we CORE people now have in each other." Thus the result of the conflict was to leave Seattle CORE seriously weakened. (Meier and Rudwick 1973, p. 311)

As recounted by Meier and Rudwick, the same fate befell other CORE affiliates. Indeed, the Seattle incident was symptomatic of a trend that was widespread throughout the movement. Once-effective insurgent organizations were rendered impotent by factional disputes that drained them of the unity, energy, and resolve needed to sustain protest activity. Thus the growing divisions within the movement not only reduced the possibility of cooperative action *between* movement groups but further diminished organizational strength by stimulating disputes *within* these groups.

THE EVOLVING "STRUCTURE OF POLITICAL OPPORTUNITIES," 1961–70

Simultaneous with organizational decline, several external processes were decreasing the political leverage exercised by blacks. These developments reversed a thirty year trend that had created a political environment increasingly favorable to insurgent political action (McAdam 1982).

Mobilization of Political Reaction and the Devaluation of the Black Vote. Between 1910 and 1960 nearly 5 million southern blacks migrated northward. This exodus was politically significant for two reasons. First, as Brooks (1974, p. 17) has observed, "for blacks it was a move, almost literally, from no voting to voting." While the total black population of the United States increased by 92 percent between 1910 and 1960, the total number of blacks voting in presidential elections increased eightfold (Weiss 1970, Wilson 1966).

Second, the black vote became less dependably Democratic than it had been in the thirties. In the 1944 and 1948 elections, had blacks reversed the proportion of the votes they gave to the two major candidates, the Republican challenger, Thomas Dewey, would have defeated his Democratic opponents, Franklin Roosevelt and Harry Truman (Brooks 1974). In the 1952 and 1956 contests, the Republican candidate, Dwight Eisenhower, was able to reverse the trend. Republican gains were especially pronounced in 1956 with Eisenhower capturing an estimated 40 percent of the black vote (Lomax 1962). As a result both parties intensified their efforts to appeal to black voters. As Glantz (1970) commented before the 1960 election, "Neither party can afford to ignore the numerical weight of the Negro vote. In the next campaign, the Democratic candidate will have the responsibility of reversing the changing image of the Democratic party, while the Republican candidate will have the responsibility of enlarging . . . the appeal of the Republican party."

The 1960 election enhanced the political significance of the black vote, as for the third time in the previous five elections, black voters were widely credited with deciding the contest. Lawson's (1976) assessment is typical:

> An analysis of the returns demonstrated that Negro ballots were enough to give the Democratic contender a winning margin in New Jersey, Michigan, Illinois, Texas, and South Carolina, all states that had supported Eisenhower in 1956. Had the Republican-Democratic division in the black districts of these states broken down in the same way as four years earlier, Richard Nixon would have become the thirty-fifth President. (p. 256)

The 1960 election was to represent the high water mark of black electoral influence. In 1964 the conservative threat posed by the Goldwater campaign altered the context of insurgency to the point where black protest came at times, to be redefined, even by allies, as a political liability. Pressure was brought on civil rights organizations to curtail protest activity during the crucial months of the presidential campaign, out of fear that protest would help Goldwater. As Brooks (1974) tells it:

. . . white liberal money men were persuaded to threaten a cutoff in funds for civil rights activity as a means of containing the wilder enthusiasm of civil rights activists. The Democratic National Committee held back releasing funds allocated for voter registration drives among blacks to assure their use for registration and not hell-raising. The message was "cool it," and Roy Wilkins called civil rights leaders together to work out a "moratorium" on demonstrations. Wilkins, King, Young and Randolph signed a call, after three hours of debate on July 29, "to observe a broad curtailment, if not total moratorium, of all mass marches, mass picketing, and mass demonstrations until after election day." (p. 237)

Although Johnson won in a landslide vote, the off-year elections of 1966 began to show mass defections from the traditional Democratic electoral coalition that had swept Kennedy and Johnson into office. Deflections were particularly heavy among the white urban ethnic groups of the industrial North. Now worried by northern riots and threatened by what they viewed as the black assault, via open housing demonstrations in their neighborhoods, these groups were unwilling to support a party that many had come to view as supportive of unacceptable black demands. In 1964 Samuel Lubell accurately forecast this trend:

> In the past, Democratic strategists have assumed that the civil rights issue helped hold together the "big city" vote. This may have been a valid political strategy as long as the civil rights cause appeared mainly a matter of improving the treatment of Negroes in the South.
>
> But the new demands of Northern Negro militants have posed sharp conflicts with what many white voters see as their own rights. Agitation over civil rights . . . could alienate enough white voters to disrupt the Democratic majorities in the urban areas. (pp. 127–28)

In 1966 the black vote held generally firm, but the white ethnics abandoned in droves. (Brink and Harris 1967). As a consequence of these defections, political strategists of both parties came to weigh the advantages of courting the black vote against the costs of antagonizing a large and ever-expanding segment of the white population.

In 1968 the Republicans sought to exploit this dilemma by devising a campaign strategy designed to play on the country's deepening racial cleavage and the post-New Deal association of blacks with the Democratic party. By reminding voters of the latter, Republicans hoped to tap the growing undercurrent of racial antagonism engendered by the changing patterns of black insurgency in the mid- to late 1960s. Consequently, a breakdown of the popular vote in 1968 along racial lines revealed that blacks retained their traditional loyalty to the Democratic party by casting 97 percent of their votes for Humphrey. By contrast, only 35 percent of the white electorate voted for the democratic presidential candidate (Converse et al. 1969, p. 1085).

The election did more than simply mirror the declining political fortunes of blacks; it contributed to them as well by electing someone with precious little political debt to blacks and considerable debt to their opponents. As Goldman reported, nothing in the substantive performance of the Nixon administration's first two years in power contradicted this expectation.

Nixon . . . came to office with substantial political debts to the South—and, as his advisors were frank to say, none at all to the blacks. The most moderate Negro leaders found their lines of communication to the White House abruptly cut. Judicial conservatives were posted to vacancies on the Supreme Court. Pressure on the South to integrate its schools relented. . . . (Goldman 1970, p. 23)

By 1970 the structure of political alignments in this country had changed considerably. Whereas the black vote had earlier constituted an electoral asset of considerable significance, the "white backlash" of the late 1960s served to render it a decided liability in many situations. The result was an overall diminution in the vulnerability of the political system to the demands of blacks and a consequent decline in the opportunities for successful insurgent activity.

The Declining Salience of the Racial Issue. Between 1961 and 1965, the salience of the "Negro question" reached such proportions that it came to be consistently identified in public opinion surveys as the most important problem confronting the country. In six of eleven polls between 1961 and 1965, "civil rights" was identified as the most important problem facing the country by more people than identified any other comparable issue. In three other polls it ranked second. Only twice did it rank as low as fourth.*

Over the same period, public support for many of the stated goals of the movement also increased steadily. Burstein (1978) has documented consistent gains in white support during the fifties and early sixties across a wide range of specific issue areas. That this support was grudging and/or hypocritical in many cases, and no doubt erosive in the face of a more meaningful test of support (i.e., fund raising, willingness to demonstrate), hardly diminishes its significance. This growing body of supportive opinion introduced a new set of political considerations into the calculations of other parties to the conflict, and in so doing helped define their response to the movement. Writing in the early 1960s, James Q. Wilson captured the nature of this dynamic. "The principal value of the white liberal . . . is to supply votes and the political pressures . . . that make it almost suicidal for an important Northern politician openly to court anti-Negro sentiment" (Wilson 1965, p. 437). The mobilization of liberal support acted, then, to enhance the bargaining position of blacks by increasing the political consequences of opposing "acceptable" black demands.

From its peak in the 1963–65 period, the issue of civil rights declined in salience during the late sixties and early seventies. This decline is depicted in Figure 17.2 which reports the proportion of survey respondents who identified "civil rights" and Vietnam as the "most important problem" facing America in a series of Gallup opinion polls between 1962 and 1971. The extent of this decline was such that by February 1971 only 7 percent of the people surveyed identified "race relations" as the country's most important problem, in con-

---

* This analysis was based exclusively on comparable Gallup polls conducted between 1961 and 1965. Smith (1980) has assembled a richer data set consisting of all similar polls conducted by the major polling organizations between 1947 and 1976. His findings are consistent with those reported here. While he does not report the rank order of "civil rights" among all problems identified in each survey, the percentage of respondents listing that as the "most important" problem remained high throughout the period. In ten of nineteen surveys, at least 20 percent of the respondents identified civil rights as the country's most important problem; in another three, the figure was between 10 and 20 percent.

trast to the 52 percent who had done so six years earlier. As Goldman (1970) has sardonically observed, "Negroes did not precisely fall from grace at [this] juncture, but they did go out of fashion" (p. 201).

One reason for the decline was the emergence of competing issues, notably Vietnam, that diverted attention from the racial conflict. As Killian (1975) has observed:

> In spite of the evidence of continued tension and growing polarization, the racial conflict that had seemed to threaten American society soon dropped from its preeminent position in public concern. Vietnam, ecology, inflation, the Arab-Israeli conflict, the energy crisis, and Watergate took their turns in preempting both the headlines of the newspapers and the interest of white Americans. (p. 146)

Another reason was the diminished organizational strength of the movement. With the disintegration of the movement's organizational core, insurgents found it increasingly hard to mount the dramatic campaigns that had earlier caught public attention. Finally, declining public support for blacks reflected efforts by politicians to discredit the more militant forms of black insurgency characteristic of the period. Thus, in the face of contradictory empir-

FIGURE 17.2 Proportion of General Public Identifying Civil Rights and Vietnam as the "Most Important Problem Confronting the Country," March 1962 Through February 1971.

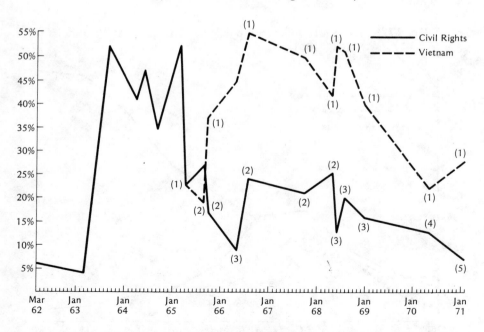

Source: Gallup, 1972: 1764, 1812, 1842, 1881, 1894, 1905, 1934, 1944, 1966, parentheses refer to the rank of Vietnam among all the problems identified in the poll.

ical evidence (cf. Fogelson 1971, Oberschall 1968), "responsible" public officials persisted in denouncing ghetto disorders as either insurrections instigated by subversive elements or exercises in rampant criminality.

THE SHIFTING RESPONSE TO INSURGENCY, 1961–70

Black insurgency was further handicapped during the late 1960s by the shifting patterns of interaction between the movement and the three other major parties to the conflict: external support groups, white opposition, and the federal government. The growing threat posed by the shifting goals and tactics of insurgents served to mobilize increased opposition. The result was a less supportive balance of opposing and supporting forces confronting the movement and a consequent decline in insurgent activity.

External Support Groups. Figure 17.3 reports the estimated level of monetary support for Big Four movement organizations during each year from 1961 to 1970. The distinct patterns for various movement organizations show a decided shift in the response of external support groups to the movement beginning around mid-decade. The shift involved a tripartite funding pattern based on the relative "acceptability" of the goals and tactics embraced by various groups. In the face of the widespread legitimacy ascribed to movement goals in the early 1960s, all four principal movement groups benefited from a consistent rise in external monetary support until the mid-1960s. As movement goals and tactics began to shift around mid-decade, so too did the response of external "sponsors."

FIGURE 17.3 External Dollar Support for SCLC, NAACP, and CORE-SNCC, 1961–70.

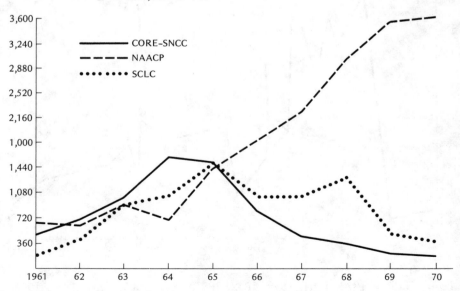

Sources: For number of movement initiated events, *Annual Index* of the *New York Times*; for financial data see Figure 17.1.

The first to experience the disaffection of liberal supporters were SNCC and CORE. After together commanding the largest share of external support between 1962 and 1965, their funding fell off rapidly after 1965. This sharp drop was prompted by the ideological shift to Black Power advocated by both groups. To quote Brink and Harris, "... the onset of black power produced sharp birth pangs for its principal advocates ... both CORE and SNCC were reduced to serious financial straits as whites deserted in droves" (Brink and Harris 1967, p. 62).

Support for SCLC also declined, but for different reasons. When SCLC's leader and chief fund raiser, Martin Luther King, publicly criticized the Vietnam war late in 1965, there was a significant loss of funds the following year. His assassination in 1968 did stimulate a brief resurgence in support, but this lasted only as long as the feelings of sympathy and guilt generated by his death.

In marked contrast to the experience of SCLC, SNCC, and CORE, the NAACP enjoyed a steep and steady rise in external funding during the late 1960s. An examination of Figure 17.3 shows that the NAACP's level of external support remained virtually constant between 1961 and 1964, while the dollar amounts received by both SCLC and SNCC-CORE increased steadily over the same period of time. After 1964, the patterns were largely reversed. Together these patterns present an inescapable conclusion: Over time, the NAACP came increasingly to be seen by external support groups as virtually the only "acceptable" funding alternative.* In response to the radicalization of SNCC and CORE and to King's antiwar stance, many groups that had earlier contributed to one of these three organizations shifted their support to the NAACP, reducing the once formidable Big Four to a single strong movement organization by the end of the decade.

White Opposition. White opposition to the movement was transformed during the decade from a regionally based, organized force of counterinsurgents to a geographically dispersed mass of people recognizable only by their common opposition to the movement. This broadened "white backlash" represented little more than a much publicized shift in public opinion rather than the organized white resistance encountered by insurgents in the South. Nonetheless, the change was to have important negative consequences for the movement.

This transformation was fueled by two trends. First, there was the rise of . Black Power as the substantive focus of insurgency. The movement's critique of America had broadened to embody a holistic attack on the complex patterns of institutional racism in which the interests of many who had earlier "supported" the movement were implicated. Second, the movement shifted from a southern to a national phenomenon. Confined almost exclusively to the South during the early 1960s, the movement posed little threat to residents of other regions of the country. With the advent of riots, open housing marches, and school busing, the comfortable illusion that the racial problem was a distinctly southern dilemma was shattered. When the movement threatened

---

* The overwhelming conservative bias in external funding is well documented in a 1970 study of corporate America's financial contributions to urban affairs programs (Cohn 1970, pp. 71, 73).

population segments earlier removed from the conflict, opposition ceased to be primarily a southern phenomenon.

The movement's shift northward also undermined the crucial conflict dynamic so evident in the earlier southern campaigns. One of the characteristics of southern supremacists was that they could be counted on to react in precisely the violent, disruptive fashion productive of media attention and federal intervention. The importance of this dynamic cannot be underestimated, for its recognition and conscious manipulation by insurgents helped produce the particularly high rates of black activism and significant victories characteristics of the years 1961–65 (Garrow 1978, Hubbard 1968, McAdam 1982).

In effect, the shift northward deprived the movement of an enemy it had learned to exploit successfully. No such convenient foil was available to the movement outside the South. Clark (1970) has captured the amorphous quality of the opposition the movement came increasingly to confront during this period:

> What do you do in a situation in which you have the laws on your side, where whites smile and say that they are your friends, but where your white "friends" move to the suburbs leaving you confronted with segregation and inferior education in schools, ghetto housing, and a quiet and tacit discrimination in jobs? How can you demonstrate a philosophy of love in response to this? What is the appropriate form of protest? One can "sit-in" in the Board of Education building, and not a single child will come back from the suburbs or from the private and parochial schools. One can link arms with the Mayor of Boston and march on the Commons, but it will not affect the housing conditions of Negroes in Roxbury. (p. 288)

In short, having developed effective tactics for one opponent, insurgents were unable to devise a suitable response for another.

Even if insurgents had been able to provoke in the North the same form of disruptive white opposition they had in the South, it is not likely that the federal government would have been as ready to intervene. The political repercussions had changed significantly. Killian (1975) wrote:

> The white people who are now resisting the movement are not the ancient foe, the southern whites. They are Jews, traditional liberal friends of blacks, now defending their middle-class surburban neighborhoods and their neighborhood schools. They are Americans of Irish, Italian, or Polish descent defending their labor unions, their neighborhood schools, and the imagined integrity of their neighborhoods .... And there are, finally, the old American Protestants as well. (p. 117)

The important characteristic of these groups is that they represented population segments vital to the political fortunes of both major parties. Consequently, the mobilization of broad-based white opposition to the movement in the late 1960s prompted a general devaluation of the political significance of blacks and, as noted earlier, a simultaneous tactical swing to the right on the part of both major parties.

The Federal Government. After 1965, and especially 1967, the grudging support that had been forthcoming in earlier years gave way to an increasingly repressive federal response to the movement. To fully describe the extent of government repression against the movement would be beyond the scope of this chapter, but two broad categories of control activities can be identified. First were the countless instances of violence, intimidation, harassment, and surveillance directed at Black Power groups active during the late 1960s. Second were the efforts to control urban riots. In both cases it is difficult to distinguish between the efforts of federal, state, and local officials, for all three levels worked together in a loosely coordinated effort to counter the perceived threat posed by the Black Power wing of the movement.

Governmental efforts to damage specific movement organizations or leaders were certainly evident earlier than 1966–70 (Marx 1976). Nevertheless, the pace of such efforts increased markedly during the late 1960s. Perhaps the most celebrated-black power group was the Black Panther party, founded in Oakland in October 1966. Typical of the treatment accorded any number of similar groups, the Panthers in the four years following their founding were subjected to a wide array of official control efforts ranging from infiltration to harassment through arrests for minor offenses to violent confrontations with law enforcement personnel.

Though unique in the extent of official attention they received, the Panthers were by no means the only group subjected to government-initiated control activities. Several other examples may help illustrate the pervasiveness of such efforts.

In Cleveland, three members of a black nationalists' group died in a 1968 shoot out with police triggered by an unsubstantiated report by an FBI informant that the group, the Black Nationalists of New Libya, were stockpiling weapons to carry out an assassination plot against moderate black leaders. (Masotti and Corsi 1969)

FBI officials planted a series of derogatory articles in papers during the SCLC-sponsored Poor Peoples Campaign in 1968 as a means of discrediting it. (Marx 1976, p. 5)

Police raided the Los Angeles office of SNCC on April 5, 1968, while chapter members were attending a memorial service for Martin Luther King (Major 1971, p. 297)

In his study of a local black power group, Helmreich reports countless instances of official violence, harassment, and intimidation directed at the organization's leadership. In the most flagrant incident, two leaders were arrested on a charge of faulty brake lights, taken to the police station, and beaten severely. (Helmreich 1973, pp. 120–21)

No fewer than 24 known black insurgent groups were subjected to tax surveillance as part of a larger effort to use the IRS to harass "extremist" groups of varying (though primarily leftist) political philosophy. (Senate Select Committee 1975, 3: 50–52)

These and other instances of repression served to diminish the pace of black insurgency in three ways. First, they increased the personal costs of movement participation significantly as members and potential recruits came to weigh their involvement against the very real threat of death, injury, or incarceration.

Second, instead of initiating new programs, Black Power groups were forced to devote increasing amounts of time and money to legal efforts aimed at preserving and defending the organization against external threats. Indeed, as Oberschall (1978) perceptively notes, the federal government's aggressive prosecution of movement activists in the late 1960s would appear to have been based, in part, on a desire to precipitate this kind of debilitating financial crisis. He writes: "[t]he government's strategy appeared to be to tie down leaders in costly and time consuming legal battles which would impede their activities and put a tremendous drain on financial resources regardless of whether the government would be successful in court" (pp. 277–78).

Finally, it would be hard to overestimate the divisive internal effect that increased government surveillance had on insurgents. Fear of informers was itself sufficient in many cases to generate the climate of suspicion and distrust needed to precipitate serious internal problems. And where fear failed to produce the desired results, agent provocateurs could be counted on to stir up dissension. As one example, Gary Marx cites a 1970 memo in which "FBI agents were instructed to plant in the hands of Panthers phony documents (on FBI stationery) that would lead them to suspect one another of being police informers" (Marx 1974, p. 435). He concludes, "Sociologists who have often observed the bickering and conflict among sectarian protest groups holding the same goals, and their ever-present problems of unity, must ask what role 'counterintelligence' activities may be playing" (ibid., p. 436).

The net effect of increased governmental repression, was to seriously weaken the capacity of the Black Power wing of the movement to sustain insurgency. As Killian observed in 1975, movement activity

> ...has subsided not because the racial crisis has passed but because white power has demonstrated that open black defiance is extremely dangerous and often suicidal. The ranks of the most dramatically defiant black leaders were decimated by imprisonment, emigration, and assassination. The best-known black nationalist organizations, such as the Black Panthers, the Republic of New Africa, the Revolutionary Action Movement, and the Student Nonviolence Coordinating Committee, have dwindled in strength. (pp. 155–56)

Intensified social control also marked the state's response to the escalation in rioting during the mid-to-late sixties. A sampling of these efforts conveys the trend of the times.

At the federal level, Congress attached antiriot provisions to the 1968 Civil Rights Act that provided harsh penalties for persons found guilty of crossing state lines or using interstate communication facilities to incite riots. This legislation provided the Justice Department with the legal basis to prosecute many black leaders in the late sixties. Furthermore, the Omnibus Crime Act of 1968 provided for a national training center to instruct local police in riot-control techniques and a program of fiscal aid to local law enforcement agencies seeking to bolster antiriot capabilities. The latter program provided 75 percent federal funding for local riot-control efforts. That there was no shortage of "takers" for the newly available funds is clear from statistics cited by Feagin and Hahn (1973).

Twenty states added antiriot sections to their penal codes between 1966 and 1969 (Feagin and Hahn 1973). Locally, ordinances were passed in many cities granting the mayor legal authority to declare martial law in the event of ghetto disorders. A more common response was simply to strengthen the riot-control capabilities of local law enforcement agencies. Webb (1969) reports that by 1969, 75 percent of the 1,267 cities providing information had instituted some form of police riot-control training. Additionally, there was a 45 percent increase in the number of cities reporting the development of riot-control plans and a 25 percent rise in those reporting that they had obtained or prepared their own riot-control manuals (Webb 1969).

The composite picture that emerges from these various sources is of a massive governmental control response designed to counter the escalation in ghetto rioting. That these combined efforts had a measurable effect on the actual handling of urban disorders is suggested by a comparison of data on the 1967 and April, 1968 riots. Perhaps most importantly, the force levels used in containing the 1968 disorders were on the average 50 percent greater than those used the previous year (Lemberg Center for the Study of Violence, 1968). Indeed, all major indices of official repression, save one, showed increases between 1967 and April 1968. The average number of injuries per disorder in 1968 was nearly 40 percent higher than in 1967. Even more spectacular was the nearly twofold increase in average number of arrests between the two years.

Not surprisingly, in the face of this massive control response, the intensity of racial disorders dropped precipitously in 1969 and 1970 (Feagin and Hahn 1973, Skolnick 1969). Confronted by governmental forces increasingly willing and able to suppress ghetto disorders, and painfully aware of the costs incurred in the earlier rioting, the pace of such actions declined sharply.

CONCLUSIONS

There are three conclusions we can draw from this study about the dynamics of movement decline. First, we should not assume an inevitable conservative trend as a social movement develops. In contradiction to the classical model, the black movement grew progressively more radical over time. In view of this and similar findings (Beach 1977), it would seem more profitable to specify which factors might dispose movements to develop in either direction.

Second, this study undermines any simplistic resource mobilization argument that equates the pace of insurgency with the absolute dollar amount of resources available to insurgents. This is not to suggest that resources are antithetical or irrelevant to the decline of insurgency. On the contrary, what is needed is a more sophisticated specification of the relationship between resources and insurgency based on a more interesting set of research questions. Are all resources of equal value? How do various sources of support differ in the constraints they place on a movement, and what effect does this have on the development of insurgency? What is the optimum distribution of resources within a movement?

Finally, in supporting a political process interpretation of black insurgency, this study should serve to remind us that the fate of any social movement is not simply a product of internal movement dynamics or external political processes but the interaction of the two. In the words of Gary Marx:

> Social movements are not autonomous forces hurling toward their destiny only in response to the oppression, intensity of commitment, and skill of activists. Nor are they epi-phenomena completely at the mercy of groups in their external environment seeking to block or facilitate them. Movements represent a complex interplay of external and internal factors. (Marx 1976, p. 1)

REFERENCES

Allen, Robert L.
  1970 *Black Awakening in Capitalist America.* Garden City, N.Y.: Doubleday.
Beach, Stephen W.
  1977 "Social Movement Radicalization: The Case of the People's Democracy in Northern Ireland." *Sociological Quarterly* 18: 305–19.
Brink, William, and Louis Harris
  1963 *The Negro Revolution in America.* New York: A Clarion Book, published by Simon and Schuster.
  1967 *Black and White.* New York: A Clarion Book, published by Simon and Schuster.
Brooks, Thomas R.
  1974 *Walls Come Tumbling Down: A History of the Civil Rights Movement, 1940–1970.* Englewood Cliffs, N.J.: Prentice-Hall.
Burstein, Paul
  1978 "Public Opinion, Demonstrations, Media Coverage, and the Passage of Anti-Discrimination Legislation." Unpublished ms., Yale University, Department of Sociology.
Clark, Kenneth B.
  1970 "The Civil Rights Movement: Momentum and Organization." Pp. 270–97 in Richard P. Young, ed., *Roots of Rebellion: The Evolution of Black Politics and Protest Since World War II.* New York: Harper & Row.
Clayton, Edward, ed.
  1964 *The SCLC Story.* Atlanta: Southern Christian Leadership Conference.
Cohn, Jules
  1970 "Is Business Meeting the Challenge of Urban Affairs?" *Fortune* 48 (March–April) 68–82.

Converse, Phillip E.; Warren E. Miller; Jerrold G. Rusk; Arthur C. Wolfe
  1969 "Continuity and Change in American Politics: Parties and Issues in the 1968 Election." *American Political Science Review* 63 (December): 1083–1105.
Downes, Bryan T.
  1970 "A Critical Reexamination of Social and Political Characteristics of Riot Cities." *Social Science Quarterly* 51, no. 2: 349–60.
Eisinger, Peter K.
  1973 "The Conditions of Protest Behaviour in American Cities." *American Political Science Review* 67 (March): 11–28.
Feagin, Joe R., and Harlan Hahn
  1973 *Ghetto Revolts, the Politics of Violence in American Cities.* New York: Macmillan.
Fogelson, Robert M.
  1971 *Violence as Protest.* Garden City, N.Y.: Doubleday.

Gallup, George H.
   1972   *The Gallup Poll, Public Opinion 1935–1971*, vol. 3. New York: Random House.
Gamson, William A.
   1975   *The Strategy of Social Protest.* Homewood, Ill.: Dorsey Press.
Garrow, David J.
   1978   *Protest at Selma.* New Haven: Yale University Press.
Gerlach, Luther P., and Virginia H. Hine
   1970   *People, Power, Change: Movements of Social Transformation.* Indianapolis: Bobbs-
          Merrill.
Gerth, Hans H., and C. Wright Mills
   1946   *From Max Weber: Essays in Sociology.* New York: Oxford University Press.
Glantz, Oscar
   1970   "The Black Vote." Pp. 248–61 in Allen Weinstein and Frank Otto Gatell,
          eds., *The Segregation Era 1863–1954.* New York: Oxford University Press.
Goldman, Peter
   1970   *Report From Black America.* New York: A Clarion Book, published by Simon
          and Schuster.
Helmreich, William B.
   1973   *The Black Crusaders: A Case Study of a Black Militant Organization.* New York:
          Harper & Row.
Hubbard, Howard
   1968   "Five Long Hot Summers and How They Grew." *Public Interest*, no. 12 (Sum-
          mer): 3–24.
Killian, Lewis M.
   1975   *The Impossible Revolution, Phase II: Black Power and the American Dream.* New
          York: Random House.
Laue, James H.
   1965   "The Changing Character of Negro Protest." *Annals of the American Academy of
          Political and Social Science* 357: 119–26.
Lawson, Steven F.
   1976   *Black Ballots: Voting Rights in the South, 1944–1969.* New York: Columbia Uni-
          versity Press.
Lemberg Center for the Study of Violence
   1968   "April Aftermath of the King Assassination." *Riot Data Review*, no. 2 (Au-
          gust), Brandeis University. Mimeographed.
Lomax, Louis E.
   1962   *The Negro Revolt.* New York: Harper & Row.
Lubell, Samuel
   1964   *White and Black, Test of a Nation.* New York: Harper & Row.
McAdam, Doug
   1982   *Political Process and the Development of Black Insurgency, 1930–1970.* Chicago: Uni-
          versity of Chicago Press.
McCarthy, John D., and Mayer N. Zald
   1973   *The Trend of Social Movement in America: Professionalization and Resource Mobiliza-
          tion.* Morristown, N.J.: General Learning Press.
   1977   "Resource Mobilization and Social Movements: A Partial Theory." *American
          Journal of Sociology* 82, no. 6: 1212–41.
Major, Reginald
   1971   *A Panther Is a Black Cat.* New York: Morrow.
Marx, Gary T.
   1974   "Thoughts on a Neglected Category of Social Movement Participant: The

Agent Provocateur and the Informant." *American Journal of Sociology* 80, no. 2: 402–42.

1976   "External Efforts to Damage or Facilitate Social Movements: Some Patterns, Explanations, Outcomes, and Complications." Paper prepared for conference on the Dynamics of Social Movements: Resource Mobilization, Tactics and Social Control, Vanderbilt University, March.

Masotti, L., and J. Corsi
1969   *Shootout in Cleveland*. Washington, D.C.: Government Printing Office.

Meier, August
1971   "Negro Protest Movements and Organizations." Pp. 20–33 in John H. Bracery, Jr., August Meier, and Elliott Rudwick, eds., *Conflict and Competition: Studies in the Recent Black Protest Movement*. Belmont, Calif.: Wadsworth.

Meier, August, and Elliot Rudwick
1973   *CORE, A Study in the Civil Rights Movement, 1942–1968*. New York: Oxford University Press.

Messinger, Sheldon L.
1955   "Organizational Transformation: A Case Study of a Declining Social Movement." *American Sociological Review* 20: 3–10.

Michels, Robert
1959   *Political Parties*. New York: Dover.

Muse, Benjamin
1968   *The American Negro Revolution*. Bloomington: Indiana University Press.

National Association for the Advancement of Colored People
1948–70   *Annual Report of the National Association for the Advancement of Colored People*. New York: NAACP.

New York Times
1948–70   *The New York Times Index*. New York: New York Times.

Oberschall, Anthony
1968   "The Los Angeles Riot of August 1965." Pp. 264–84 in James A. Geschwender, ed., *The Black Revolt*. Englewood Cliffs, N.J.: Prentice-Hall.
1973   *Social Conflict and Social Movements*. Englewood Cliffs, N.J.: Prentice-Hall.
1978   "The Decline of the 1960's Social Movements," Pp. 257–89 In Louis Kriesberg, ed., *Research in Social Movements, Conflicts, and Change*, Vol. 1. Greenwich, Conn.: JAI Press.

Perrow, Charles
1979   "The Sixties Observed." In Meyer N. Zald and John McCarthy, eds., *The Dynamics of Social Movements: Resource Mobilization, Social Control, and Tactics*. Cambridge, Mass.: Winthrop.

Rustin, Bayard
1965   "From Protest to Politics: The Future of the Civil Rights Movement." *Commentary*, February, pp. 27–32.

Skolnick, Jerome H.
1969   *The Politics of Protest*. New York: Simon and Schuster.

Smith, Tom W.
1980   "America's Most Important Problem—A Trend Analysis, 1946–1976." *Public Opinion Quarterly* 44, no. 2: 164–80.

U.S. Congress, Senate Select Committee to Study Governmental Operations with Respect to Intelligence Activities
1976   *Final Report. Hearings*, Vol. I–VII. Washington, D.C.: Government Printing Office.

Webb, Horace S.
  1969   "Police Preparedness for Control of Civil Disorders." *Municipal Yearbook, 1969*. Washington, D.C.: International City Management Association.
Weiss, Nancy J.
  1970   "The Negro and the New Freedom." In Allen Weinstein and Frank Otto Gatell, eds., *The Segregation Era 1863–1954*, pp. 129–42. New York: Oxford University Press.
Wilson, James Q.
  1965   "The Negro in Politics." In Talcott Parsons and Kenneth B. Clark, eds., *The Negro American*, pp. 423–47. Boston: Houghton Mifflin Company.
  1966   "The Negro in American Politics: The Present." In John P. Davis, ed., *The American Negro Reference Book*, pp. 431–57. Englewood Cliffs, New Jersey: Prentice-Hall.
Zinn, Howard
  1965   *SNCC*. Boston: Beacon Press.

19

The Student Non-Violent Coordinating Committee: Rise and Fall of a Redemptive Organization

Emily Stoper

The Student Non-Violent Coordinating Committee (SNCC) presents an enigma to the political analyst, an enigma left unsolved in descriptive histories by former members (Zinn 1964, Lester 1968, Forman 1972, Sellers with Terrell 1973). SNCC was founded in 1960 for the purpose of coordinating the sit-in movement then sweeping the South in an attempt to integrate bus stations, lunch counters, and the like. The following year, with the integration of public facilities largely achieved, SNCC moved into voter registration work among poor blacks in the rural Deep South. Most of its members in this period from 1960 to 1963 were black southern college dropouts. After several years of almost total frustration in this effort, SNCC decided to bring its case to the nation. In order to dramatize the disenfranchisement of blacks in the Deep South, it threw all its efforts behind a challenge to the seating of the all-white Mississippi delegation at the 1964 Democratic National Convention.

Here was the beginning of SNCC's seeming success. The convention offered a compromise that had the effect of expelling the white Mississippi delegates and seating some of the black challengers. The following year, a federal Voting Rights Act was passed, which sent federal registrars to the southern states, something SNCC had been demanding for years. The registrars effectively ended the mass disenfranchisement of blacks.

Meanwhile, in 1964 SNCC had gained a large number of new, highly capable, and enthusiastic members. Then in 1966 it achieved national fame when its chairman, Stokely Carmichael, enunciated the slogan "Black Power."

After this cavalcade of apparent successes, what did SNCC do? It rapidly faded out of existence! Depth interviews with about fifty former SNCC members suggest to me that the solution to this enigma (success leading to failure) lies in SNCC's almost unique organizational ethos and in the tension between that ethos and SNCC's pursuit of purposive goals.

SNCC's ethos was a product of its unusual incentive structure, which made it a "redemptive organization," one type of purposive organization in the typology that includes purposive, solidary, and material organizations (according to their incentive structure). This typology was developed by Clark and Wilson (1961) and refined by Wilson (1973). Wilson (1973) describes a redemptive organization as one that

> seeks not only to change society and its institutions, but also to change its members by requiring them to exemplify in their own lives the new order. The way in which goals are sought is as important as their substance. Moral and political enthusiasm are to be made evident in the routine activities of the members and in all organizational meetings. (p. 47)

SNCC fits this description very well. This study of SNCC extends and elaborates on the characteristics of redemptive organizations. First, I discuss what SNCC as a redemptive organization was *not*.

SNCC's members (who were all full-time activists) certainly did *not* join because of material incentives. Their salaries, which were paid very irregularly, ranged from $10 to $60 a week, with the mode about $10.

Nor did they join out of a belief in SNCC's ideological correctness, as did members of the Socialist and Communist parties. SNCC had no formal ideology. Its members plucked ideas from the works of Albert Camus, Karl Marx, Mao Tse-tung, Malcolm X, Frantz Fanon, and others, but there were no basic SNCC principles on which they all agreed.

SNCC does not fit Max Weber's famous classification of organizations as either bureaucratic, charismatic, or traditional (Gerth and Mills 1958). SNCC was obviously not held together by a bureaucracy or bureaucratic incentives. Almost all of its members were activists in the field, and the office staff was kept to a bare minimum.

Nor were SNCC's members drawn together by a few charismatic leaders at the top. Leadership in SNCC tended to be decentralized at the level of a state or local project. No one controlled the organization from the national office in Atlanta. Even at the project level, SNCC members rejected leadership. In many interviews activists actually denied that there were leaders in SNCC at all—because the word "leader" connoted to them a person who manipulated others, thus distorting the purpose of an organization.

SNCC did, of course, have leaders, and they were an important source of its redemptive ethos. Such men as Bob Moses in Mississippi, Charles Sherrod in southwest Georgia, and Bill Hansen in Arkansas were highly effective leaders not so much because of their intellectual acumen or organizing skills as because of their moral courage, a quality that gave others a sense of hope for personal and social redemption. They were praised for this quality again and again in interviews.

SNCC's redemptive ethos consisted partly of a set of attitudes toward the world that were exemplified by the lives of these leaders. These attitudes constituted both more than and less than an ideology. They were both broader and deeper than ideology in the sense that they embraced life style as well as political ideas and in that they called for a commitment in action as well as a mere affirmation of belief. They were also less explicit than ideology. Nowhere was there a pamphlet stating authoritatively that "this is what you must believe to be a SNCC member." One would have been hard put between 1961 and 1965 to say precisely which ideas were basic to the SNCC world view. There was a high level of agreement among members about many things, but no clearly stated central tenets.

The redemptive ethos was more than a set of attitudes. It was also a strong sense of intimacy, solidarity, and loyalty among SNCC members in the face of what was increasingly seen as an implacably hostile world. The world was also seen in highly moral terms, more and more as time passed. SNCC was good; those who were not with it were against it, they were evil. One did not make compromises because one does not negotiate about matters of good and evil.

To sum up, SNCC was a redemptive organization because it had

1. A moral ethos, consisting of a set of broad attitudes, shared by almost all members, involving a rejection of ideology (formal sets of beliefs)
2. A sense of superiority of other institutions and to individual nonmembers
3. A very high rate of activism among members
4. Pervasiveness, that is, an important influence on all or almost all aspects of its members' lives
5. A belief in the equality of all members, which leads to the rejection of bureaucracy and of all formal leadership structures

A redemptive political organization is in many ways analogous to a religious sect, as distinguished from a church, in the work of Ernst Troeltsch (1958) and others. For example, it possesses a total rather than a segmental hold over its members. Virtually all SNCC members were totally absorbed in SNCC work at all times. In sects, too, spirituality or grace is something to be lived or at least sought at every moment, not merely occasionally or one day a week (see Knox 1950). Like a sect, SNCC practiced the "priesthood of all believers"; every member was actively engaged in spreading its message.

SNCC's redemptive ethos gave its members the feeling, common in sects, of belonging to an elect group with special enlightenment. It played a role analogous to that of faith or "inner light" in sects; the members considered it superior to mere doctrine. For SNCC, moral impatience took the place of a systematic body of ideas, just as for sects millenialism takes the place of theology.

In sects, the "inner light" perceived by a member is expressed in spontaneous displays of religious feeling ("holy rolling"). Similarly, SNCC expected its members' moral and political enthusiasm to help them initiate new projects and experimental tactics. Going even further in a religious direction, the members of the Freedom High, a small, mostly white group within SNCC in 1963 and 1964, thought that SNCC members should strive chiefly for personal perfection (salvation). All of these are characteristics of sects as described by Wilson (1959).

But the Freedom High was short-lived; most of its adherents were soon driven out of SNCC. For SNCC was *not* a sect; it was a political organization, and its political goal (racial justice) was central to its existence. My thesis is that it was the tension between its sectlike qualities and its political purposiveness that eventually destroyed SNCC.

A number of factors made SNCC a redemptive organization. The first of these was its origin in the sit-in movement, with that movement's emphasis on moral confrontation with the evil of segregation and its quasi-religious tone (supplied by the many divinity students who helped lead it).

The second factor was the youthfulness of the membership. Zinn (1964) found that most Mississippi SNCC members in 1963 were 15 to 22 years old. Only the very young had the freedom from family responsibilities, the energy and the physical stamina necessary for SNCC work. And the very young are also often very moralistic. As Keniston (1968) and Fishman and Solomon (1963) show, the young see with fresh eyes the rampant injustice and suffering to which their parents have become calloused. And they have a shorter time perspective for the correction of these injustices than even those adults who perceive that they do exist. Moreover, they are less forgiving of those who cooperate in perpetuating the evils of the world.

For many reasons, these young people chose to concentrate their crusade against injustice in the rural counties of the Deep South, especially Mississippi. One of these reasons was that Mississippi, which had a reputation as the most racist state in the union, had some of the appeal of the conversion of the worst sinner. Also, little work was being done there by other black groups, mainly because of the white terror. In tackling the rural Deep South, SNCC could enjoy a sense of a special and superior mission, which proved to be an important source of solidarity.

SNCC's choice of locale became the chief cause of its difficulties in the next few years. Almost every SNCC member was jailed at least once in the next few years on such charges as "disturbing the peace" or "parading without a permit." Going to jail became almost an initiation rite. Nearly every male SNCC member (and many females) had been beaten, either in jail or on the street. SNCC offices were fire-bombed, its members were shot at (and sometimes hit), many of its close associates were actually murdered. Through all this, SNCC was almost entirely nonviolent (not in principle, but out of tactical necessity). This experience of persecution was probably the most important factor in shaping SNCC's moral ethos. It made SNCC righteously angry, defiant, uncompromising, and filled with suspicion as to the goodwill and sincerity of those who had never faced the terror. Until the beginning of 1964 most of SNCC's efforts were devoted to surviving in the face of fear and to helping its clientele, the poor blacks of the Deep South, overcome that fear and achieve political freedom.

After the spring of 1964 SNCC began to experience the tension between its ethos and its political effectiveness. Five crises in rapid succession destroyed it: (1) the challenge to Mississippi's delegation to the Democratic National Convention, (2) the sudden influx of several hundred whites into the organization, (3) the bad results of SNCC's inability to get along with other civil rights groups, (4) the loss of a financial base, and (5) an attempt to shift the base of operations from South to North. I shall describe these one by one.

THE CONVENTION CHALLENGE

In August 1964 a SNCC-founded and SNCC-backed organization called the Mississippi Freedom Democratic Party (FDP) attempted to have its delegates seated as representatives of Mississippi in place of the regular delegates at the Democratic National Convention. The narrative that follows comes from the *New York Times* (1964) and from interviews. The FDP delegates had been selected in a political process that paralleled the regular method of delegate selection in Mississippi but (unlike the regular Mississippi Democratic Party's practice) excluded no one on grounds of race. (Of course, almost no whites had chosen to participate in the FDP conventions.)

There was a further basis for the FDP challenge—that the regulars were unwilling to pledge support for the nominees of the convention, as required by a convention rule. (Most of the regulars later publicly endorsed Barry Goldwater, the Republican candidate for President.)

Ultimately, after a great deal of backroom negotiations, demonstrations, and impassioned pleas, the Credentials Committee of the Convention offered the following compromise, which was approved by a voice vote of the convention: all of the regulars who signed the loyalty oath would be seated, plus two delegates-at-large from the FDP, with voting rights but without the right to sit in the Mississippi seating section. The rest of the FDP delegates were welcomed as honored guests of the convention. Moreover, it was promised that the call to the 1968 convention would announce that states which practiced racial discrimination in the selection of their delegates would be denied seating.

All the 1964 regulars did eventually withdraw from the convention; almost the entire FDP delegation did take the regulars' seats on the floor (but only two of their votes); and four years later, in 1968, the regulars (as well as half the regulars from Georgia) were denied their seats because of racial discrimination in the selection procedure.

However, to SNCC the compromise was totally unacceptable and was taken as evidence of pervasive racism and hypocrisy within the Democratic Party. First, the regulars lost their seats *not* as a penalty for racial discrimination but because they themselves chose to protest against the offering of the compromise by leaving and also to refuse to sign the loyalty oath to the convention's nominees. So the principle that delegates chosen in Jim Crow elections were unacceptable was not established. The change in the call to the 1968 convention was considered meaningless because it forbade discrimination against voters and most of Mississippi's blacks were *not* voters and had little prospect of registering. (This was before the passage of the 1965 Voting Rights Act.) Moreover, the FDP's right to represent Mississippi was not acknowledged since its delegates were designated "at large"; nor was its right even to choose its own delegates, since the two with voting rights were specified by the convention.

SNCC thought it had gone quite far by expressing its willingness to accept another compromise (suggested by Representative Edith Green of Oregon) that treated FDP equally with the regulars. And it was deeply insulted at being treated *worse* than people whom it considered totally immoral.

In spite of all this, white and black liberals generally thought the compromise was generous and were puzzled at SNCC's rejection of it. The FDP delegates themselves (who were almost all local Mississippi blacks) seemed much more inclined to accept the compromise than were their SNCC advisers. SNCC's rejection of the compromise meant that it defined the convention challenge as a failure. This felt failure was in turn an important factor in causing the period of depression and turmoil that SNCC went through during the following year, and also in the fact that the FDP never again regained the organizing momentum of the heady summer of 1964.

Almost any other organization, recognizing the slowness with which so vast and decentralized an institution as the Democratic party shifts its commitments, would have seen the proffered compromise as a victory. In fact, the Southern Christian Leadership Conference (SCLC, Martin Luther King's group), the NAACP, the AFL-CIO, and most of SNCC's other allies urged SNCC to accept the compromise.

But SNCC by its nature as a redemptive organization could not accept the kind of partial commitment implied in the compromise. In discussing the convention in the interviews, SNCC members often spoke of backroom negotiations, of deals, of pressure, and of betrayals. It apparently shocked them that the Democratic Party operated so amorally that it seemed to regard the FDP and the Mississippi regulars chiefly as political rivals who must both be at least partly accommodated, rather than as the forces of right and justice fighting against the forces of evil and racism. The fact that the northern liberals in the party had important links to the southern conservatives (on whom they depended for votes in presidential elections) indicated to SNCC that these liberals were totally useless as allies of SNCC. A partial commitment was worse than no commitment at all, because it opened the door to betrayal (see Carmichael and Hamilton 1967). Moreover, concessions in practice were meaningless without concessions in principle. Having been immersed in its own moral universe for several years, SNCC simply could not accept the moral universe of the mainstream of the American political system, in which "compromise" is not a dirty word but the very basis of all activity.

THE INFLUX OF WHITES

Simultaneously with the crisis created by the convention challenge, SNCC was undergoing another deep struggle. This one concerned the aftermath of the Mississippi Summer Project, in which over 800 whites, mostly northern students, came into Mississippi in the summer of 1964 to work with SNCC in organizing the blacks of Mississippi around the convention challenge, and also to draw national attention to the persecution of civil rights workers in that state. Over a hundred of these whites stayed on to work in Mississippi after the summer. Since before this SNCC had rarely numbered more than 100 members (and only about 60 in late 1963), the increase in numbers alone meant a transformation of the organization. These mostly intelligent and aggressive new members could have provided the basis for a vastly expanded and far better publicized organizing effort. Instead, SNCC in Mississippi in the fall of 1964 and winter and spring of 1965 was almost paralyzed. The situation in Mississippi affected the entire organization profoundly. In almost every month in that period, there was a national SNCC staff meeting (membership meeting) lasting a week to ten days. The sessions were stormy and often lasted far into the night. The major disputes were (1) how to socialize so many new members into the organization at once, especially since they differed from the old members in social class, race, and level of education; (2) whether whites could ever organize black people effectively; (3) how SNCC should be structured and where its centers of power should be.

The meetings were a sign of the fact that SNCC was no longer functioning as a redemptive organization. It was too big, it was too diverse, and it had too many members who had never shared the unifying experience of the terror (and since they were white, never fully would). SNCC met the problem by tightening its structure, driving out the newcomers (and those old-timers who were white or were closely associated with whites), and thus trying to restore the old SNCC. But this proved futile. Too much talent was lost, too many people were left disoriented by the long internal struggle, and for too many people the tension between SNCC's redemptive ethos and their personal desire to be effective opponents of racial injustice became painfully manifest. Many of those who left SNCC in early 1965 joined more moderate civil rights groups or the "war on poverty." Many others, unwilling to dilute their principles, dropped out of politics entirely.

The expulsion of the whites pointed up a major problem: racism within SNCC. Before 1964, when there were only a small number of highly dedicated whites in SNCC, their presence had not created serious problems. After the Summer Project and convention challenge, however, some blacks in SNCC began to question both the effectiveness and the motives of the large number of new white members. The new whites were enthusiastic, self-confident, mostly better educated than the blacks and often more skilled at typing, expressing their ideas at meetings, putting out newsletters, and other organizing abilities. Therefore, in many places they began to take over the day-to-day and week-to-week decision making. This angered the blacks who had been working in SNCC for several years and were really much better at the essential work of communicating with and encouraging local black people. The whites, in fact, tended to reinforce the tendency of local blacks to defer to white people. For example, a white volunteer who asked a local black person to vote might receive the reply "yessir, boss!"

Blacks in SNCC also began to question the motives of the whites for coming to work in the Deep South. The whites seemed to have come to learn about life or to find themselves, to help the poor benighted black people and earn their gratitude, to act on an ideology, to satisfy a need for engagement or political activity, to play the political game, to atone for guilt, to escape themselves, and for any number of other reasons that did not seem legitimate to the blacks. None of these motives could form a satisfactory basis for a redemptive commitment.

Probably the blacks in SNCC also had motives that were not totally altruistic, but they were right in believing that the whites' commitment would never have the same meaning as their commitment. The blacks, after all, were fighting in their own cause, whose outcome would directly affect their personal destinies. The whites were merely giving a little of their time to somebody else's cause. (On the whole question of white-black relations within SNCC, see also Levy 1968 and Poussaint 1966.)

If SNCC had not been a redemptive organization, it could probably have dealt with the fact that different members had different levels and types of commitment. But the complete equalitarianism and the complete unity of sentiment necessary to sustain the redemptive ethos were incompatible with different types of membership. After all, a redemptive ethos involves seeing everyone in the world as either "sinners" or "saved." Partial salvation, partial commitment, is not possible.

For almost any organization, the absorption of so many new members, especially new members who were different in important ways from the old members, would be a serious problem—but few would have been so crippled by the crisis as SNCC. Most would have been sustained by the tremendous opportunities for renewal and expansion of activity presented by the new members. In fact, it would be difficult to think of another example of an ongoing voluntary organization that went into a rapid decline a few months after tripling its membership.

PROBLEMS WITH OTHER CIVIL RIGHTS GROUPS

At about this time (the spring of 1965), SNCC faced another serious problem. It began to reap the consequences of its long-term bad relations with other civil rights organizations. SNCC people had always despised the NAACP, regarding it as a corrupt group concerned chiefly with gaining advantages for the black middle class. (SNCC's clientele had, with few exceptions, always been the poorest of the poor.) However, SNCC had a policy of never publicly attacking the NAACP or any other black group, a policy it almost always adhered to.

By the spring of 1965, the national leadership of the NAACP had become very concerned about Communists in SNCC. A few white conservatives had been saying for some time that SNCC was Communist-infiltrated, but now the NAACP became one of the most zealous participants in a broad attack by liberals and liberal groups on alleged Communist influence in SNCC (see Kopkind 1965a, Evans and Novak 1966).

The NAACP has always been meticulous in maintaining the "purity" of its own membership and associates, so as not to antagonize powerful anticommunist liberals or give its racist enemies extra fuel for attacking it. SNCC could not understand such toadying to one's enemies and to doubtful allies at the expense of one's own people. SNCC refused even to reply to the charges. Its leaders would say only that SNCC did not require a loyalty oath and that they personally were unconcerned about fighting the battles of the 1930s, 1940s, and 1950s. They might have added that SNCC's redemptive ethos was totally incompatible with that of the Communist Party and that a person who joined SNCC either adapted to that ethos or left. What SNCC did, instead, was to take a moral stand against McCarthyism. Its failure to deny the charges explicitly hurt it a good deal with the liberals who were its chief financial backers. But the last thing SNCC would do would be to compromise its principles by yielding to McCarthyistic (or any other external) pressures. After the 1964 Democratic National Convention, it was extremely suspicious of the commitment of liberals and the NAACP anyway—and when they began to attack it publicly, SNCC became even more alienated from them.

The spring of 1965 also saw SNCC come into conflict with SCLC and Dr. Martin Luther King, this time far more dramatically than ever before. Both SNCC and SCLC had been working in Selma, Alabama, on voter registration, SNCC for two years, SCLC for a few months. Progress was very slow, and therefore SCLC decided to sponsor a march to the state capital at Montgomery 50 miles away to demand voting rights for black people. The march would be in defiance of an order by Governor George Wallace. SNCC opposed the march as yet another one of Dr. King's tactics that (in SNCC's view) would give him a lot of glory overnight and undermine the long-term efforts to develop local people's confidence in their ability to achieve political goals on their own. The SNCC project in Selma decided not to participate officially in the march. The march eventually became three marches; the first one, in which the nonviolent marchers were turned back at a bridge near Selma by police led by Sheriff James Clark and using whips, guns, horses, and teargas; the second march, two days later, in which by prior agreement with the police the marchers turned back at the same bridge ("making secret deals with Jim Clark" was the way SNCC members described this, since neither SNCC nor the public had not been told of the agreement); and a third march, two weeks after the first, in which an estimated 3,200 people participated, including hundreds of Northern whites, protected by almost 4,000 federal soldiers. This march provided the push necessary to bring the Voting Rights bill, which had been languishing in committee, up to the floor of Congress and get it passed. The Voting Rights Act sent large numbers of federal registrars to the Deep South, who quickly accomplished what SNCC and other black groups had been vainly attempting for years: the mass registration of black voters in the South.

So Dr. King's "glory-seeking" had resulted in an enormous success for the entire civil rights movement—but not a success for SNCC. SNCC defined its goal not as the passage of specific laws but as teaching people (which did not mean federal registrars) to act politically on their own behalf. Of course, the Voting Rights Act opened up previously undreamed-of possibilities for the self-organization of black people in the South—but not at all in the way SNCC had been hoping. SNCC envisioned its followers as developing a kind of "alternative politics" for America—a politics that was more decentralized, idealistic, intimate, noncoercive—in short, more redemptive. The Voting Rights Act in effect coopted the people whom SNCC had been counting on to build the new politics by luring them into standard two-party politics.

In the year that followed passage of the Voting Rights Act, most of SNCC's projects in the Deep South (with the notable exception of Stokely Carmichael's Lowndes County Freedom Organization) were either dead or dying. It was clear that SNCC was going to have to change if it was to continue to exist.

THE MOVE NORTH

The logical direction for SNCC to look at this point was North and to the cities. By 1966 the political awakening of black urban youth that had begun with the 1964 and 1965 riots had become quite widespread. Moreover, the continuing mechanization of southern agriculture was driving increasing numbers of blacks northward and cityward. There were fewer and fewer southern counties with black majorities, and two northern cities (Washington and Newark) by then had populations more than half black.

But SNCC faced severe problems in moving. Its membership (staff) had been decimated, and it faced strong competition in the North with other groups in recruiting new members.

LOSS OF A FINANCIAL BASE

Moreover, its financial base had all but disappeared, partly because of its own behavior (such as sending Stokely Carmichael to Havana and Hanoi, and also issuing a strongly anti-Israeli pamphlet, thus alienating its anticommunist and Jewish supporters). No doubt it was also the case that white liberals were becoming chary of supporting blacks now that they were getting so militant.

SNCC's only hope at this point seemed to be to form alliances with other groups. It had always been able to work harmoniously with the Congress of Racial Equality (CORE) in the South because CORE's southern chapters had a redemptive ethos similar to SNCC's. But now, in 1967, a planned alliance with national CORE for the purpose of forming a new political apparatus for black people never got off the ground. And a working alliance with the Black Panthers in 1968 lasted only five months, ending in bitterness and violence. It would have been very surprising, in the light of the explanation offered here, if SNCC had been able to maintain an alliance with the urban-bred Panther party, which had such a different ethos.

So SNCC never took hold in the North. Its redemptive ethos, so dependent on a particular mix of circumstance, belief, and background, was like a delicate plant. It was not easily transplanted into new soil—nor could it survive, under changing conditions, in the old soil. SNCC could not change its ethos, and given that ethos, it was capable only of limited responses to political opportunities—and mostly self-destructive ones. So SNCC flowered and died in a very brief span of years.

What can be concluded from this strange tale of success through failure and failure through success? I say success through failure because during the 1961–63 period when SNCC was encountering almost total frustration in its voter registration campaigns, its members described it as the most "meaningful" and "beautiful" group they had ever known. I say success also because in spite of the hardships, danger, and frustration of SNCC life, SNCC in that period always had a stream of new members to replace the old. And the old members left not in disillusion but in exhaustion (they usually lasted no more than a year). The many ex-SNCC members interviewed were almost universally very positive in their feelings toward SNCC. This was true even of the whites who were forced out in the spring of 1965.

SNCC's failure through success is more obvious. The compromise offered at the 1964 convention, the advent of so many talented new members, the passage of the Voting Rights Act, the national fame that Stokely Carmichael brought with his "Black Power" slogan—all these look, to the outsider, like successes and opportunities for more success. Yet within SNCC they were experienced as failures and portents of greater failure.

That SNCC was a strange kind of organization is clear. Very few other political organizations have resembled it, even radical ones. For example, the Socialist and Communist parties in America, far from being redemptive, have been basically ideological organizations.

SNCC has sometimes been compared with the Industrial Workers of the World (IWW), also know as the Wobblies. As Renshaw (1967) relates, in the 1905–20 period, the IWW challenged the conservative, bread-and-butter unions of the day by being radical and visionary. Yet the IWW was very different from SNCC. It was bureaucratic and large, with a peak membership of about 100,000. Its disputes over strategy and structure were fought out among the top leaders in the language of European radical ideologies (Marxism and syndicalism), whereas SNCC's disputes directly involved the entire organization and had little to do with any ideologies.

SNCC has also been compared with the Students for a Democratic Society (SDS), and there are a number of similarities in values and attitudes between members of the two groups. In fact, before 1965, when it was engaged in small-scale community organizing, SDS did seem to have a redemptive organization. But SDS then began organizing students around the issues of the Vietnam war, the draft, and student power. It became a large organization with thousands of members, some very active, most of them almost entirely inactive. Moreover, some of the leaders began a serious effort to develop an ideology, in order to explain to people how their problems were caused by deep-rooted failures of the American system. Other leaders continued to hold the more redemptive viewpoint that to explain this to people was to preclude their discovering it through experience, which was the only way to gain real knowledge. So SDS after 1965 retained some redemptive characteristics but was too large and diffuse to be really a redemptive organization (on SDS, see Kopkind 1965b, Blumenthal 1967, Jacobs 1968, Brooks 1965).

The Weathermen (now called the Weather Underground), which split off from SDS, does seem to have been redemptive. Its members lived together in collectives of ten to thirty people in which they studied revolutionary doctrine, wrote, organized, and participated in Maoist-style self-criticism sessions. Kifner (1970) describes them as having a "quality approaching religious fanaticism." The result of its redemptive spirit was a burning moral outrage that led it to commit acts of violence which in turn resulted in its being driven underground and eventually into virtual extinction.

No wonder SNCC did not have the instinct for staying alive in a political world. It was held together almost entirely by incentives that are atypical of political organizations. Just as SNCC's incentive structure was nonpolitical, so its contribution was also nonpolitical, or rather prepolitical.

That contribution was a challenge to the extreme rationality and individualism of the American system. This challenge came not through anything SNCC taught but precisely through its redemptive nature. SNCC offered its members a kind of total universe that made possible a full commitment, an unmediated caring about the values and the people in that universe. Many of its members report that before 1964, they often experienced a sense of harmony and certainty that is rarely felt by other Americans. Their lives were not fragmented. Instead of filling a series of largely unrelated roles (parent, employee, citizen), they filled only one role: SNCC worker. Instead of balancing in their heads a multiplicity of values, all of them tentative, they had one certain, absolute set of beliefs. The group provided a world order that is far more complete and stable than any that individuals could assemble for themselves.

The SNCC outlook stands most sharply in contrast to that of the liberal —the person who makes a point of seeing every issue from all perspectives and of being always prepared to trade off his or her values for each other. The liberal is a specialist in living with a minimum of conflict in a complex, atomized, shifting world. Without the liberal, the American system could hardly exist. The liberal makes possible the relatively peaceful coexistence of many highly diverse groups. The liberal is the keystone of a society that fails to give its members any sort of total viewpoint or meaning.

It was to this society that the early SNCC offered an alternative. But the pressures and the temptations proved too great for that alternative to last. The history of SNCC after 1964 is the history of the gradual breakdown of the earlier total universe leading to its dissolution.

But the SNCC experience offered a kind of model, a definition, a direction to the rest of the New Left. Some of SNCC's members became prominent in other New Left groups. Tom Hayden, after working in SNCC during 1961, went on to become one of the founders of SDS in 1962. Mario Savio, a 1964 summer volunteer, that fall became the best-known leader of Berkeley's Free Speech Movement. The Black Panther Party took its name from the nickname of a SNCC project, Stokely Carmichael's Lowndes County Freedom Organization. SNCC's ethos served a kind of prepolitical role by presenting a model of an alternative politics to the New Left and a critique of America's values that is of potential interest to many more people—though very few outside the New Left heard the message. It was very hard to understand, and it got mixed up with the more frightening simultaneous Black Power message coming from SNCC.

In short, SNCC's contribution was precisely that it was a redemptive political organization. There are probably thousands of redemptive organizations, from motorcycle gangs to religious sects. They are rarely explicitly political. (Those that are political, like SNCC and also CORE in the South in the early 1960s, tend to be very short-lived or to have a very short redemptive phase.) Those Americans who feel the need for the rewards of intimacy and moral certainty offered by a redemptive ethos do not generally seek them in politics. SNCC is of interest because it attempted to do both things: to be political and to offer its members the satisfactions of a redemptive ethos. The story of how it failed provides an illustration of the reason the American political system is not likely to provide its citizens with a sense of community or meaning for their lives.

SNCC's story also shows the limitations of compromises, concessions, and reforms as a government strategy for dealing with dissident groups. Most groups, even radical ones, can be influenced to some extent by these three basic techniques of American government and can even work temporarily with reformist groups for reformist ends, as the Communist party did during the Popular Front and as the Black Panthers are doing now. But to a redemptive group a compromise is always an implied insult (because it denies the absoluteness of the group's moral right); a concession is always a trick (because it is never given in a redemptive spirit but may sway people from the redemptive group's position); and a reform is always a sham (because it does not change the underlying immoral or amoral system). The rejection of the convention compromise makes perfect sense in these terms. If the government is faced with further redemptive political challenges—by the remnants of the New Left, by young people, by black people, by women—it can expect further rebuffs to any concessions it offers.

But in another way a redemptive group is extremely vulnerable to offers of reform. Its lack of adaptability means that its base—of both financial supporters (white liberals, for SNCC) and active followers (poor rural southern blacks, for SNCC)—can easily be stolen. The redemption-oriented core of active members is then left impotent and frustrated and more morally offended than ever. I do not know what effect this usually has—whether it stimulates other, even more angry redemptive challenges like the Weatherman; whether it reinforces the determination of nonredemptive reformist groups like SCLC to continue "working within the system"; whether it encourages redemptive groups like SDS to transform themselves into something else; or whether it merely increases apathy and cynicism and a kind of simmering anger among the excluded groups (like blacks and youth) to which redemptive organizations seem to appeal. Probably all four to different degrees. In any case, this will have to be the subject of further research.

REFERENCES

Blumenthal, R.
   1967   "SDS: Protest Is Not Enough." *Nation* 204 (22 May): 656–60.

Brooks, T. R.
    1965   "Voice of the New Campus Underclass." *New York Times Magazine*, 7 November, 25–27.
Carmichael, S., and C. V. Hamilton
    1967   *Black Power*. New York: Vintage.
Clark, P. B., and J. Q. Wilson
    1961   "Incentive Systems: A Theory of Organizations." *Administrative Science Quarterly* 6 (September): 129–66.
Diamond, M.
    1956   "Socialism and the Decline of the American Socialist Party." Ph.D. dissertation, University of Chicago.
Evans, R., and R. Novak
    1966   *Boston Globe*, 7 September.
Fishman, J. R., and F. Solomon
    1963   "Youth and Social Action, I: Perspectives on the Student Sit-in Movement." *American Journal of Orthopsychiatry* 33 (October): 872–82.
Forman, J.
    1972   *The Making of Black Revolutionaries: A Personal Account*. New York: Macmillan.
Gerth, H. H., and C. W. Mills, eds.
    1958   *From Max Weber*. New York: Oxford University Press.
Howe, I., and L. Coser
    1957   *The American Communist Party: A Critical History, 1917–57*. Boston: Beacon Press.
Jacobs, J.
    1968   "SDS: Between Reform and Revolution." *Nation* 206 (10 June): 753–57.
Keniston, K.
    1968   *Young Radicals*. New York: Harcourt, Brace and World.
Kifner, J.
    1970   "Vandals in the Mother Country." *New York Times Magazine*, 4 January, 14–16.
Knox, R. A.
    1950   *Enthusiasm: A Chapter in the History of Religion*. Oxford: Clarendon Press.
Kopkind, A.
    1965a   "Of, by, and for the Poor." *New Republic* 152 (19 June): 15–19.
    1965b   "New Radicals in Dixie: Those Subversive Civil Rights Workers." *New Republic* 152 (10 April): 13–16.
Lester, J.
    1968   *Look Out, Whitey! Black Power's Gon' Get Your Mama!* New York: Dial.
Poussaint, A. F.
    1966   "The Stresses of the White Female Worker in the Civil Rights Movement in the South." *American Journal of Psychiatry* 123 (October): 401–7.
Renshaw, P.
    1967   *The Wobblies: The Story of Syndicalism in the United States*. Garden City, N.Y.: Doubleday.
Sellers, C., with R. Terrell
    1973   *The River of No Return*. New York: Morrow.
Troeltsch, E.
    1958   *Protestantism and Progress*. Boston: Beacon Press.
Student Nonviolent Coordinating Committee
    n.d.   "Some Aspects of Black-White Problems as Seen by Field Staff." SNCC. Mimeographed.

Wilson, B.
  1959 "An Analysis of Sect Development." *American Sociological Review* 24 (February): 3–15.
Wilson, J. Q.
  1973 *Political Organizations*. New York: Basic Books.
Zinn, H.
  1964 *SNCC: The New Abolitionists*. Boston: Beacon Press.

20

Repression and the Decline of Social Movements: The Case of the New Religions

David G. Bromley and
Anson D. Shupe, Jr.

Social movements represent organized efforts to effect change in the established social order. For a variety of reasons, many social movements do not succeed in achieving their goals (Gamson 1975). For example, they may adopt inappropriate strategies, they may lack the capacity either to attract or to socialize a sufficient number of new members to survive; they may fail to develop a viable financial base; the sociocultural environment in which they emerge may change; the issues to which they address themselves may be supplanted by more pressing concerns. Another major factor affecting the course of social movements is repression by the larger society. In general, the more sweeping the change a social movement seeks to implement, the greater the conflict with the larger society. If conflict ensues between a social movement and the larger society, the potential for repression is great, given the likelihood of a significant power imbalance. What have been termed the "new religions," or more pejoratively, "cults," in the United States graphically illustrate the effects of repression on social movements.

A motley assortment of new religious movements appeared on the American scene amid a general resurgence of religiosity in the United States during the 1970s. These movements included several groups of Eastern origin, such as

This chapter is the product of joint effort. Authorship is random and does not indicate any difference in contribution.

Hare Krishna; sectarian offshoots of fundamentalist Christian churches, such as Children of God, and quasi-religious groups, such as Scientology. The best-known and most visible of the new religious movements was the Unification Church, which incorporated a syncretic blend of Eastern philosophy and Christian theology. The vast majority of converts to these movements were young adults (i.e., late teens through late twenties), individuals whose ideal-ism suggests that during the 1960s they might well have participated in one of the politically oriented activities of that decade (e.g., Peace Corps, civil rights, Black Power, anti-Vietnam war).

Although none of these movements attained an active membership of more than a few thousand, they quickly became the targets of social repres-sion. By the end of the 1970s the momentum of these movements had been slowed dramatically. While numerous factors contributed to the declining for-tunes of these movements, social repression was a key element. Attempts to suppress the new religions were initiated and coordinated by a loose coalition of groups comprised principally of fundamentalist Christians and families of members of the new religions, which we have termed the Anti-Cult Movement (hereafter ACM). The ACM's chief target was the Unification Church, more popularly known as the "Moonies," which was considered by the anticultists to be the archetypical "cult." We have, therefore, selected the Unification Church as an illustrative case through which to analyze the process of repres-sion in the decline of the new religions. The data presented here are based on our several years of study of the Unification Church (Bromley and Shupe 1979) and the Anti-Cult Movement (Shupe and Bromley 1980).

THE UNIFICATION MOVEMENT

In 1936, Sun Myung Moon claimed to have received a vision in which Je-sus Christ announced to him that he, Moon, had been chosen by God to attempt to complete restoration of the physical Kingdom of God on earth. He founded the Unification Church in South Korea in 1954; the first missionaries were dispatched to America in 1959. The Unification Church languished in obscurity until Moon's personal arrival in the United States in 1971 attracted large numbers of enthusiastic, youthful followers. At least in America the Uni-fication Church actually was much more than a church and can be more pro-ductively viewed as a social movement. Therefore, we shall henceforth refer to the Unification Church as the Unificationist Movement, or UM. The nature and scope of change sought by the UM is reflected in its religiously based ideology. According to the *Divine Principle*, all of mankind's contemporary problems can be traced to the original sin of Adam and Eve. Instead of the perfect, spiritual union planned for the pair by God, Eve allowed herself to be physically seduced by Satan. As a result, all future human generations were traceable to satanic rather than divine parentage. All of human history, then, has been a struggle between the forces of God and Satan. The effects of satanic influence evidence themselves in such problems as divorce, pornography, promiscuity, interpersonal alienation, individualistic and ego-centered life styles, and even war. In modern times, on an international level, the satanic forces are represented by nations advocating godless communism and the divine forces by God-fearing democratic nations.

At periodic intervals mankind has earned, and God has offered, opportunities for full restoration to God. At these times, messianic figures (such as Noah, Abraham, Moses, and King Solomon) have been sent by God to lead the restoration effort. Each mission has failed, owing mainly to human error and recalcitrance. Jesus was the last such messiah, but he too failed to complete the restoration process. Now, nearly two thousand years later, another opportunity for restoration has been earned, and a new messiah is to appear. Moon himself is thought by UM members to be either the messiah or a forerunner prophet. Should mankind fail to seize this divinely preferred opportunity, thousands of years will pass before another such opportunity can be earned.

The UM's organizational structure was consistent with the thrust of its ideology. Because human societies have been so pervasively corrupted by satanic influence, a broad range of institutions had to be reformed or transformed. Thus, for example, the UM established the Unification Theological Seminary to train future religious leaders; a daily newspaper, The News World, was founded in New York City to emphasize the UM's world view in the context of contemporary events; preeminent concern was devoted to establishing "perfect," "God-centered" families that would serve as the building blocks of the new social order; an organization was created to warn of the dangers of communism (Freedom Leadership Foundation); a campus-based affiliate (Collegiate Association for the Research of Principles) was erected to stimulate discussion of the *Divine Principle* and recruit new members for the UM; and the International Cultural Foundation was established to unify all human knowledge and reveal its divine linkages. Moon and a small circle of close advisers were ultimately responsible for the creation of each of these organizations, as well as for their basic goals and philosophy. Yet on a day-to-day basis these organizations proceeded autonomously. Constant personal monitoring of the organizational apparatus was not necessary because Moon periodically replaced the top leadership of each organization. This strategy avoided the problems of entrenched bureaucracy and of leaders who pursued their separate organizational interests. Leaders owed their allegiance and job security to Moon.

In addition, because sweeping change had to be achieved almost immediately, the UM avidly sought new members, financial resources, and public visibility to underpin its world-transforming goals. Most members were engaged in one or more of these three activities on a full-time basis. Mobile fundraising and witnessing teams crisscrossed the country in search of new members and financial resources to sustain the movement. Elaborate nationwide tours were arranged so that Moon could personally bring his message to America.

Finally, because the contemporary world had been so thoroughly corrupted, UM members withdrew from it. UM centers were organized communally with all members living as "brothers" and "sisters" under the tutelage of Moon and his wife, their "spiritual parents." Only highly ritualized contacts were maintained with outsiders, usually in the context of proselytizing or fund-raising activites.

THE ANTI-CULT MOVEMENT

The ACM emerged as a result of parental misgivings about their children's conversions to new religious movements. The first group that came to their attention was the Children of God, which, like the UM, was organized communally and actively recruited young adults. Parents of converts to the Children of God banded together into FREECOG (The Parents Committee to Free Our Sons and Daughters from the Children of God). It was not long after the formation of FREECOG that parents became aware of the existence of other new religious movements with characteristics that they found disturbingly similar to those displayed by the Children of God. As parents who took the lead in forming the ACM began to realize that the Children of God was not the only new religious movement recruiting young adults, they expanded the list of groups with which they were concerned to include the Hare Krishna, Divine Light Mission, Scientology, and a number of other groups. Gradually they began to perceive a "cult" problem.

Although the ACM opposed all new religions, the UM quickly replaced the Children of God as its arch nemesis. Early in the 1970s the UM began actively recruiting young adults and achieved rapid growth, while most members of the Children of God migrated to Europe when their leader, Moses David Berg, prophesied that the United States would soon be destroyed in a holocaust. The UM presented an easy target. Moon's nationwide speaking tours created high visibility for the groups. The general public was annoyed by the UM's aggressive solicitation campaigns and angered by the large amounts of money that public solicitation generated. The UM's overt intrusions into politics (such as lobbying for economic and military aid to South Korea and vigorously supporting Richard Nixon throughout the Watergate crisis) offended many Americans. Moon's thinly disguised claims to be the messiah enraged many Christians.

As the ACM grew, two separate but interrelated sets of organizations developed. First, there were anticult associations composed of parents of converts to new religious movements, which bore names such as the American Family Foundation, Citizens Engaged in Freeing Minds and the Individual Freedom Federation. These groups served as support and information networks for parents whose children had converted to a new religion, conducted "education" campaigns to warn the public of the danger posed by cults, and sought to mobilize public officials to take formal legal action against cults. Second, there was a loose network of deprogrammers, that is, individuals who tried to neutralize the effects of brainwashing techniques that cults allegedly used to gain and maintain control over their members. These individuals worked with parents to "rescue cult members." While on some occasions parents were able to convince their offspring to withdraw voluntarily from a new religious movement, frequently this was not the case. In such circumstances deprogrammers would physically abduct converts, hold them in isolation, and attempt to find some means of inducing them to recant their faith. If strong emotional pressure from parents was effective, deprogrammers would exploit family loyalties. If biblical refutation was effective, deprogrammers would quote chapter and verse. If discrediting testimony from ex-members created uncertainty in converts, apostates were brought in. Of course, if individuals agreed to leave a new religion after encounters with deprogrammers, these outcomes buttressed ACM claims that they had indeed been brainwashed.

The anticult associations and deprogrammers remained separate organizationally despite considerable informal cooperation. The associations were more concerned with mobilizing allies, while the deprogrammers were involved in direct action. Further, not all parents could support physical abduction and deprogramming, despite their personal anguish over their offsprings' course. Finally, deprogrammers were vulnerable to legal prosecution for false imprisonment, kidnapping, and violation of civil rights. Through organizational separation the anticult associations, which were seeking public and governmental support, avoided open entanglement in violations of the law. Nevertheless, each wing of the ACM gained support from the other. The associations' calls for public action were strengthened by the deprogrammers' apparent success at breaking cult-imposed mind control, and the fact that deprogrammers always proceeded with parental blessing reduced their vulnerability to legal prosecution.

SOURCES OF CONFLICT

Given the UM's commitment to total, imminent transformation of the social order, there was a high potential for conflict with a broad range of established institutions. The two institutions most directly and seriously threatened by the UM were the familial and the religious, and these two formed the nucleus of the Anti-Cult Movement. Among the diverse array of churches in the United States it was the fundamentalist churches that were most unequivocally hostile to the UM because of the latter's threat to these churches' spiritual authority. For fundamentalist clergy and members alike, it was the UM's rejection of Jesus as *the* messiah that was the chief source of discontent. As the founder of the Christian church Jesus was the link through which church leaders claimed their spiritual authority. At the same time, Jesus was the source of authority through which individual church members oriented their interpersonal relationships. Norms governing a variety of behaviors (e.g., drug and alcohol use, sexual behavior, and husband-wife relationships) were closely linked to religious beliefs. Because the UM defined Jesus as having failed in his divinely mandated role, a new messiah (and source of authority) would supplant him. Since the new messiah would condemn and restructure existing churches (as Moon and the UM were in fact beginning to do), the UM's doctrine clearly posed a threat to fundamentalist church leaders and members alike.

For families, it was the "loss" of a son or daughter to a "cult" that precipitated opposition to the UM. The frequently rapid shift from an apparent-aly well established course toward a conventional occupational/domestic career to what seemed to be a total, lifelong commitment to the UM's world-transforming quest left parents bewildered, frightened, and angry. In addition, UM members participated in a fictive kinship system in which Moon and his wife were designated as "true parents" (as opposed to biological parents), and UM members became one's "brothers" and "sisters." Thus both parental authority and family membership were also threatened. From parents' perspective, years of sacrifice, future success and happiness, and even family unity had suddenly and inexplicably been endangered. Unable to communicate with or dissuade their offspring, parents concluded that something must have happened (or been done) to them to have produced such abrupt, irrational, and unacceptable changes.

Both the churches and families agreed that youthful UM converts had been victimized, the churches contending that UM members were victims of satanically inspired deception and parents arguing that their offspring had been drugged, hypnotized, or brainwashed. Fundamentalists and parents, therefore, took the lead in opposing the UM, although their interests did vary somewhat. The fundamentalist churches concentrated on rejecting the UM's legitimacy as a Christian religion so that their own authority would be preserved. Families frequently sought a more extreme solution through abducting and restraining their errant offspring until the latter recanted their faith. Alternatively, families sought ways of discrediting the UM as an organization albeit with the same ultimate goal of "rescuing" their sons or daughters.

THE RISE AND FALL OF THE UM

The first UM missionaries arrived in the United States in 1959, but despite frenetic efforts to gain converts and publicize their message, they were greeted with overwhelming apathy. Through the 1960s the UM managed to recruit no more than a few hundred members. Moon paid brief visits to his fledgling movement in 1965 and 1969 but did not move to America until 1971. By this time the UM may have had as many as 500 members. With Moon's arrival came a massive overhaul of the UM's organization as members were required to devote their full time and energy to working toward the movement's goals. The result was a revitalization of the movement.

During the first half of the 1970s the UM enjoyed considerable success on a number of fronts. Following Moon's arrival in America in 1971, the UM organized a series of national speaking tours in which Moon brought his spiritual message to virtually every major metropolitan area in the country. Full-time UM membership grew to between 3,000 and 7,000. The fund-raising teams that became a standard fixture at airports, bus stations, and shopping centers yielded revenues of $25 million to $50 million annually. A number of new organizational components were established. For example, the Collegiate Association for the Research of Principles (CARP), the UM's campus evangelical group, and the International Cultural Foundation, which was to promote the search for absolute values and the unity of science, were both established in 1973. Two years later, the Unification Theological Seminary, which was to train future church leaders, and the *News World*, the New York City daily newspaper with the goal of publicizing the UM's worldview, were founded.

By the middle of the decade, however, the UM's momentum was slowed substantially. Membership stabilized as high rates of turnover continued to plague the movement. The UM continued to raise large amounts of money through public solicitation, but this revenue came at the expense of constant legal challenges and public hostility. The *News World* found few businesses interested in advertising space. The Unification Theological Seminary was denied accreditation. The Collegiate Association for the Research of Principles was denied permission to organize on most college campuses. Conferences sponsored by the International Cultural Foundation were boycotted by many scholars. Local communities rose up in resistance wherever the UM attempted to establish church centers or purchase property. So, although the UM remained affluent, active, and visible, its growth was blunted. Much of the resistance to the UM can be traced to a concerted ACM campaign to discredit and disrupt its activities.

THE DYNAMICS OF REPRESSION

The ACM sought to repress the UM and other "cults"; successful repression was dependent on a substantial power imbalance between the partisans in the conflict. Neither the UM or the ACM possessed significant sanctioning capacity. Therefore, both sides thus were heavily reliant upon gaining allies in attempting to exert social control on the other. It was the relatively greater success of the ACM in forming alliances with other groups within the society the determined the outcome of the conflict.

The UM never was able to marshal a significant number of allies and hence was at a continuous disadvantage in its struggle with the ACM. With the exception of civil liberties organizations and some liberal academicians, the UM had few supporters. Even these groups were primarily concerned with defending religious liberty and not the UM itself. Other groups occasionally provided the UM with some measure of protection if their own interests were endangered by repression of the UM. For example, courts at the appellate level reversed numerous lower court decisions that would have legitimated the use of force or limited free expression of religious beliefs. By contrast, the ACM was highly successful in mobilizing allies to its cause and so possessed a significant advantage in the balance of power. Among the ACM's most important allies were mainline churches, a variety of governmental agencies, and the media. Other groups were willing to support the ACM because (1) they shared the same value orientations or (2) they perceived some real or potential threat to their own interests.

CHURCH SUPPORT FOR THE ACM

Fundamentalist churches were able to discredit the UM among their membership, but they were not able to exclude the UM from the Christian community without support from other churches. Mainline churches supported fundamentalist initiatives for several reasons. First, UM fund-raising and witnessing teams frequently identified themselves as Christian. Mainline churches felt it was imperative to "expose" these claims as public suspicion began to affect their own solicitation campaigns. Second, most UM members were drawn from families affiliated with mainline denominations; these churches felt obligated to support parents who were unalterably opposed to their offsprings' UM membership. Finally, the UM openly engaged in partisan political activity and lobbying, publically defending President Richard Nixon at the height of the Watergate crisis and pressing for military and political support for South Korea (the "New Israel" from which the new messiah was to appear). Mainline denominations were distressed at this flagrant disregard for the carefully constructed, uneasy boundary between church and state, and they felt compelled to disavow the UM's intrusion into the political sphere.

While the UM did not pose an imminent threat to the major denominations, the challenge was sufficient for them to rally with the fundamentalists in locating the UM outside the purview of legitimate Christianity and, more specifically, in excluding the UM from legitimating organizations (such as national, state, and local councils of churches). One result of this exclusion was that the UM was significantly hindered in its capacity to reach important segments of the population from which it hoped to win acceptance and support. Since the UM was dependent on a strategy of persuasion, this symbolic ostracism was a significant sanction. Further, substantive sanctions were more easily imposed on the UM by other institutions once religious gatekeepers had declared the UM to be illegitimate. For example, the UM was consistently denied access to college campuses and prevented from establishing affiliated student organizations largely as a result of its marginal status as a church. For similar reasons, the UM's Unification Theological Seminary was denied accreditation by the New York Regents. Lack of accreditation, in turn, meant that credits earned at the seminary were not transferable to other universities, the faculty was not eligible for a number of benefit and retirement programs, foreign students wishing to attend the seminary could not obtain student visas, and students were ineligible for a range of state and federal scholarship funds. Various other courtesies extended to most churches by the media, such as free announcement of church-sponsored services and activities, also were denied to the UM. A number of churches conducted "educational campaigns" that warned parents and youth of the danger of "cults," and some provided space and facilities for ACM organizational meetings. In sum, then, the alliance of fundamentalist and mainline denominations had the effect of both locating the UM outside the boundaries of legitimate Christianity and encouraging or allowing other groups to deny crucial access or resources to the UM.

GOVERNMENTAL SUPPORT FOR THE ACM

In general the ACM was more successful in mobilizing symbolic than substantive support from various components of the government. At the local level ACM organizations were able to mount systematic lobbying campaigns and gain the imposition of some sanctions against the UM. For example, solicitation statutes originally enacted to control peddlers and vagrants were simply redirected against UM fund-raising teams. These mobile fund-raising teams crisscrossed the country soliciting donations in any heavily trafficed public area. They approached passers-by, usually identifying themselves as members of a "Christian youth group" and requesting donations for their work. On some occasions they offered small trinkets as "gifts" to stimulate contributions. Because fund-raisers identified themselves in a way that local residents believed was misleading, local charitable funds were being siphoned off, and public mistrust of all solicitation was increased, resistance mounted rapidly. Control tactics varied from setting up complex application procedures to denying UM members solicitation permits to simply escorting fund-raisers out of town. These harassment campaigns had mixed effects. On the one hand, appellate courts systematically rejected this use of local ordinances as an infringement of religious liberty. On the other hand, the UM was forced to divert time, energy, and money away from pursuing movement goals to deal with literally hundreds of these local conflicts. In addition, such cases were always reported in the media and often provided an opportunity for the ACM to publicize the full range of its allegations against the UM.

At the state level, the anticultists were less successful in mobilizing substantive sanctions, but they did manage to achieve some symbolic victories, which had the effect of denigrating and discrediting the UM. ACM leaders pressured their district representatives to launch investigations of "cults." These lobbying efforts resulted in the formation of special committees to hold public hearings on "cults" in a number of states (e.g., Vermont 1977), and in some instances legislation was introduced attempting to distinguish between a "legitimate" and a "pseudo-religion" (e.g., New York 1977) or to hinder UM fund-raising (e.g., Minnesota 1978). The best single illustration of legislation sponsored by the ACM was a conservatorship bill that passed both houses of the legislative in New York in 1980 and 1981 before being vetoed by Governor Carey. This bill was a model for legislation introduced in the legislatives of Connecticut, Oregon, and Texas during the 1980–81 legislative sessions. Conservatorship legislation originally was intended to allow family members to assume temporary guardianship of elderly relatives who became incapable of independently conducting their personal and financial affairs. The proposed revisions of these laws allowed parents to petition for a court hearing that could culminate in a temporary (45 days) conservatorship over their adult offspring who had joined a new religious movement. A conservatorship could be granted if parents could demonstrate that their offspring had undergone psychological deterioration as a result of coercive persuasion by groups that misrepresented themselves or their activities. Because criteria were extremely vague (e.g., blunted emotional responses, inadequate diet, manipulation and control of environment, performance of repetitious tasks), such legislation promised relative ease in documenting abuses. Of course, once an order of conservatorship had been granted, it was possible for parents to engage a deprogrammer.

These hearings, investigations, and bills rarely culminated in governmental action against "cults"; rather, they represented a means of responding to constituency pressures without committing the government to substantive action. Public officials recognized the questionable wisdom and legality of attempting to pass legislation that broached the issue of religious freedom. By conducting public hearings, legislators attempted to provide a "cooling out mechanism" and to symbolically align themselves with the anticultists. The UM, of course, was compelled to defend itself every time a hearing or investigation was conducted. More important, such proceedings were accorded substantial media coverage, and the ACM allegations were incorporated in official reports that had the effect of discrediting the UM (e.g., New York 1979).

The ACM was able to gain any semblance of federal support on only a few occasions. There were simply too many crosscutting interests at the federal level, and the ACM was too small and poorly financed to mobilize federal officials. A few legislators, such as Senator Robert Dole and Representative Leo Ryan, took a personal interest in the conflict and sided with the ACM. For example, Dole held informal hearings in his Senate offices on two occasions. Parents, former UM members, and ACM supporters provided testimony in one-sided hearings, and transcripts of the proceedings were published (e.g., CEFM 1976). Like the proceedings of state hearings, the "Dole hearings" testimony was funneled to the public through the media and had the effect of discrediting the UM. For the most part, however, the ACM was able to gain access to federal forums only when governmental interests were themselves threatened, as in the "Koreagate" scandal or the tragedy at Jonestown. In the former case, for example, UM members testified that they had been ordered to engage in lobbying activity on behalf of South Korea (U.S. Government 1978). Taken as a whole, this continuous flow of governmental hearings, investigations, and direct action on local, state, and federal levels was highly damaging to the UM. The mere fact that so many allegations were being made enhanced the credibility of the ACM's claims and aroused public suspicion that the UM must be fundamentally fraudulent and nefarious.

The deprogramming wing of the ACM received both direct and indirect support from law enforcement agencies and courts. In many instances when a UM member was forcibly abducted for deprogramming (often with parents present), the police chose to regard the incident as a "family dispute" and refused to become involved (Bromley, Shupe, and Ventimiglia 1980; Patrick and Dulack 1976). Parents and deprogrammers also were successful in convincing local judges to issue either writs of *habeus corpus* so that UM members could be shown in court to be mentally incompetent or temporary conservatorships, which remanded UM members to parental custody so that deprogramming could be undertaken. During the 1970s literally hundreds of deprogrammings took place, and only in a handful of cases were deprogrammers prosecuted and convicted. Even in instances where deprogrammers were prosecuted, judges and juries usually dismissed charges or levied only token penalties. As one after another of its legal tactics were reversed on appeal, deprogrammers found new means of avoiding conviction. So, despite the considerable risks involved, deprogrammings continued throughout the 1970s with devastating consequences for the UM.

The most important consequence for the ACM of "successful" deprogrammings was the bolstering of its brainwashing ideology. Enough individuals who were deprogrammed ultimately left the UM to buttress ACM allegations that brainwashing (i.e., programming) had taken place. Most devastating were public statements by former UM members that they had themselves been brainwashed, had helped to brainwash others, and had only escaped UM domination as a result of deprogramming. These first-person accounts significantly shaped public perception of the UM (e.g., Edwards 1979, Wood and Vitek 1979, Underwood and Underwood 1979) and were the single most effective weapon in the ACM's campaign to discredit the UM. The UM was at an inherent disadvantage in combating charges from ex-members. The complex motives and pressures involved in cases of individuals trying to change sides in an intense conflict were simply much more difficult to convey than was the ACM's stereotypical brainwashing imagery (for a discussion of the defection process, see Oliver 1980, Shupe and Bromley 1980). Given the fact that public suspicion toward the UM was already high, ex-members' stories were readily and uncritically accepted.

MEDIA SUPPORT FOR THE ACM

The media certainly aided the ACM cause more than any other single institution. The steady flow of negative media coverage was the single most important factor shaping the public image of the UM. In part, the media indirectly supported the ACM simply by reporting the numerous conflicts between the UM and other groups within the larger society. Media representatives also directly supported the ACM through highly sympathetic coverage. From the perspective of journalists and talk-show hosts, ACM members appeared to be normal, reputable middle-class parents with no apparent axes to grind. It was difficult for media representatives to believe that such ordinary citizens would jeopardize their careers, expend their life savings, and risk legal prosecution to have their offspring abducted and deprogrammed if their allegations were groundless. Some investigative reporters did attempt to gain firsthand experience by covertly attending UM recruitment sessions. However, because they began such ventures already suspicious of the UM, were looking for a sensational story, and the UM's communal life style was no more appealing to them than to ACM members, the tone of their stories was predictably negative.

By the mid-1970s, media coverage of the UM was overwhelmingly negative (Bromley, Shupe, and Ventimiglia 1980). ACM versions of the conflict were uncritically reported in newspaper and magazine articles, television documentaries, books by apostates, and even "cult episodes" worked into regular television series. Once "cults" had become a major "story," the media began competing to produce the most sensational coverage. For example, virtually every magazine appealing to teenagers and homemakers printed at least one exposé of "cults." Magazines such as *McCalls* (Rasmussen 1976), *Seventeen* (Remsberg and Remsberg 1976) and *Good Housekeeping* (Crittenden 1976) ran articles with titles such as "How Sun Myung Moon Lures America's Children," "Why I Left the Moon Cult," and "The Incredible Story of Ann Gordon." These stories created the impression that innocent children were being plucked off the streets and college campuses and reduced to automatons obedient to Moon's will. Because most individuals' only contact with the UM was through the media, the UM's inability to manage its public identity was disastrous to its efforts to gain legitimacy and public support.

CONCLUSIONS

In this chapter we have sought to demonstrate the importance of repression as a factor in the decline of social movements. By the end of the 1970s, the UM was in an embattled position, spending much of its time and resources in defensive actions. Repression was not the only factor accounting for the UM's failure to achieve its goals. From a historical perspective, no social movement with the goal of total world transformation has been successful, and the UM certainly made its share of tactical and organizational errors. However, that is not the issue. What is significant from our perspective is the tremendous impact societal repression has on the potential for social change. Social movements, like the UM and other new religions, that seek more than modest, limited change inevitably provoke conflict with groups possessing a strong vested interest in the status quo. The prospects are not favorable for such movements. As we have shown in this case, the forces arrayed against them are formidable to the point of being overwhelming. Such movements may survive, but they rarely are able to fully succeed. Thus, while modern societies may spawn large numbers of social movements, the social order remains remarkably stable.

One final observation is in order with respect to repression. Usually this term evokes an image of naked force and violence, but what this case study has shown is that repression can be far more subtle. In this conflict there was relatively little violence. Further, the ACM was a small, poorly financed, and factionalized movement. Yet, despite all its organizational problems, the ACM was impressively successful in its campaign against the new religions. We can only speculate as to what might have happened if powerful groups within the society had perceived their interests to be more directly and seriously threatened. What is clear is the awesome capacity for repression of significant social change possessed by established institutions, a capacity that does not necessarily require overt use of force. Much of the order we perceive in the social order is literally a reflection of the social distribution of power. The potential for social change is limited by those same power realities.

REFERENCES

Bromley, David, and Anson Shupe
    1979   *Moonies in America*. Beverly Hills, Calif.: Sage.
Bromley, David; Anson Shupe; and Joseph Ventimiglia
    1980   "The Role of Anecdotal Atrocities in the Social Construction of Evil." In James Richardson, ed., *The Deprogramming Controversy*. New Brunswick, N.J.: Transaction Press.
CEFM (National Ad Hoc Committee Engaged in Freeing Minds)
    1976   *A Special Report. The Unification Church: Its Activities and Practices*, vols. 1 and 2. Arlington, Tex.: National Ad Hoc Committee.

REPRESSION AND THE DECLINE OF SOCIAL MOVEMENTS

Crittenden, Ann
1976 "The Incredible Story of Ann Gordon and Reverend Sun Myung Moon." *Good Housekeeping*, October, pp. 86ff.

Edwards, Christopher
1979 *Crazy for God.* Englewood Cliffs, N.J.: Prentice-Hall.

Gamson, William
1975 *The Strategy of Social Protest.* Homewood, Ill.: Dorsey Press.

Holy Spirit Association for the Unification of World Christianity
1977 *Divine Principle.* Condensed Version. Washington, D.C.

Minnesota
1978 Section 309.50, Subdivision 10 of Minnesota Statutes. 1976. Amendment of Chapter 601 (H.F. 1248), Charitable Funds Regulation of Solicitation. 70th Minnesota Legislature.

New York
1977 Proposed Bill AB 9566-A (Section 240.46 "Promoting a Pseudo-Religious Cult") to State Assembly, Albany, 5 October.
1979 *Public Hearing on Treatment of Children by Cults.* New York: State Assembly, 9–10 August. Reprinted by American Family Foundation.
1981 Proposed Bill 7912 ("An Act to Amend the Mental Hygiene Law") to the State Assembly, Albany, 31 March.

Oliver, Donna
1980 "The Role of Apostates in the Mobilization of Countermovements." Master's thesis, University of Texas at Arlington.

Patrick, Ted, and Tom Dulack
1976 *Let Our Children Go!* New York: Dutton.

Rasmussen, M.
1976 "How Sun Myung Moon Lures America's Children." *McCalls*, September, pp. 102ff.

Remsberg, C., and B. Remsberg
1976 "Why I Left the Moon Cult." *Seventeen*, July, pp. 107, 117, 127.

Shupe, Anson, and David Bromley
1980 *The New Vigilantes: Deprogrammers, Anti-Cultists, and the New Religions.* Beverly Hills, Calif.: Sage.

Underwood, Barbara, and Betty Underwood
1979 *Hostage to Heaven.* New York: Clarkson Potter.

U.S. Government
1978 *Investigations of Korean-American Relations.* Report of the Subcommittee on International Organizations of the Committee on International Relations, U.S. House of Representatives. Washington, D.C.: Government Printing Office.

Vermont
1977 *Report of the Senate Committee for the Investigation of Alleged Deceptive, Fraudulent and Criminal Practices of Various Organizations in the State.* Montpelier, January.

Wood, Allan, and J. Vitek
1979 *Moonstruck.* New York: Morrow.

21

The New York City Transit Strike of 1980: A Case Study of Organizing a Movement Within an Institutionalized Social Movement

Steve Burghardt

Unlike many social activists, organizers of rank-and-file trade union caucuses are confronted not with an unorganized mass but with an institutionalized movement.[1] After a century of activism, the labor movement has created a framework of laws, formal procedures, and guidelines that have institutionalized collective bargaining. Originally these gains were designed to protect workers' job rights and enhance their potential power in negotiations with management. Yet this institutionalization also spelled the demise of labor as a social movement by making it more difficult to employ political techniques outside the established framework. Caucus organizers recognize the importance of procedural guarantees, yet their quest for union reform often requires decentralized, fluid organizations that are more responsive to spontaneous actions and rank-and-file issues. These activists are often hard-pressed to maintain the necessary "pro-union" credibility while organizing internally based initiatives.

These difficulties were amply illustrated in 1980 during the ten-day strike by the New York City Transport Workers Union (Local 100). The strike reflected an attempt by rank-and-file groups within the union both to wrest power from a leadership it felt was no longer in touch with the members and to gain a better contract for the members. Despite tremendous opportunities at the outset, they failed; they were unable to resolve the conflict between their basic support for the union and the need to go beyond institutionalized procedures, rules, and conventions of present labor actions if they were to win.

The strike began auspiciously enough. On April 1, at 12:32 a.m., just one half hour after their old contract had expired, 23 members of the 45-person Local 100 executive board (most of them newly elected) angrily turned down the TWU leadership's proposed final offer of a 7.5 percent wage hike for each of two years. The city, its politicians, and its trade union officials were stunned. The scenario by which the city would grudgingly accept the union's final offer and prevent a strike had been worked out previously—in accordance with standard practice—behind the scenes. This offer would have meant a loss in real wages because inflation was much higher than the proposed 7.5 percent wage gain. The offer also involved the loss of coffee break and clean-up times. While hardly an attractive settlement, the TWU leadership had agreed to it because they "understood" the city's precarious financial position and because they had long-standing relationships with city officials that they had no desire to undermine through "unrealistic" demands. The militant 23-person majority of the executive board one vote upset this relationship.

A closer look at this majority, however, revealed that its unity would have to be strengthened quickly if it was to withstand the response by the union leadership, politicians, the press, and others hostile to wide-ranging objectives and a more militant approach. The majority, forming a Coalition for a Good Contract Committee, was in fact an amalgam of three different groups, each led by individuals who had run against the other leaders for top TWU slots and lost because of the divided votes. Here, in brief, are profiles of the three dissident groups.

The Coalition of Concerned Transit Workers. Led by Henry Lewis, a black motorman of the Muslim faith, and Frank Troia, an Italian motorman, the Coalition was the preeminent dissident group in 1978 when the membership almost defeated the negotiated contract; the vote was 12,200 for the contract to 10,800 against. Lewis and Troia's militant opposition to "sell-out misleadership" struck a responsive chord throughout the local that year, especially among motormen and conductors. Their regular rank-and-file meetings, held in restaurants and social clubs throughout the outer boroughs of New York City, had between 50 and 100 TWUers in attendance. But Lewis and Troia never took advantage of this enthusiasm to mold a strong organization, preferring to use a nicely printed newspaper to "do their work," as they put it. By early 1980 the Coalition was still well known but not as well organized as it had been. Nevertheless, Lewis's and Troia's personal popularity and recognition by the media made them important figures in the coalition that was to run the 1980 strike, even though neither was elected to an executive board seat.

Unity Caucus. The group that benefited most from the CCTU's lack of organizational cohesion was the Unity Caucus. In 1978 the group's limited but united strength was in the "cars and shops," the craft maintenance division of the local. Influenced but not controlled by members of the Communist party, Unity never held open meetings. It preferred to develop a small newsletter and participate in well-organized demonstrations that were antileadership but vague about Unity leaders' aspirations. This less boisterous approach, although undemocratic in its functioning, did allow Unity to extend its influence between 1978 and early 1980 to the point where the caucus and its leader, Arnold Cherry, were viewed as the most powerful rank-and-file group in the local. This perception was validated when 11 of its members were elected to the executive board.

Committee of Concerned Transit Workers. The Committee was an older group, led and dominated by George MacDonald, a white Vietnam veteran. Looser in structure than Lewis and Troia's Coalition, the Committee held few formal meetings and was less antagonistic than the other groups to the present leadership. It attracted many white transit workers dissatisfied with present conditions but unwilling to join the other groups. The Committee was always perceived as MacDonald's forum for running for higher office, but it became clear over time that it had staying power beyond its leader, electing ten of its members to the executive board.

The election of 21 dissident union members to the executive board in February 1980, all of them to groups established outside the present union leaders' influence, was a clear sign that the leadership was in trouble. Coupled with two long-time dissidents from the bus drivers' division, the groupings, if united, would form a majority. The leadership was nervous and quickly adopted a number of the three groups' demands: a 30 percent wage increase; no "give-backs," or changes in work rules to increase productivity;[2] and opposition to any layoffs became part of Local 100 President John Lawe's program. The leaders realized there would have to be some sense of militant victory if they were to stave off an "embarrassing" strike. Since the three groups did not have a united leadership and were generally vague on union problems beyond militancy and the election of new leaders, Lawe and his followers reasoned that there was some chance they could break off at least one dissident to ensure their power in negotiations.

The three groups outflanked Lawe. Immediately after the executive board elections, they formed a Coalition for a Better Contract. Meeting together for the first time about one month before the strike deadline, the three groups agreed to work together to force a strike. The agreement was as simple as it was clear: If Lawe did not negotiate a settlement with at least 10 percent annual wage increases (20 percent over two years), they would strike. Period.

And strike they did. After the Coalition voted down Lawe's "7.5 percent solution," at the luxurious Sheraton Center Hotel, where negotiations had taken place, conductors and motormen, still dressed in their blue-suited work clothes, hugged each other in the joy of anticipation over a *real* fight ahead, one they felt the union, now seemingly controlled by the new Coalition, could win. The power to force 3.5 million riders to find alternative forms of transportation to work, with corresponding havoc for businesses in the city, was now in their hands. All they had to do was use it well.

TEN DAYS OF STRIKING: FROM MILITANCE TO DISSOLUTION

The strike began with widespread enthusiasm. Interviews on television and radio found every worker demanding "at least 30 percent" before they would go back to work. The Coalition leadership of Cherry, MacDonald, and Lewis appeared in the press almost as often as did John Lawe. All 220 transit work sites were surrounded by chanting, exuberant workers expecting to win.

At the same time, political and economic leaders, led by New York City Mayor Edward Koch, blasted the strike as "illegal," "disastrous for the city," and "against the public good." Perhaps more important, Mayor Koch decided on the adroit tactic of going out every morning to the Brooklyn Bridge, exhorting the thousands of stranded employees trudging across to "hang tough" and "stay united to win" this battle with the workers. As the perceived leader of the city, elected on a fiscally conservative platform, Koch's appearances heightened tension and potential conflict by suggesting strongly that the transit workers had created an "us" vs. "them" fight—and the "us" was all the city against 33,000 selfish, overpaid transit employees.

Meanwhile, John Lawe, who personally had nothing to gain from a successfully led anti-Lawe Coalition strike, spent most of his time in closed negotiations with management. Wanting disorganization, he left the actual running of the strike to a few hired staff members and the newly formed and organizationally weak Coalition. His distant behavior inside the union would become an effective complement to Koch's publicly antagonistic words. To outsiders, the plan seemed obvious: Koch and Transit Authority officials responsible for negotiation would keep attacking, marshaling public opinion to force the strikers to retreat; Lawe, once the retreat had begun, would step in and hammer out a new contract (thus ensuring his position as a "responsible" leader while showing the dissidents to be "irresponsible hotheads"). Only if the Coalition could remain cohesive enough to maintain internal unity and attract some public support could this plan be defeated.

Unfortunately, by the fourth day there had been little change. Koch was holding forth on the bridge, Lawe was sequestered, and the membership seemed united and firm. But the Coalition itself was under strain. In addition to trying to run the strike through a makeshift organization (using one small room in the union building to do so), the leaders were concentrating less on building the strike and its support than on trying to replace Lawe at the bargaining table. Instead of using their 23 votes to make a quick replacement, Coalition leaders spent precious time fighting over who would represent the group. The one long Coalition meeting held during the strike took over four hours on this item alone. Other business, especially matters related to the strike, was tabled to meetings that were scheduled but never held.

By the seventh day, the internal dynamics of the Coalition and the corresponding resistance led by Koch (publicly) and Lawe (privately) had begun slowly to turn the momentum toward conciliation. A quick spot check of transit shops showed poorer attendance, less militancy. Many workers complained of "nothing to do." Two meetings called by Henry Lewis for the Coalition leadership to discuss strategy had been ignored, first by MacDonald, then by Cherry. Lawe began to talk about "movement" in the negotiations; Koch, leery of direct confrontation with the transit workers, shifted his oratory from the Brooklyn Bridge to the Manhattan Bridge.

By the ninth day, it was clear that the strike was losing momentun. The Coalition had done nothing to mobilize the membership, which grew discouraged at the inactivity. The one public demonstration—a march across the Brooklyn Bridge—drew less than 80 supporters, and they were lost among the thousands marching to work. Attempts by some militants to disrupt traffic were put down vigorously by the press and union leadership alike, furthering the decline of support. There seemed to be little happening to keep the strike alive, even though workers still talked uniformly of high wage increases "no matter what."

The tenth day ended it all. A dissident member of the executive board, Arthur Morris, went on previously scheduled military leave without checking with the Coalition leadership, thus ending the Coalition's majority. With a slight increase added to the original offer, Lawe convened the board, broke a tie vote, and using what he called "the power of the presidency," proclaimed the strike over. Coalition members were furious and demanded another vote be held after Morris returned.

That second vote was never taken. The next day, trains and buses were running, transit workers were proclaiming their satisfaction at being back at work. Within a month the political outcomes were obvious. First, the contract was ratified by a 3–1 margin, a far greater victory for Lawe then either he or the Coalition (which had waged a "Vote no!" campaign) had expected. There would be a 9 percent increase in 1980, another 8 percent in 1981, and a cost-of-living adjustment of about 3 percent over two years, making it a 20 percent wage package. This was much higher than Koch had wanted, and he considered the settlement a personal defeat. TWU workers also felt defeated because New York State's Taylor Law, which imposes stiff fines on striking public employees (two days' pay for each day on strike) wiped out the entire first-year increase. As the union leadership had no plans to try to stop the fines—the leaders assumed that a $70 loss per paycheck for four months would serve as a harsh reminder as to who was "responsible"—the fines canceled the major gains of the strike.

Moreover, the Transit Authority gained an important precedent. For the first time, the union openly gave back certain contractural rights won in previous contracts, ranging from limits on overtime to trimming of wash-up time, coffee breaks, and the like.

As for political alignments of power in the union, the three groups within the Coalition have collapsed, and the Coalition itself is gone. Henry Lewis is isolated in his elected, middle-level role as chairman of the conductors' division, a potentially excellent organizing slot but one ill suited to his flamboyant style. At present he is working with the Black United Front, a Brooklyn-based community group. Arnold Cherry and George MacDonald opposed one another for a vice-presidential slot on the executive board. MacDonald, who a week before the election mysteriously dropped his opposition to the contract, surfaced at the executive board election with Lawe's backing, thus realizing the earlier fears of Lewis, Troia, and Cherry. MacDonald was elected easily. As for Cherry, he went back to school and is working on a Ph.D. in public administration. Many of the other rank and filers seemed too discouraged to carry on more work. Caucuses are far weaker than they were in 1978.

John Lawe still runs the TWU executive board—but not the entire union

—with an iron hand. While a few dedicated rank and filers on the board continue to oppose him, he has been able to ram through any vote he has needed —including $365,000 in budget items for "incidental expenses," a financial cover for costs incurred in the "good life" many union officials have come to expect; expense account meals; convention junkets; and so forth. What began on April 1, 1980, as a militant, insurgent-led strike that shocked the city and intimidated union officials was by June of the year little more than a bitter memory. As of this writing, John Lawe plans to leave his local office to run for International president; George MacDonald, now firmly pro-Lawe, is set to replace him, running on a platform of "young, responsible leadership." No one seems to be opposing him.

THE PROBLEM OF INSTITUTIONALIZATION

The failure of the three groups within the Coalition to forge a body strong enough to counter union officials' actions (or, in this case, inaction) and mobilize the effective organization needed to win a good settlement can be traced to a number of errors. Most of these errors flow from an underestimation of the difficulties faced by an insurgent group inside an institutionalized movement like labor—a broader problem that all trade unionists at some time need to consider. The historical successes of the trade union movement, based as they were on a century of conflict and struggle,[3] make opposition to established leaders a difficult task. To be effective, dissidents must prove their loyalty to the union (thus showing their respect for those previously hard-fought victories) while posing a genuine alternative to established leaders (and therefore creating a "better" union than before). To be loyal to an institution and critical of its leadership is to walk a perilously fine line. There are three reasons why the institutionalization of the labor movement has undercut labor dissidents' effectiveness.

1. Unlike most other organizations, labor's institutionalization occurred after militant and often bloody sacrifices were made by workers. Workers fought for over a century for certain job-related rights before attaining them, (e.g., the right to organize a union without harrassment; the guarantee of formal procedures between labor and management, which ended personalistic criteria for hiring, firing, and promotion; collective bargaining and the establishment of grievance procedures).[4] None of these rights was won easily. Other movements may have faced initial hostility, but rarely did it last as long or become as violent as labor disputes. The bosses were militantly opposed to trade unions and worked for years to defeat them. Because it was through the union that battles were fought and won, the union as an institution understandably came to be viewed as the workers' most important tool, to be protected from outside interference at all costs. Given labor's history, it is no accident that outsiders are viewed with suspicion and that officials' calls of "union busting" are listened to very carefully. Most union histories are filled with outside interference, police and management spies, and "deputy sheriffs" bent on union destruction.[5] Today's militants must carefully state their criticisms about union problems if they are to avoid an "antiunion" label.

  2. Institutionalization breeds an emphasis on the maintenance of organizational means, not ends. Organized labor's transformation from a militant, grass-roots, and heterogeneous movement in the 1930s to a conservative, well-established, and integrated institution by the 1950s has been documented elsewhere.[6] That transformation created new ideas and norms about the purpose of organization. The unionism of the Thirties often sought to organize large numbers in order *to fight management* over workplace issues. Shop floor actions were both more democratic and more militant than those permitted by collective bargaining contracts. Institutionalized labor organizations today work with management, and they seek members primarily to increase union revenue. As Michels wrote years ago in analyzing the powerful German socialist trade unions:

> The history of the international labor movement furnishes innumerable examples of the manner in which the party becomes inert as the strength of its organization grows; it loses its revolutionary impetus, becomes sluggish, not in respect to action alone, but also in the sphere of thought. More and more tenaciously does the party cling to what it calls "ancient and glorious tactics," the tactics which have continued to increase membership. More and more invincible becomes its aversion to all agressive actions.[7]

  3. Once elected to office, most leaders use their status and power to remain in power, and to increase their control. Lipset and others have noted that trade union leaders, once they become labor officials, acquire status and income, which most are loath to lose. As Lipset has written, "if the social distance between the trade union leader's position as an official and his position as a regular worker is great, his need to retain the former will be correlatively great."[8] Officials have used their office to maintain power in any number of ways—limiting discussion at meetings, controlling the means of internal communication, and using political skills (e.g., parliamentary procedure, organizing demonstrations) to thwart dissidents less polished then they. As Gamson has suggested, a trade union rank-and-file group has to be prepared to match these skills and at least equalize the power of communication if they are to thwart institutionalized power.[9]

  These problems are inherent in large-scale organizations and have been written about for years by Michels, Lipset, Gamson, and others. Each has documented the tendency of social movements to atrophy once they are accepted by the mainstream; each has analyzed why leaders alter their original goals of social change to maintain the power and prestige of their official positions. The TWU dissidents were not ignorant of these problems and addressed them at varying stages of their groups' growth. Yet, almost every time, the wrong tactical choices were made on how to proceed in their political and organizational development. Dissident leaders consistently articulated problems in terms of conservatism and overinstitutionalization; but they refused, even when suggestions were made, to pose different objectives in the own work. By holding on to the objective of merely replacing old leaders with new ones (themselves), after they initially acted as if they wanted to shake-up old institutional relationships, they confused their membership and eventually undercut their strategic effectiveness.

For example, their initial prestrike rhetoric and demands promised rank-and-file participation, condemning the antidemocratic methods of past leadership. Dissident leaders also suggested that the rank and file work toward a sustained level of militancy—wildcats, train slow-downs, free rides—that would contribute to victory in the upcoming negotiations. However, once the leaders attained a semblance of power (the executive board majority), their actions undercut this rallying point. The resulting disorganization and disorientation within the Coalition and its leadership than allowed the well-trained and previously established power of the union leadership to reassert itself, carefully marshaling pro-union sentiment, concern with "responsible leadership," and the like to regain full control over the membership.

Specific errors, while apparently "only tactical," grew out of a misunderstanding of the above dimensions of institutionalization. Dissidents misunderstood both the power of the officials and the corresponding weaknesses in their own loosely formed groupings. They thus failed to draw out the actual causes for "misleadership" and to apply them to the institutionalized procedures of the union itself, seeing only that new leaders were needed. Had they understood that "misleadership" was another name for institutionalized relations between labor and management that were breaking down in the fiscal crisis,[10] they might have prepared differently. They did not, and they were defeated.

What were their specific errors?

1. Failure to use the two years between the 1978 and 1980 contracts to organize and train insurgent group members. Lewis and Troia's CCTU had between 50 and 100 people attending their regular meetings in the Fall of 1978. Instead of using those meetings to organize these members into workplace units around current campaign issues (especially job safety), Lewis antagonized members by orating on any number of issues—the evils of John Lawe, the necessity of militancy, and so on. When it was pointed out repeatedly that such orations were effective only as brief introductions, Lewis and Troia both explained that "one's willingness to sacrifice for the greater cause" would keep people active. By the end of 1979, CCTU meetings with five or six members in attendance were sad testimony to a different answer.

The Unity Caucus was less rhetorical but equally disinterested in rank-and-file involvement. As a Communist party activist highly influential within the group put it, "Our meetings are to get things done, not talk. If people have things to say, let them write to our newsletter and then they can distribute it." Thus, while concerned with reaching the rank and file, Unity had no corresponding interest in the members' reaching them—a method of organizing (and leadership) not readily distinctive from that of the entrenched officials. MacDonald's Committee of Concerned Transit Workers was no different.

This lack of previous organization cannot be overstressed. First, the dissidents did not recognize that mobilizing antiofficial sentiment is far easier than creating sentiment for genuine alternatives to past practices. The election of dissidents to the executive board was a signal for change, but not necessarily a willingness to completely change the way in which the union functioned. Their electoral success also lulled the dissidents into ignoring the necessity for organizing a grass-roots operation powerful enough to withstand future official opposition. Instead, the dissidents' combination of militant rhetoric and inadequate preparation ended them. In short, to raise the specter of new labor-management relations without being prepared for the withering blast of resistance that would inevitably follow was a shortcut to disaster.

2. The most telling signal that the Coalition's unity was fragile occurred in the late 1979 local presidential campaign. At a meeting the three leaders held right before ballots were drawn up, Lewis volunteered to step down and run for a lesser office on a joint slate. Amazingly, even though all three were on record for a strike if higher wages were not forthcoming, MacDonald and Cherry refused the offer, thus sealing the defeat of all three. (The combined vote total of Cherry and Lewis was over 53 percent; Lawe's 40 percent vote was the first plurality victory in the local's history.) The difference between the rhetoric of unity and the reality of personal power could not be more evident than in the inability of the dissidents to divide the union offices between them rather than compete for them.

3. The internal divisions among the three groups could not be papered over through the creation of a "coalition," nor could its one-vote majority on the executive board easily replace years of entrenched power and organizational savvy. But the majority's existence did create an opening wedge that could have developed power if, after calling the strike, they had seized the initiative and had gained control over strike operations. When suggestions were made to call a Local 100 meeting at Madison Square Garden (a commonly practice among other unions), at which members could be organizationally prepared to act together to build public support, all three Coalition leaders recoiled from the suggestion as "too difficult for the membership"—exactly the refrain past officials had used to discourage widespread activity by suggesting rank-and-file ignorance.

4. Instead, wishing to prove their institutional loyalty to the union (as it was now under attack from the press and politicians), the executive board of the Coalition passed its one substantive motion—*a declaration of support for John Lawe's leadership.* By confusing institutional loyalty and leadership support, their action undercut their other cries of "misleadership."

The declaration's result was to undermine any chance of running the strike effectively, for the officials, having been given responsibility for the strike by the Coalition and yet fully aware that the dissidents were out to replace them, made no serious efforts to organize a tightly run, militant strike. The Coalition had no awareness of how "critical support" within a united front between officials and themselves would work. It meant to stand *publicly united* with all who were part of the strike (including the officials) while urging that the strike proceed by reliance on shop floor committees and not just paid union officials, and by holding joint union-community rallies. These ideas were rejected out of hand. As a Coalition member put it, "We have only one president, and in this situation we back him." "Backing" meant that the opposition would make no moves to take the political and organizational leadership of the strike away from Lawe.

5. All of these internal problems—failing to prepare members before the strike, declining to elect a joint slate, not seizing initiative and control over the

strike, confusing loyalty to the union with public support for officials—was compounded by the dissident leaders' poor public relations. In fact this was due to inexperience, but the general attitude suggests more about their perceptions on how to build a solid grass-roots movement.

First, Coalition leaders felt that other unions should come to them to offer aid; they would not request aid. This was politically naive, for the offers of official aid from other unions (such as AFSCME's D.C. 37 and the United Federation of Teachers) would have to come from leaders who, like Lawe, were opposed to and in the past had been threatened by the kind of insurgent militancy in the TWU Coalition.

Second, no attempts at winning public support were made throughout the strike. Because most people assumed there was a serious fiscal crisis created in large part by high labor costs, they followed the lead of politicians like Mayor Ed Koch much more readily than they would have supported angry workers. But there were numerous pro-mass-transit groups in New York City, and there were a few opportunities for joint rallies that could have altered people's perception about the nature of the strike. Such rallies were never called, thus further isolating the workers as the strike wore on.

THE TWU STRIKE AND ITS IMPLICATIONS FOR THE LABOR MOVEMENT

These tactical errors, flowing out of mistaken perceptions about the causes for present-day labor leadership problems, ruined the strike effort and allowed the once defensive local officials to regain control over TWU operations. But the story of the TWU strike, from the five years of ineffective leadership in delivering on past contracts to the tactical errors of the insurgents while on strike, is also an example of problems facing organized labor in the 1980s.

The nation's economic crisis has led to a myriad number of solutions, most of which seek to redefine the institutional relationships between labor and management that have existed for so many years. As David Gordon has noted,[11] the call for "reindustrialization"[12] sweeping the nation is call for ending the material basis for traditional labor-management relations. In the past, smooth official managerial relations were maintained through tradeoffs of "higher productivity" (more output per worker) for higher wages (more real income per worker).[13] As long as the economy expanded, such tradeoffs were possible; in today's economic climate, "reindustrialization" calls for greater productivity *without* increases in real income. Labor officials once emphasized the "ancient and glorious tactic" of greater membership and labor peace partially because the ever-expanding economy made such institutionalized tradeoffs possible. Today's underproductivity, slow growth, and high inflation rates—all of which are expected to continue in the 1980s[14]—have disoriented union officials, be they John Lawe or the United Auto Workers' Doug Fraser.[15] They have been hard pressed to come up with solutions that better workers' lives and incomes, and they are unsure of what to do. The present stagnation in the size of organized labor—down from 33 percent of the work force in the mid-Fifties to less than 20 percent today[16]—is concrete testimony to trade union officials' ineffectiveness in reaching their constituency.

The economic difficulties have deepened other problems facing labor today, including the harsh rightward drift in politics and the increasing public antagonism to labor's demands. Given such problems, and the breakdown of the institutionalized procedures of the past, unionists who wish to revitalize the labor movement in the 1980s have at least three primary strategic tasks before them.

1. They must create widespread rank-and-file involvement in their unions if they are to shorten the distance between leaders and members. The use of "one glorious tactic" that Michels alluded to was the process by which leaders, through their ongoing relations with management, separate themselves from the ranks in order to concentrate on "more important business"—increasing membership size (and dues), maintaining labor peace through contract provisions, and so forth. The norm has been established that leaders *do* for members, not that members create issues and elect leaders to carry out their bidding. The weight of present political and employer activity has made this elitist notion of union official behavior no longer tenable. Without the mobilized and involved activity and ideas of far larger numbers of workers, unions and their leaders cannot expect to be heard. Therefore, as much as possible, dissidents must organize the disaffection felt by so many into activity—campaigns on job safety problems, workshop committees to collect and disseminate information, and attention to other substantive issues (from union democracy to lower wages)—*before* they decide to run for office. For, as the transit dissidents found out, without a strong organization behind them, popular insurgents cannot withstand hostility to their efforts.

2. Rank-and-file activists must distinguish support for unionism from criticism of particular union officials. The need to protect unions from outside attack is going to grow in the Eighties as more political and economic leaders attempt to cut costs and increase productivity. Union officials can and will use this attack to discourage dissent within their membership. Since labor activists rarely begin from a position of strength, they will have to work in coalitions containing large numbers of officials who are antagonistic to their ideas about democratic unionism or shop floor militancy. Activists will have to learn to support the goals of these coalitions without capitulating to their official leadership on how the group should perform all its tasks. Otherwise, they will not be able to educate their members to the broader issues of union revitalization without succumbing to either organizational irrelevance or political passivity.[17] "Organizational irrelevance" occurs when some activists overreact and condemn all actions by officials *because* they are officials (a form of "political sectarianism"). "Political passivity" develops when dissidents passively accept all directives from leadership in order to enhance their short-term organizational effectiveness (often called "opportunism").

3. Activists must reassess their past community and political alignments. Since the New Deal, trade union officials have relied on and supported strong ties within the Democratic party. Most community liaisons, when they occur, have also been channeled through this relationship by working with various district

Democratic clubs and officials. As today's economic impasse has changed many union supporters into fiscal conservatives, it has become more difficult for labor to pass any of its legislative objectives.[18] Such long-term inability to meet working-class needs provides an opportunity for trade union activists and other progressives to give active consideration to the notion of a Labor party.

Additionally, the weak links between public service workers and the public breeds antagonism. As services continue to deteriorate through cutbacks, the antagonism must be turned into alliances demanding more and better services if they are to create a serious alternative to present-day public assumptions.

While the New York City transit strike was a small story of a transitory event, it illustrates in microcosm the problems of organizing within the trade union movement. Organizing social movements is always difficult. But ordinary problems are compounded when one is organizing within the institutionalized outcomes of a previous social movement because one must challenge established patterns of action and power relationships without appearing to threaten the institution. This is why it is so important for rank-and-file organizers, perhaps even more than community organizers, to develop caucuses with solid roots in shops and offices, to encourage members' participation in decision making, and to educate members about the political context in which their actions occur. For without those roots, the political confidence and staying power of trade union initiatives will be little different than that witnessed in New York in the spring of 1980.

NOTES

1. By "institutionalized movement" I mean a movement in which the language and rituals of behavior are movement-oriented—highly inflammatory, spontaneous, open to activism on a wide scale—while the procedures and actual forms of concrete activity are primarily limited to institutionalized guidelines established by the courts, legislatures, and contract bargaining.
2. Roughly speaking, "productivity" means the cost of work one gets out of a worker minus the costs of production. The desired goal of services like transit is to cost only what they take in from tokens, bridge tolls, and the like. Thus, every coffee break, as it is "free time" that does not generate revenue, is viewed as a "loss of productivity."
3. There are innumerable studies of the trade union movement. Some of the most often cited are Thomas R. Brook's *Toil and Trouble* (New York: Delta Press, 1972); *History of the Labor Movement*, vol. 1–4 (New York: International Publishers, 1976–79); and Irving Bernstein's *The Lean Years* (Boston: Houghton Mifflin, 1960).
4. For a more conservative discussion of gains that have become institutionalized, see Derek C. Bok and John T. Dunlap, *Labor and the American Community* (New York: Simon and Shuster, 1966).
5. See Bernstein, *Lean Years*; and Farrell Dobbs, *Teamster Rebellion* (New York: Pathfinder Press, 1971). Both are examples of spies and agents inside the labor movement.
6. Brooks, *Trial and Trouble; History of Later Movement*, esp. vol. 4.
7. Robert Michels, *Political Parties* (Glencoe, Ill.: Free Press, 1949), p. 337.
8. Martin Lipset, Martin Trow, and James Coleman, *Union Democracy* (New York:

Doubleday, 1956), p. 118. For descriptions of this dynamic, see also Steven Brill, *Teamsters* (New York: Quadrangle Press, 1978; and David Greenstone, *Labor and American Politics* (Chicago: Univ. of Chicago Press, 1971), esp. chap. 1, 2.

9. William Gamson, *Strategies for Social Protest* (New York: Houghton Mifflin, 1969), p. 112.

10. For two timely analyses on the city crisis and its effect on unionism, see William K. Tabb's "Domestic Economic Policy Under Carter," and the Institute for Labor Education and Research's "Labor Unions In Transition', both in *U.S. Capitalism in Crisis* (New York: Union for Radical Political Economics, 1978).

11. David Gordon, a leading Marxist economist, was so quoted in the *New York Times*, 18 October 1980; later, Mario Cuomo, in an editorial entitled "Reindustrialization," (*New York Times*, 9 October 1980) admitted the same. As Cuomo is lieutenant governor of New York, it seems that many are of the same opinion on the nature of the solutions proposed to resolve the economic crisis.

12. "Reindustrialization" is a term most commonly used to describe the process of revitilizing less economical U.S. firms, especially auto, steel, and rubber. Both liberal and conservative politicians and economists seek revitilization through smaller social service budgets and lower taxes, freeing the firms to invest their additional funds in new plants and modernize old ones. More progressive alternatives in the U.S. have not yet been clearly developed, although Great Britain's Lucas Aerospace shop steward's councils have advanced and implemented some fascinating ideas on how to save jobs and revitalize certain industries. See Dave Albury, "Alternative Plans and Revolutionary Strategy," *International Socialism*, 2, no. 6 (Autumn 1979): 85–96.

13. See Brooks, *Trial and Trouble*, esp. chaps. 7, 8.

14. Leonard Silk, "The Economic Scene: Outlook for the 1980's," *New York Times*, 18 August 1980, p. D-2.

15. "U.A.W. Convention a Time of Demoralization and Fear," *New York Times*, 28 August 1980, p. 23.

16. Bureau of Labor Statistics, Annual Report, 1978.

17. Samuel Friedman, "The Teamsters for a Democratic Union and the Problems of Political Reform" (New York: Convention of the Society for the Study of Social Problems, 1980), nicely analyzes dilemmas that even self-consciously political activists have when confronting the combined tasks of union reform and political education. The Teamsters for a Democratic Union, begun in 1974 by around 20 activists (many of them socialists), is the only *national* rank-and-file movement in the country today, with approximately 6,000 members in 50 chapters. Their merger with the more conservative and legislatively oriented PROD was a victory for the more activist-oriented TDUers, especially since national attention had focused on the PROD organization. However, the problems of when and how to inject criticism of leaders through the raising of political issues that many may perceive as less than direct trade union issues (such as racism, sexism) continue to be serious issues before the group, as Friedman suggests.

18. See "Labor Faces a Challenge as It Plans Leadership Shift," *New York Times*, 15 November 1979, p. 1.

Index

About the Authors

Jo Freeman is the author of *The Politics of Women's Liberation* (Longman, 1975), winner of the 1975 American Political Science Association prize as the Best Scholarly Work on Women and Politics, and the editor of *Women: A Feminist Perspective* (Mayfield, 1975, 1979). After receiving her Ph.D. in political science from the University of Chicago, she taught for four years in New York and spent two years in Washington, D.C., as a Staff Associate in Employment Policy at the Brookings Institution, an APSA Congressional Fellow, and a writer for *In These Times*. She then entered New York University School of Law as a Root-Tilden Scholar and received her J.D. in 1982. Her involvement in social movements began while she was an undergraduate at the University of California at Berkeley in the early Sixties where she participated in the civil rights and free speech movements. After two years as a civil rights worker in Alabama, Mississippi, Georgia, and Chicago, she became a founder of the women's liberation movement in 1967 and editor of its first newsletter. She has published articles on feminism, social movements, law, public policy, sex-role socialization, organizational theory, education, and party politics in scholarly journals, popular magazines, and numerous anthologies.

David G. Bromley received his Ph.D. from Duke University. An associate professor and chairman of sociology at the University of Hartford, Connecticut, his primary interests are social movements, deviance, and political sociology. He and Anson D. Shupe, Jr., are engaged in a long-range study of new religious movements and the countermovements emerging as a response to them. In addition to numerous articles, Bromley and Shupe have co-authored *Moonies in America: Cult, Church and Crusade* (Sage Publications, 1979), *The New Vigilantes: Deprogrammers, Anti-Cultists and the New Religions* (Sage Publications, 1980), and *Strange Gods: The Great American Cult Scare* (Beacon Press, 1981).

Steve Burghardt, MSW and Ph.D., is an assistant professor of urban policy and practice at the Hunter School of Social Work. He has authored *The Other Side of Organizing* (Schenkman, 1981). Active for nine years in organizing trade union–community coalitions around public-sector cutbacks, Burghhardt continues to work with rank-and-file transit workers. He is also helping to develop a Human Services Activists Network with other human service workers in New York.

Leonard Davidson developed a fascination with sociology as a child by observing Philadelphia schoolyard basketball rituals. His interests shifted to T-groups, minority employment, tenants' unions, and other social and political developments while he was an MIT graduate student in Cambridge, Massachusetts. He received his doctorate in 1973 from MIT's Sloan School of Management. Bored with mid-Seventies "mellow" during six years as a professor of organization behavior at the University of Florida, he co-founded the Papier Mâché Giants of America Discovery Contest and renovated an 1880's Florida dress shop into The Gamery—a three-story bar-restaurant-entertainment-arts complex. He has returned to Philadelphia as a neon artist and an organization development consultant at the Center for the Study of Adult Development.

Lynn Dwyer received her undergraduate degree in zoology and a master's degree in sociology from the University of Tennessee at Knoxville before going on to a Ph.D. in anthropology from the American University. Her participant-observation study of the anti-nuclear-power-plant movement began with her dissertation research on the middle Tennessee movement in 1974. Before beginning this research, she had long been interested in politics and social change and had participated in the environmental movement. Her study of local antinuclear activities evolves from her background interests and her present occupation—teaching at Tennessee State University.

Ernest Evans is an assistant professor in the politics department of Catholic University. He received his Ph.D. in political science in 1977 from MIT. His work has focused on the politics of radical movements, particularly those movements that use violence to achieve their aims. His academic interests have been heavily influenced by two personal experiences: (1) His grandfather, a union official who lived in Birmingham, Alabama, throughout the civil rights struggles of the Fifties and Sixties, was subjected to repeated death threats from the Ku Klux Klan because of his unyielding defense of the rights of blacks in his union and because of his outspoken opposition to racism; and (2) he witnessed firsthand the activities of groups like SDS while an undergraduate at Brown University from 1968 to 1972.

James A. Geschwender is a professor and chairperson of sociology at the State University of New York at Binghamton. He has published extensively in the fields of social movements and racial/ethnic stratification since receiving his Ph.D. at Michigan State University. His two most recent books are *Racial Stratification in America* (William C. Brown, 1978) and *Class, Race and Worker Insurgency* (Cambridge University Press, 1977). He became involved as a participant in the defense of Waiahole-Waikane in 1976–77 while on sabbatical in Hawaii. He did not initially intend to write about it inasmuch as he was convinced from historical precedent that it would end in defeat and felt that publishing on another movement failure would aid only his own professional career. He reassessed this position after an apparent victory was won, hoping that analysis of the struggle would provide information of use elsewhere.

David P. Gillespie specializes in organizational evaluation and research methods. He has completed field research on several groups of emergent economic and political organizations: housing cooperatives in East Lansing, Michigan, farming cooperatives in Nepal, and tenant associations in Madison, Wisconsin. These studies focus on member socialization, internal control, collective decision making, and tactics available to small voluntary organizations for controlling their environments. After receiving his Ph.D. in sociology from the University of Wisconsin, Madison, he lectured for several years on public policy at Michigan State University's Madison College. He has now joined Standard Oil of Ohio, where he consults on organization research and planning.

Alan E. Gross, the single father of Matthew and Molly Gross, is a professor and former chair of the psychology department at the University of Maryland. He has written on male sexuality and male responsibility for contraception. As a straight, white male who played active supporting roles in the civil rights movement of the Sixties, the women's movement of the Seventies, and the gay rights movement of the Eighties, he has been frustrated in searching for a political *and* personal cause. His recent involvement in the men's movement has been important for him personally; however, as described in this volume, the movement has not yet had a significant social impact.

Luther P. Gerlach is a professor of anthropology at the University of Minnesota. After receiving his Ph.D. from the University of London with additional certificates in African and Islamic Law, he focused his research on social cultural change and particularly on social and religious movements. With Virginia H. Hine he has co-authored *People, Power, Change: Movements of Social Transformation* (Bobbs-Merrill, 1970) and *Lifeway Leap: The Dynamics of Change in America* (University of Minnesota Press, 1973). His model of the structure and function of social movements was developed through study of the Charismatic renewal movement in the U.S. and Central America, and on the Black Power movement in the U.S., but it was influenced by his earlier study of the social and economic organization of the Digo and Duruma peoples of Kenya, East Africa. This model helped him predict the rise of ecology and energy concerns movements on which he is now doing research.

J. Craig Jenkins is an assistant professor of sociology at the University of Missouri-Columbia and a research associate for the Center for Policy Research in New York. He received his Ph.D. in sociology from the State University of New York at Stony Brook and is the author of *The Politics of Insurgency: The Farm Worker Movement and the Politics of the 1960s* as well as articles on social movements and political change. His interest in the United Farm Workers stemmed from having been an SDS "fellow traveler" in the late 1960s and from various UFW support activities throughout the past two decades.

Roberta Ann Johnson graduated magna cum laude and Phi Beta Kappa as a political science major from Brooklyn College. She was a Woodrow Wilson Fellow at Harvard University where she earned an M.A. and Ph.D. in political science. An author of numerous articles on minorities and on women, she has also written *Puerto Rico: Commonwealth or Colony?* (Praeger, 1980). She has taught at the University of California, Santa Cruz, at the University of Missouri where she was academic coordinator for the Institute on Black Women in America, and at San Francisco State University where she was coordinator of women's studies. Roberta currently works in San Francisco for the Office for Civil Rights, U.S. Department of Education.

Bennett W. Judkins was born in 1947 in a small textile mill town in southern Virginia and later moved to the coal-mining region of western Virginia. His mother, an occupational health nurse in both the coal and textile industries, was extremely influential in developing his interest in the field of workers' health. He received his Ph.D. from the University of Tennessee where he completed a dissertation on the Black Lung Movement. He is currently chairperson and associate professor of sociology at Belmont Abbey College, North Carolina, and is involved in continuing research on occupational health issues in the textile industry.

Ronald Lawson received a Ph.D. in 1970 at the University of Queensland in his native Australia. He then came to Columbia University's sociology department and Bureau of Applied Social Research as a postdoctoral Visiting Scholar and Research Associate during 1971–73. He has been an associate professor in the urban studies department of Queens College, City University of New York, and director of its housing program since 1977. He has completed a large study of the tenant movement in New York City and also a study of the political organization of New York City's real estate industry. He is now studying the impact of tenant-oriented strategies on the social process of housing abandonment and assessing the success of New York City's low-income cooperative housing established in the early 1970s. His movement experience includes having been a "foot soldier" in the antiwar movement in Australia while in graduate school, a committee member and president of his building's tenant organization during the late Seventies in New York, and prominent in academic and religious groups within the gay liberation movement nationally since 1975.

Deborah LeVeen is on the faculty of the Urban Studies Program at San Francisco State University. She received her doctorate in political science from the University of Chicago. Her contribution to this volume is based on her dissertation, which studied community organizations in the ethnically and socioeconomically diverse neighborhood of Uptown on Chicago's north side. She has been active in local political and women's groups and helped found the Native American Policy Network, an organization of social scientists and policy practitioners seeking to promote policy-relevant research on Native American Issues.

Douglas McAdam is an assistant professor of sociology at George Mason University, Virginia. His work in the social movement field includes authoring *Political Process and the Development of Black Insurgency, 1930–1960* (1982) and several related articles and papers. He has also co-authored *The Politics of Privacy* (New American Library, 1980).

Frederick D. Miller observed the transformation of SDS into Weathermen while working for a left-wing undergraduate newspaper at the City College of New York in the late Sixties. He continued to keep his eye on these events while pursuing a doctorate in social psychology at Harvard, studying both social movements and psychological issues in social perception and cognition. During five years of teaching at New York University, he researched community organizing and social cognition. Since 1980, he has been with Bell Telephone Laboratories, designing the human user interfaces of computer systems.

Robert Ross received his Ph.D. from the University of Chicago and is an associate professor of sociology at Clark University. He was among the founders of SDS, serving as a member of the executive committee and as vice-president. He worked in the SDS Economic Research and Action Project as a community organizer in the mid-Sixties. From 1968–69 Ross served as the executive director of the New University Conference, a New Left organization of graduate students and faculty members. In the last few years he has consulted closely with Massachusetts Fair Share, a statewide community organization of low- and moderate-income citizens, and has worked as a staff consultant with the Massachusetts Coalition to Save Jobs. Ross wrote an earlier version of the article in this volume in 1968 as an attempt to understand why he and other members of the founding group of SDS were marginal within the organization.

Anson D. Shupe, Jr., is an associate professor of sociology at the University of Texas at Arlington and associate director of its Center for Social Research. He received his Ph.D. in political sociology from Indiana University, but his studies of religious and political movements began during his undergraduate studies at Waseda University in Tokyo. Shupe first studied the post-World War II "new religions" in Japan before branching into "mail-order" religions in the United States, new religions (both imported and indigenous) in the United States, and fundamentalist movements such as the Moral Majority. He has authored or co-authored five books and numerous articles on religious and political movements.

Ron Smith, Ed.D., trained as an education psychologist at the University of Tennessee. He now works as a research psychologist for a federal agency in Washington. His current research examines the influence of male-male interpersonal dynamics on co-worker performance. His involvement in the men's movement includes membership on the Steering Committee of the First National Men and Masculinity Conference; co-coordinator of the *Men's Awareness Network Newsletter*; and work with other men to form a national organization focusing on men's issues, sexism, and feminism. He has also worked as a higher education administrator at the West Virginia Institute of Technology.

Emily Stoper is a professor and acting chair in the political science department at California State University, Hayward, where she also co-chairs the women's studies program. She was active in the civil rights movement in the Sixties as well as in the peace movement and, more recently, the women's movement.

Barrie Thorne, associate professor of sociology at Michigan State University, received her Ph.D. in sociology from Brandeis University. She is co-editor with Marilyn Yalom of *Rethinking the Family: Some Feminist Questions* (Longman, 1981) and with Nancy Henley of *Language and Sex: Difference and Dominance* (Newbury House, 1975). She has contributed chapters to seven books, has written many articles, and is now working on an ethnography of gender arrangements in elementary schools. From her 1967–69 experiences as a participant and observer in the draft resistance movement and the New Left, she became a member of one of the women's collectives that in 1969 formed Bread and Roses, a socialist feminist group in Boston.

Barbara Strudler Wallston is an associate professor of psychology at George Peabody College of Vanderbilt University. Her major areas of research are the psychology of women and health psychology. She is a past president of the Division on the Psychology of Women in the American Psychological Association and is currently a member of APA's Committee on Women in Psychology. She has published many journal articles, including one on the male sex role. Her interest in the men's movement has primarily been an avocation; she is the only women to have attended all eight National Men and Masculinity Conferences.